PandoraHeart

Jun Mochizuki

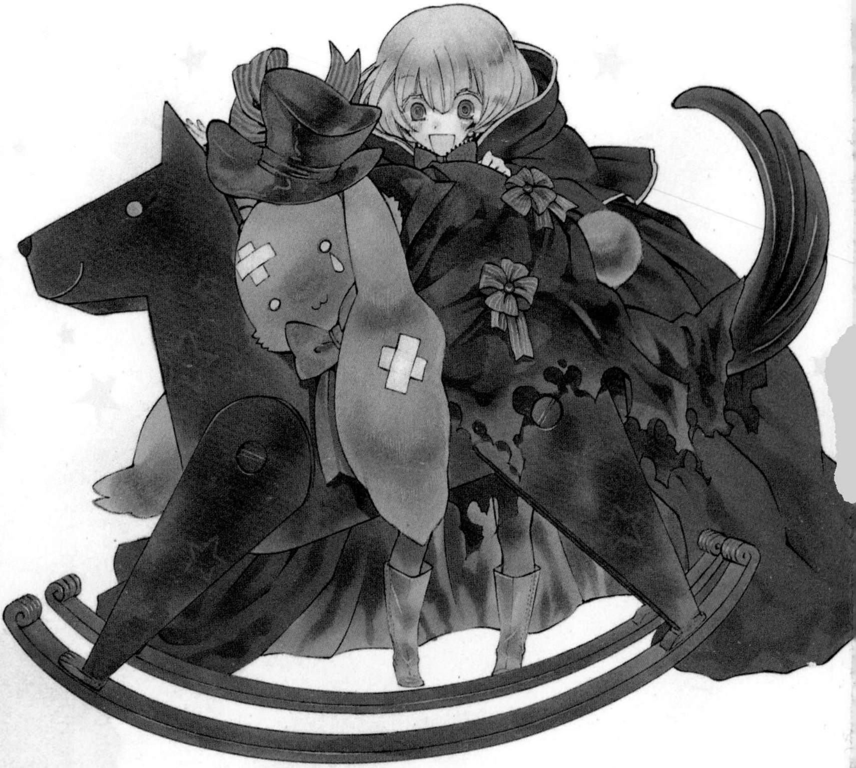

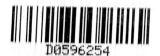

CONTENTS

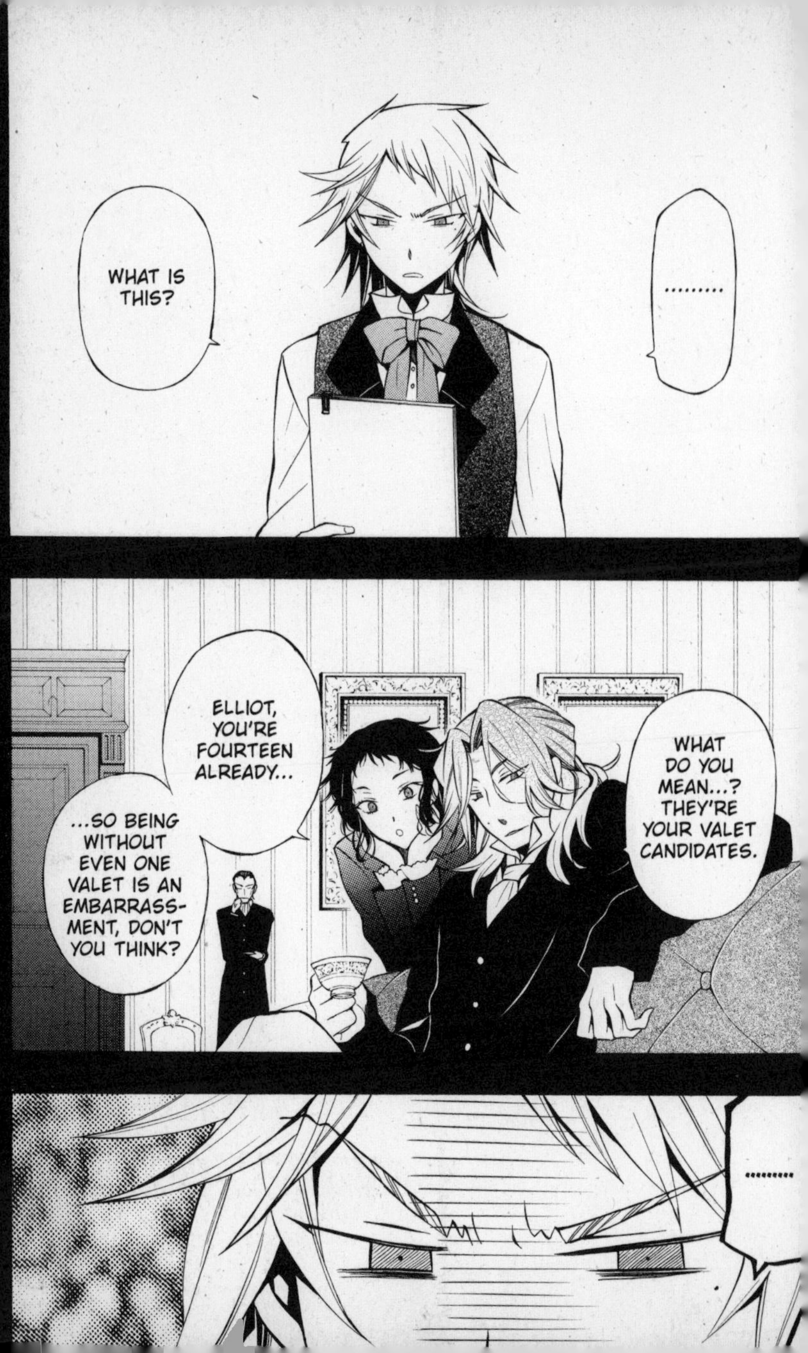

....
WHAT IS THIS?
WHAT DO YOU MEAN...? THEY'RE YOUR VALET CANDIDATES.
ELLIOT, YOU'RE FOURTEEN ALREADY...
...SO BEING WITHOUT EVEN ONE VALET IS AN EMBARRASS-MENT, DON'T YOU THINK?
....

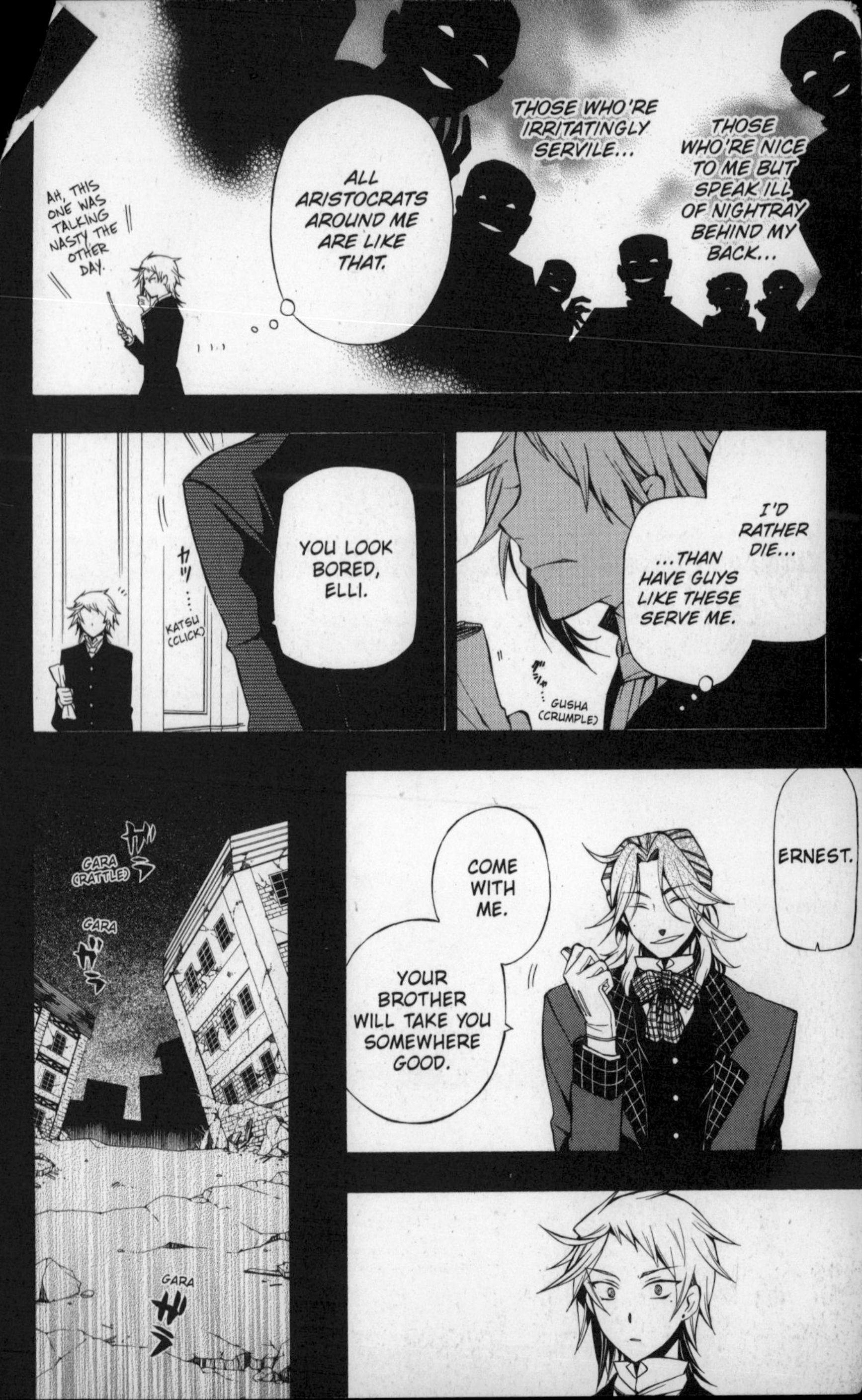
THOSE WHO'RE NICE TO ME BUT SPEAK ILL OF NIGHTRAY BEHIND MY BACK...
THOSE WHO'RE IRRITATINGLY SERVILE...
ALL ARISTOCRATS AROUND ME ARE LIKE THAT.
AH, THIS ONE WAS TALKING NASTY THE OTHER DAY.
I'D RATHER DIE...
...THAN HAVE GUYS LIKE THESE SERVE ME.
GUSHA (CRUMPLE)
YOU LOOK BORED, ELLI.
KATSU (CLICK)
ERNEST.
COME WITH ME.
YOUR BROTHER WILL TAKE YOU SOMEWHERE GOOD.
GARA (RATTLE)
GARA
GARA

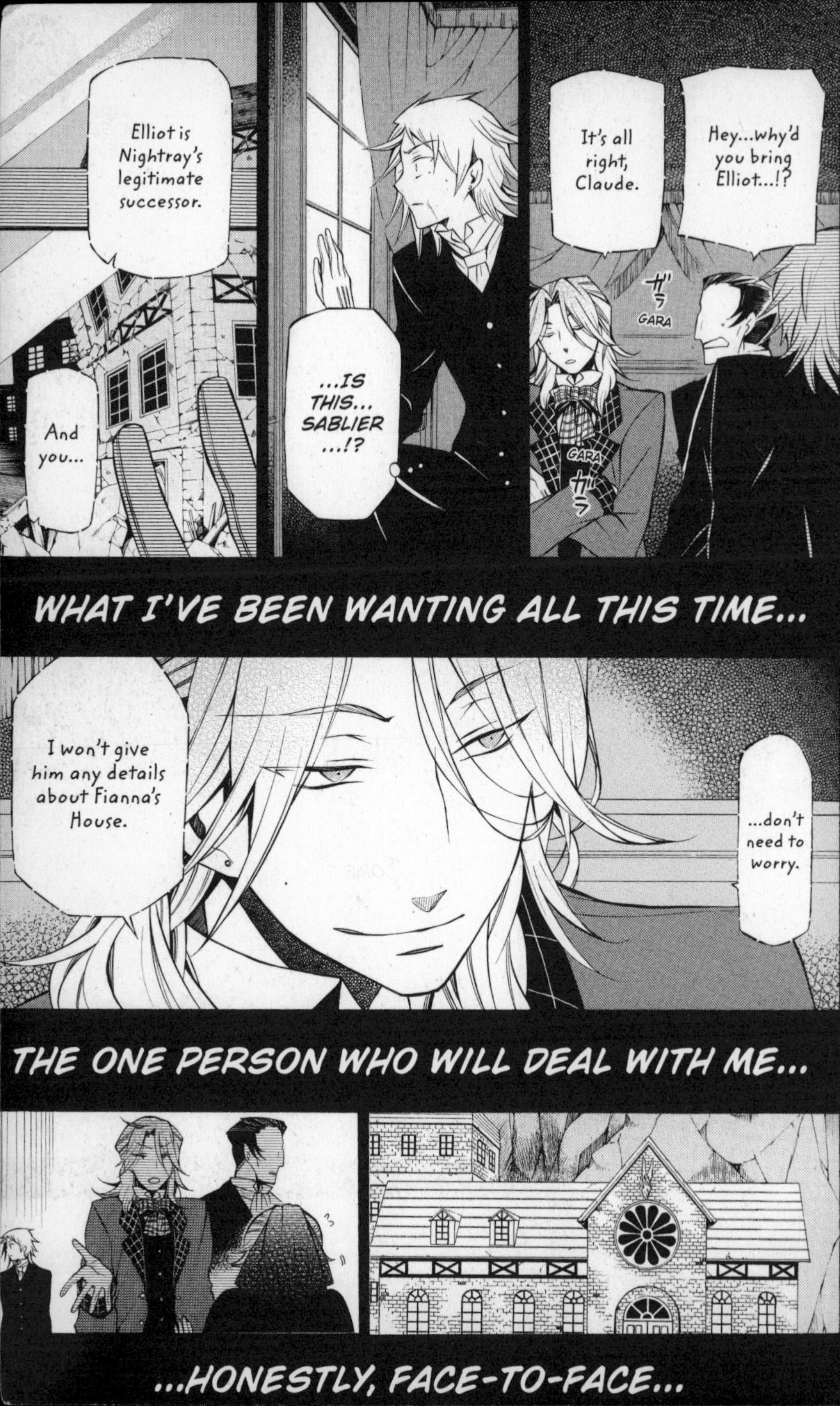
Hey...why'd you bring Elliot...!?
It's all right, Claude.
ガラ
GARA
GARA
ガラ
...IS THIS... SABLIER ...!?
Elliot is Nightray's legitimate successor.
And you...
WHAT I'VE BEEN WANTING ALL THIS TIME...
...don't need to worry.
I won't give him any details about Fianna's House.
THE ONE PERSON WHO WILL DEAL WITH ME...
...HONESTLY, FACE-TO-FACE...

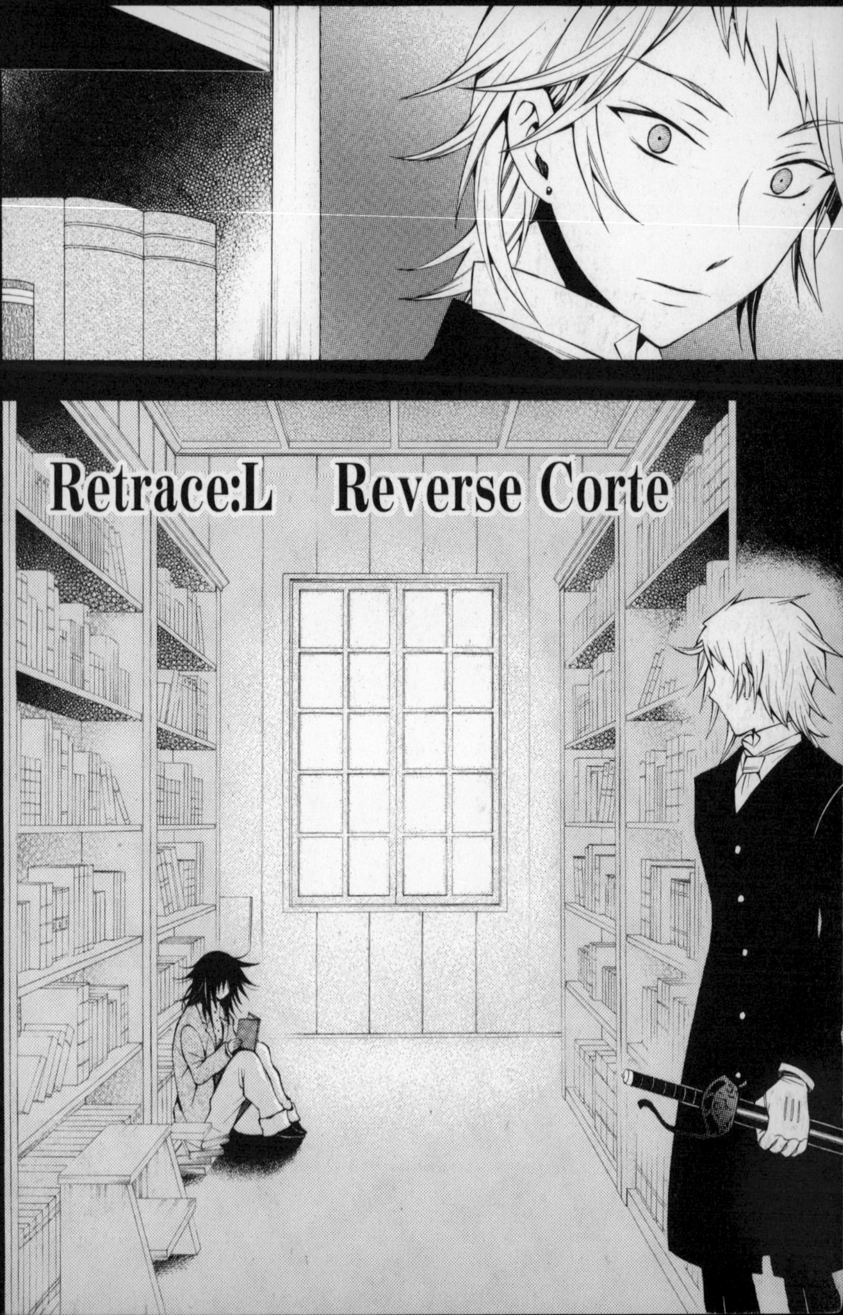
Retrace:L Reverse Corte

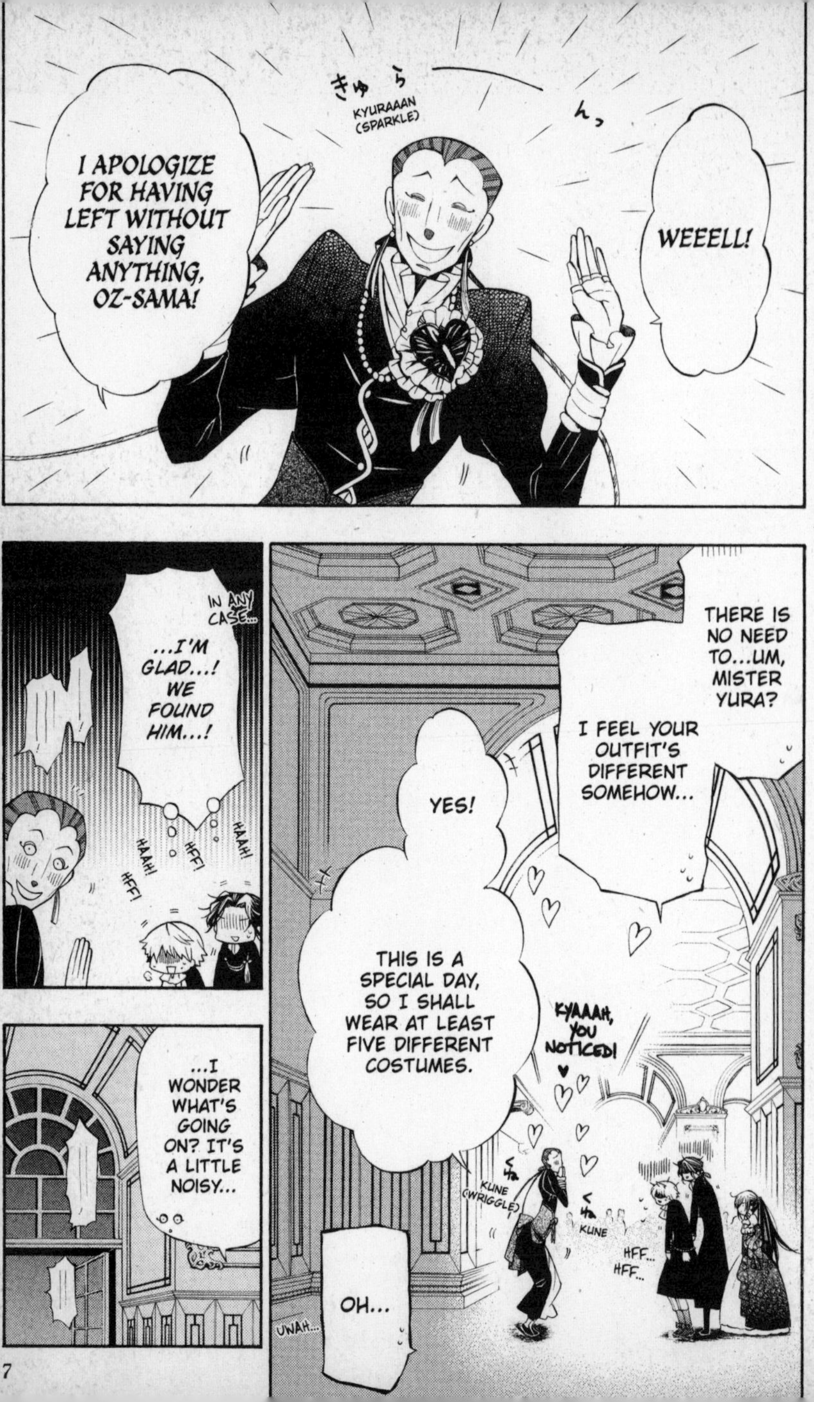
WEEELL!
きゅらん
KYURAAAN (SPARKLE)
I APOLOGIZE FOR HAVING LEFT WITHOUT SAYING ANYTHING, OZ-SAMA!
THERE IS NO NEED TO...UM, MISTER YURA?
I FEEL YOUR OUTFIT'S DIFFERENT SOMEHOW...
YES!
KYAAAH, YOU NOTICED!
THIS IS A SPECIAL DAY, SO I SHALL WEAR AT LEAST FIVE DIFFERENT COSTUMES.
KUNE (WRIGGLE)
KUNE
HFF... HFF...
OH...
UNWAH...
IN ANY CASE...
...I'M GLAD...! WE FOUND HIM...!
HAAH! HFF! HAAH! HFF!
...I WONDER WHAT'S GOING ON? IT'S A LITTLE NOISY...

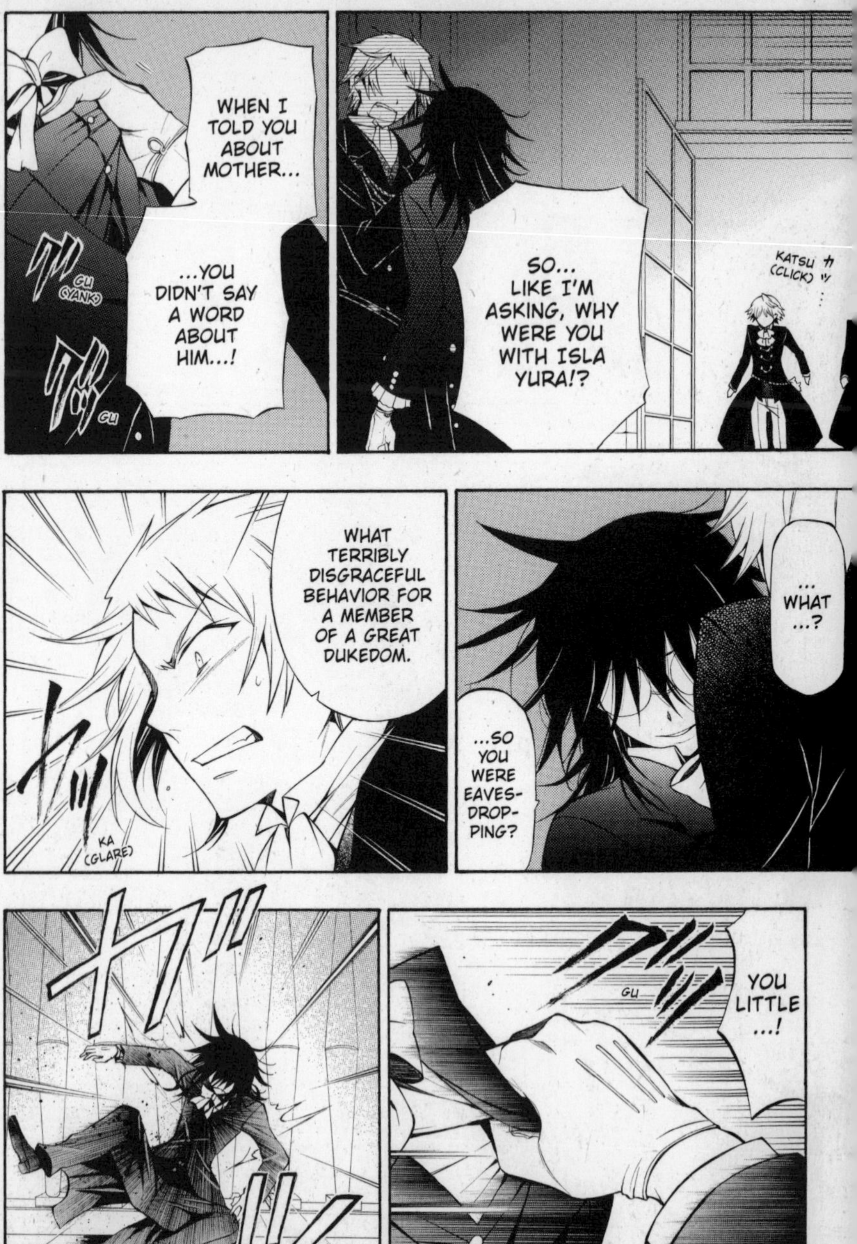
KATSU (CLICK)
SO... LIKE I'M ASKING, WHY WERE YOU WITH ISLA YURA!?
WHEN I TOLD YOU ABOUT MOTHER...
...YOU DIDN'T SAY A WORD ABOUT HIM...!
GU (YANK)
GU
... WHAT ...?
...SO YOU WERE EAVES-DROPPING?
WHAT TERRIBLY DISGRACEFUL BEHAVIOR FOR A MEMBER OF A GREAT DUKEDOM.
KA (GLARE)
YOU LITTLE ...!
GU
GA (WHAM)

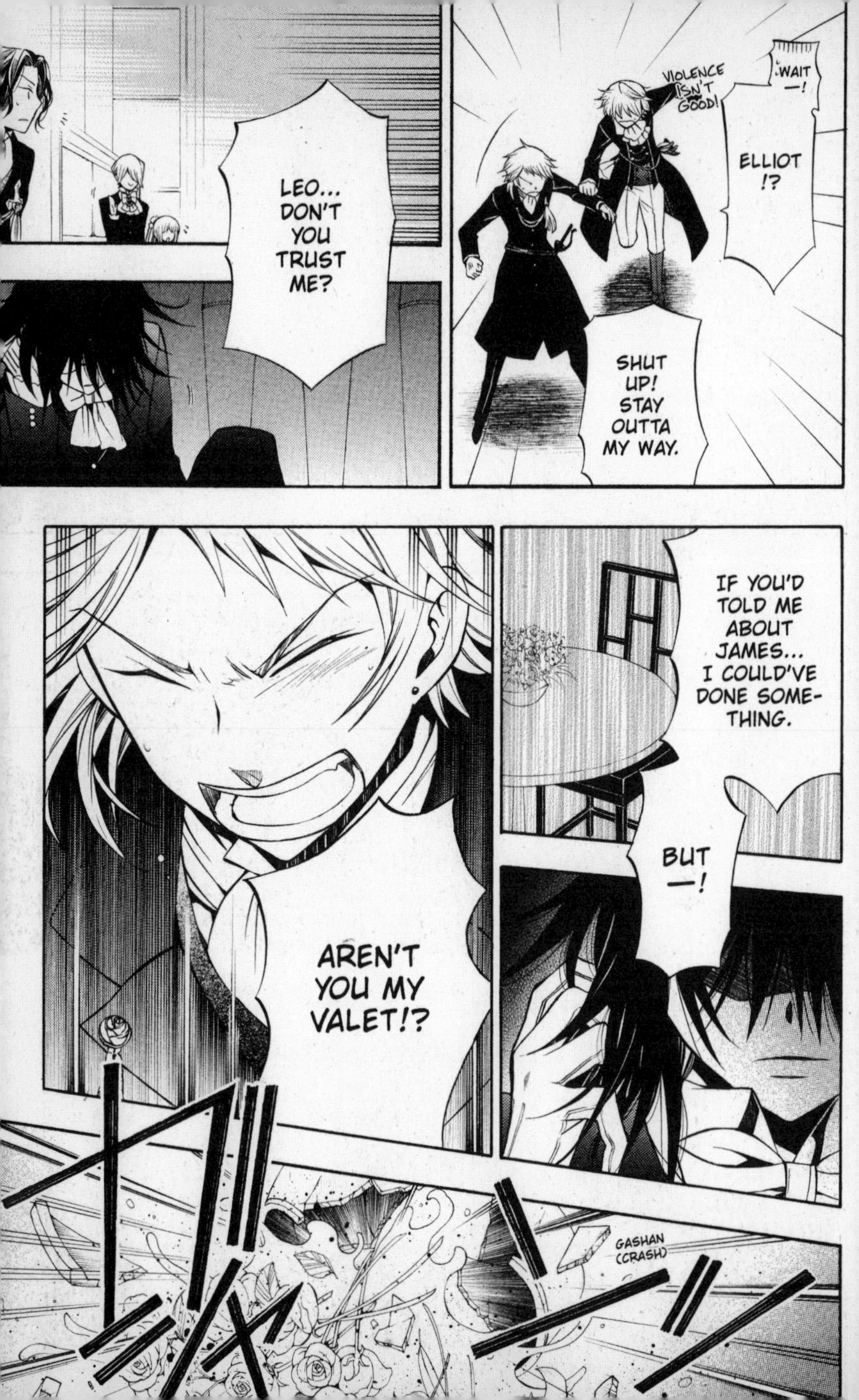
...WAIT—!
ELLIOT!?
VIOLENCE ISN'T GOOD!
SHUT UP! STAY OUTTA MY WAY.
LEO... DON'T YOU TRUST ME?
IF YOU'D TOLD ME ABOUT JAMES... I COULD'VE DONE SOME-THING.
BUT—!
AREN'T YOU MY VALET!?
GASHAN (CRASH)

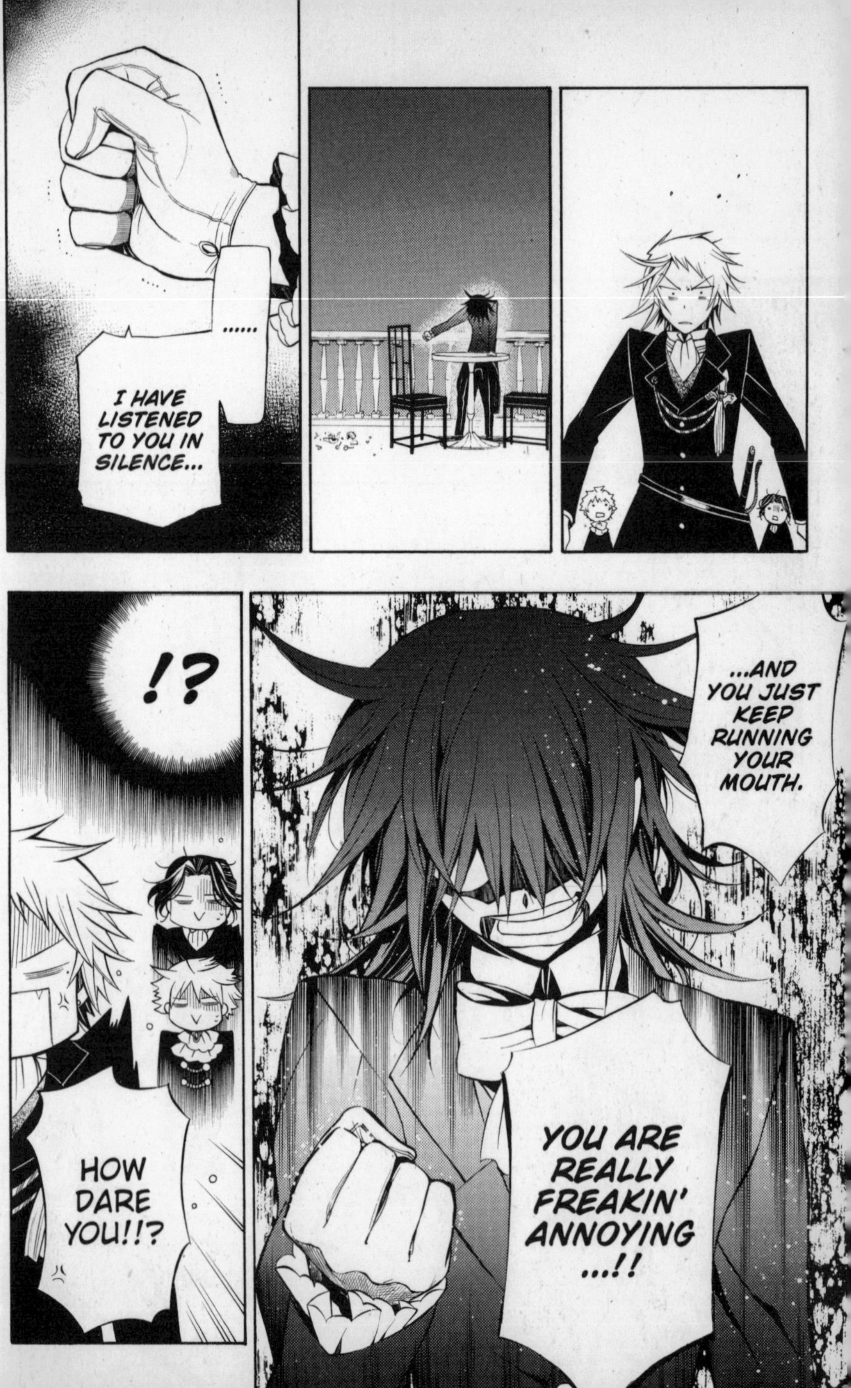
......
I HAVE LISTENED TO YOU IN SILENCE...
...AND YOU JUST KEEP RUNNING YOUR MOUTH.
YOU ARE REALLY FREAKIN' ANNOYING ...!!
!?
HOW DARE YOU!!?

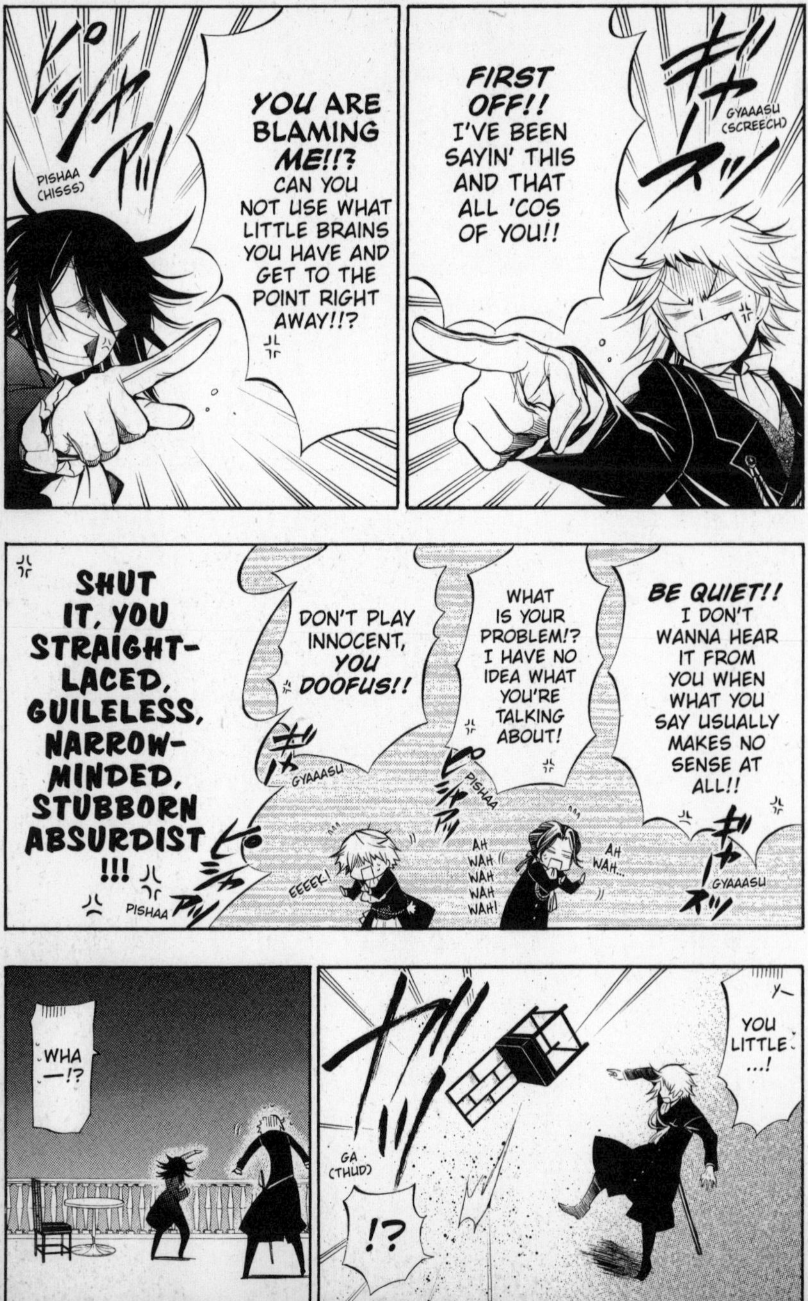
GYAAASU (SCREECH)
FIRST OFF!! I'VE BEEN SAYIN' THIS AND THAT ALL 'COS OF YOU!!
PISHAA (HISSS)
YOU ARE BLAMING ME!!? CAN YOU NOT USE WHAT LITTLE BRAINS YOU HAVE AND GET TO THE POINT RIGHT AWAY!!?
BE QUIET!! I DON'T WANNA HEAR IT FROM YOU WHEN WHAT YOU SAY USUALLY MAKES NO SENSE AT ALL!!
GYAAASU
WHAT IS YOUR PROBLEM!? I HAVE NO IDEA WHAT YOU'RE TALKING ABOUT!
PISHAA
AH WAH...
AH WAH WAH WAH WAH!
DON'T PLAY INNOCENT, YOU DOOFUS!!
GYAAASU
EEEEK!
SHUT IT, YOU STRAIGHT-LACED, GUILELESS, NARROW-MINDED, STUBBORN ABSURDIST!!!
PISHAA
YOU LITTLE...!
GA (THUD)
!?
WHA—!?

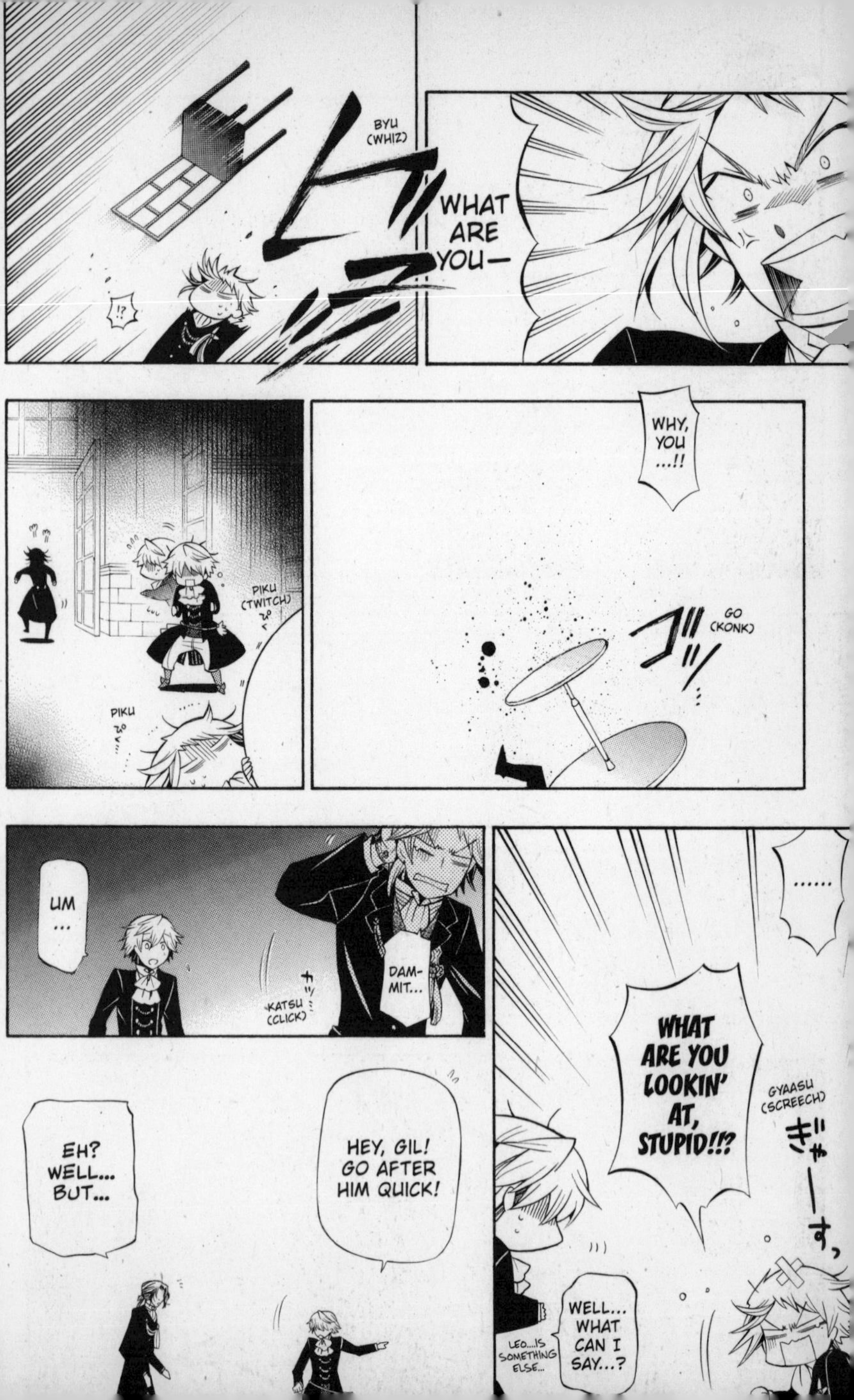
WHAT ARE YOU—
BYU (WHIZ)
!?
WHY, YOU ...!!
GO (KONK)
PIKU (TWITCH)
PIKU
....
......
WHAT ARE YOU LOOKIN' AT, STUPID!!?
GYAASU (SCREECH)
ぎゃーすっ
WELL... WHAT CAN I SAY...?
LEO...IS SOMETHING ELSE...
DAM-MIT...
KATSU (CLICK)
UM ...
HEY, GIL! GO AFTER HIM QUICK!
EH? WELL... BUT...

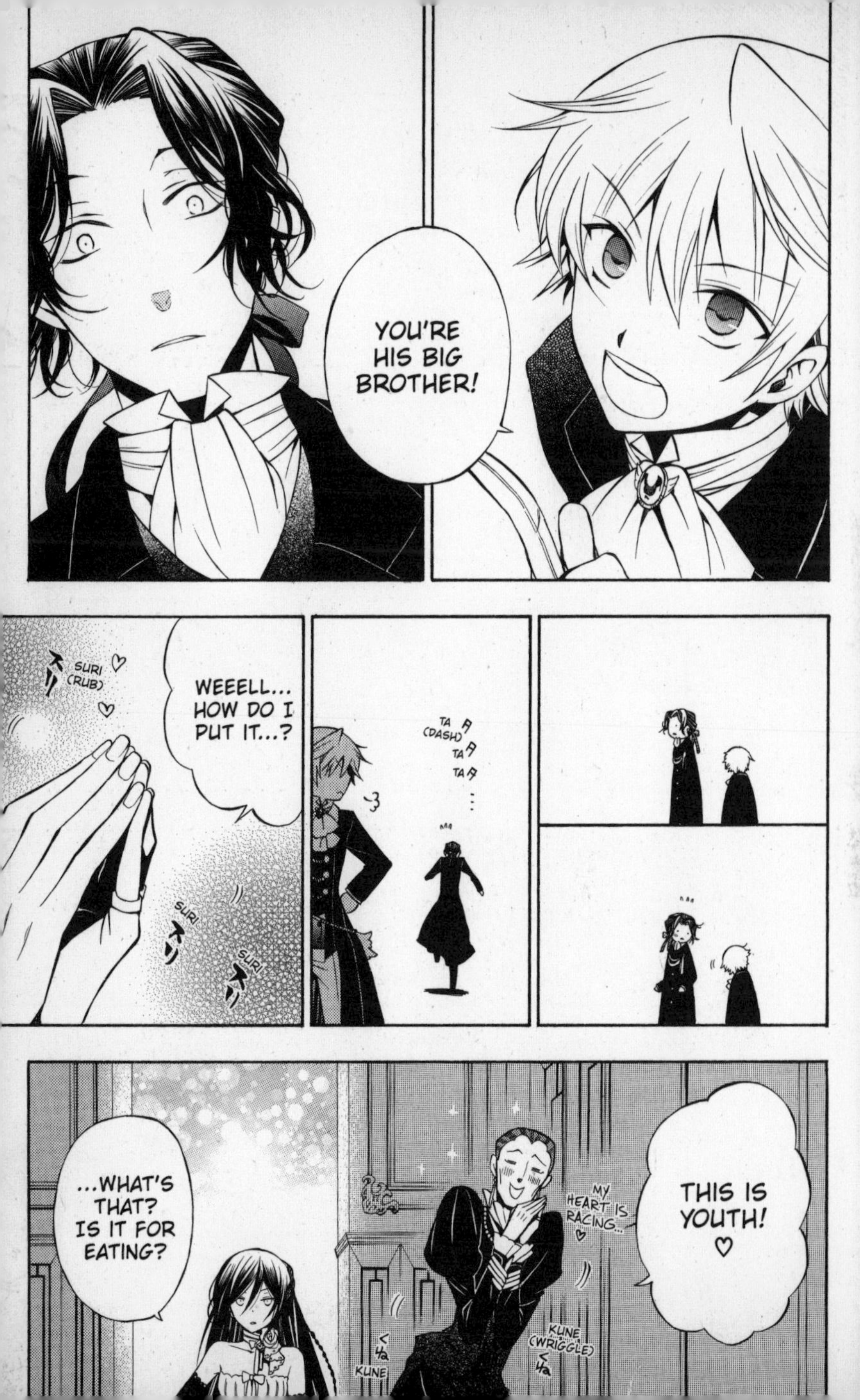
YOU'RE HIS BIG BROTHER!
TA (DASH) TA TA
...
SURI (RUB)
WEEELL... HOW DO I PUT IT...?
SURI SURI
THIS IS YOUTH! ♡
MY HEART IS RACING... ♡
KUNE (WRIGGLE)
KUNE
...WHAT'S THAT? IS IT FOR EATING?

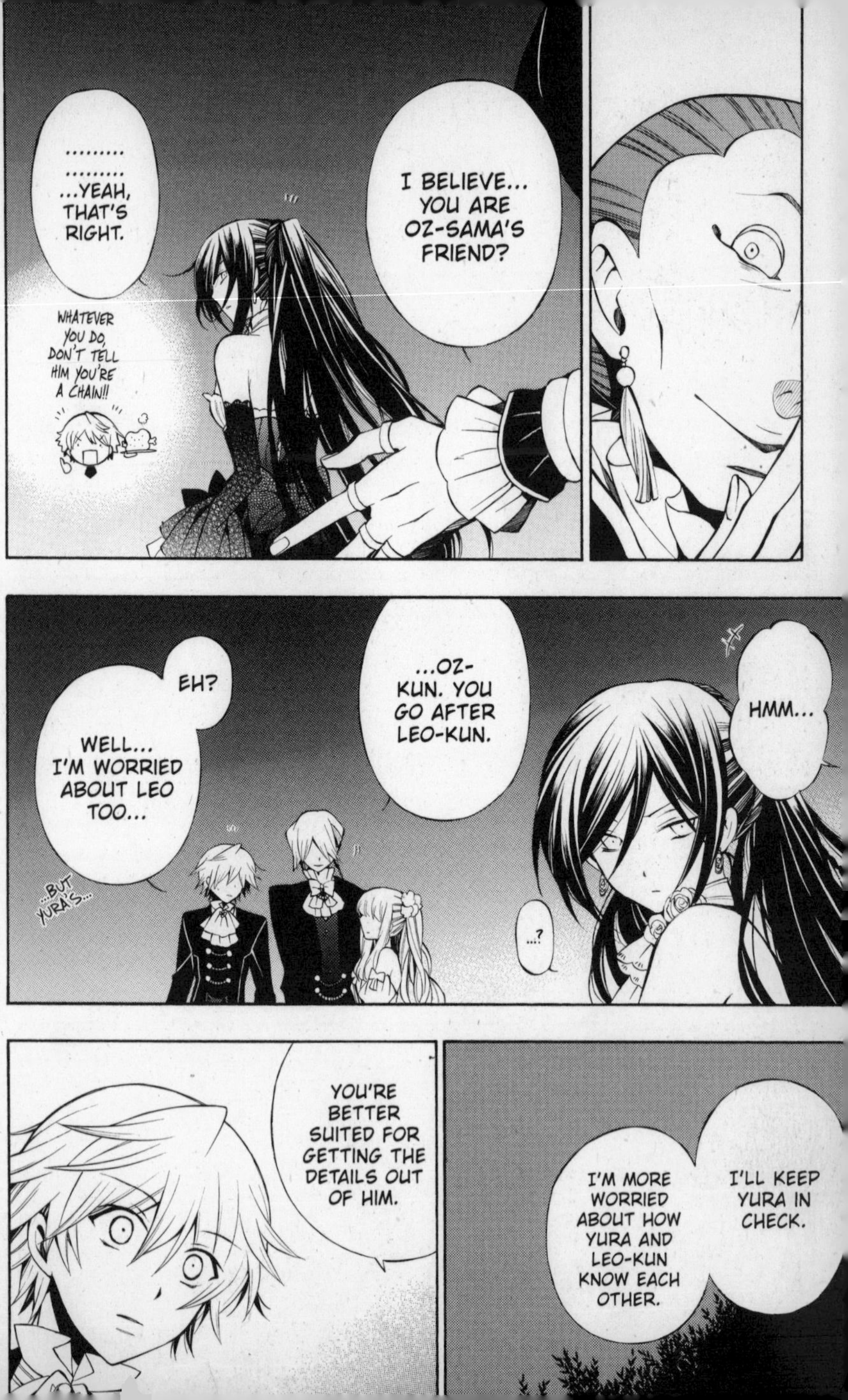
I BELIEVE... YOU ARE OZ-SAMA'S FRIEND?
....YEAH, THAT'S RIGHT.
WHATEVER YOU DO, DON'T TELL HIM YOU'RE A CHAIN!!
HMM...
...?
...OZ-KUN. YOU GO AFTER LEO-KUN.
EH?
WELL... I'M WORRIED ABOUT LEO TOO...
...BUT YURA'S...
I'LL KEEP YURA IN CHECK.
I'M MORE WORRIED ABOUT HOW YURA AND LEO-KUN KNOW EACH OTHER.
YOU'RE BETTER SUITED FOR GETTING THE DETAILS OUT OF HIM.

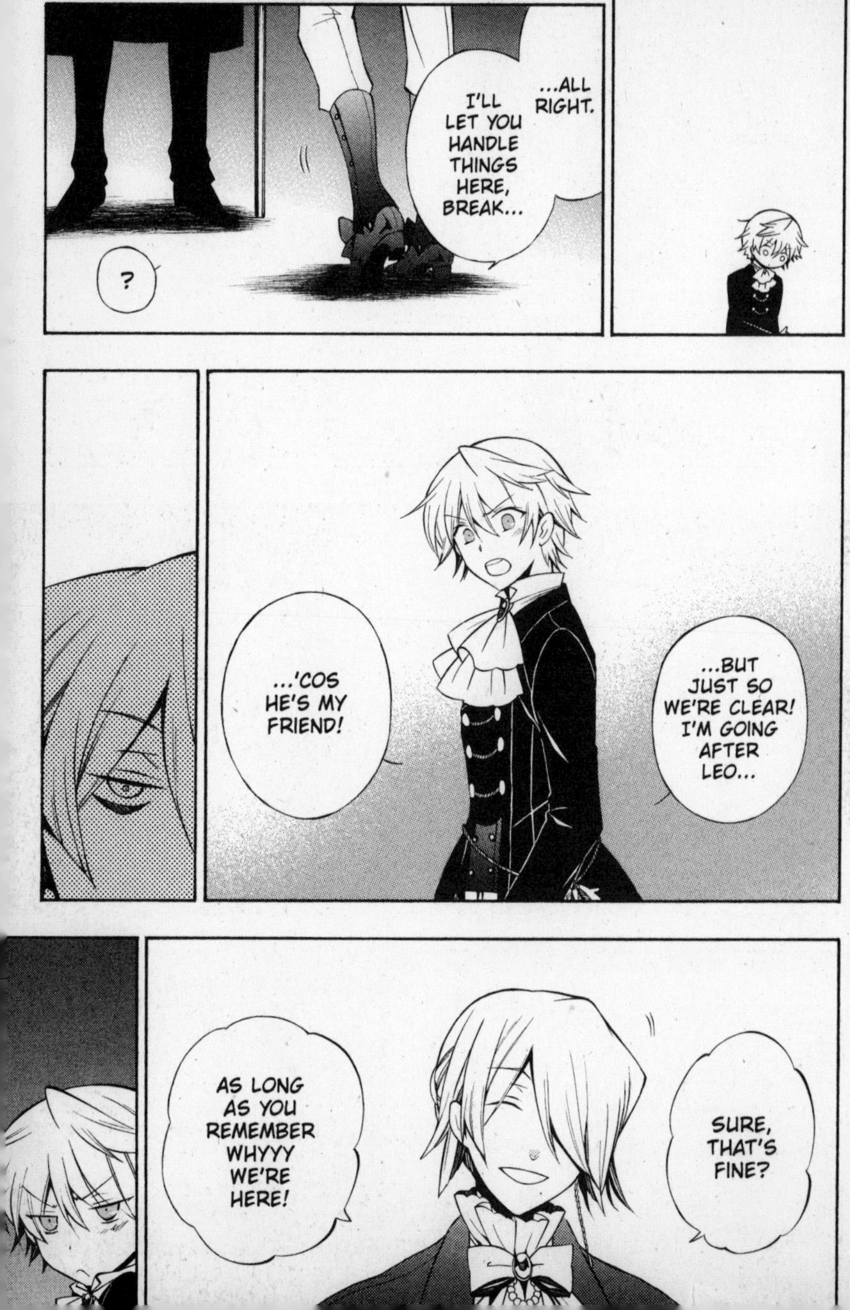
...ALL RIGHT.
I'LL LET YOU HANDLE THINGS HERE, BREAK...
?
...BUT JUST SO WE'RE CLEAR! I'M GOING AFTER LEO...
...'COS HE'S MY FRIEND!
SURE, THAT'S FINE?
AS LONG AS YOU REMEMBER WHYYY WE'RE HERE!

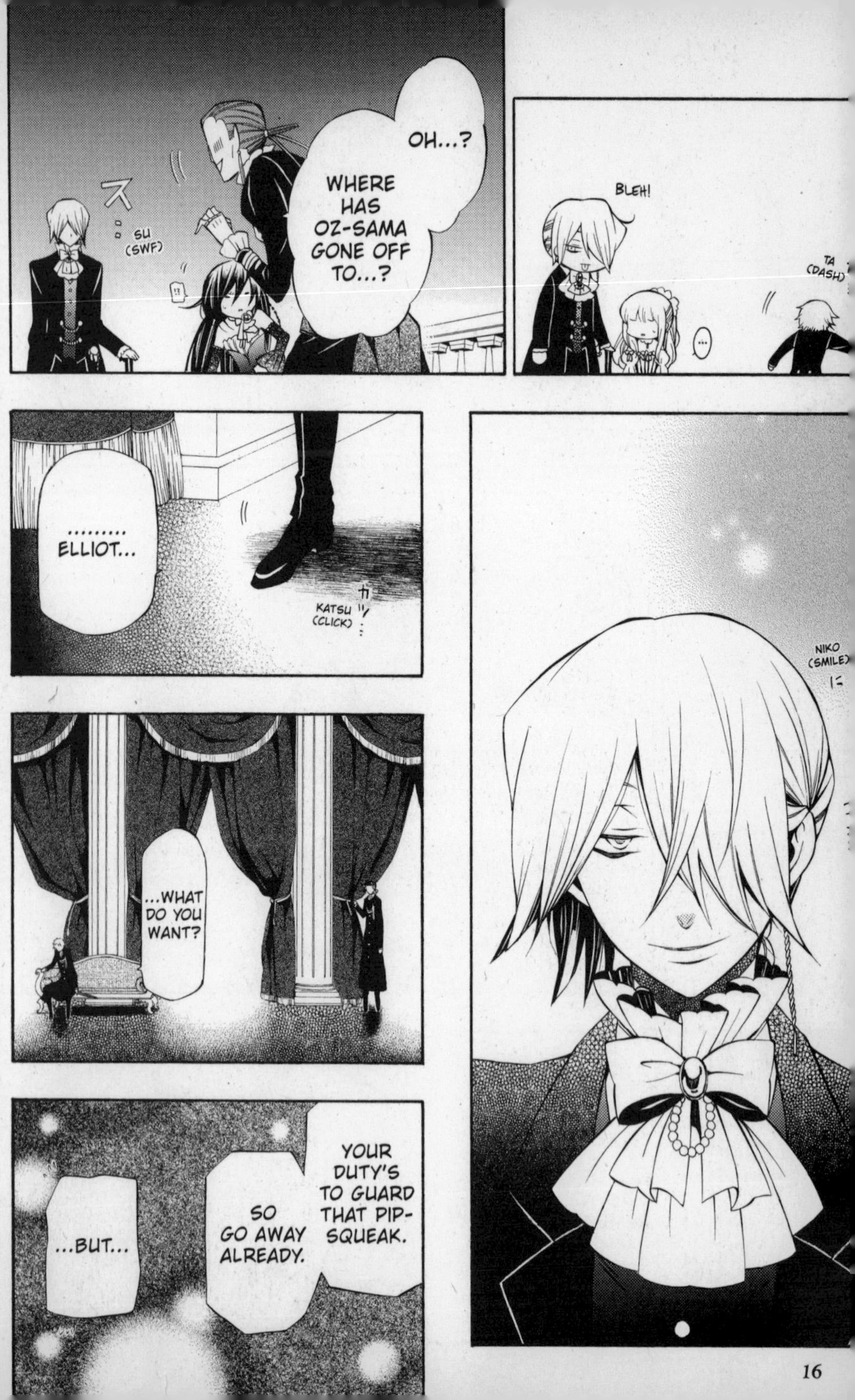
BLEH!
TA (DASH)
...
OH...? WHERE HAS OZ-SAMA GONE OFF TO...?
SU (SWF)
!?
NIKO (SMILE)
.........ELLIOT...
KATSU (CLICK)
...WHAT DO YOU WANT?
YOUR DUTY'S TO GUARD THAT PIP-SQUEAK.
SO GO AWAY ALREADY.
...BUT...

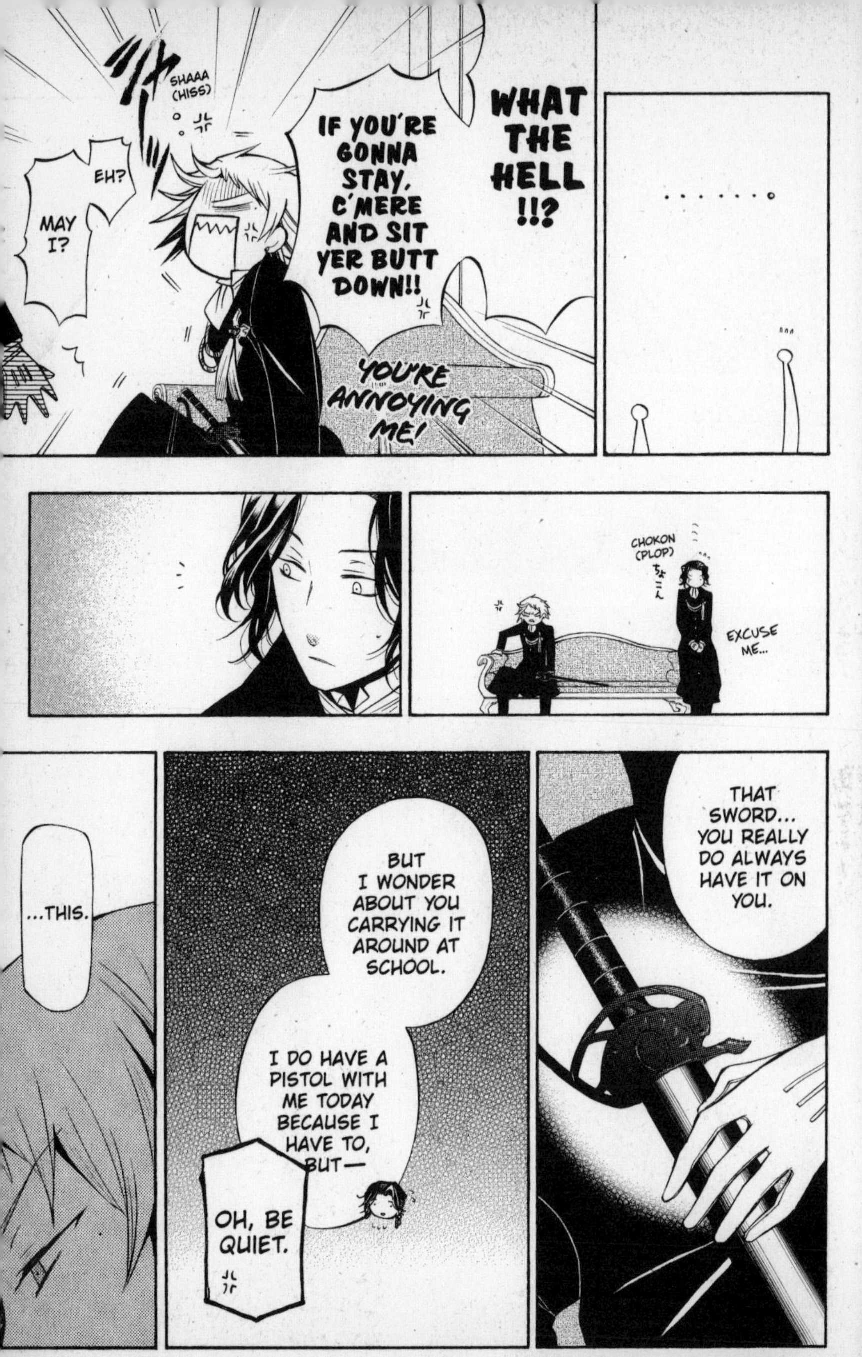

.......。
WHAT THE HELL!!?
IF YOU'RE GONNA STAY, C'MERE AND SIT YER BUTT DOWN!!
YOU'RE ANNOYING ME!
SHAAA (HISS)
EH?
MAY I?
CHOKON (PLOP)
ちょこん
EXCUSE ME...
THAT SWORD... YOU REALLY DO ALWAYS HAVE IT ON YOU.
BUT I WONDER ABOUT YOU CARRYING IT AROUND AT SCHOOL.
I DO HAVE A PISTOL WITH ME TODAY BECAUSE I HAVE TO, BUT—
OH, BE QUIET.
...THIS.

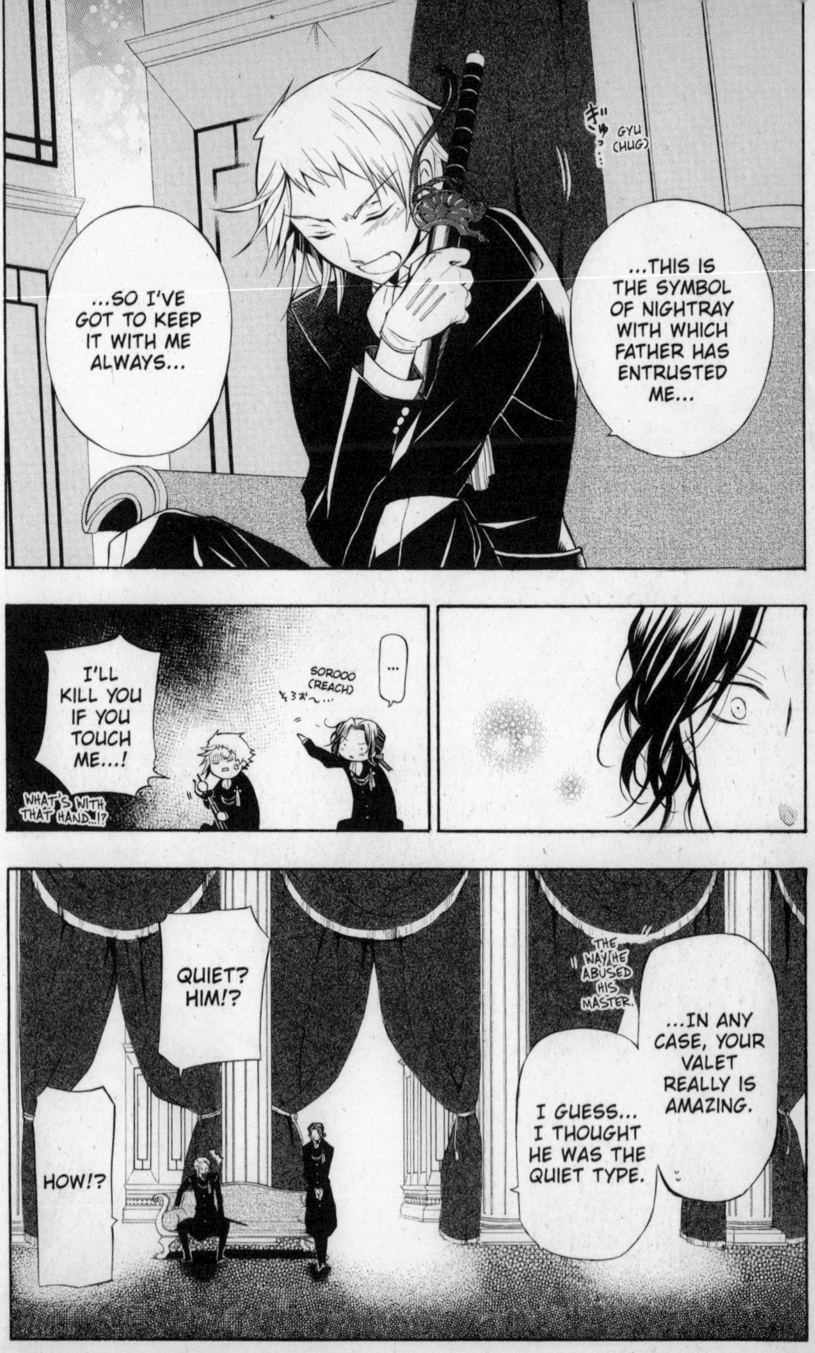
GYU (HUG)
...THIS IS THE SYMBOL OF NIGHTRAY WITH WHICH FATHER HAS ENTRUSTED ME...
...SO I'VE GOT TO KEEP IT WITH ME ALWAYS...
...
SOROOO (REACH)
I'LL KILL YOU IF YOU TOUCH ME...!
WHAT'S WITH THAT HAND...!?
THE WAY HE ABUSED HIS MASTER.
...IN ANY CASE, YOUR VALET REALLY IS AMAZING.
I GUESS... I THOUGHT HE WAS THE QUIET TYPE.
QUIET? HIM!?
HOW!?

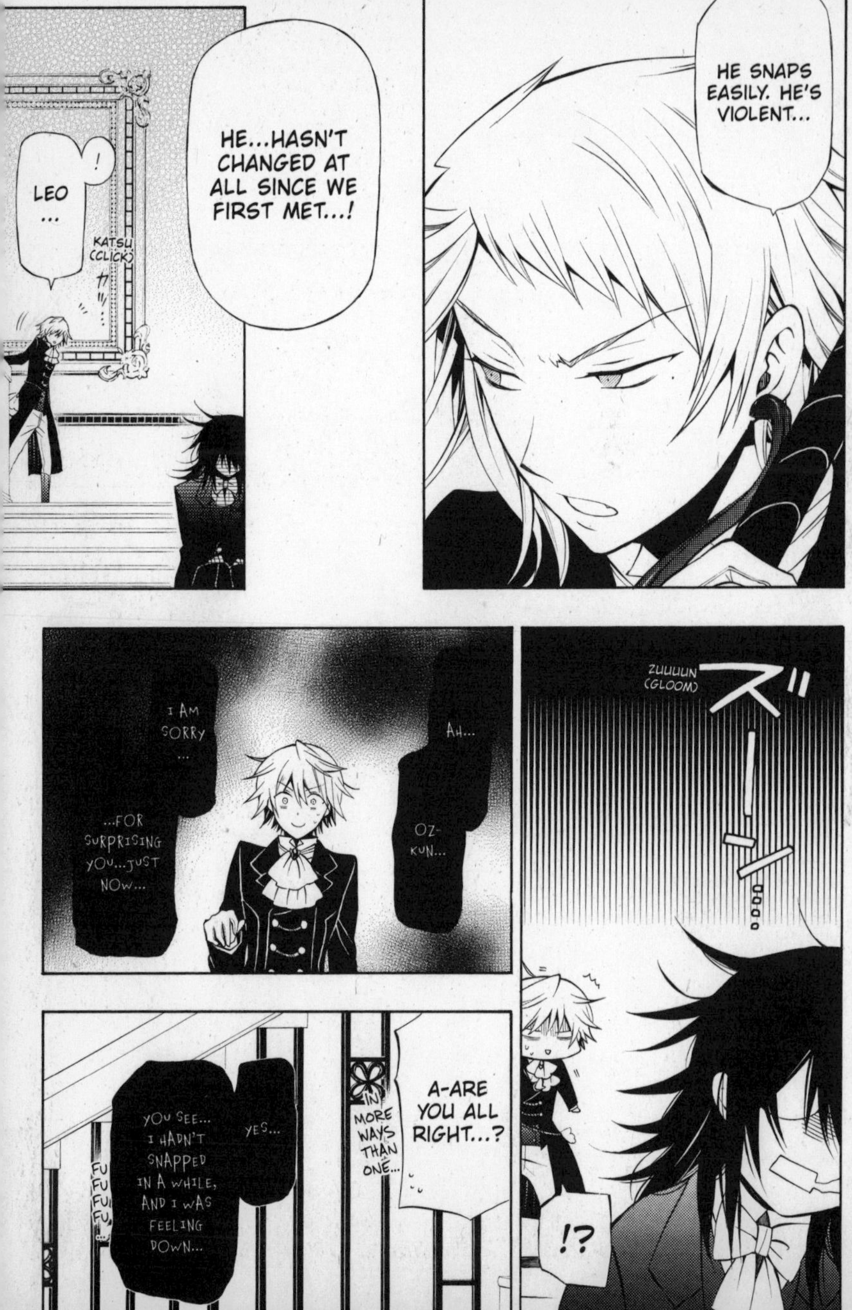
HE SNAPS EASILY. HE'S VIOLENT...
HE...HASN'T CHANGED AT ALL SINCE WE FIRST MET...!
!
LEO ...
KATSU (CLICK)
ZUUUUN (GLOOM)
AH... OZ-KUN...
I AM SORRY ...
...FOR SURPRISING YOU...JUST NOW...
A-ARE YOU ALL RIGHT...?
IN MORE WAYS THAN ONE...
YES...
YOU SEE... I HADN'T SNAPPED IN A WHILE, AND I WAS FEELING DOWN...
FU FU FU FU...
!?

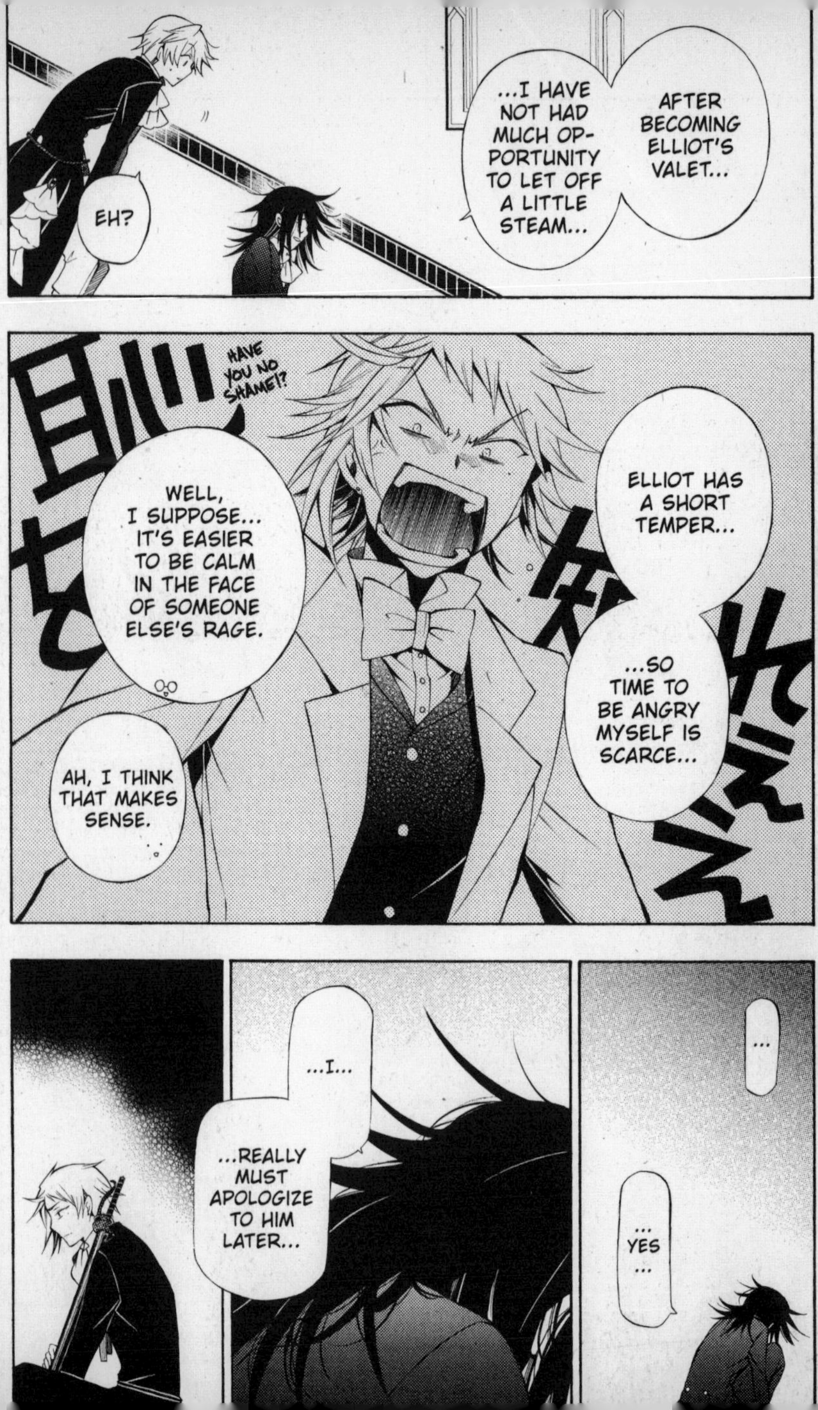
AFTER BECOMING ELLIOT'S VALET...
...I HAVE NOT HAD MUCH OP-PORTUNITY TO LET OFF A LITTLE STEAM...
EH?
ELLIOT HAS A SHORT TEMPER...
...SO TIME TO BE ANGRY MYSELF IS SCARCE...
HAVE YOU NO SHAME!?
WELL, I SUPPOSE... IT'S EASIER TO BE CALM IN THE FACE OF SOMEONE ELSE'S RAGE.
AH, I THINK THAT MAKES SENSE.
...
...YES...
...I...
...REALLY MUST APOLOGIZE TO HIM LATER...

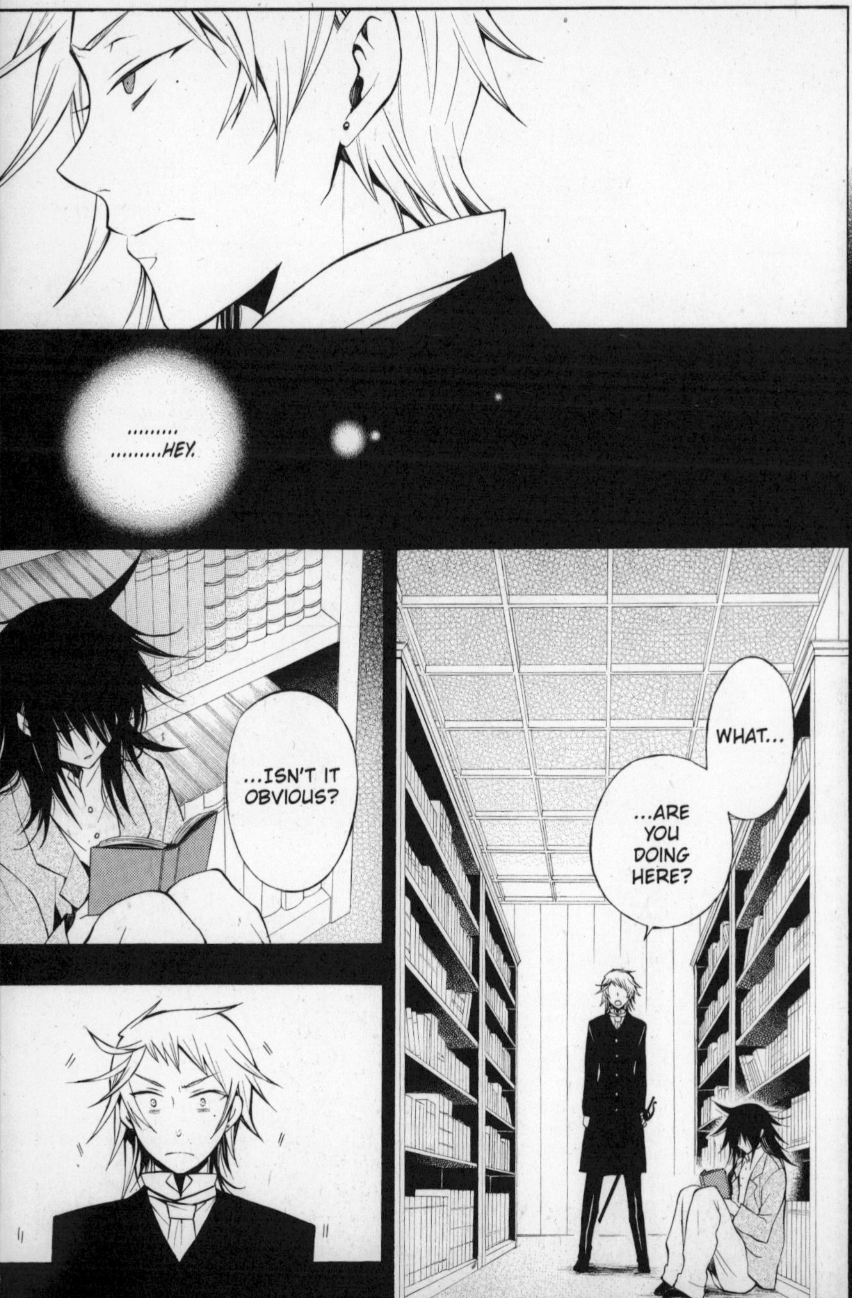
....
.........HEY.
WHAT...
...ARE YOU DOING HERE?
...ISN'T IT OBVIOUS?

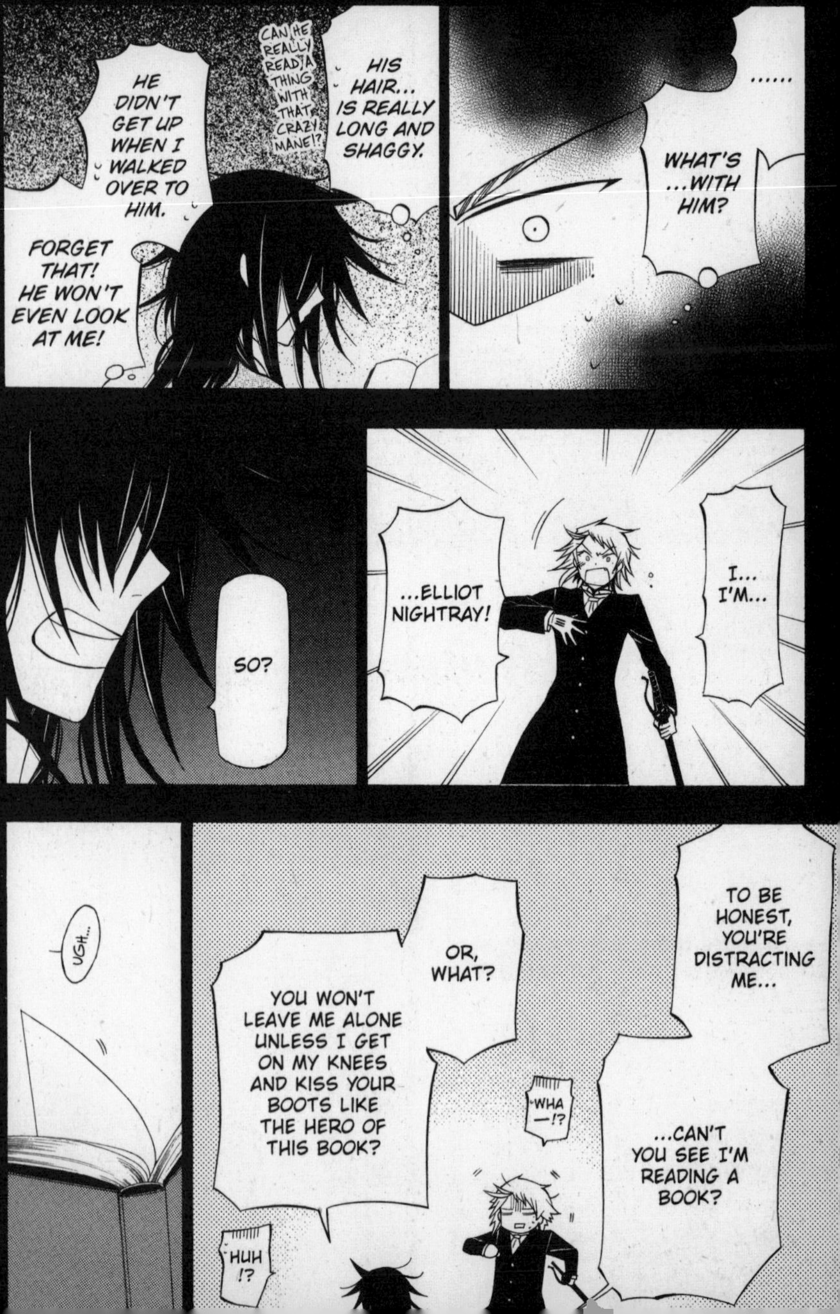
......
WHAT'S ...WITH HIM?
HIS HAIR... IS REALLY LONG AND SHAGGY.
CAN HE REALLY READ A THING WITH THAT CRAZY MANE!?
HE DIDN'T GET UP WHEN I WALKED OVER TO HIM.
FORGET THAT! HE WON'T EVEN LOOK AT ME!
I... I'M...
...ELLIOT NIGHTRAY!
SO?
TO BE HONEST, YOU'RE DISTRACTING ME...
...CAN'T YOU SEE I'M READING A BOOK?
OR, WHAT?
YOU WON'T LEAVE ME ALONE UNLESS I GET ON MY KNEES AND KISS YOUR BOOTS LIKE THE HERO OF THIS BOOK?
WHA—!?
HUH!?
UGH...

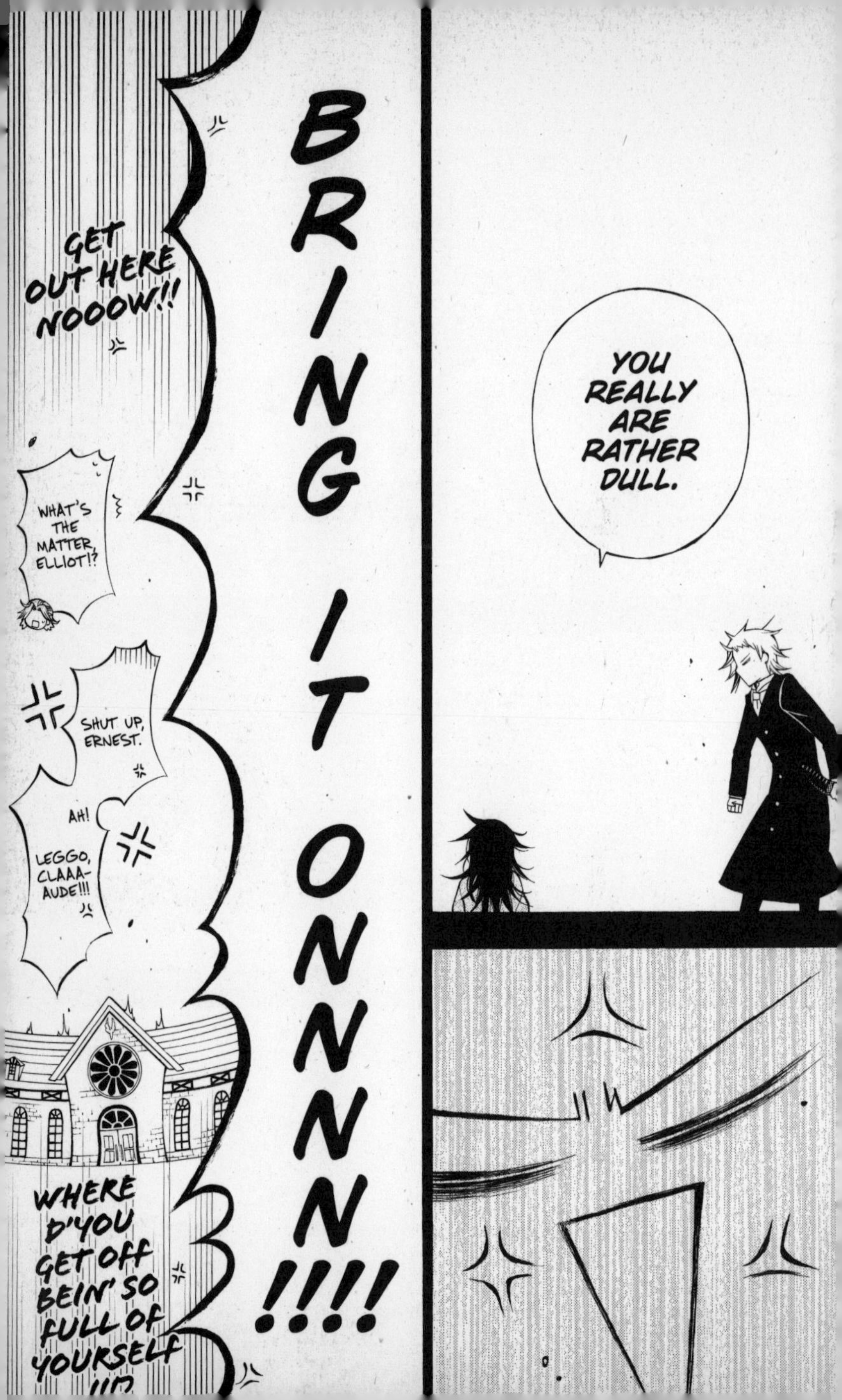
YOU REALLY ARE RATHER DULL.
BRING IT ONNNN!!!!
GET OUT HERE NOOOW!!
WHAT'S THE MATTER, ELLIOT!?
SHUT UP, ERNEST.
AH!
LEGGO, CLAAA-AUDE!!!
WHERE D'YOU GET OFF BEIN' SO FULL OF YOURSELF

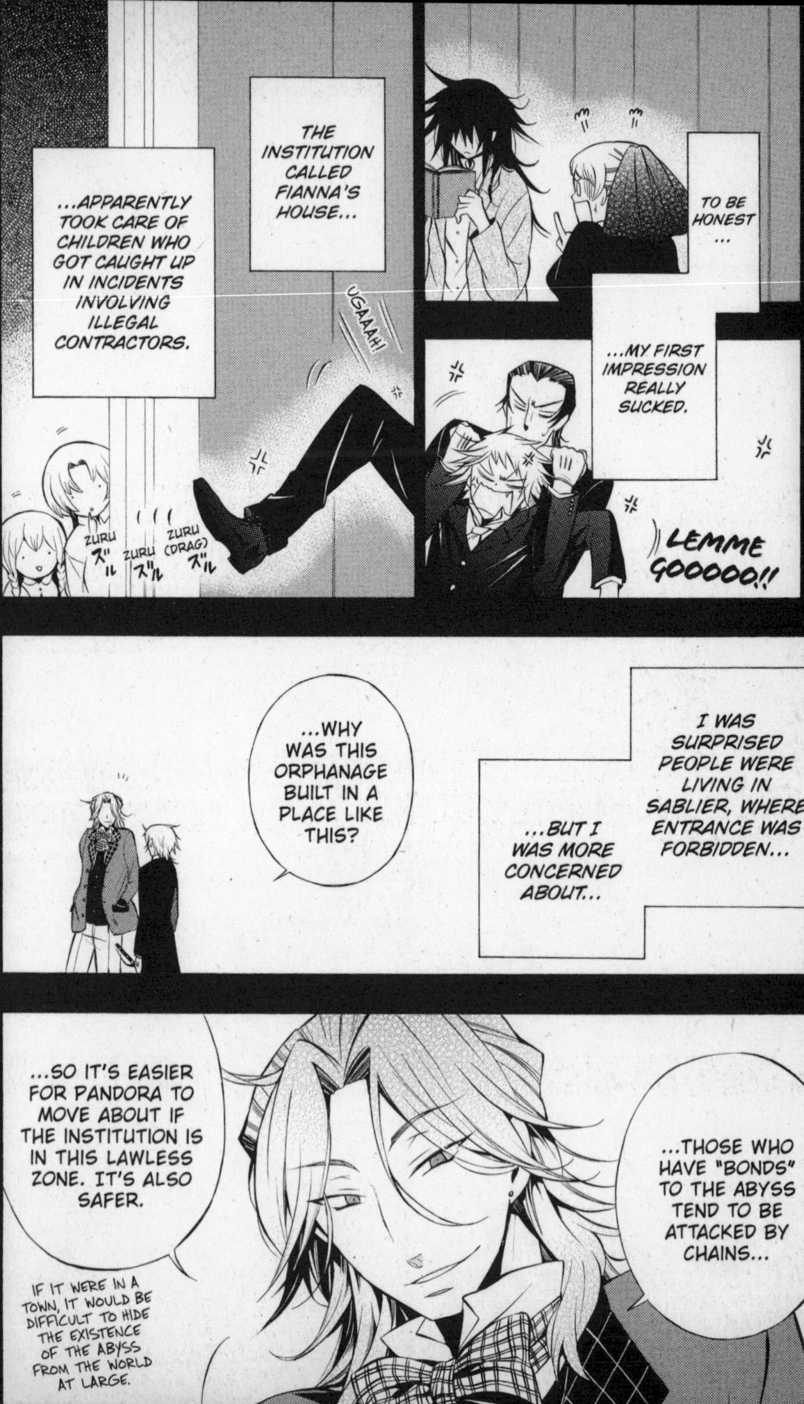
TO BE HONEST ...
...MY FIRST IMPRESSION REALLY SUCKED.
LEMME GOOOOO!!
THE INSTITUTION CALLED FIANNA'S HOUSE...
...APPARENTLY TOOK CARE OF CHILDREN WHO GOT CAUGHT UP IN INCIDENTS INVOLVING ILLEGAL CONTRACTORS.
UGAAAH!
ZURU
ZURU
ZURU (DRAG)
I WAS SURPRISED PEOPLE WERE LIVING IN SABLIER, WHERE ENTRANCE WAS FORBIDDEN...
...BUT I WAS MORE CONCERNED ABOUT...
...WHY WAS THIS ORPHANAGE BUILT IN A PLACE LIKE THIS?
...THOSE WHO HAVE "BONDS" TO THE ABYSS TEND TO BE ATTACKED BY CHAINS...
...SO IT'S EASIER FOR PANDORA TO MOVE ABOUT IF THE INSTITUTION IS IN THIS LAWLESS ZONE. IT'S ALSO SAFER.
IF IT WERE IN A TOWN, IT WOULD BE DIFFICULT TO HIDE THE EXISTENCE OF THE ABYSS FROM THE WORLD AT LARGE.

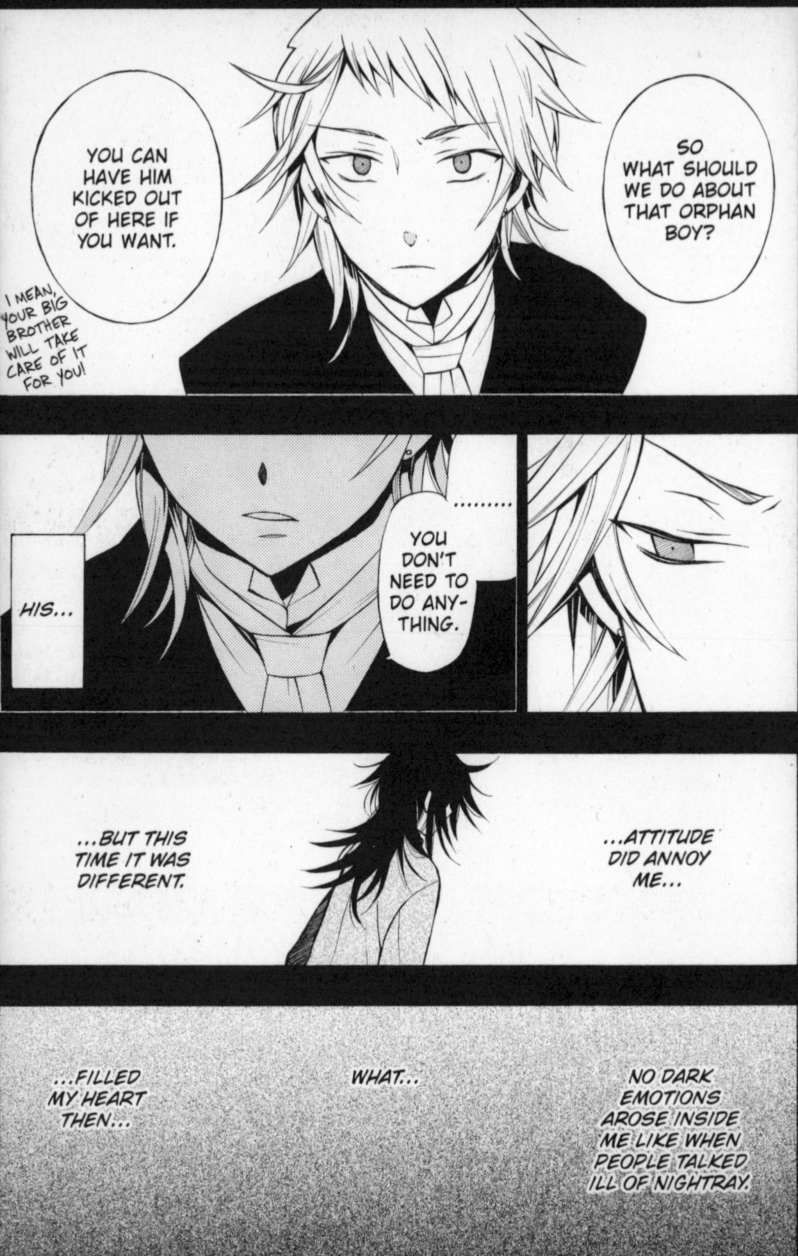
SO WHAT SHOULD WE DO ABOUT THAT ORPHAN BOY?
YOU CAN HAVE HIM KICKED OUT OF HERE IF YOU WANT.
I MEAN, YOUR BIG BROTHER WILL TAKE CARE OF IT FOR YOU!
....
YOU DON'T NEED TO DO ANY-THING.
HIS...
...ATTITUDE DID ANNOY ME...
...BUT THIS TIME IT WAS DIFFERENT.
NO DARK EMOTIONS AROSE INSIDE ME LIKE WHEN PEOPLE TALKED ILL OF NIGHTRAY.
WHAT...
...FILLED MY HEART THEN...

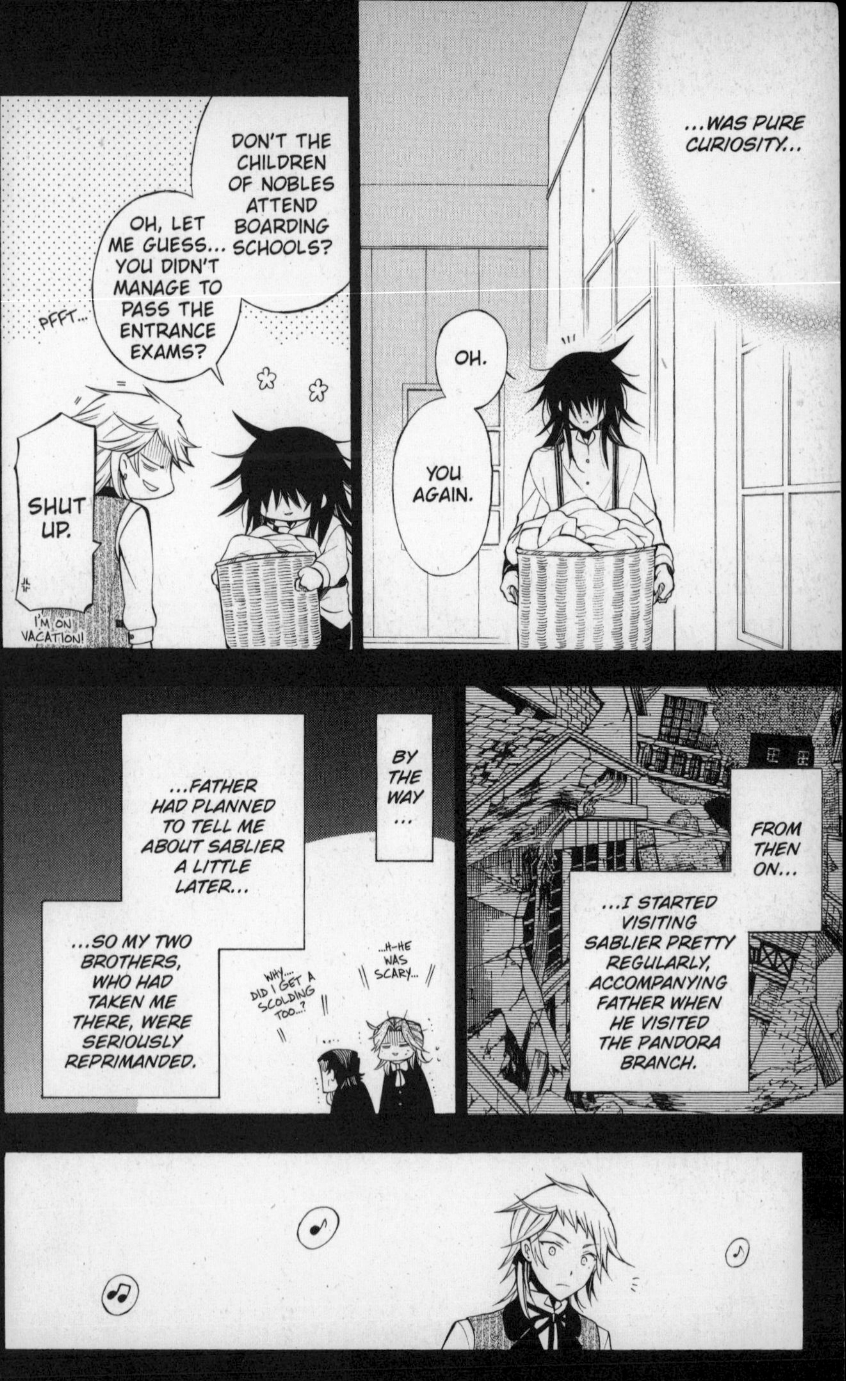
...WAS PURE CURIOSITY...
OH.
YOU AGAIN.
DON'T THE CHILDREN OF NOBLES ATTEND BOARDING SCHOOLS?
OH, LET ME GUESS... YOU DIDN'T MANAGE TO PASS THE ENTRANCE EXAMS?
PFFT...
SHUT UP.
I'M ON VACATION!
FROM THEN ON...
...I STARTED VISITING SABLIER PRETTY REGULARLY, ACCOMPANYING FATHER WHEN HE VISITED THE PANDORA BRANCH.
BY THE WAY...
...FATHER HAD PLANNED TO TELL ME ABOUT SABLIER A LITTLE LATER...
...SO MY TWO BROTHERS, WHO HAD TAKEN ME THERE, WERE SERIOUSLY REPRIMANDED.
...H-HE WAS SCARY...
WHY... DID I GET A SCOLDING TOO...?

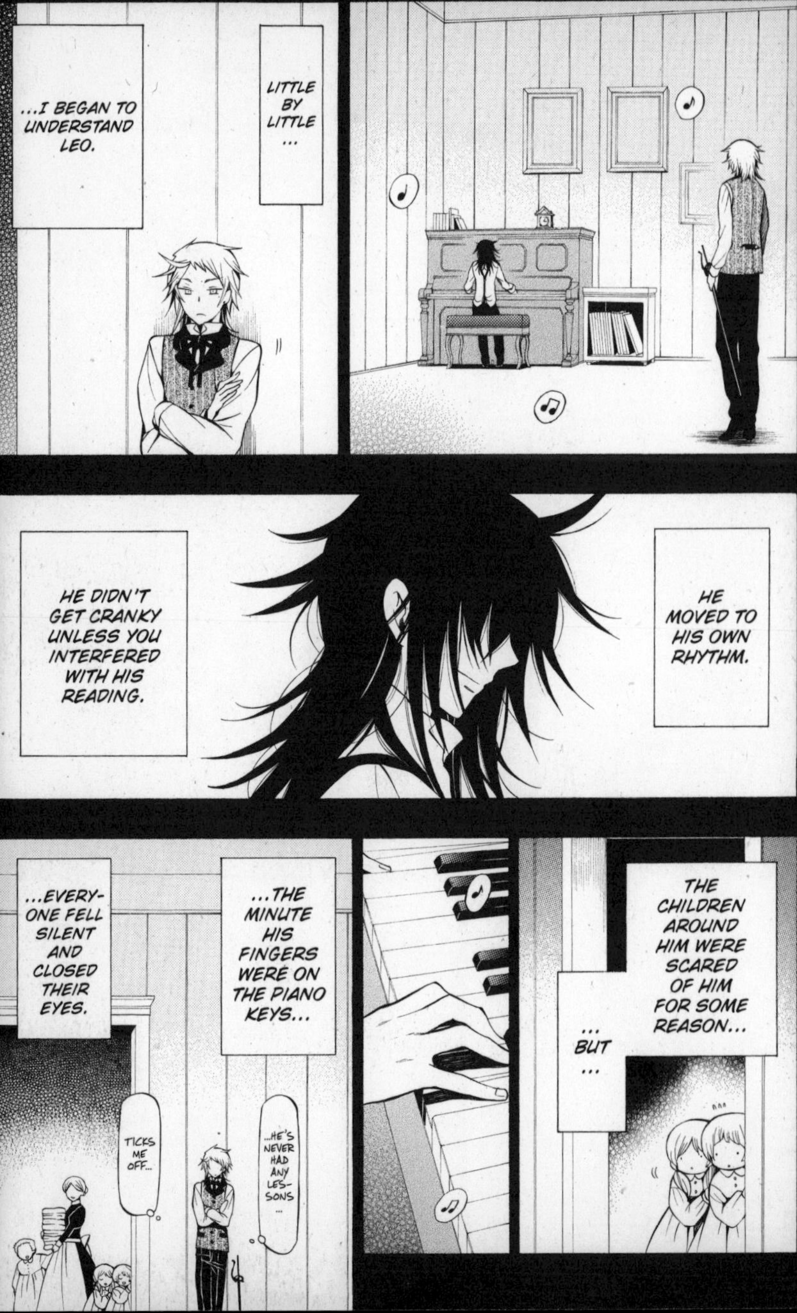
LITTLE BY LITTLE ...
...I BEGAN TO UNDERSTAND LEO.
HE MOVED TO HIS OWN RHYTHM.
HE DIDN'T GET CRANKY UNLESS YOU INTERFERED WITH HIS READING.
THE CHILDREN AROUND HIM WERE SCARED OF HIM FOR SOME REASON...
... BUT ...
...THE MINUTE HIS FINGERS WERE ON THE PIANO KEYS...
...EVERYONE FELL SILENT AND CLOSED THEIR EYES.
...HE'S NEVER HAD ANY LESSONS ...
TICKS ME OFF...

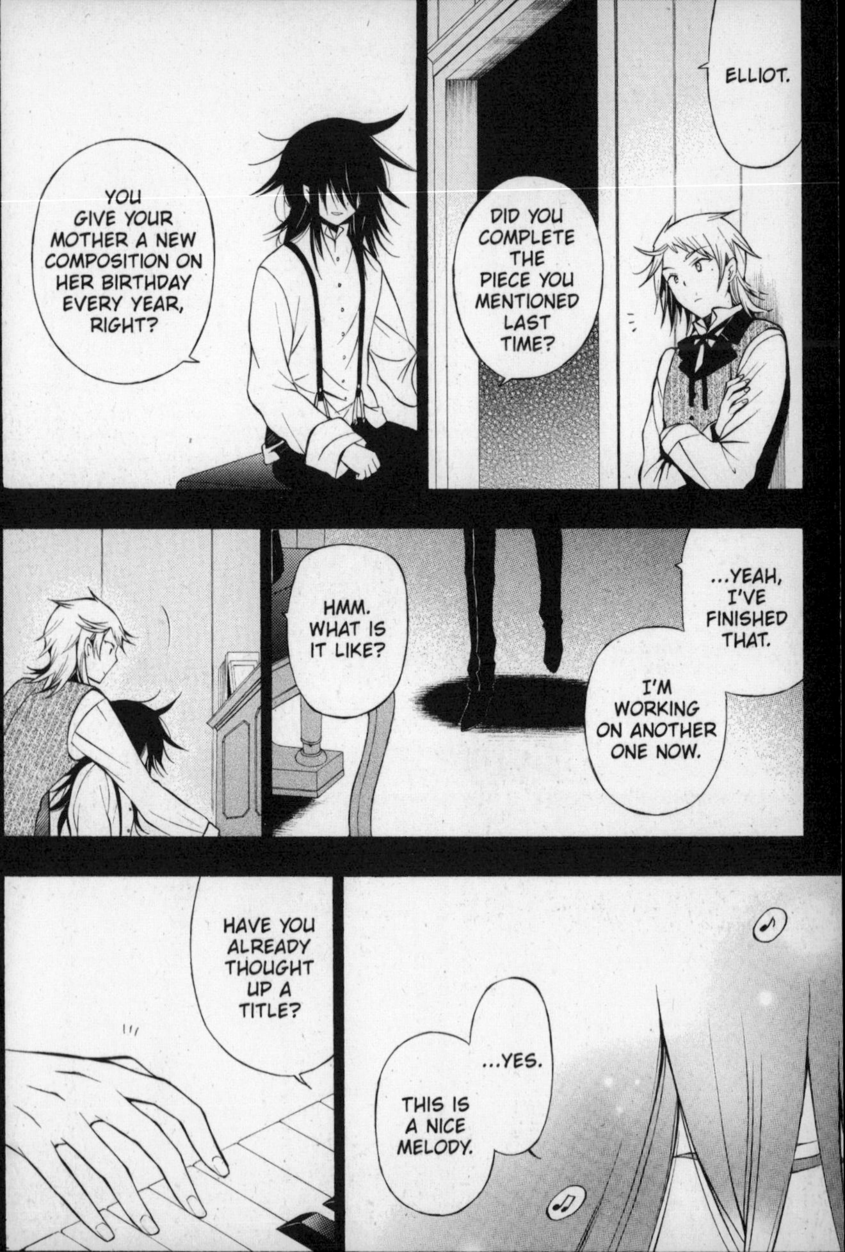
ELLIOT.
DID YOU COMPLETE THE PIECE YOU MENTIONED LAST TIME?
YOU GIVE YOUR MOTHER A NEW COMPOSITION ON HER BIRTHDAY EVERY YEAR, RIGHT?
...YEAH, I'VE FINISHED THAT.
I'M WORKING ON ANOTHER ONE NOW.
HMM. WHAT IS IT LIKE?
...YES.
THIS IS A NICE MELODY.
HAVE YOU ALREADY THOUGHT UP A TITLE?

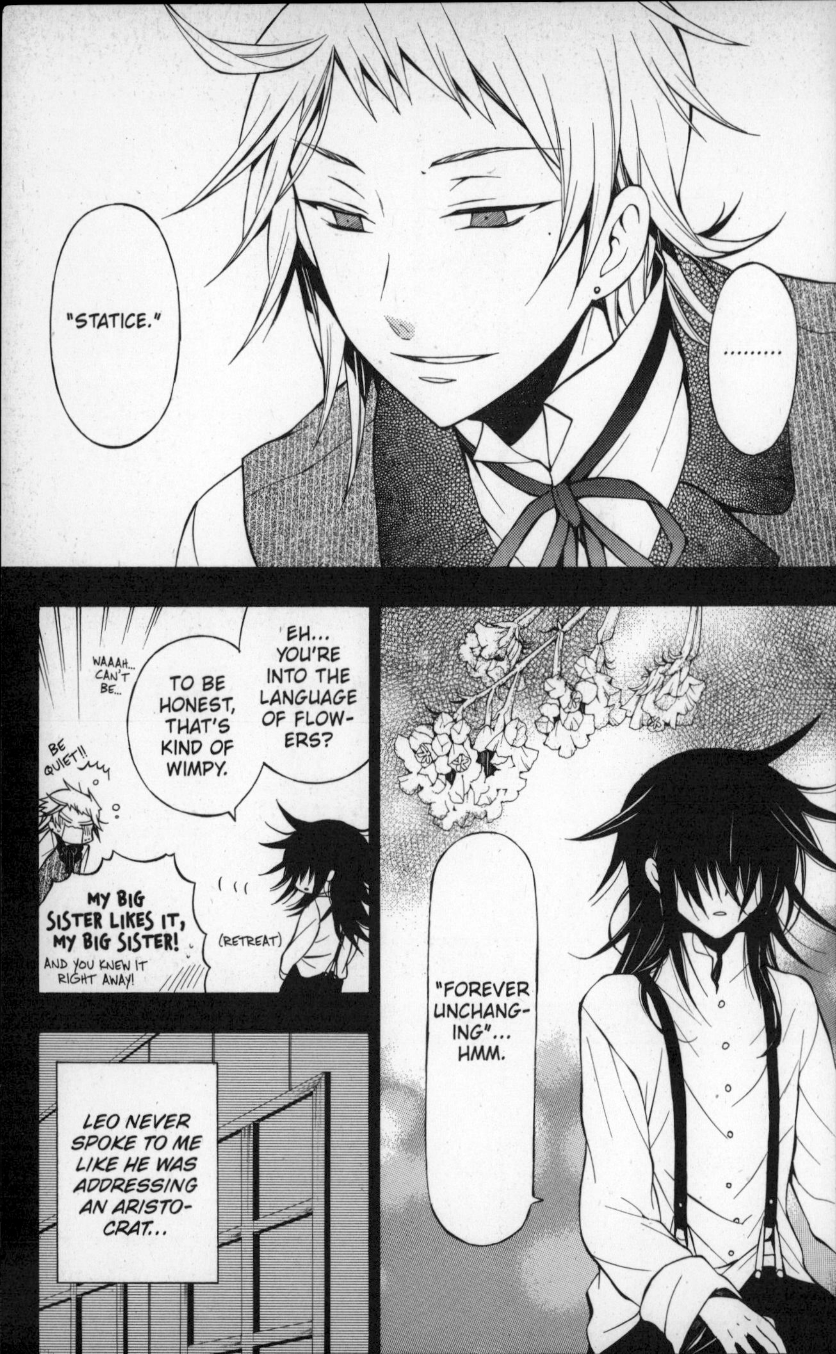
....
"STATICE."
"FOREVER UNCHANGING"... HMM.
EH... YOU'RE INTO THE LANGUAGE OF FLOWERS?
TO BE HONEST, THAT'S KIND OF WIMPY.
WAAAH... CAN'T BE...
BE QUIET!!
(RETREAT)
MY BIG SISTER LIKES IT, MY BIG SISTER!
AND YOU KNEW IT RIGHT AWAY!
LEO NEVER SPOKE TO ME LIKE HE WAS ADDRESSING AN ARISTOCRAT...

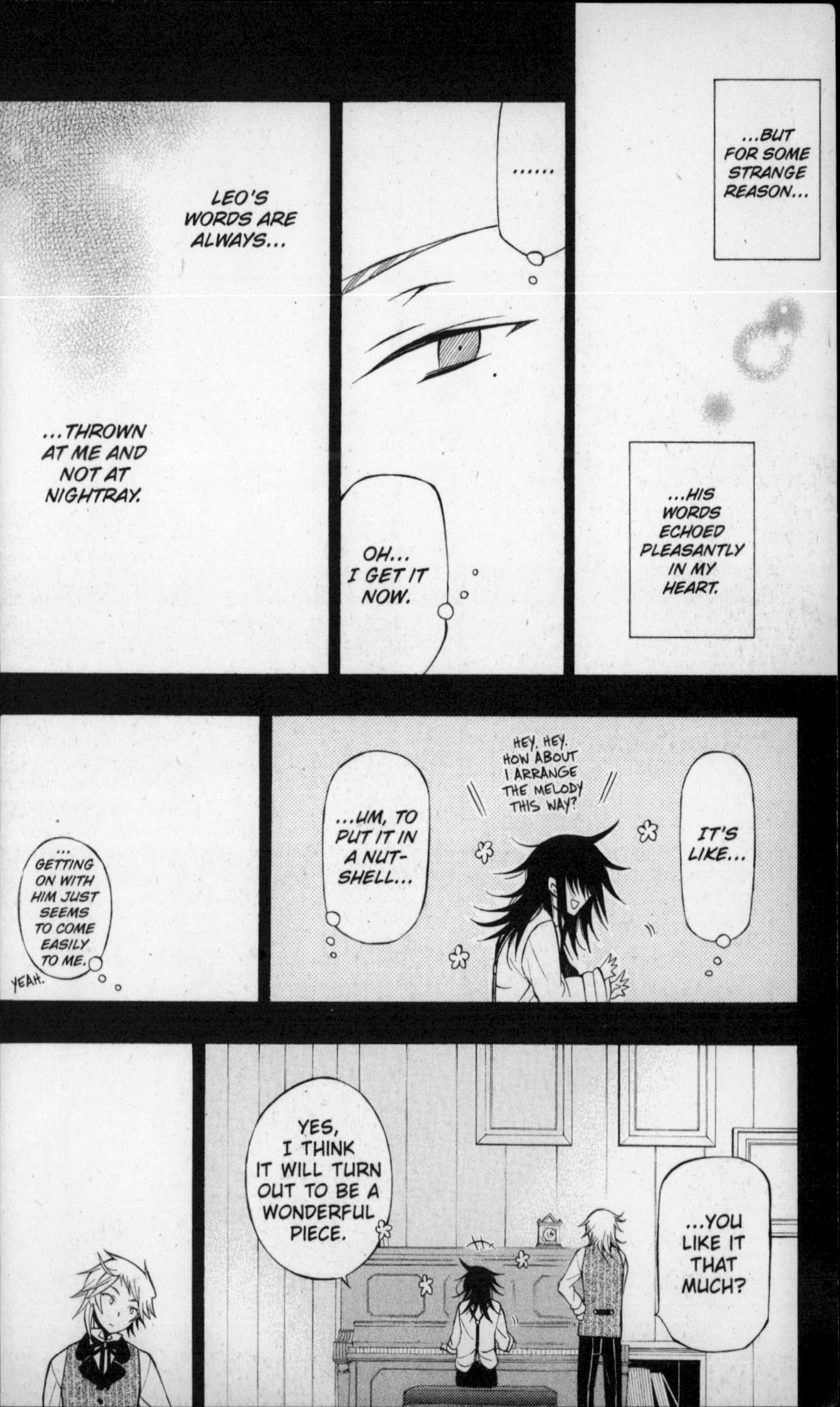
...BUT FOR SOME STRANGE REASON...
...HIS WORDS ECHOED PLEASANTLY IN MY HEART.
......
OH... I GET IT NOW.
LEO'S WORDS ARE ALWAYS...
...THROWN AT ME AND NOT AT NIGHTRAY.
IT'S LIKE...
HEY, HEY. HOW ABOUT I ARRANGE THE MELODY THIS WAY?
...UM, TO PUT IT IN A NUT-SHELL...
...GETTING ON WITH HIM JUST SEEMS TO COME EASILY TO ME.
YEAH.
...YOU LIKE IT THAT MUCH?
YES, I THINK IT WILL TURN OUT TO BE A WONDERFUL PIECE.

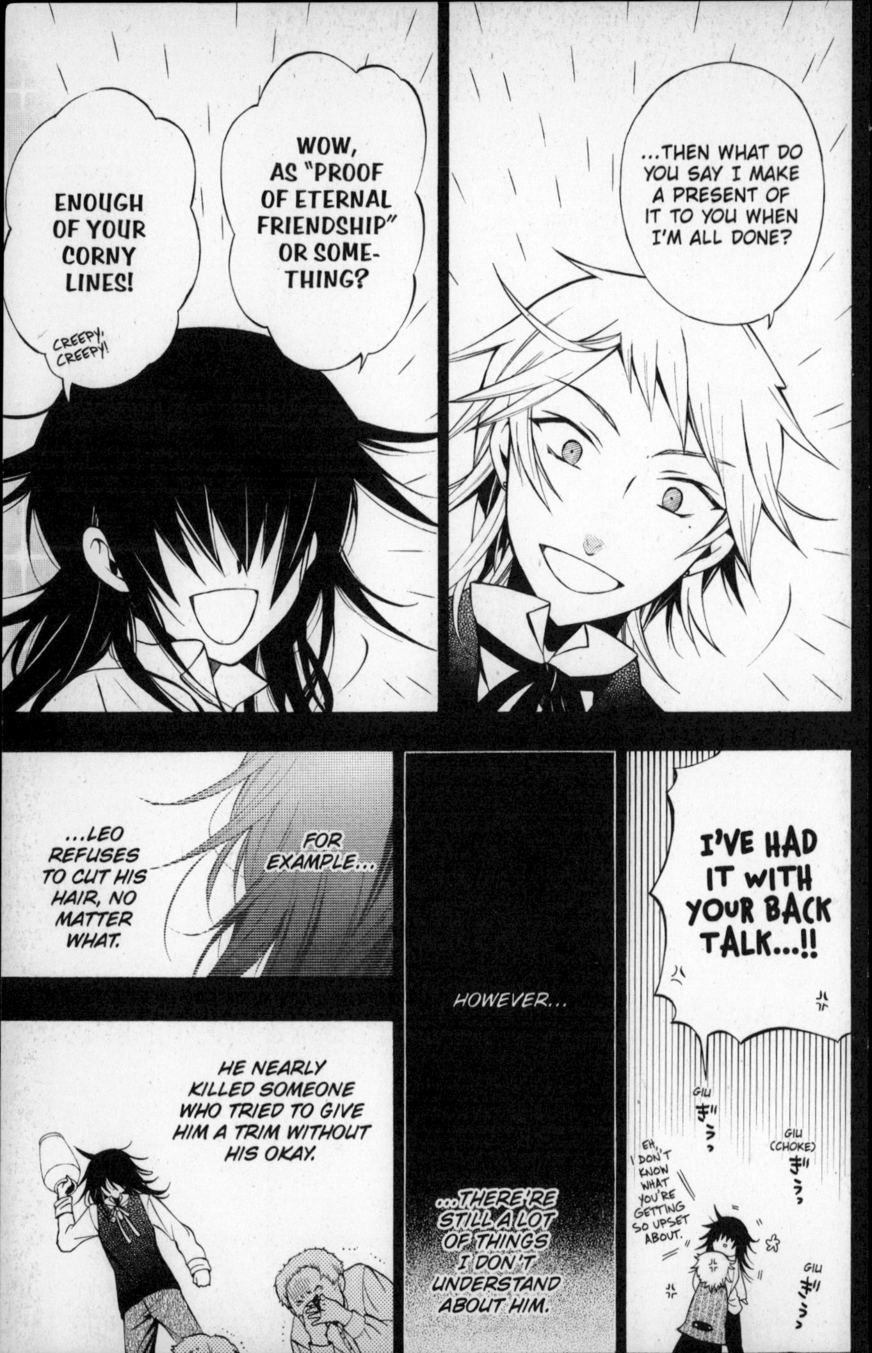
...THEN WHAT DO YOU SAY I MAKE A PRESENT OF IT TO YOU WHEN I'M ALL DONE?
WOW, AS "PROOF OF ETERNAL FRIENDSHIP" OR SOME-THING?
ENOUGH OF YOUR CORNY LINES!
CREEPY, CREEPY!
I'VE HAD IT WITH YOUR BACK TALK...!!
GIU
GIU (CHOKE)
EH, I DON'T KNOW WHAT YOU'RE GETTING SO UPSET ABOUT.
GIU
HOWEVER...
...THERE'RE STILL A LOT OF THINGS I DON'T UNDERSTAND ABOUT HIM.
FOR EXAMPLE...
...LEO REFUSES TO CUT HIS HAIR, NO MATTER WHAT.
HE NEARLY KILLED SOMEONE WHO TRIED TO GIVE HIM A TRIM WITHOUT HIS OKAY.

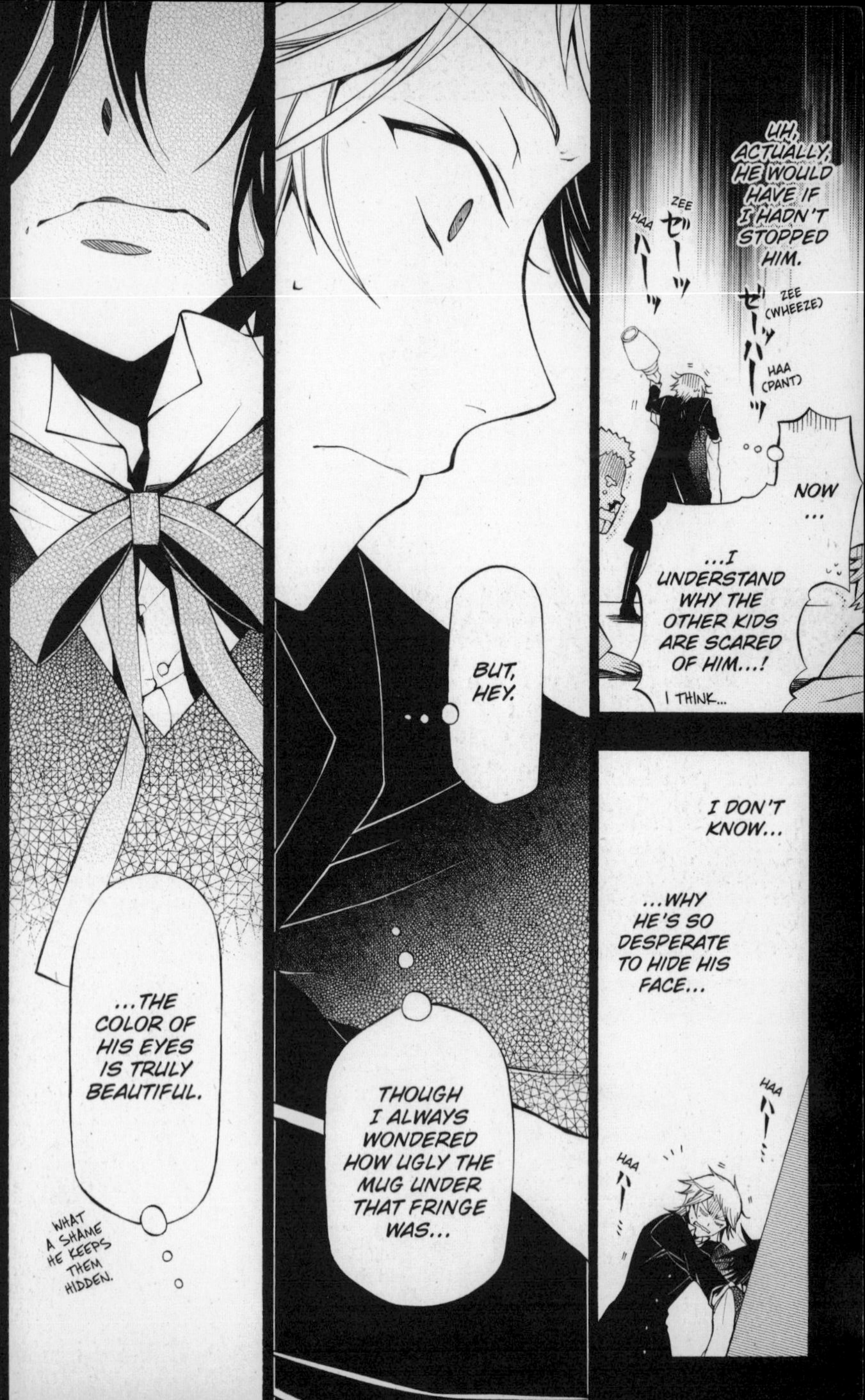
UH, ACTUALLY, HE WOULD HAVE IF I HADN'T STOPPED HIM.
ZEE ゼーッ
HAA ハーッ
ZEE (WHEEZE) ゼーッ
HAA (PANT) ハーッ
NOW...
...I UNDERSTAND WHY THE OTHER KIDS ARE SCARED OF HIM...!
I THINK...
I DON'T KNOW...
...WHY HE'S SO DESPERATE TO HIDE HIS FACE...
HAA ハー
HAA ハー
BUT, HEY.
THOUGH I ALWAYS WONDERED HOW UGLY THE MUG UNDER THAT FRINGE WAS...
...THE COLOR OF HIS EYES IS TRULY BEAUTIFUL.
WHAT A SHAME HE KEEPS THEM HIDDEN.

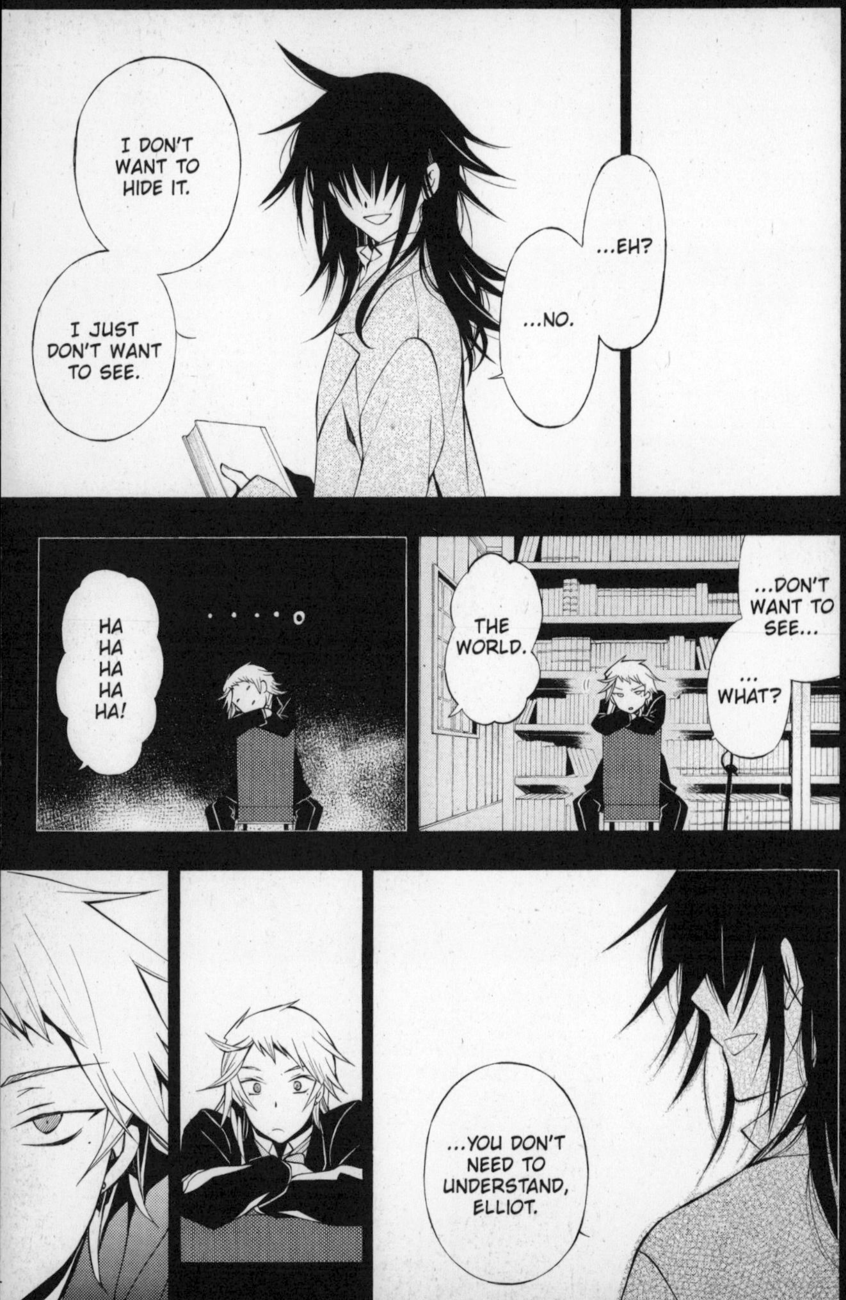
...EH?
...NO.
I DON'T WANT TO HIDE IT.
I JUST DON'T WANT TO SEE.
...DON'T WANT TO SEE...
...WHAT?
THE WORLD.
.....O
HA HA HA HA HA!
...YOU DON'T NEED TO UNDERSTAND, ELLIOT.

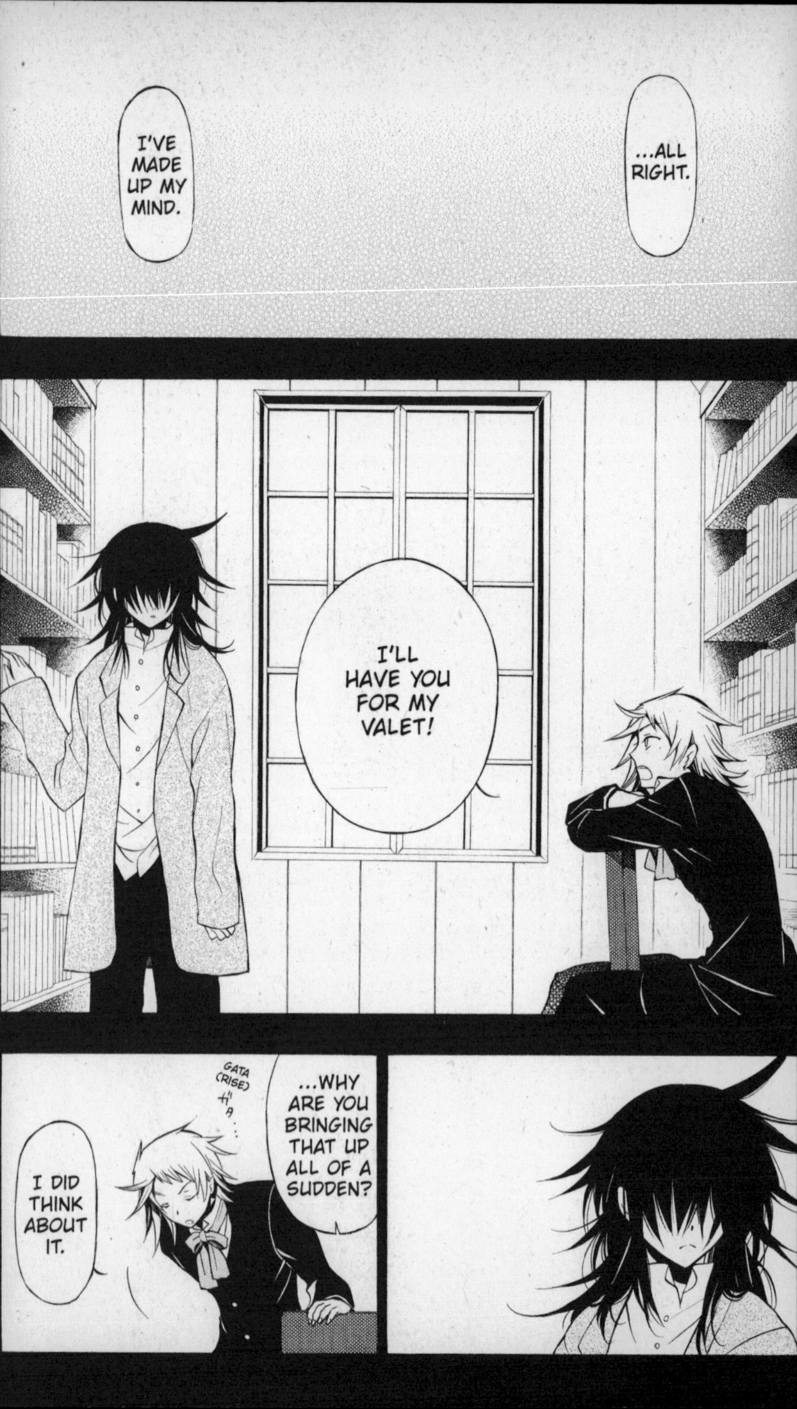
...ALL RIGHT.
I'VE MADE UP MY MIND.
I'LL HAVE YOU FOR MY VALET!
...WHY ARE YOU BRINGING THAT UP ALL OF A SUDDEN?
GATA (RISE)
I DID THINK ABOUT IT.

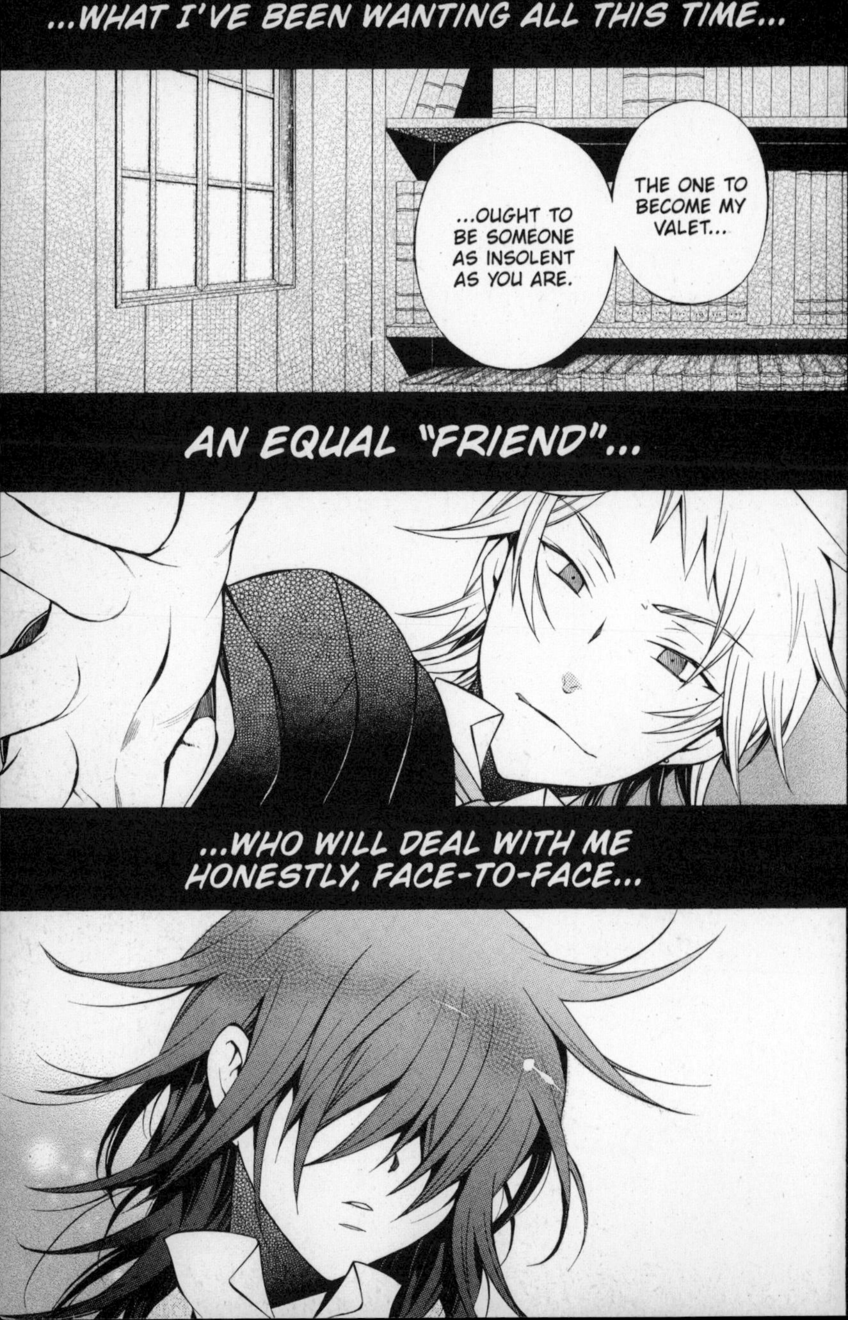
...WHAT I'VE BEEN WANTING ALL THIS TIME...
THE ONE TO BECOME MY VALET...
...OUGHT TO BE SOMEONE AS INSOLENT AS YOU ARE.
AN EQUAL "FRIEND"...
...WHO WILL DEAL WITH ME HONESTLY, FACE-TO-FACE...

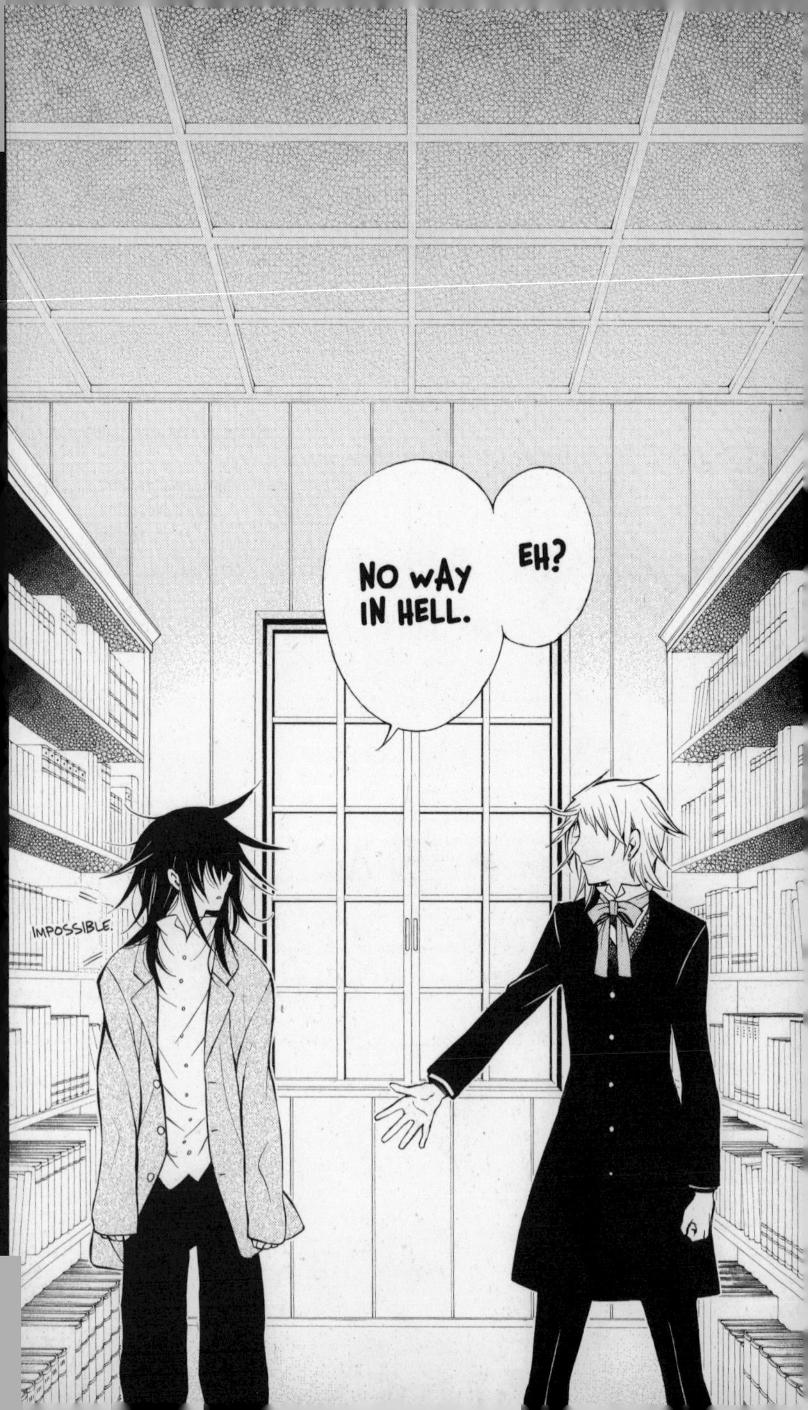
EH?
NO WAY IN HELL.
IMPOSSIBLE.

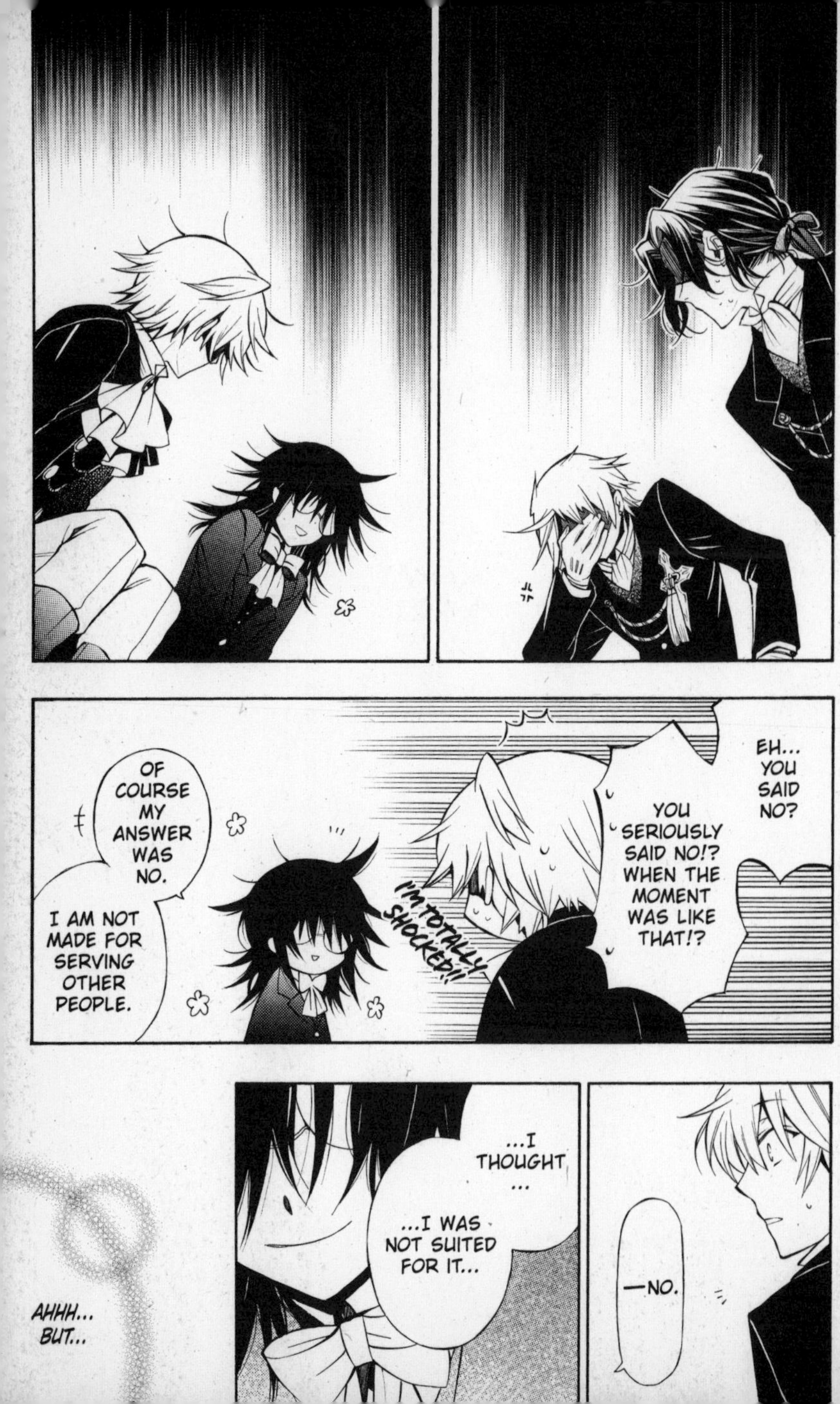
EH... YOU SAID NO?
YOU SERIOUSLY SAID NO!? WHEN THE MOMENT WAS LIKE THAT!?
I'M TOTALLY SHOCKED!!
OF COURSE MY ANSWER WAS NO.
I AM NOT MADE FOR SERVING OTHER PEOPLE.
—NO.
...I THOUGHT ...
...I WAS NOT SUITED FOR IT...
AHHH... BUT...

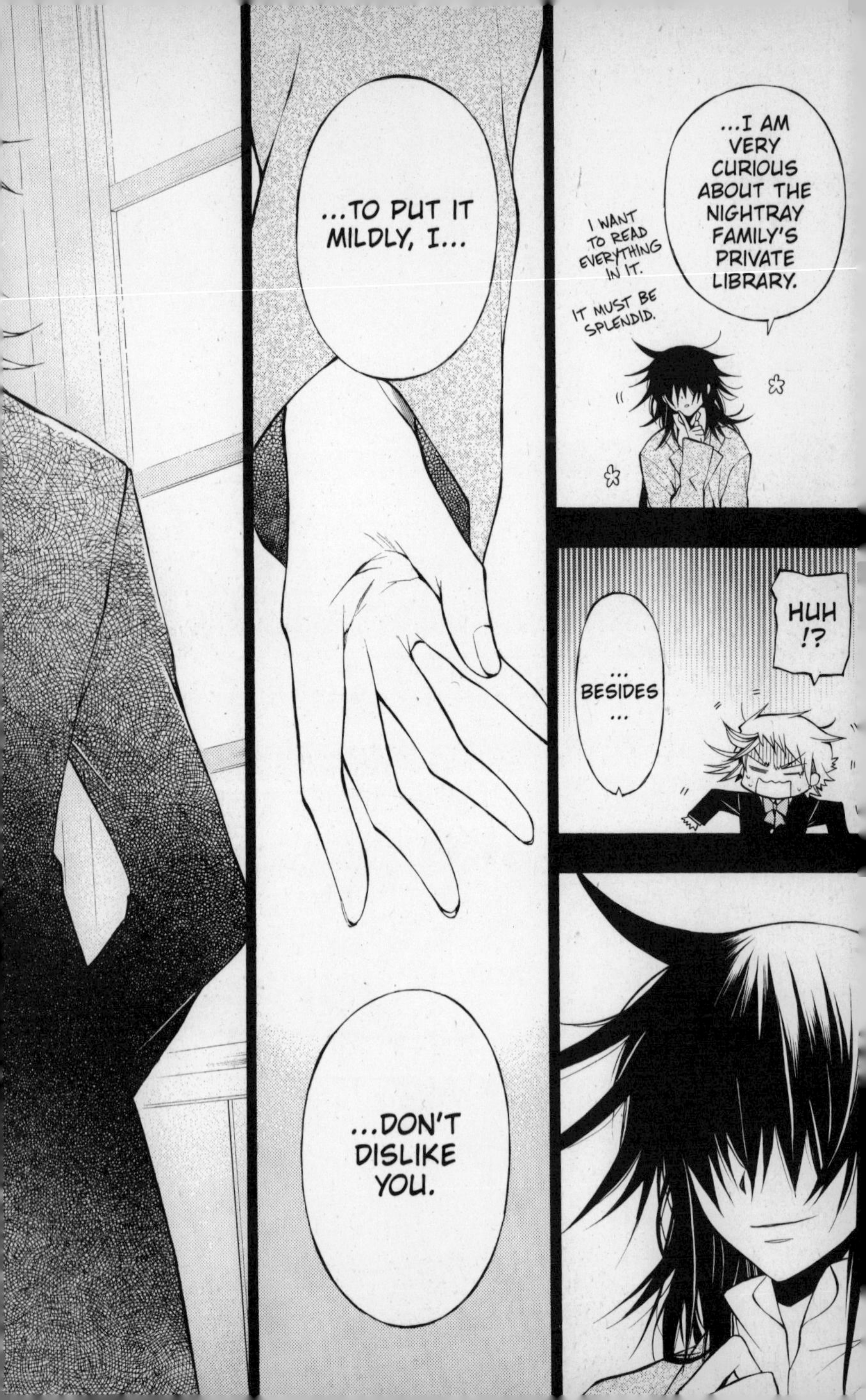
...I AM VERY CURIOUS ABOUT THE NIGHTRAY FAMILY'S PRIVATE LIBRARY.
I WANT TO READ EVERYTHING IN IT.
IT MUST BE SPLENDID.
HUH !?
... BESIDES ...
...TO PUT IT MILDLY, I...
...DON'T DISLIKE YOU.

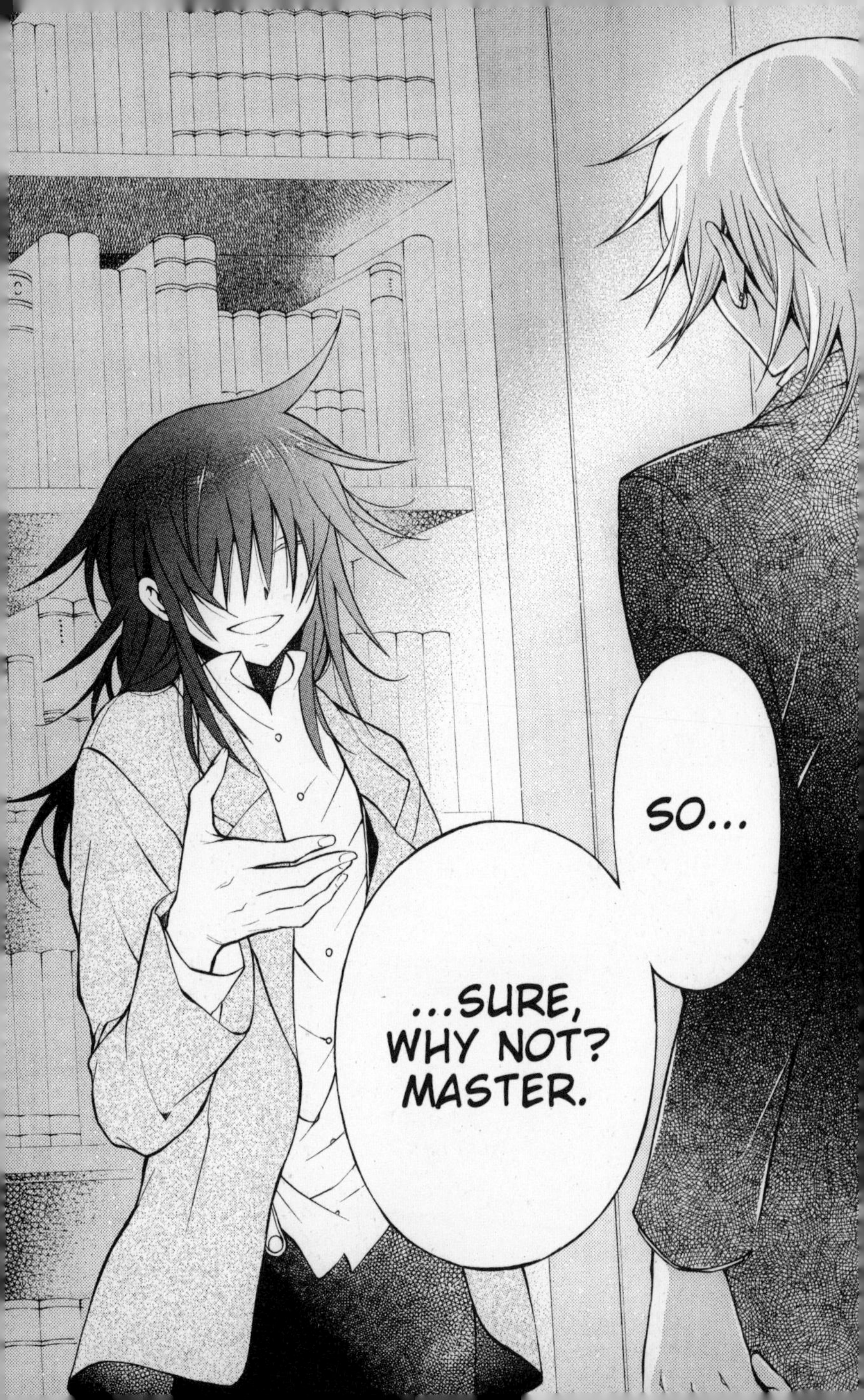
SO...
...SURE, WHY NOT? MASTER.

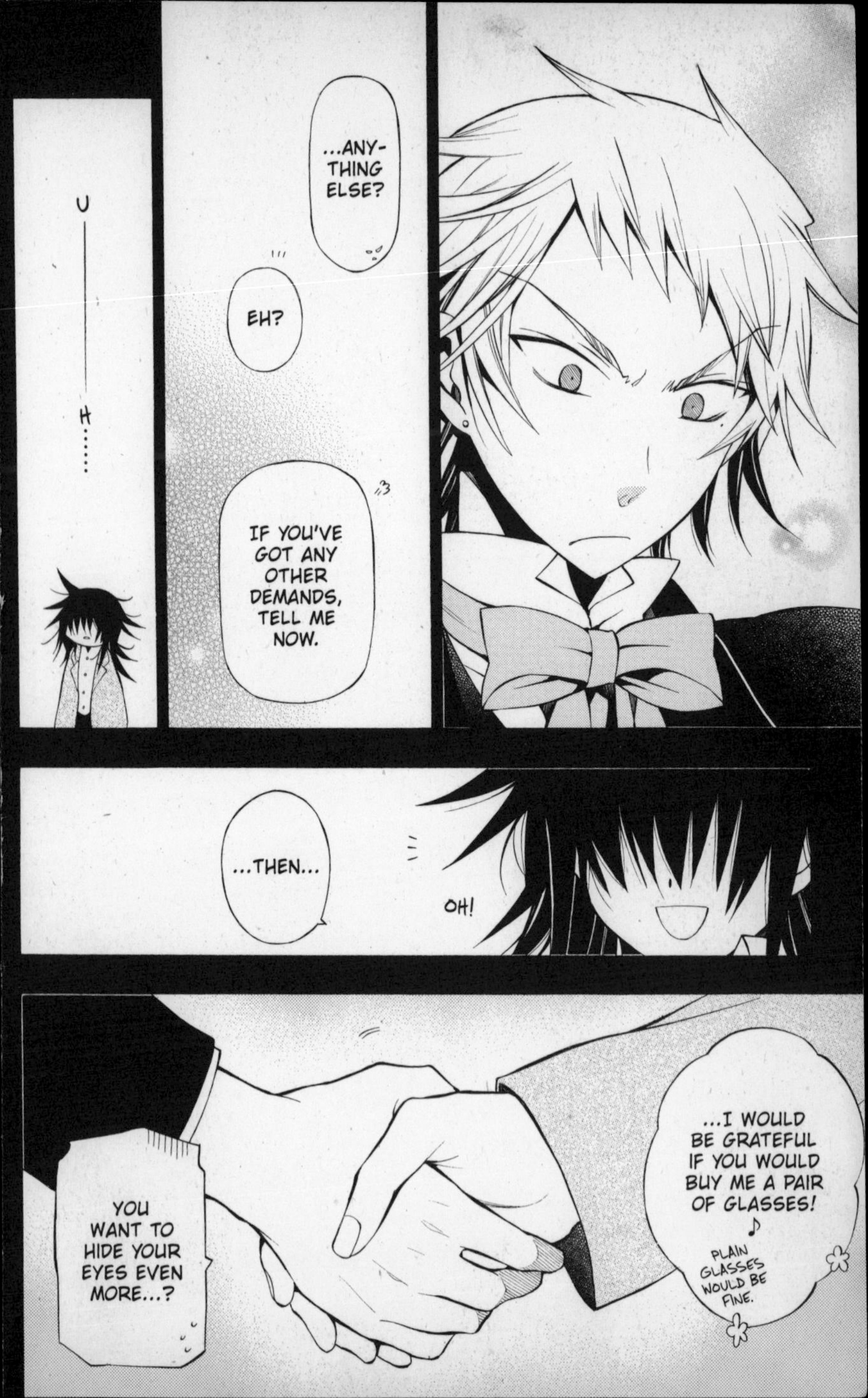
...ANY-THING ELSE?
EH?
IF YOU'VE GOT ANY OTHER DEMANDS, TELL ME NOW.
U——H......
OH!
...THEN...
...I WOULD BE GRATEFUL IF YOU WOULD BUY ME A PAIR OF GLASSES! ♪
PLAIN GLASSES WOULD BE FINE.
YOU WANT TO HIDE YOUR EYES EVEN MORE...?

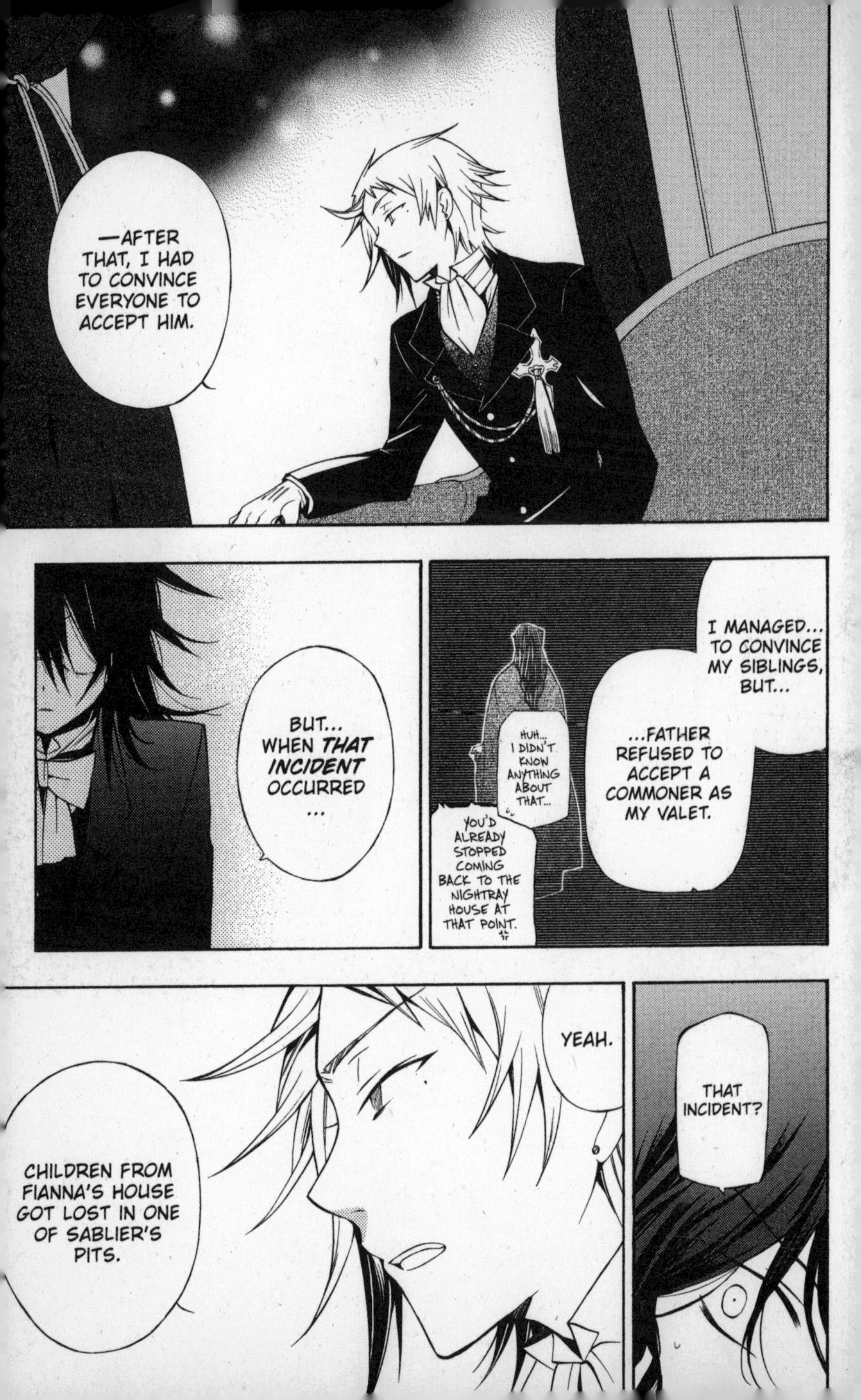
—AFTER THAT, I HAD TO CONVINCE EVERYONE TO ACCEPT HIM.
I MANAGED... TO CONVINCE MY SIBLINGS, BUT...
...FATHER REFUSED TO ACCEPT A COMMONER AS MY VALET.
HUH... I DIDN'T KNOW ANYTHING ABOUT THAT...
YOU'D ALREADY STOPPED COMING BACK TO THE NIGHTRAY HOUSE AT THAT POINT.
BUT... WHEN *THAT INCIDENT* OCCURRED ...
THAT INCIDENT?
YEAH.
CHILDREN FROM FIANNA'S HOUSE GOT LOST IN ONE OF SABLIER'S PITS.

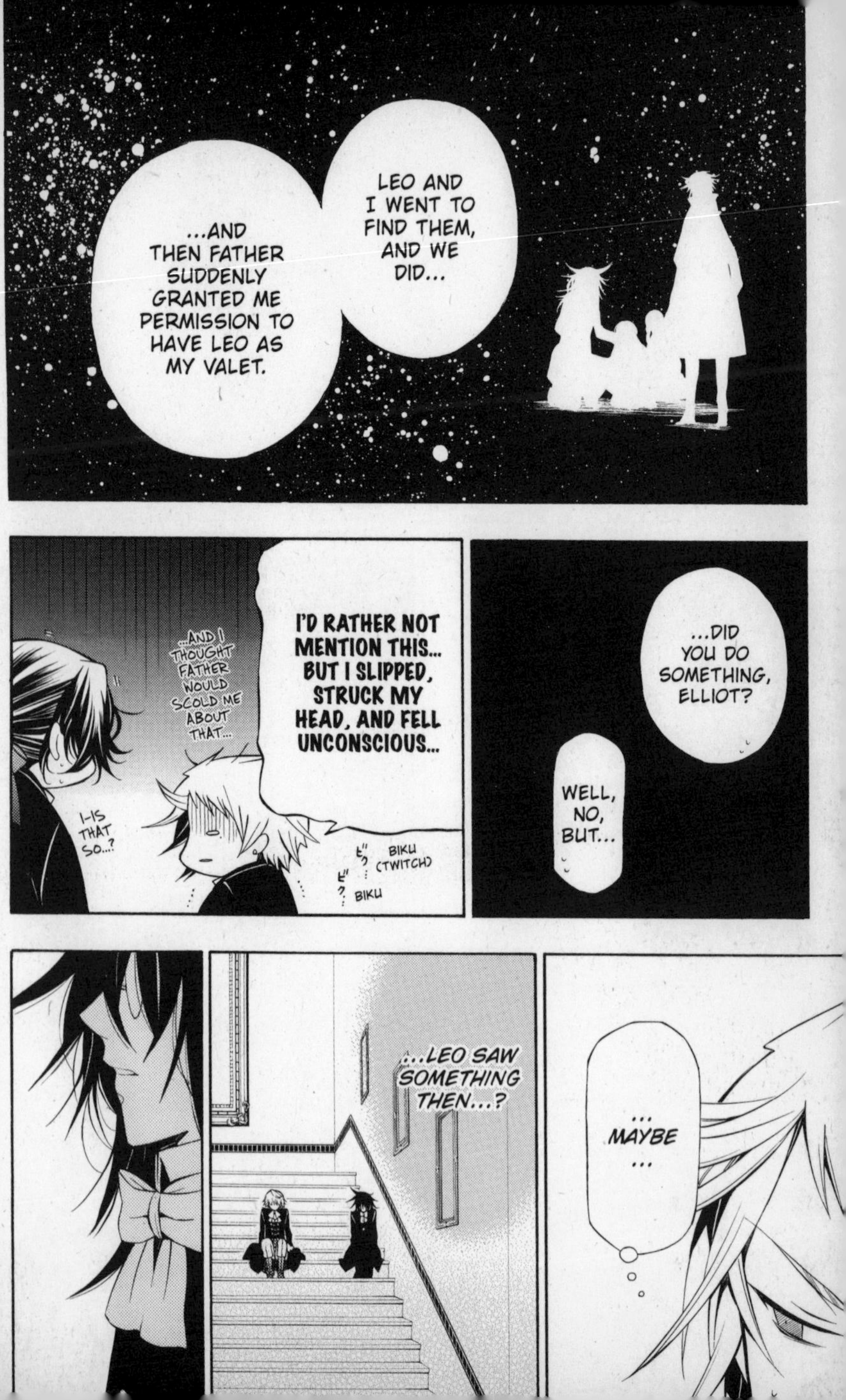
LEO AND I WENT TO FIND THEM, AND WE DID...
...AND THEN FATHER SUDDENLY GRANTED ME PERMISSION TO HAVE LEO AS MY VALET.
...DID YOU DO SOMETHING, ELLIOT?
WELL, NO, BUT...
I'D RATHER NOT MENTION THIS... BUT I SLIPPED, STRUCK MY HEAD, AND FELL UNCONSCIOUS...
BIKU (TWITCH)
BIKU
...AND I THOUGHT FATHER WOULD SCOLD ME ABOUT THAT...
I-IS THAT SO...?
...MAYBE...
...LEO SAW SOMETHING THEN...?

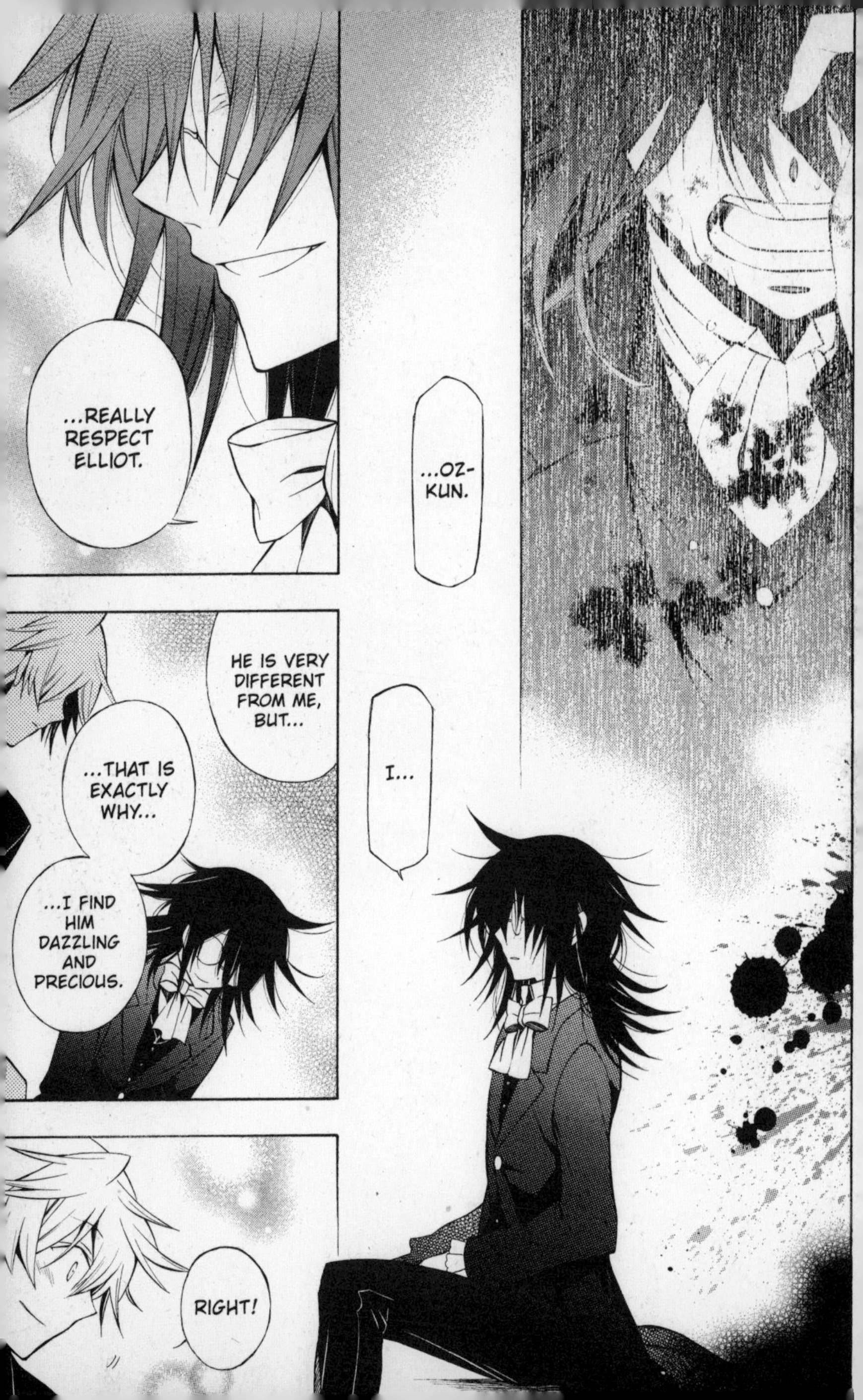
...OZ-KUN.
I...
...REALLY RESPECT ELLIOT.
HE IS VERY DIFFERENT FROM ME, BUT...
...THAT IS EXACTLY WHY...
...I FIND HIM DAZZLING AND PRECIOUS.
RIGHT!

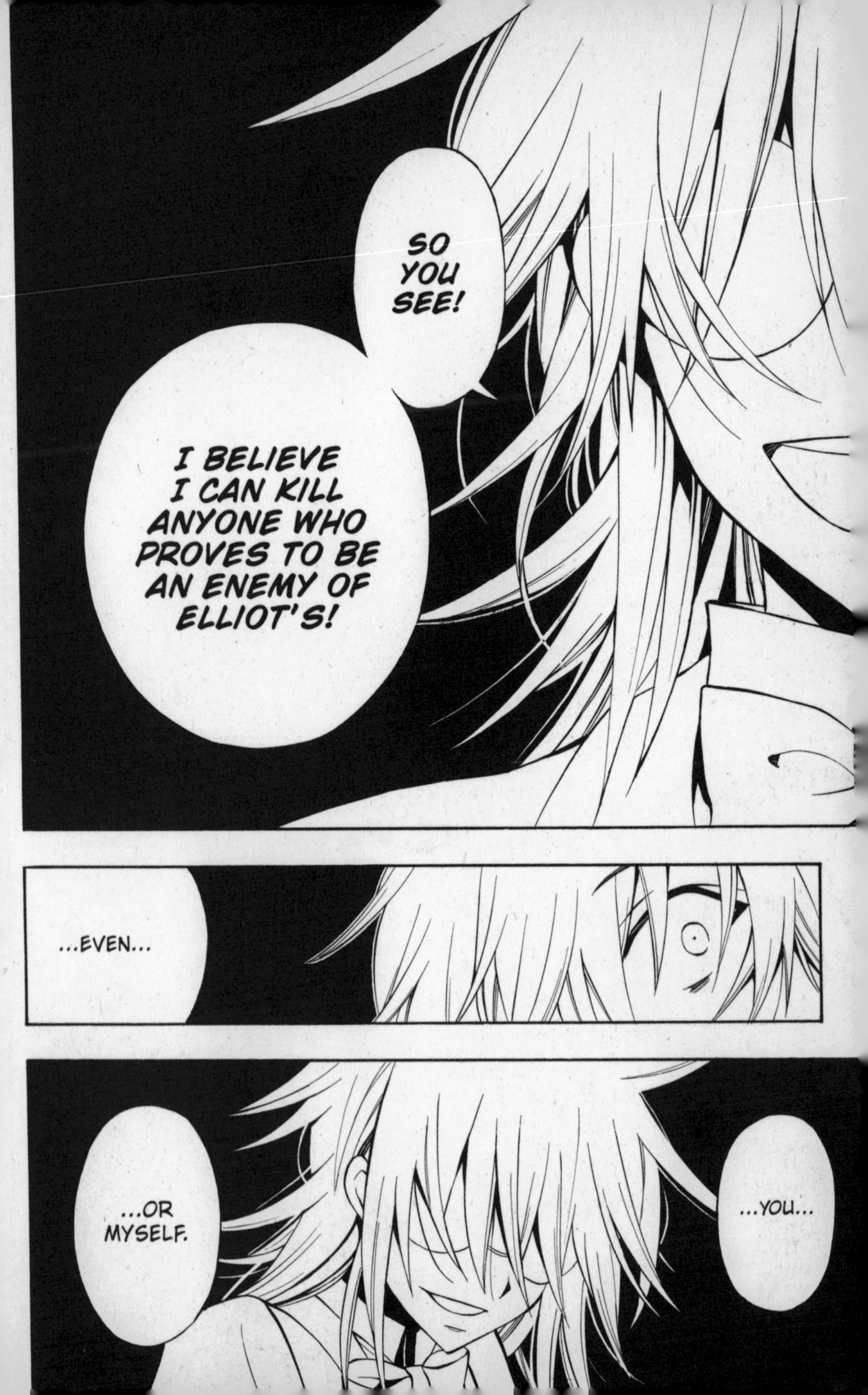
SO YOU SEE!
I BELIEVE I CAN KILL ANYONE WHO PROVES TO BE AN ENEMY OF ELLIOT'S!
...EVEN...
...YOU...
...OR MYSELF.

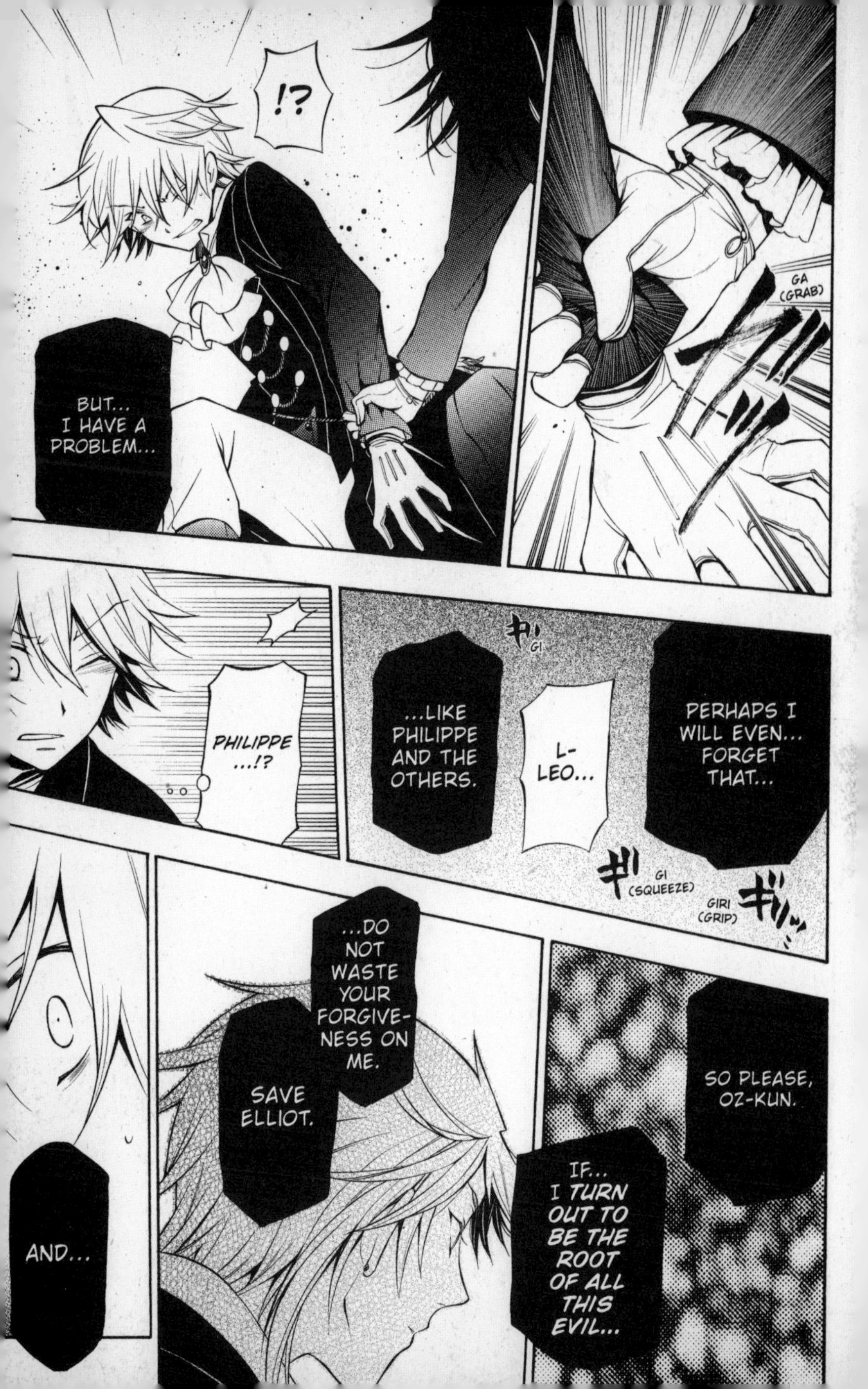
GA (GRAB)
!?
BUT... I HAVE A PROBLEM...
PERHAPS I WILL EVEN... FORGET THAT...
GI
L- LEO...
...LIKE PHILIPPE AND THE OTHERS.
GI (SQUEEZE)
GIRI (GRIP)
PHILIPPE ...!?
SO PLEASE, OZ-KUN.
IF... I TURN OUT TO BE THE ROOT OF ALL THIS EVIL...
...DO NOT WASTE YOUR FORGIVENESS ON ME.
SAVE ELLIOT.
AND...

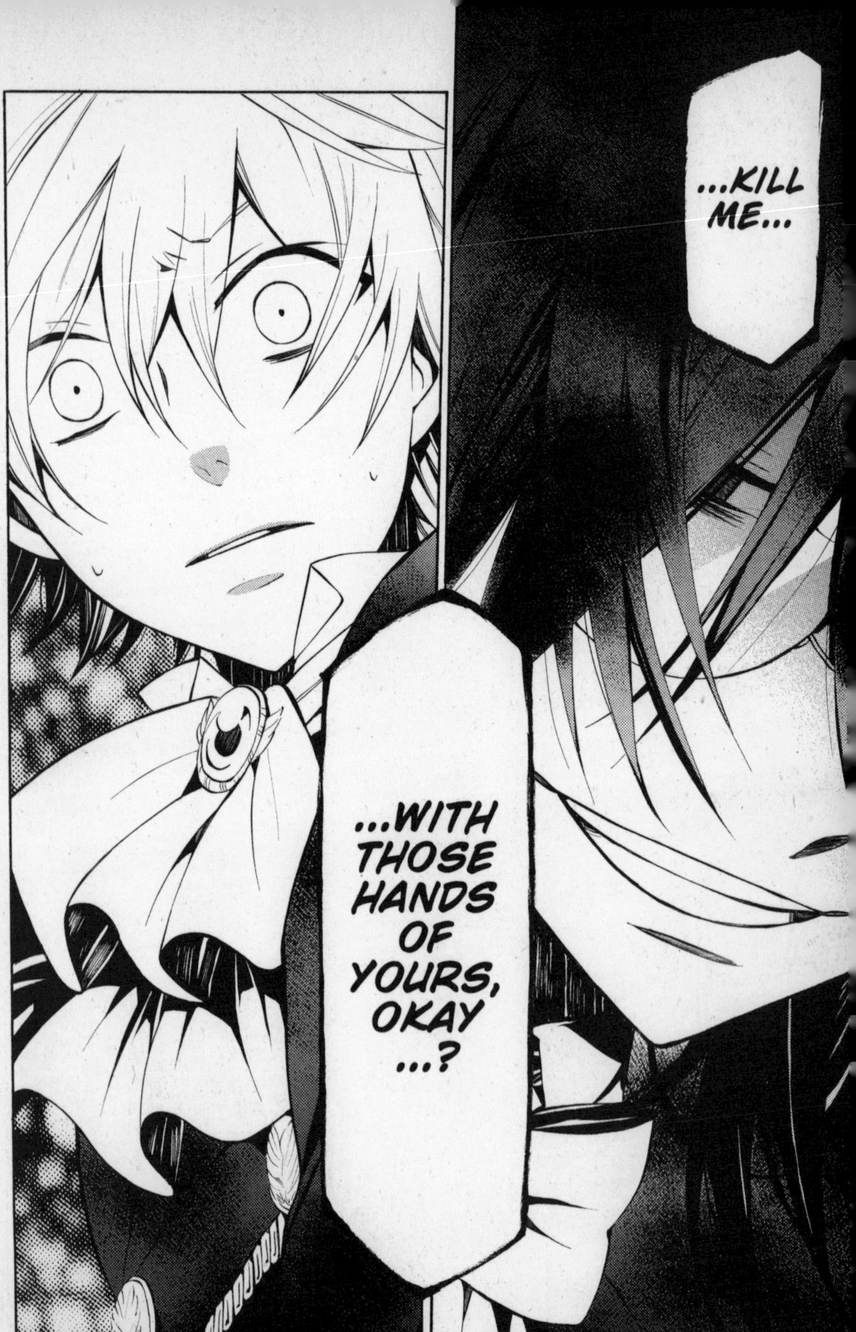
...KILL ME...
...WITH THOSE HANDS OF YOURS, OKAY ...?

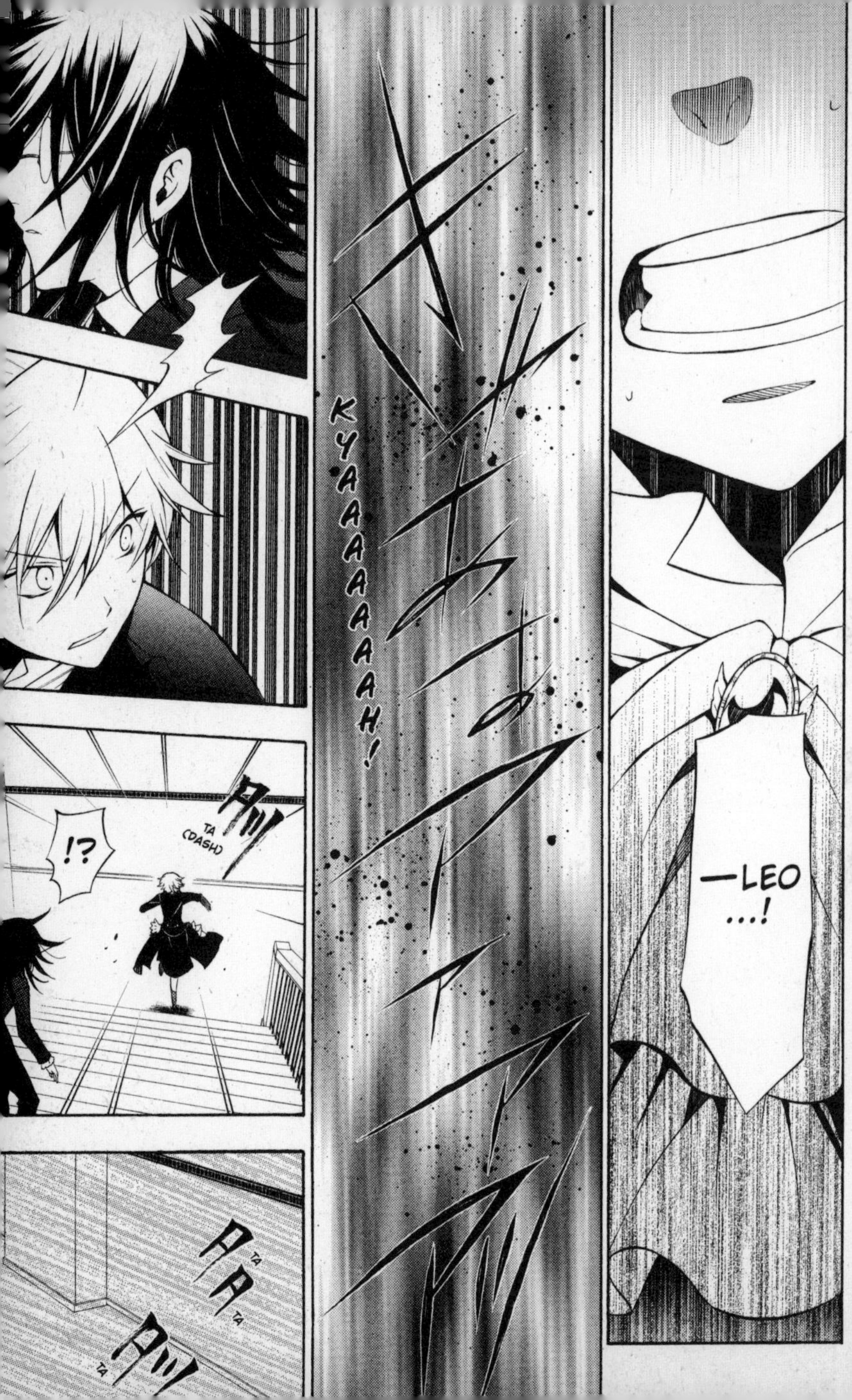
—LEO
...!
KYAAAAAAAAAH!
TA
(DASH)
!?
TA
TA
TA

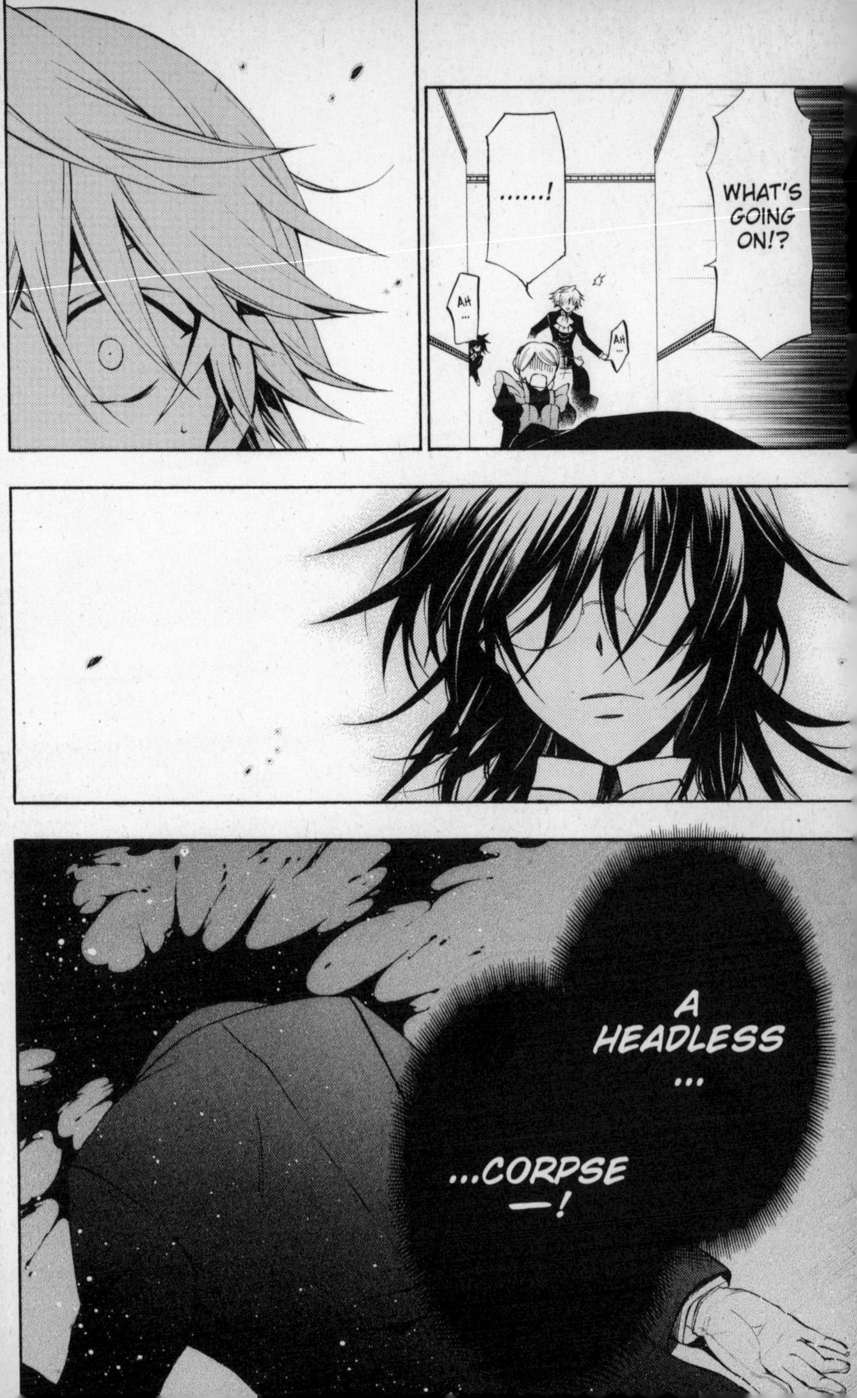
WHAT'S GOING ON!?
......!
AH ...
AH ...
A HEADLESS ...
...CORPSE —!

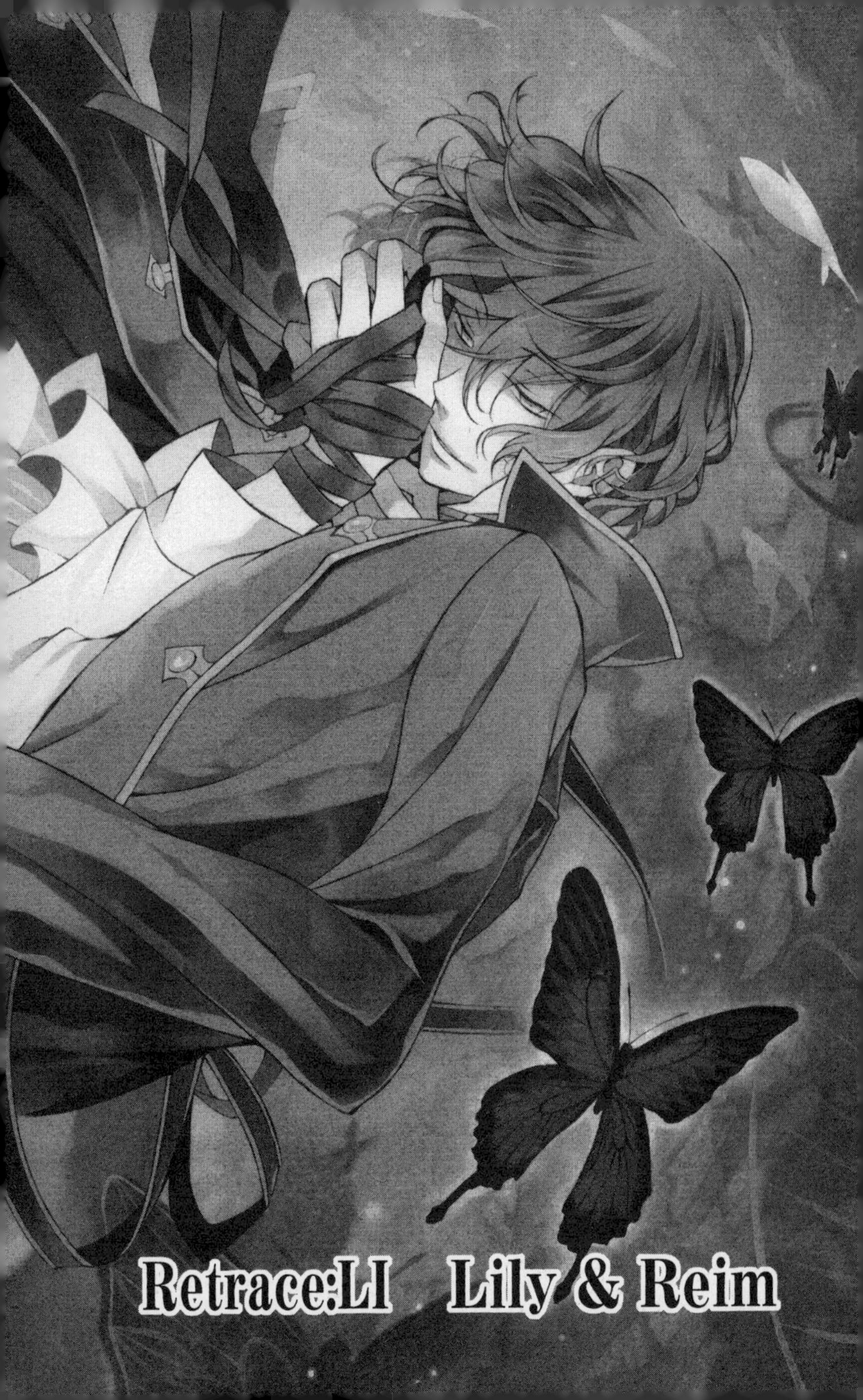

Retrace:LI Lily & Reim

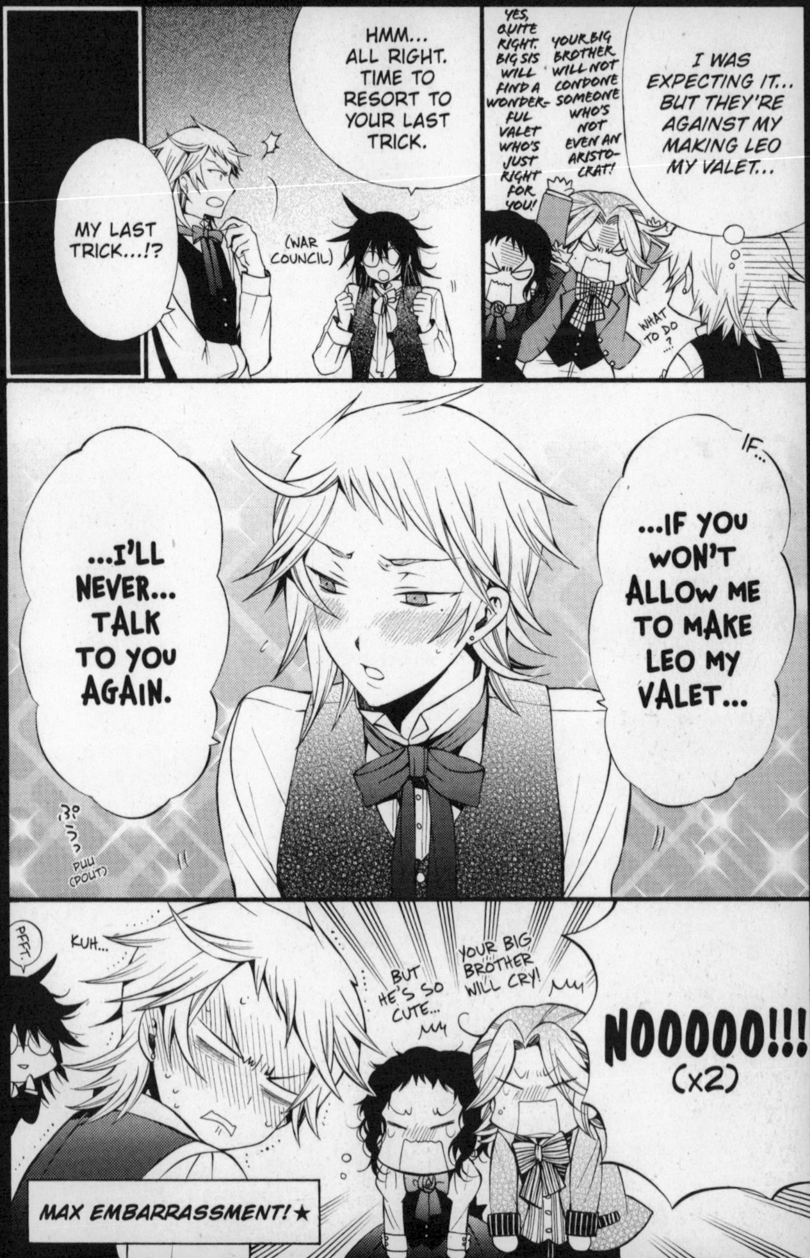
I WAS EXPECTING IT... BUT THEY'RE AGAINST MY MAKING LEO MY VALET...
YOUR BIG BROTHER WILL NOT CONDONE SOMEONE WHO'S NOT EVEN AN ARISTOCRAT!
YES, QUITE RIGHT. BIG SIS WILL FIND A WONDERFUL VALET WHO'S JUST RIGHT FOR YOU!
WHAT TO DO...?
HMM... ALL RIGHT. TIME TO RESORT TO YOUR LAST TRICK.
(WAR COUNCIL)
MY LAST TRICK...!?
IF...
...IF YOU WON'T ALLOW ME TO MAKE LEO MY VALET...
...I'LL NEVER... TALK TO YOU AGAIN.
PUU (POUT)
NOOOOO!!! (x2)
YOUR BIG BROTHER WILL CRY!
BUT HE'S SO CUTE...
KUH...
PFFT.
MAX EMBARRASSMENT!★

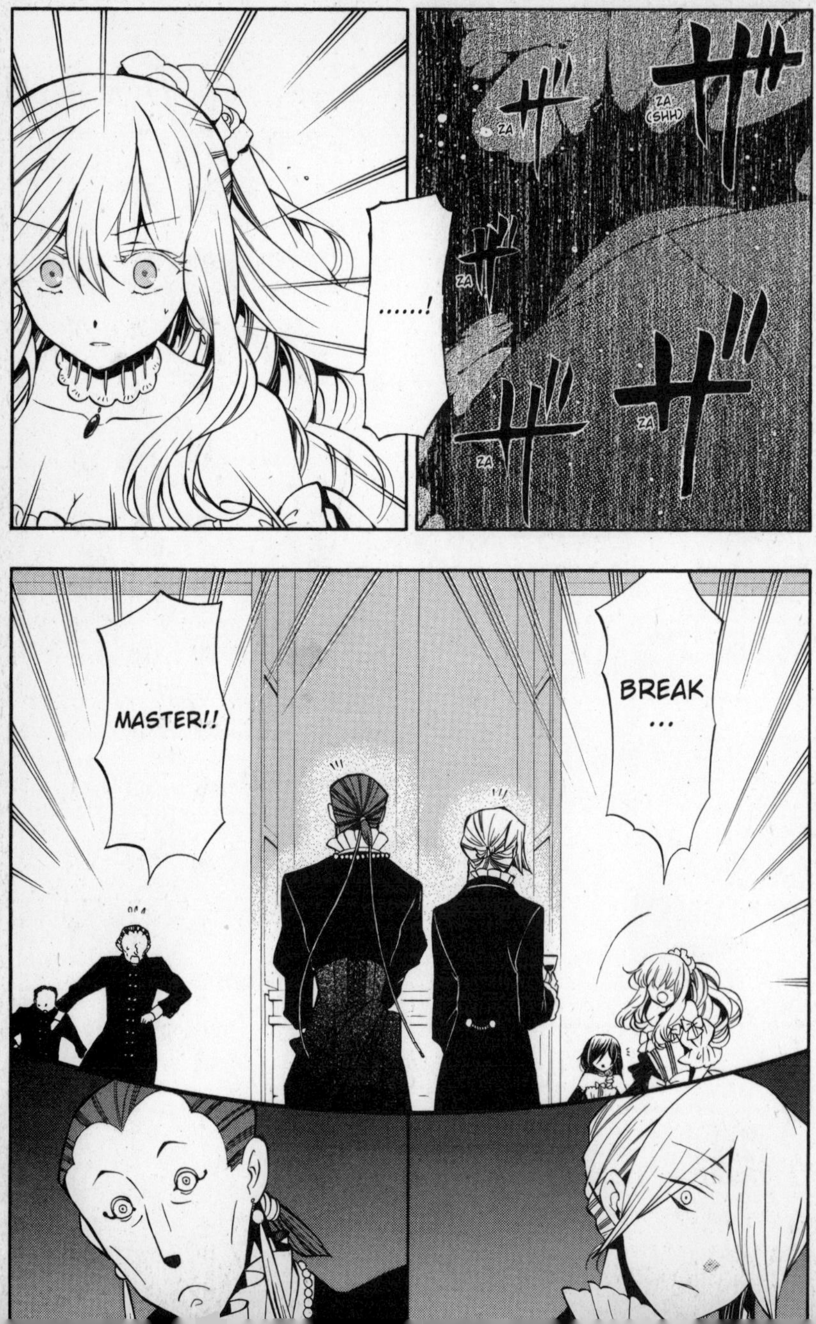
ZA (SHH)
ZA
ZA
ZA
ZA
......!
BREAK ...
MASTER!!

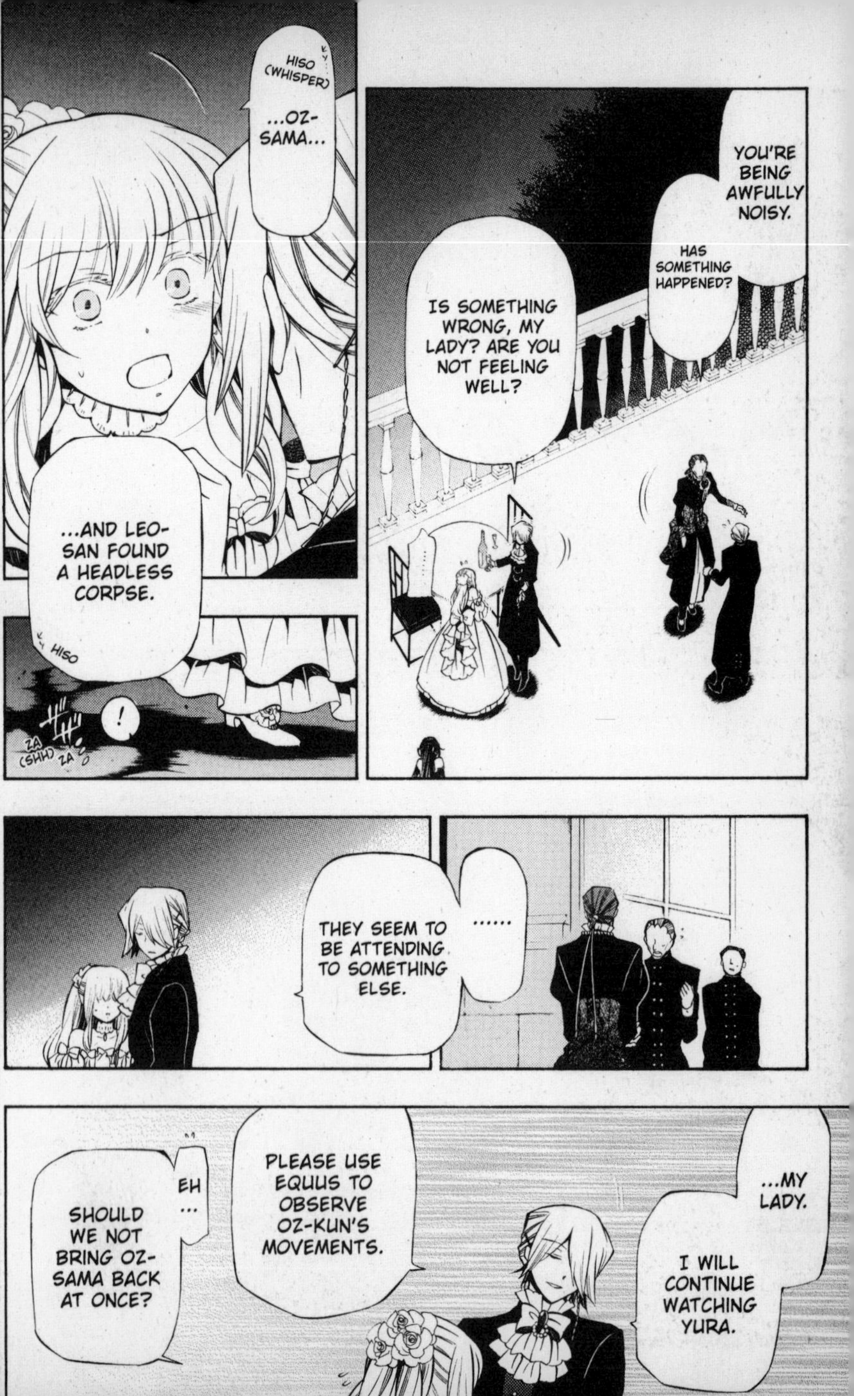
YOU'RE BEING AWFULLY NOISY.
HAS SOMETHING HAPPENED?
IS SOMETHING WRONG, MY LADY? ARE YOU NOT FEELING WELL?
HISO (WHISPER)
...OZ-SAMA...
...AND LEO-SAN FOUND A HEADLESS CORPSE.
HISO
!
ZA (SHH) ZA
......
THEY SEEM TO BE ATTENDING TO SOMETHING ELSE.
...MY LADY.
I WILL CONTINUE WATCHING YURA.
PLEASE USE EQUUS TO OBSERVE OZ-KUN'S MOVEMENTS.
EH...
SHOULD WE NOT BRING OZ-SAMA BACK AT ONCE?

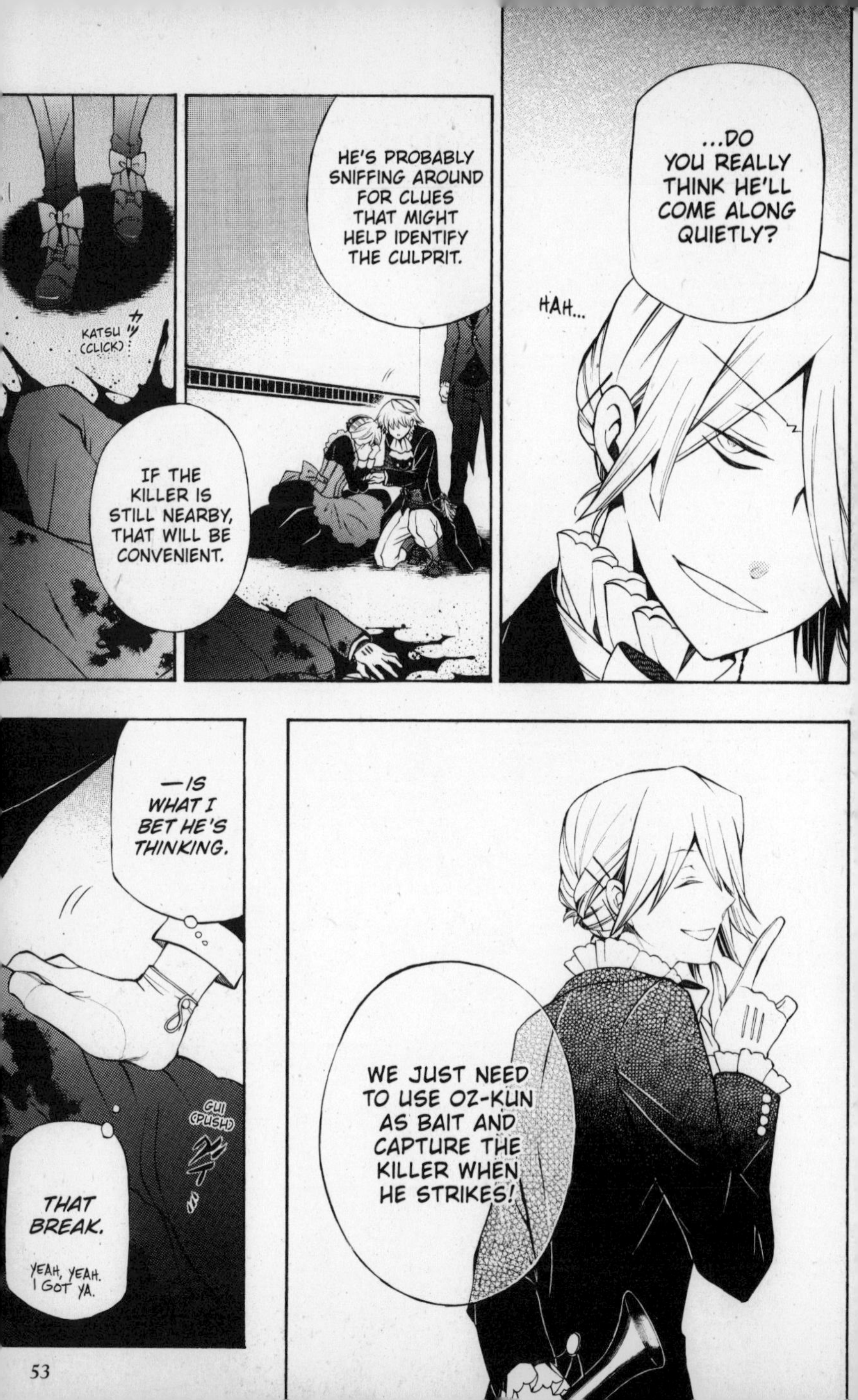
...DO YOU REALLY THINK HE'LL COME ALONG QUIETLY?
HAH...
HE'S PROBABLY SNIFFING AROUND FOR CLUES THAT MIGHT HELP IDENTIFY THE CULPRIT.
IF THE KILLER IS STILL NEARBY, THAT WILL BE CONVENIENT.
KATSU (CLICK)
WE JUST NEED TO USE OZ-KUN AS BAIT AND CAPTURE THE KILLER WHEN HE STRIKES!
—IS WHAT I BET HE'S THINKING.
GUI (PUSH)
THAT BREAK.
YEAH, YEAH. I GOT YA.

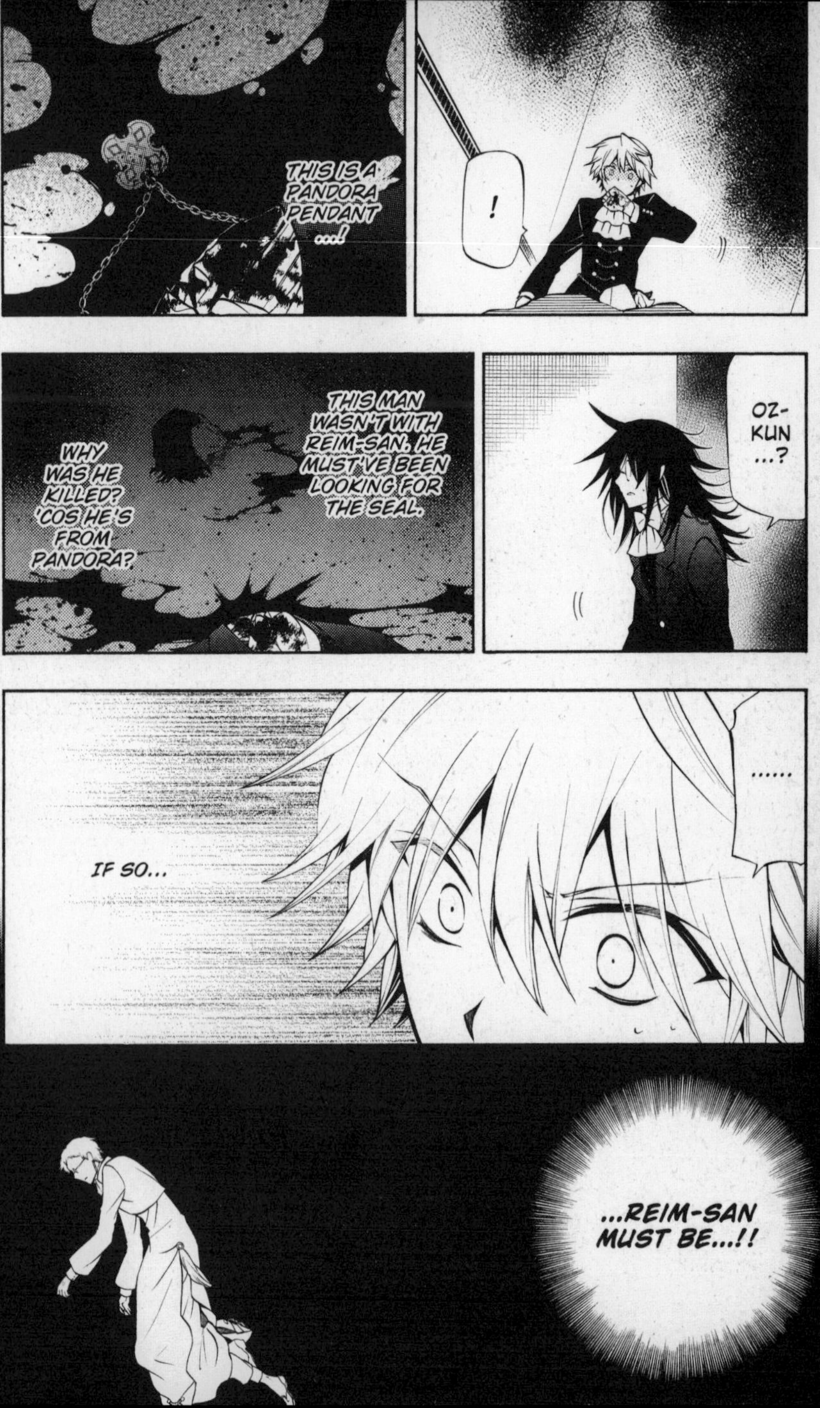
!
THIS IS A PANDORA PENDANT ...!
OZ-KUN ...?
THIS MAN WASN'T WITH REIM-SAN. HE MUST'VE BEEN LOOKING FOR THE SEAL.
WHY WAS HE KILLED? 'COS HE'S FROM PANDORA?
......
IF SO...
...REIM-SAN MUST BE...!!

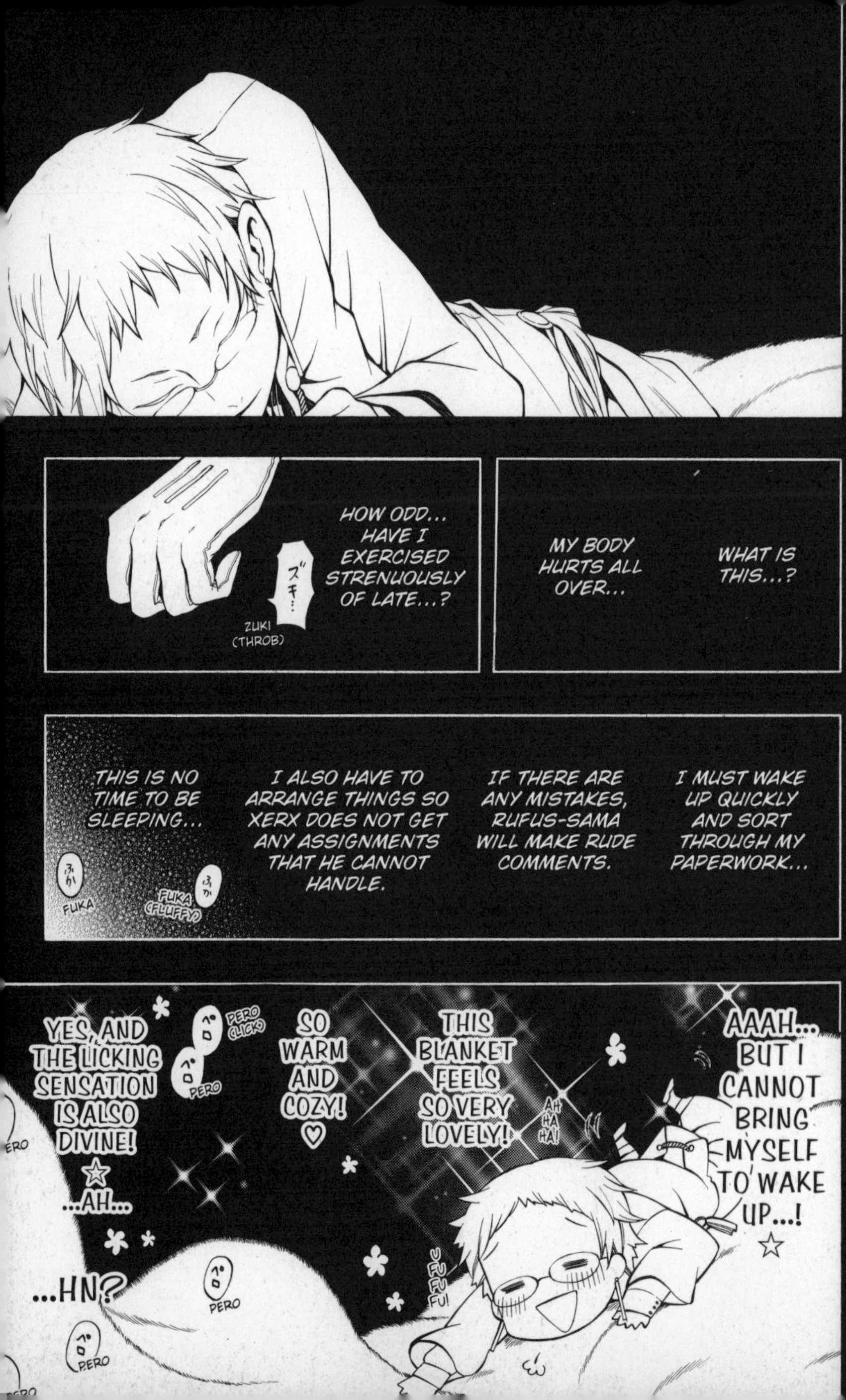
WHAT IS THIS...?
MY BODY HURTS ALL OVER...
HOW ODD... HAVE I EXERCISED STRENUOUSLY OF LATE...?
ズキ…
ZUKI (THROB)
I MUST WAKE UP QUICKLY AND SORT THROUGH MY PAPERWORK...
IF THERE ARE ANY MISTAKES, RUFUS-SAMA WILL MAKE RUDE COMMENTS.
I ALSO HAVE TO ARRANGE THINGS SO XERX DOES NOT GET ANY ASSIGNMENTS THAT HE CANNOT HANDLE.
THIS IS NO TIME TO BE SLEEPING...
ふか
FUKA (FLUFFY)
ふか
FUKA
AAAH... BUT I CANNOT BRING MYSELF TO WAKE UP...! ☆
AH HA HA!
THIS BLANKET FEELS SO VERY LOVELY!
SO WARM AND COZY! ♡
ペロ
PERO (LICK)
ペロ
PERO
YES, AND THE LICKING SENSATION IS ALSO DIVINE! ☆ ...AH...
UFUFUFU!
ペロ
PERO
...HN?
ペロ
PERO

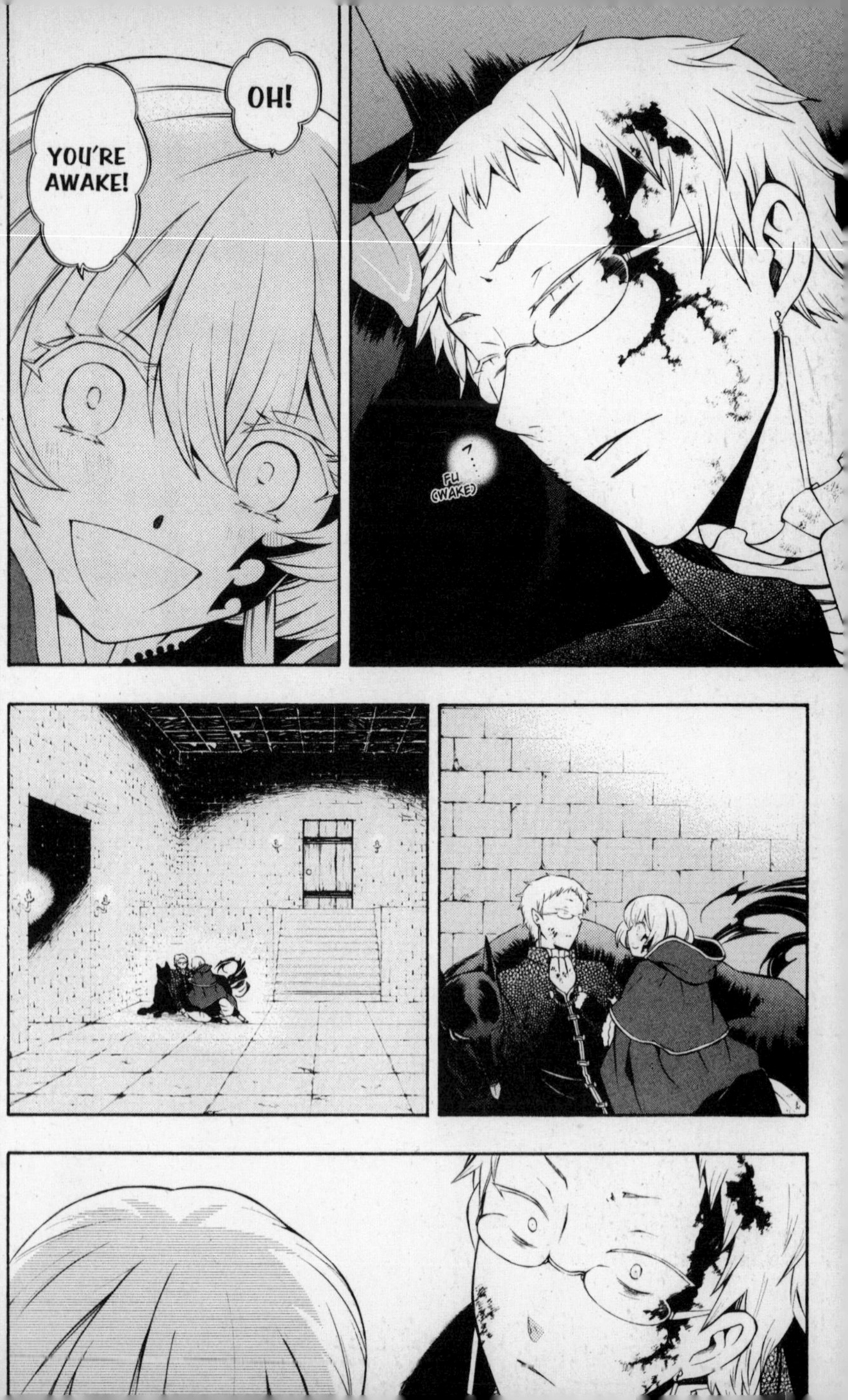
FU
(WAKE)
OH!
YOU'RE AWAKE!

DO
(THUMP)

!! ....

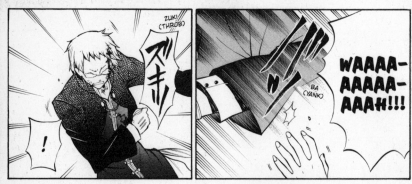

ZUKI
(THROB)

!

BA
(YANK)

WAAAAA-
AAAAA-
AAAH!!!

...HE.

AGH!

DOSA
(THUD)

WHAT'RE
YOU
DOIIING!?

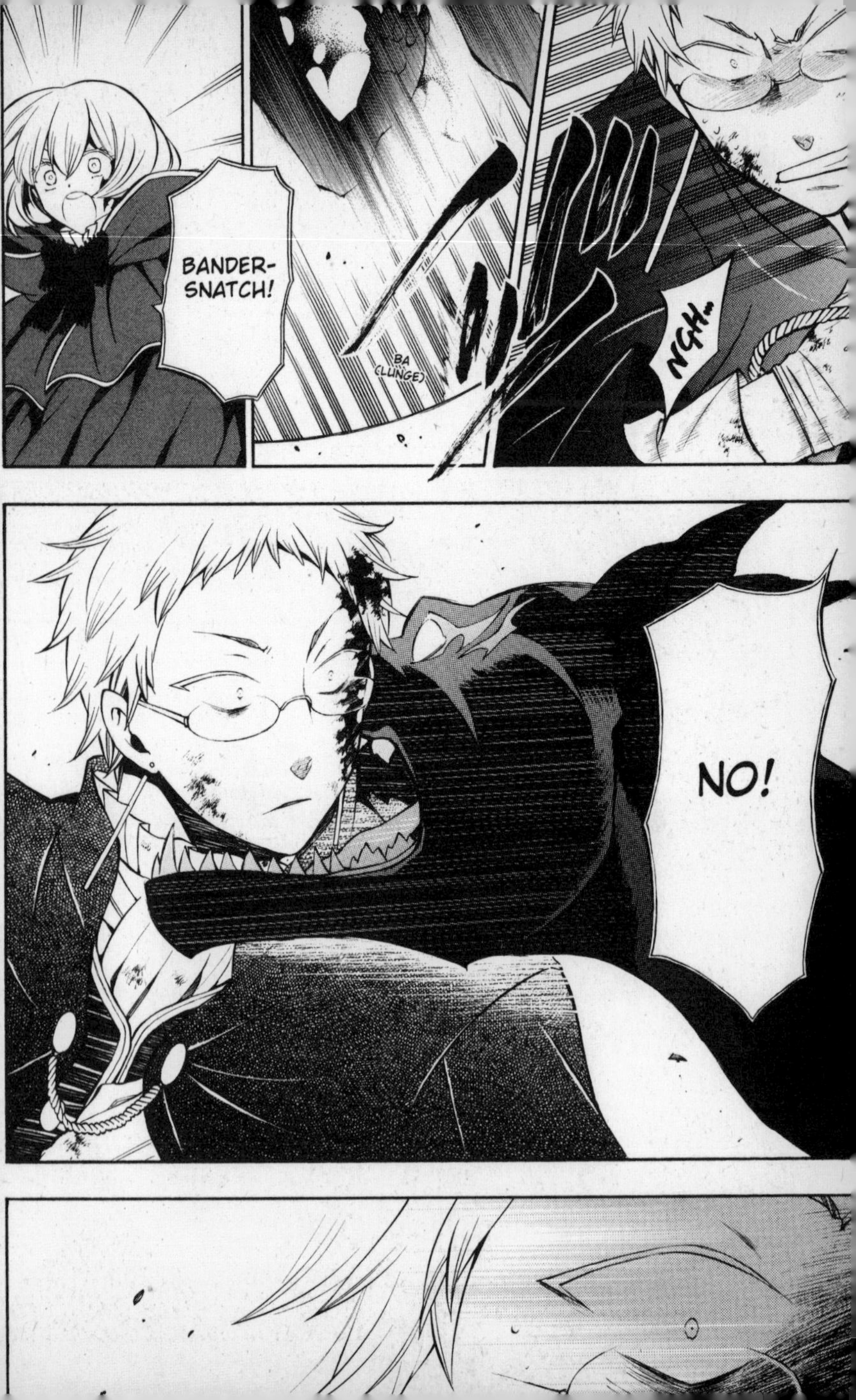
NGH...
BA (LUNGE)
BANDER-SNATCH!
NO!

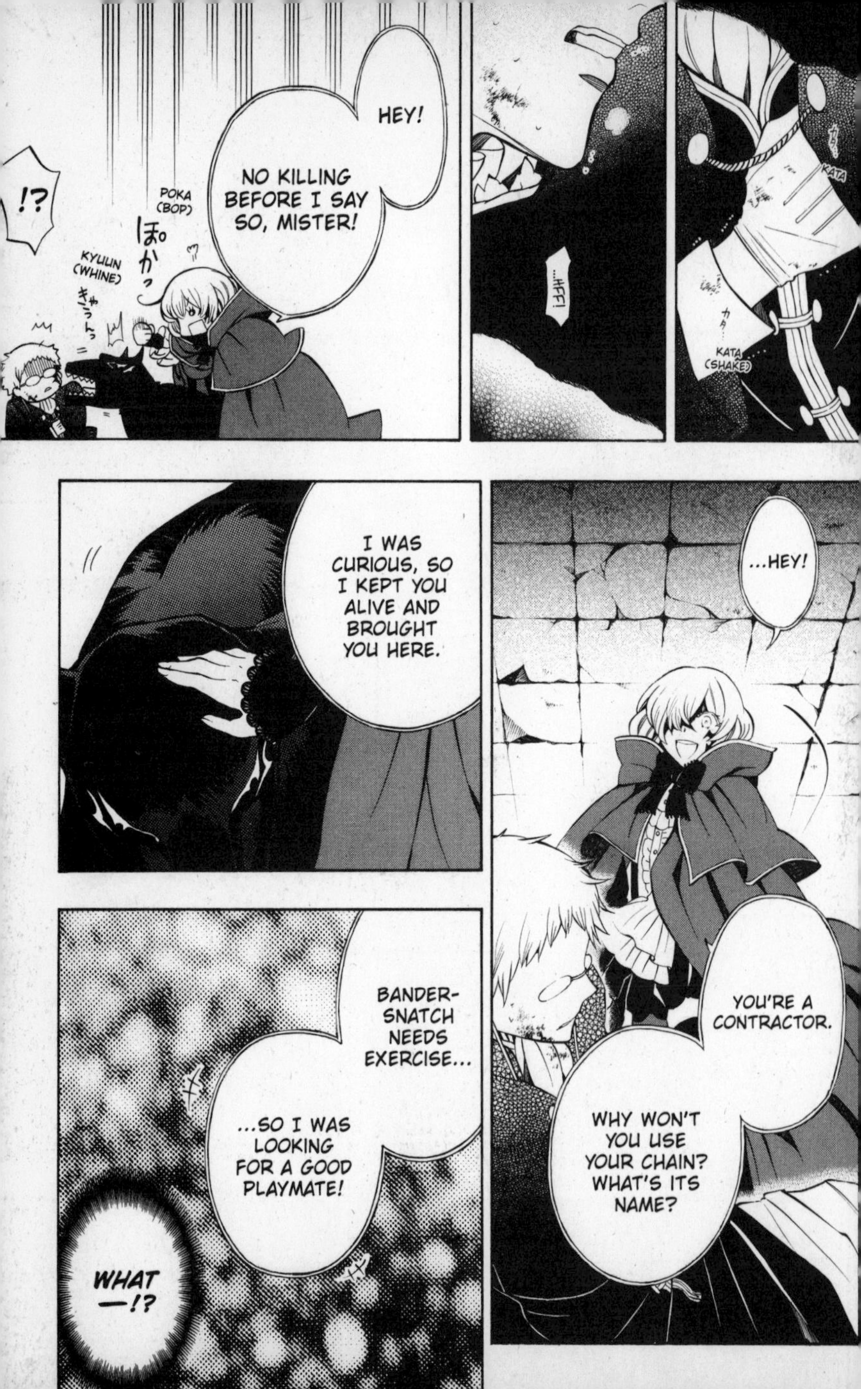
カタ
KATA
カタ…
KATA (SHAKE)
...HFF!
HEY!
NO KILLING BEFORE I SAY SO, MISTER!
ぽかっ
POKA (BOP)
きゃうんっ
KYUUN (WHINE)
!?
...HEY!
YOU'RE A CONTRACTOR.
WHY WON'T YOU USE YOUR CHAIN? WHAT'S ITS NAME?
I WAS CURIOUS, SO I KEPT YOU ALIVE AND BROUGHT YOU HERE.
BANDER-SNATCH NEEDS EXERCISE...
...SO I WAS LOOKING FOR A GOOD PLAYMATE!
WHAT—!?

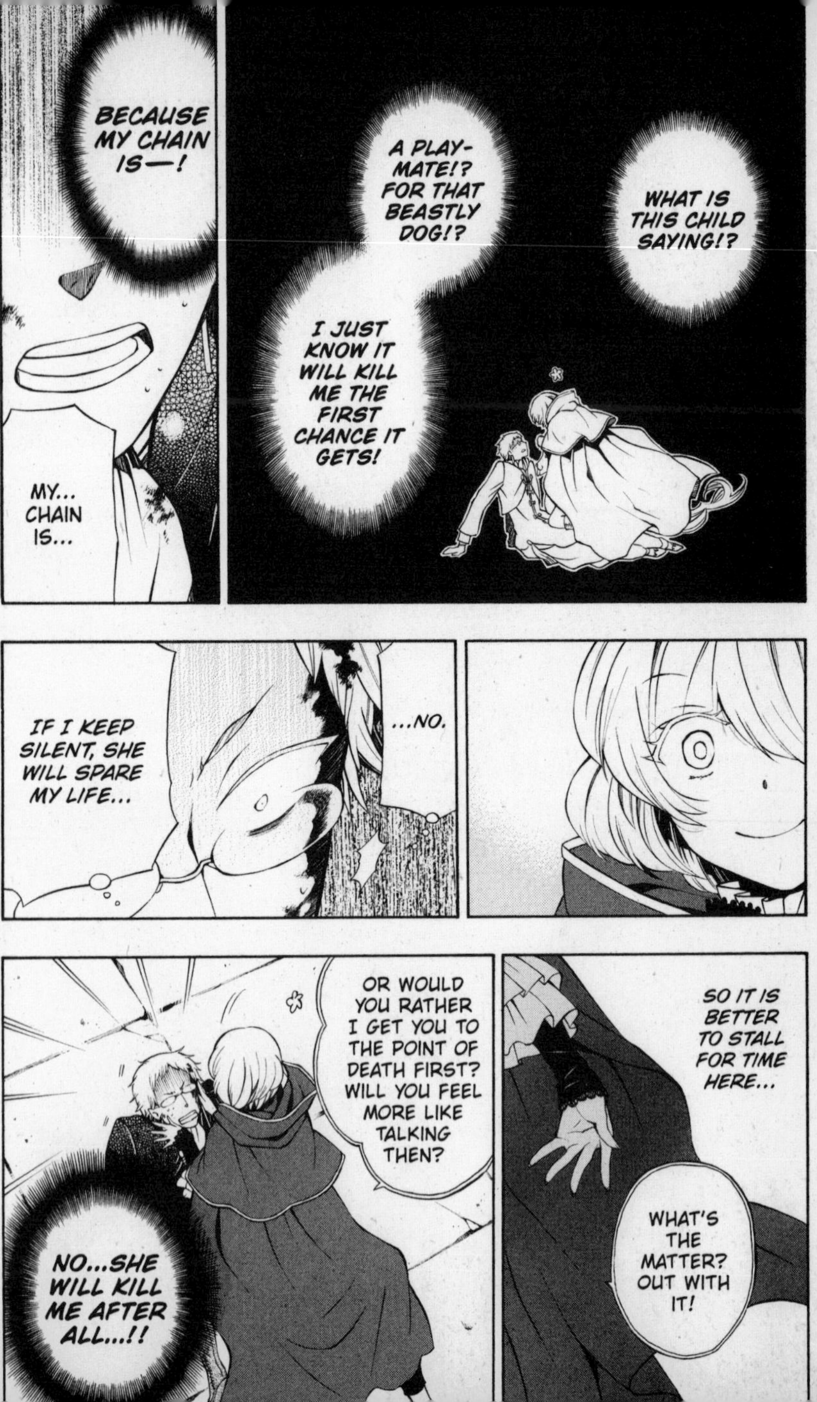
WHAT IS THIS CHILD SAYING!?
A PLAY-MATE!? FOR THAT BEASTLY DOG!?
I JUST KNOW IT WILL KILL ME THE FIRST CHANCE IT GETS!
BECAUSE MY CHAIN IS—!
MY... CHAIN IS...
...NO.
IF I KEEP SILENT, SHE WILL SPARE MY LIFE...
SO IT IS BETTER TO STALL FOR TIME HERE...
WHAT'S THE MATTER? OUT WITH IT!
OR WOULD YOU RATHER I GET YOU TO THE POINT OF DEATH FIRST? WILL YOU FEEL MORE LIKE TALKING THEN?
NO...SHE WILL KILL ME AFTER ALL...!!

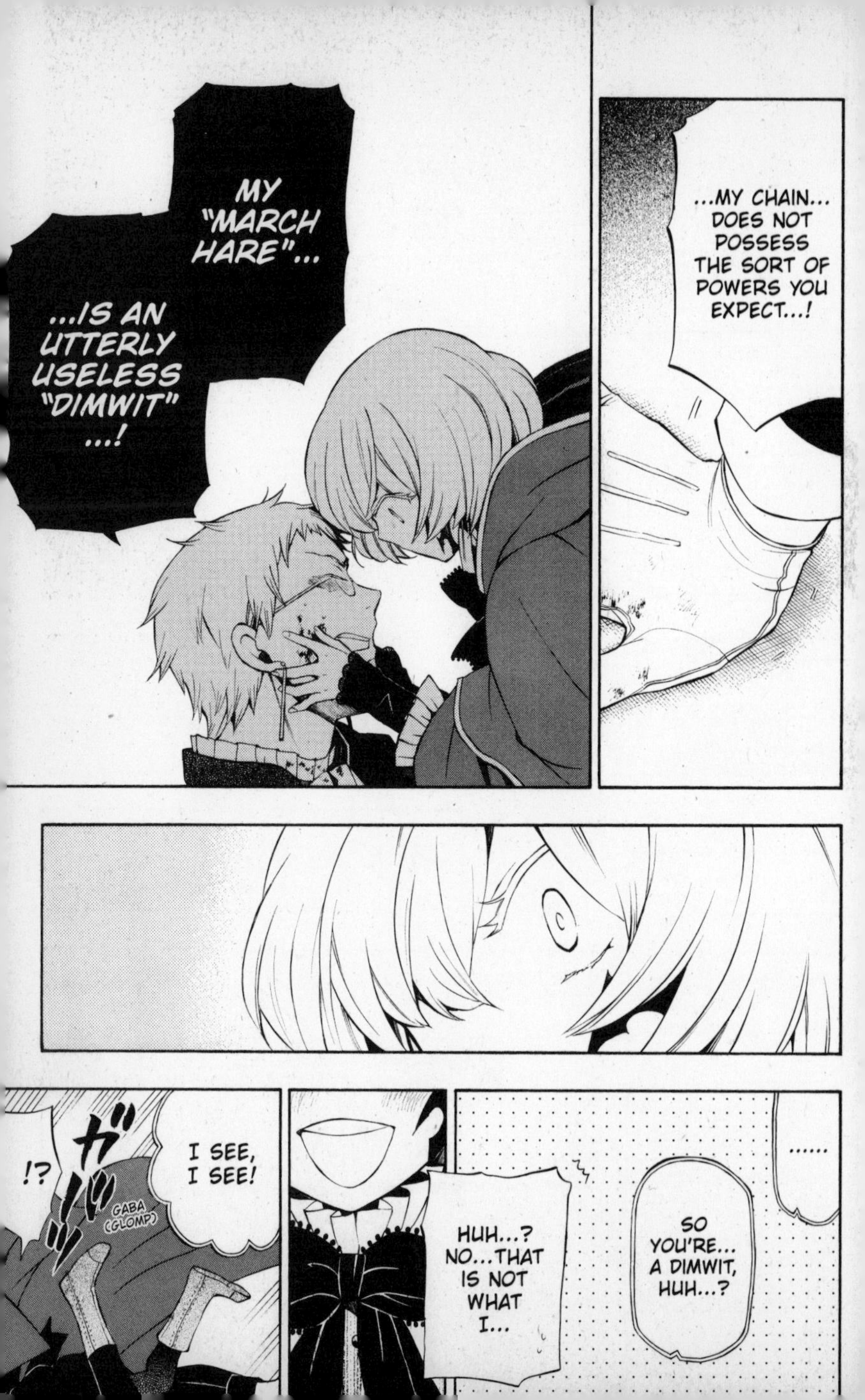
...MY CHAIN... DOES NOT POSSESS THE SORT OF POWERS YOU EXPECT...!
MY "MARCH HARE"...
...IS AN UTTERLY USELESS "DIMWIT" ...!
......
SO YOU'RE... A DIMWIT, HUH...?
HUH...? NO...THAT IS NOT WHAT I...
I SEE, I SEE!
!?
GABA (GLOMP)

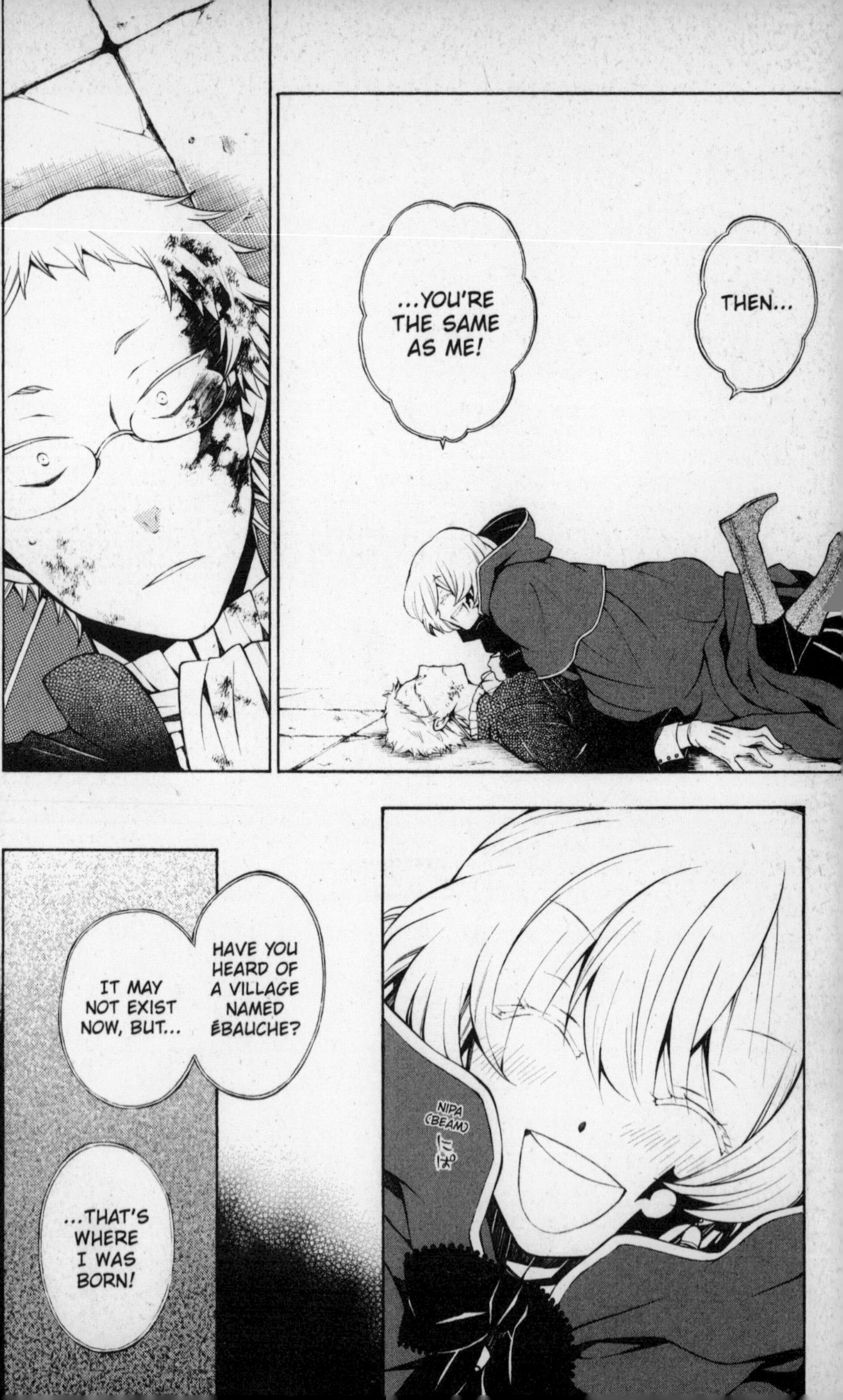
THEN...
...YOU'RE THE SAME AS ME!
NIPA (BEAM)
にぱ
HAVE YOU HEARD OF A VILLAGE NAMED ÉBAUCHE?
IT MAY NOT EXIST NOW, BUT...
...THAT'S WHERE I WAS BORN!

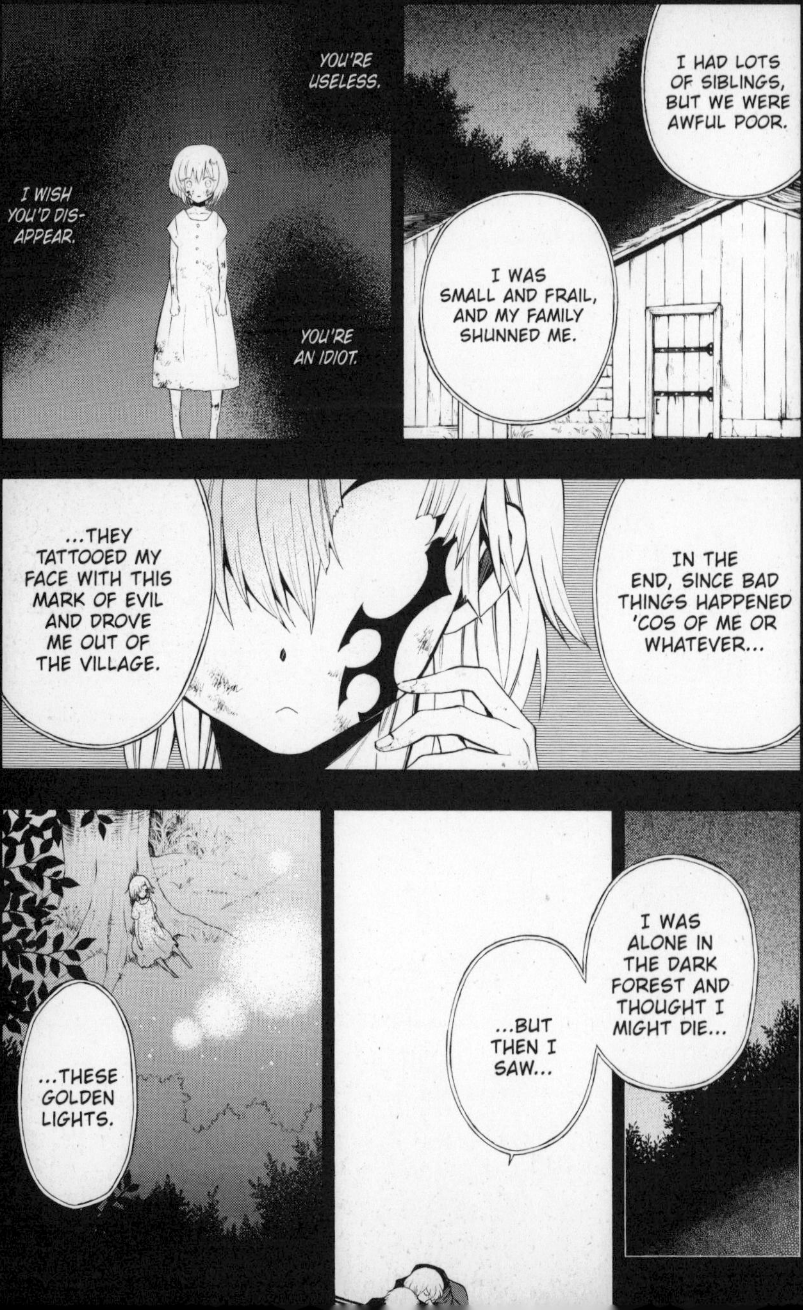
I HAD LOTS OF SIBLINGS, BUT WE WERE AWFUL POOR.
I WAS SMALL AND FRAIL, AND MY FAMILY SHUNNED ME.
YOU'RE USELESS.
I WISH YOU'D DIS-APPEAR.
YOU'RE AN IDIOT.
IN THE END, SINCE BAD THINGS HAPPENED 'COS OF ME OR WHATEVER...
...THEY TATTOOED MY FACE WITH THIS MARK OF EVIL AND DROVE ME OUT OF THE VILLAGE.
I WAS ALONE IN THE DARK FOREST AND THOUGHT I MIGHT DIE...
...BUT THEN I SAW...
...THESE GOLDEN LIGHTS.

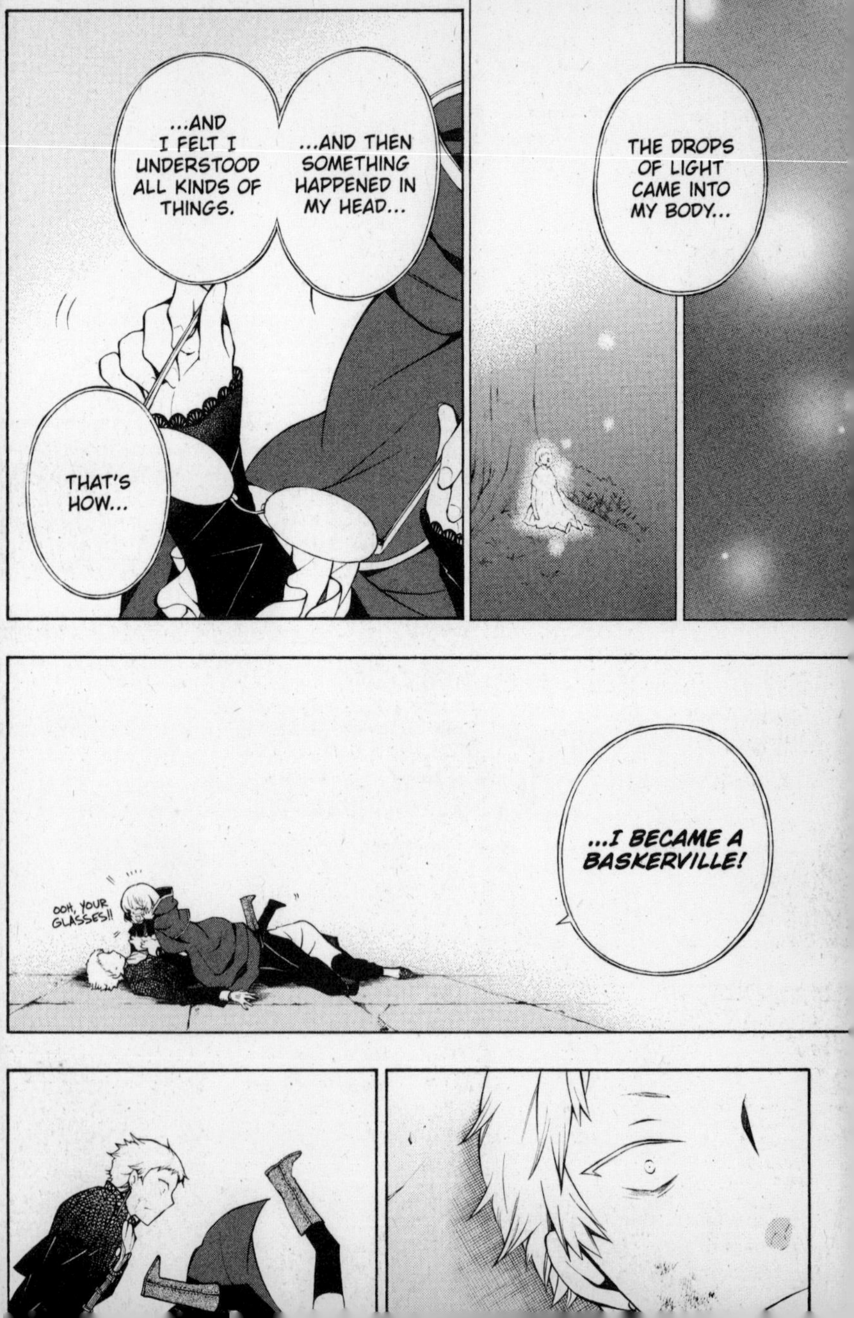
THE DROPS OF LIGHT CAME INTO MY BODY...
...AND THEN SOMETHING HAPPENED IN MY HEAD...
...AND I FELT I UNDERSTOOD ALL KINDS OF THINGS.
THAT'S HOW...
...I BECAME A BASKERVILLE!
OOH, YOUR GLASSES!!

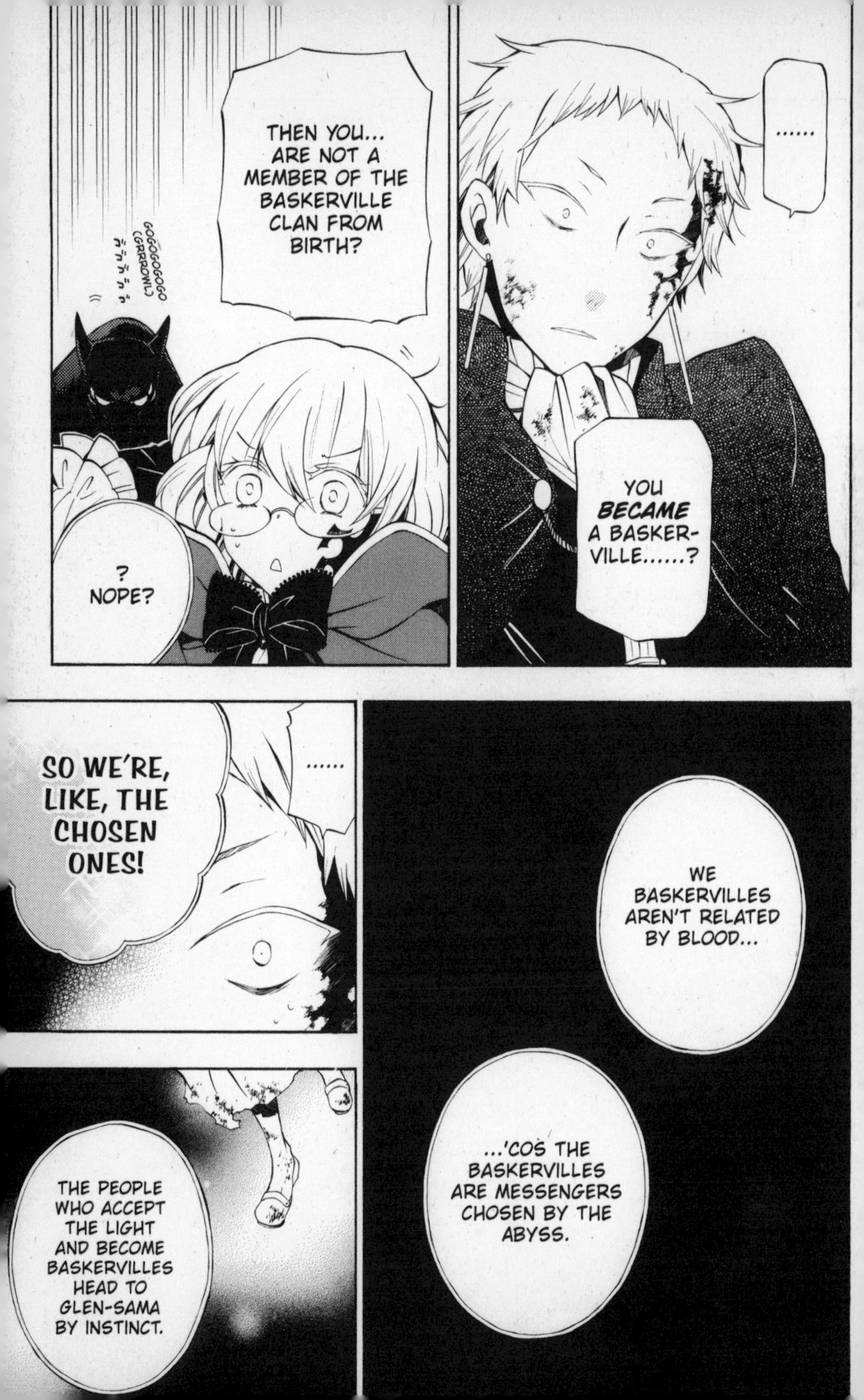
......
YOU *BECAME* A BASKERVILLE......?
THEN YOU... ARE NOT A MEMBER OF THE BASKERVILLE CLAN FROM BIRTH?
GOGOGOGOGO (GRRROWL)
? NOPE?
WE BASKERVILLES AREN'T RELATED BY BLOOD...
...'COS THE BASKERVILLES ARE MESSENGERS CHOSEN BY THE ABYSS.
......
SO WE'RE, LIKE, THE CHOSEN ONES!
THE PEOPLE WHO ACCEPT THE LIGHT AND BECOME BASKERVILLES HEAD TO GLEN-SAMA BY INSTINCT.

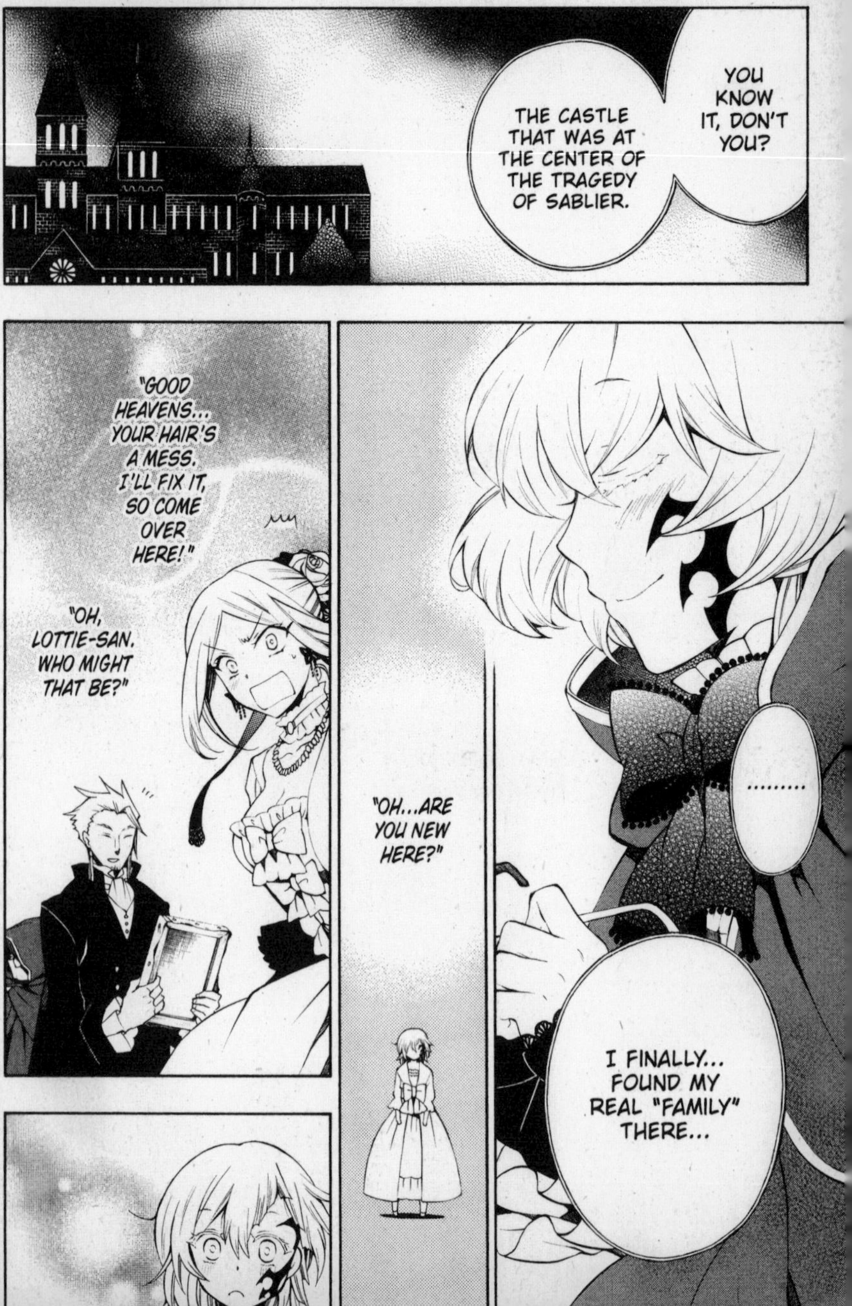
YOU KNOW IT, DON'T YOU?
THE CASTLE THAT WAS AT THE CENTER OF THE TRAGEDY OF SABLIER.
....
I FINALLY... FOUND MY REAL "FAMILY" THERE...
"OH...ARE YOU NEW HERE?"
"GOOD HEAVENS... YOUR HAIR'S A MESS. I'LL FIX IT, SO COME OVER HERE!"
"OH, LOTTIE-SAN. WHO MIGHT THAT BE?"

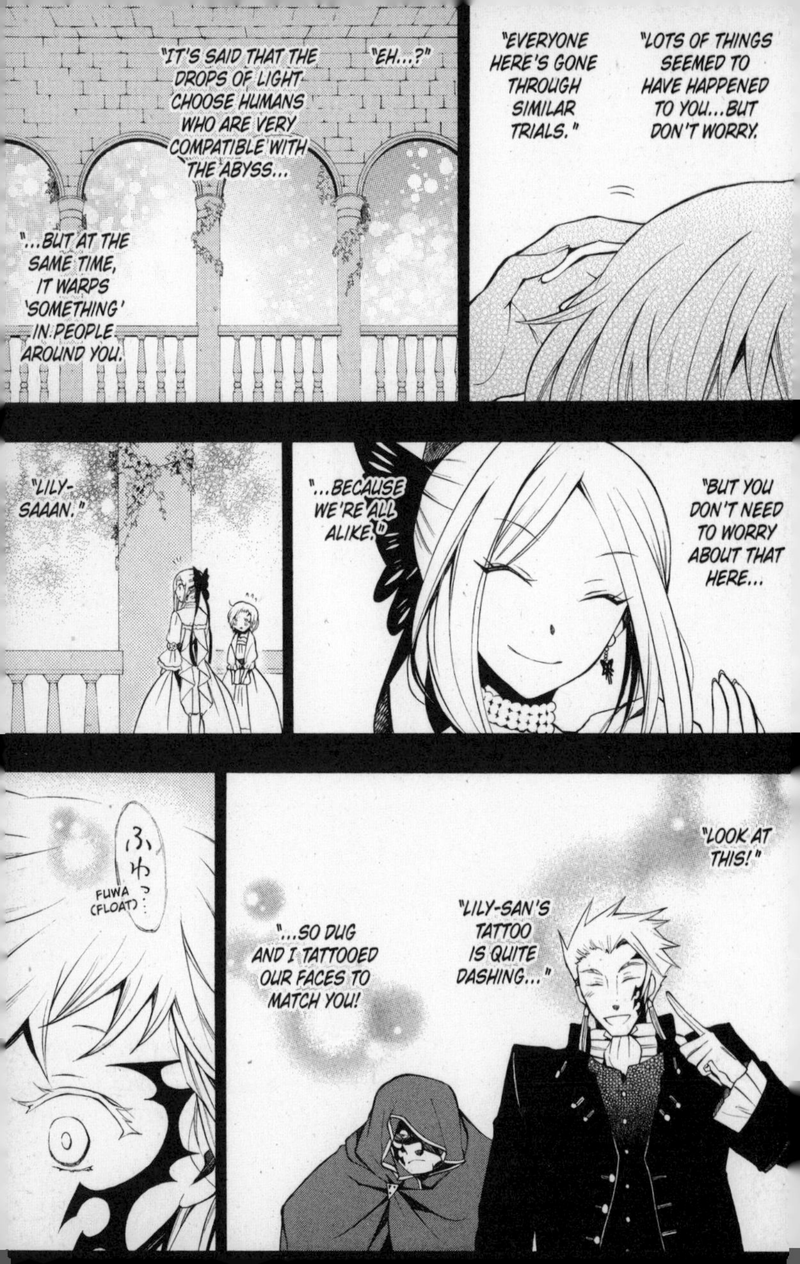
"LOTS OF THINGS SEEMED TO HAVE HAPPENED TO YOU...BUT DON'T WORRY.
"EVERYONE HERE'S GONE THROUGH SIMILAR TRIALS."
"EH...?"
"IT'S SAID THAT THE DROPS OF LIGHT CHOOSE HUMANS WHO ARE VERY COMPATIBLE WITH THE ABYSS...
"...BUT AT THE SAME TIME, IT WARPS 'SOMETHING' IN PEOPLE AROUND YOU.
"BUT YOU DON'T NEED TO WORRY ABOUT THAT HERE...
"...BECAUSE WE'RE ALL ALIKE."
"LILY-SAAAN."
"LOOK AT THIS!"
"LILY-SAN'S TATTOO IS QUITE DASHING..."
"...SO DUG AND I TATTOOED OUR FACES TO MATCH YOU!
ふわっ
FUWA (FLOAT)

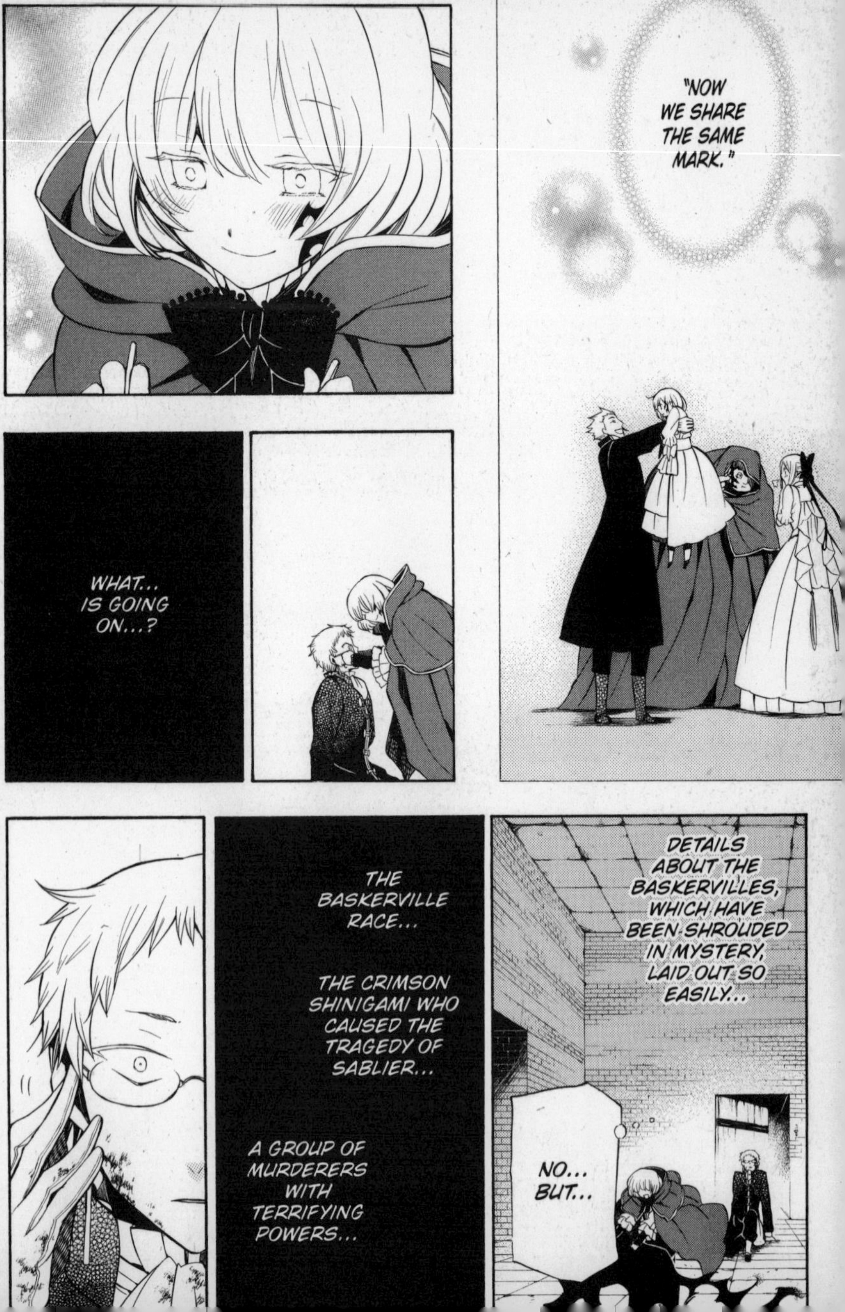
"NOW WE SHARE THE SAME MARK."
WHAT... IS GOING ON...?
DETAILS ABOUT THE BASKERVILLES, WHICH HAVE BEEN SHROUDED IN MYSTERY, LAID OUT SO EASILY...
NO... BUT...
THE BASKERVILLE RACE...
THE CRIMSON SHINIGAMI WHO CAUSED THE TRAGEDY OF SABLIER...
A GROUP OF MURDERERS WITH TERRIFYING POWERS...

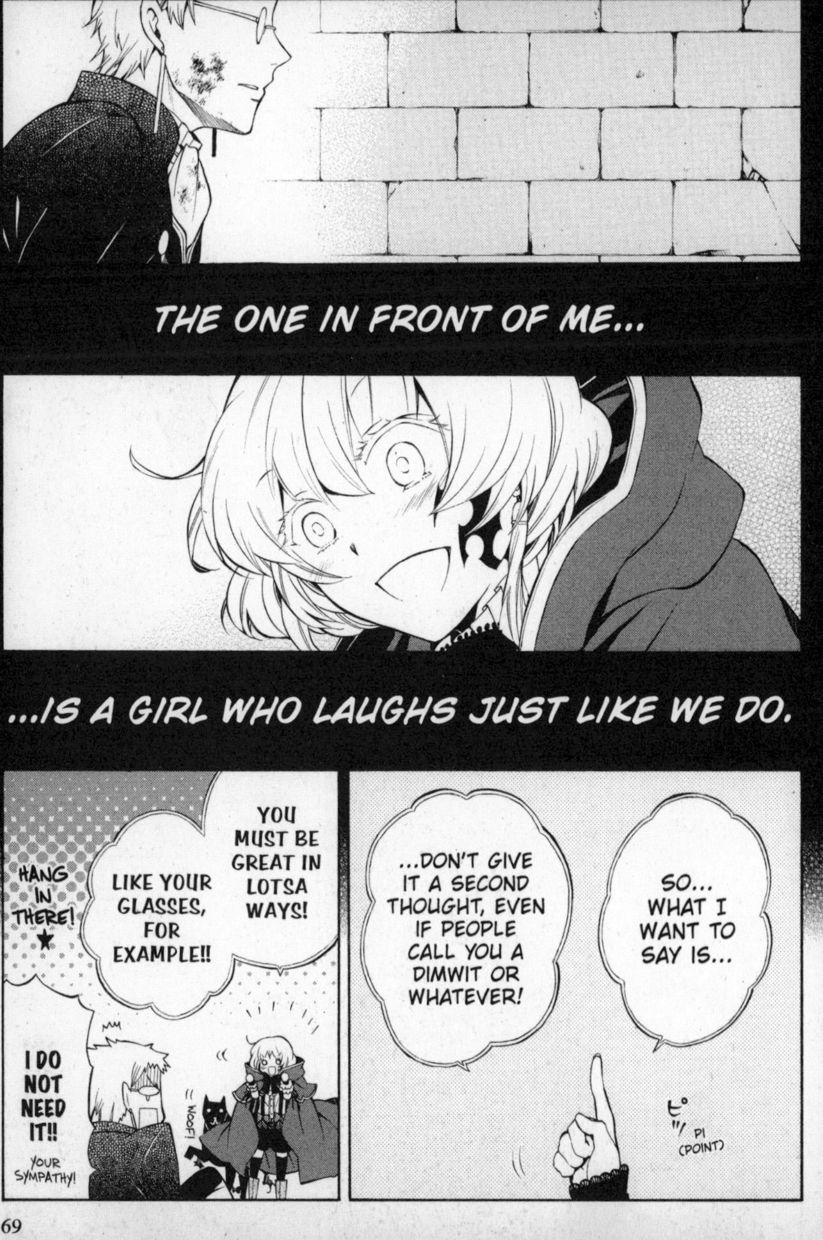
THE ONE IN FRONT OF ME...
...IS A GIRL WHO LAUGHS JUST LIKE WE DO.
SO... WHAT I WANT TO SAY IS...
...DON'T GIVE IT A SECOND THOUGHT, EVEN IF PEOPLE CALL YOU A DIMWIT OR WHATEVER!
ピッ PI (POINT)
YOU MUST BE GREAT IN LOTSA WAYS!
LIKE YOUR GLASSES, FOR EXAMPLE!!
HANG IN THERE! ★
I DO NOT NEED IT!!
YOUR SYMPATHY!
WOOF!

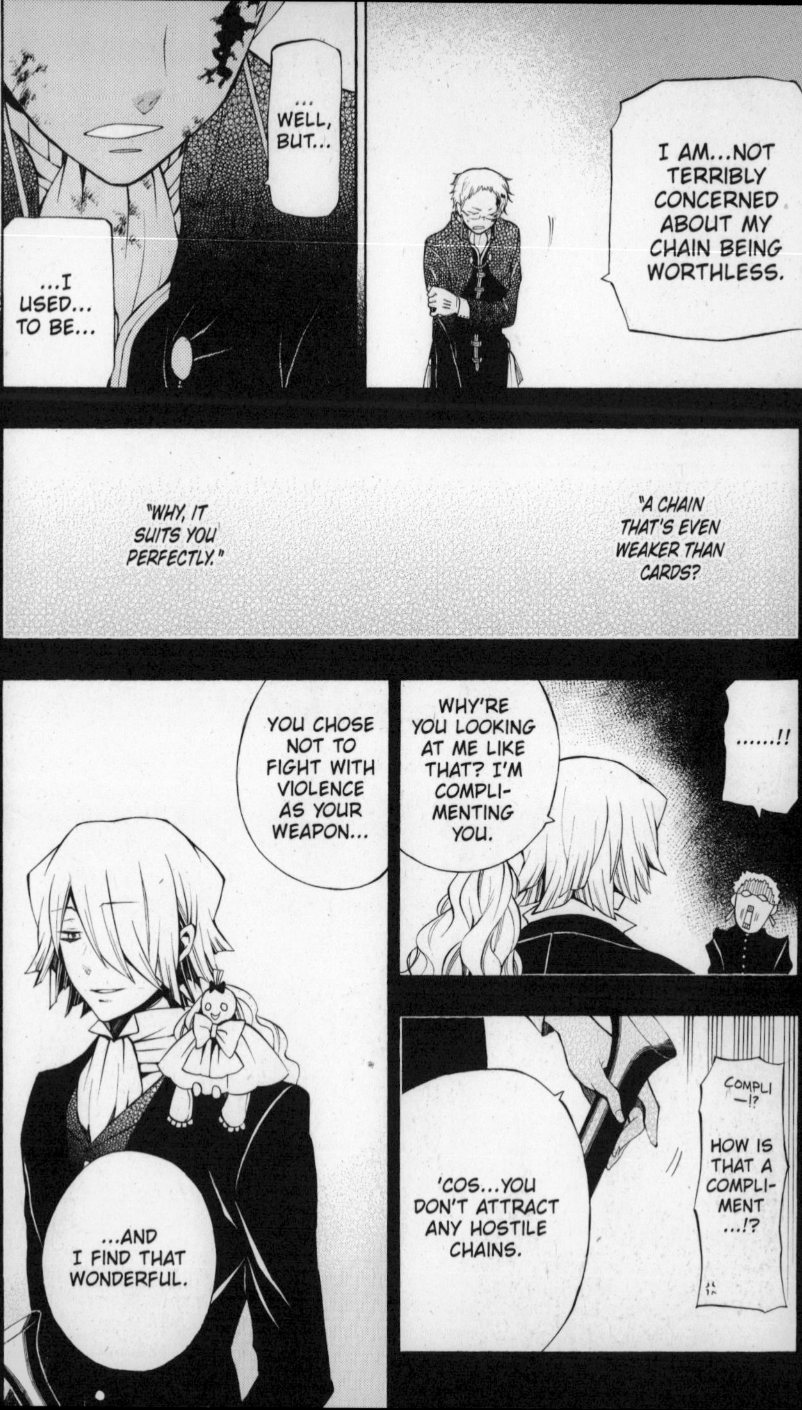
I AM...NOT TERRIBLY CONCERNED ABOUT MY CHAIN BEING WORTHLESS.
...WELL, BUT...
...I USED... TO BE...
"A CHAIN THAT'S EVEN WEAKER THAN CARDS?
"WHY, IT SUITS YOU PERFECTLY."
......!!
WHY'RE YOU LOOKING AT ME LIKE THAT? I'M COMPLI-MENTING YOU.
COMPLI—!?
HOW IS THAT A COMPLI-MENT ...!?
'COS...YOU DON'T ATTRACT ANY HOSTILE CHAINS.
YOU CHOSE NOT TO FIGHT WITH VIOLENCE AS YOUR WEAPON...
...AND I FIND THAT WONDERFUL.

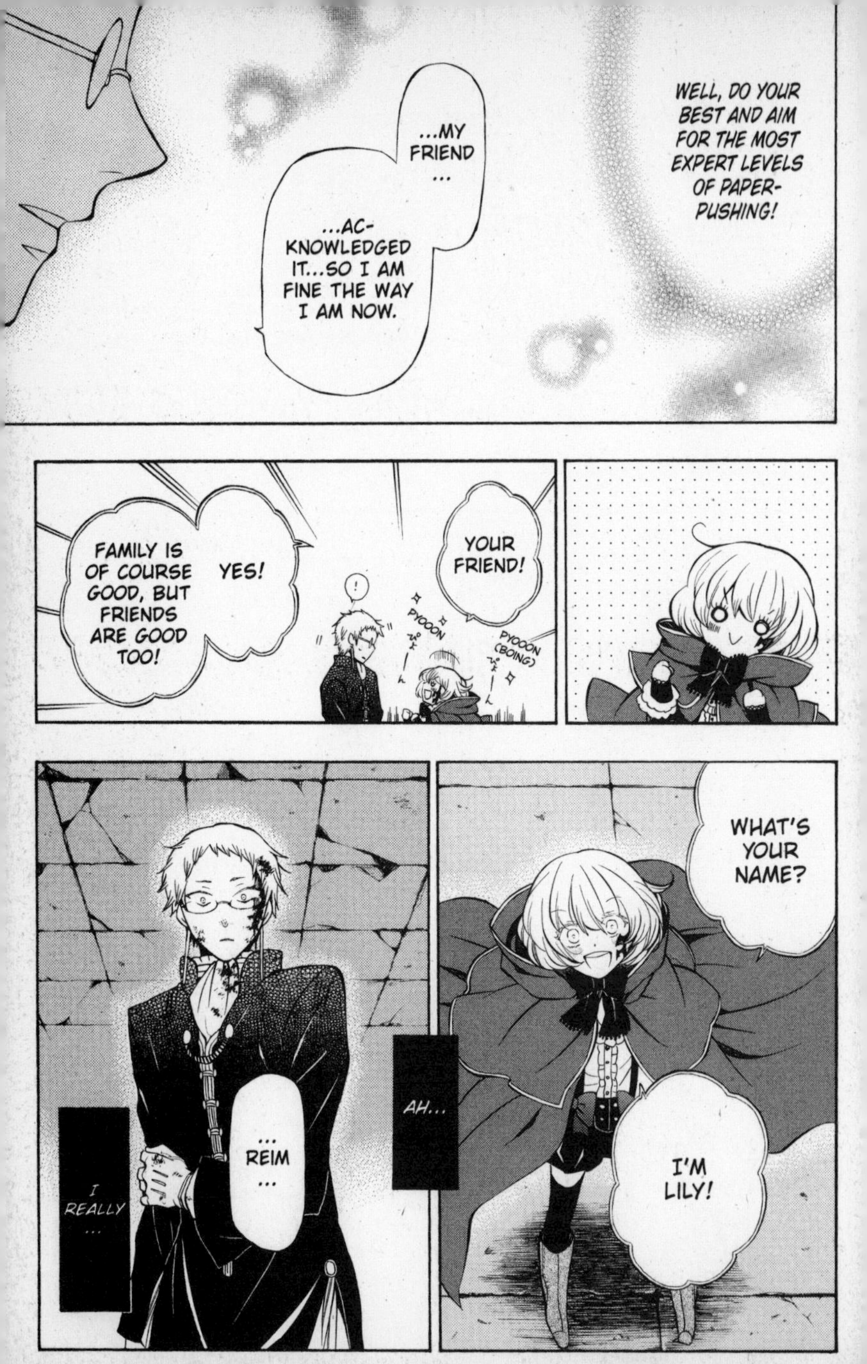
WELL, DO YOUR BEST AND AIM FOR THE MOST EXPERT LEVELS OF PAPER-PUSHING!
...MY FRIEND ...
...AC-KNOWLEDGED IT...SO I AM FINE THE WAY I AM NOW.
YOUR FRIEND!
PYOOON (BOING)
PYOOON
!
YES!
FAMILY IS OF COURSE GOOD, BUT FRIENDS ARE GOOD TOO!
WHAT'S YOUR NAME?
I'M LILY!
AH...
... REIM ...
I REALLY ...

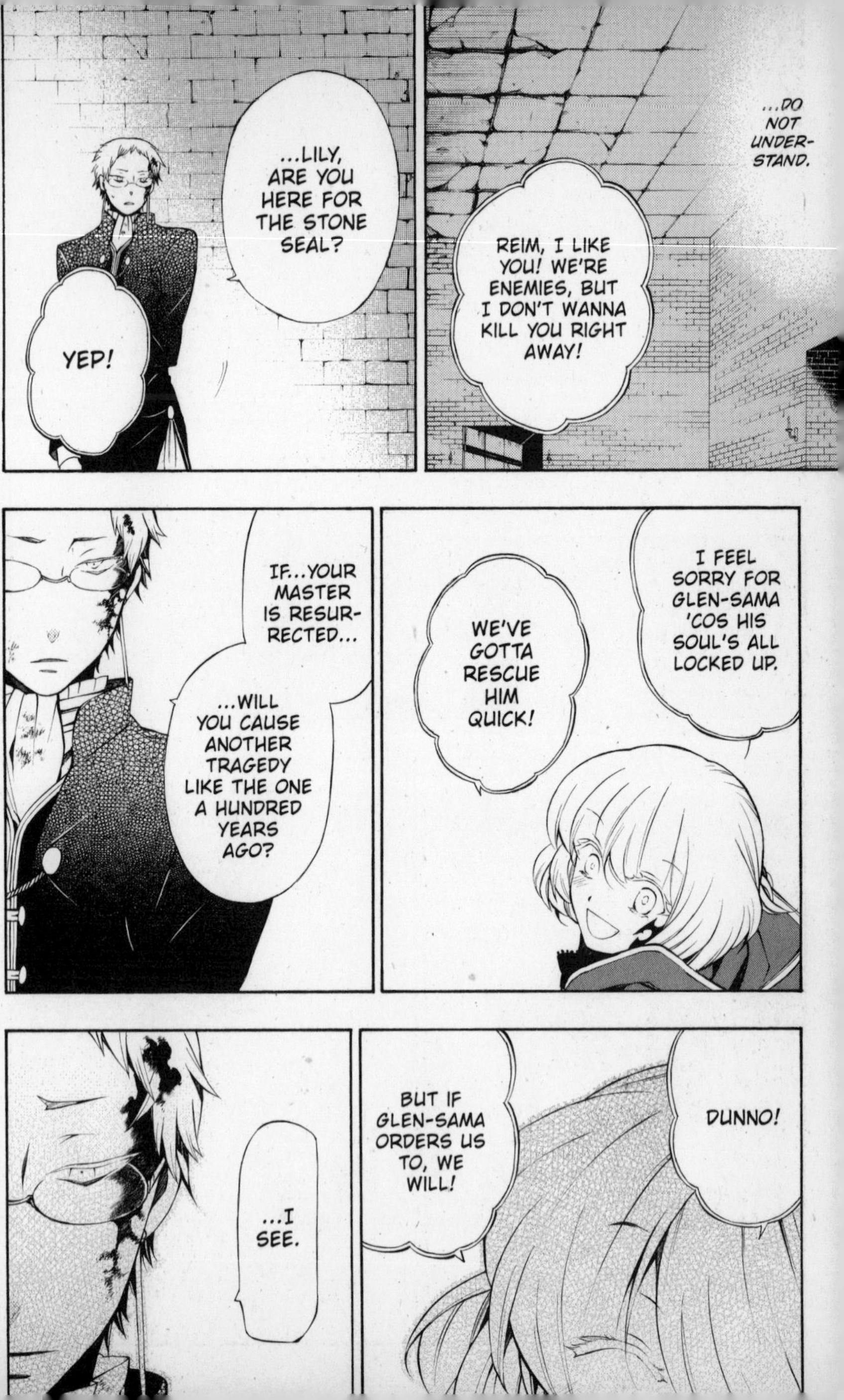
...DO NOT UNDERSTAND.
REIM, I LIKE YOU! WE'RE ENEMIES, BUT I DON'T WANNA KILL YOU RIGHT AWAY!
...LILY, ARE YOU HERE FOR THE STONE SEAL?
YEP!
I FEEL SORRY FOR GLEN-SAMA 'COS HIS SOUL'S ALL LOCKED UP.
WE'VE GOTTA RESCUE HIM QUICK!
IF...YOUR MASTER IS RESURRECTED...
...WILL YOU CAUSE ANOTHER TRAGEDY LIKE THE ONE A HUNDRED YEARS AGO?
DUNNO!
BUT IF GLEN-SAMA ORDERS US TO, WE WILL!
...I SEE.

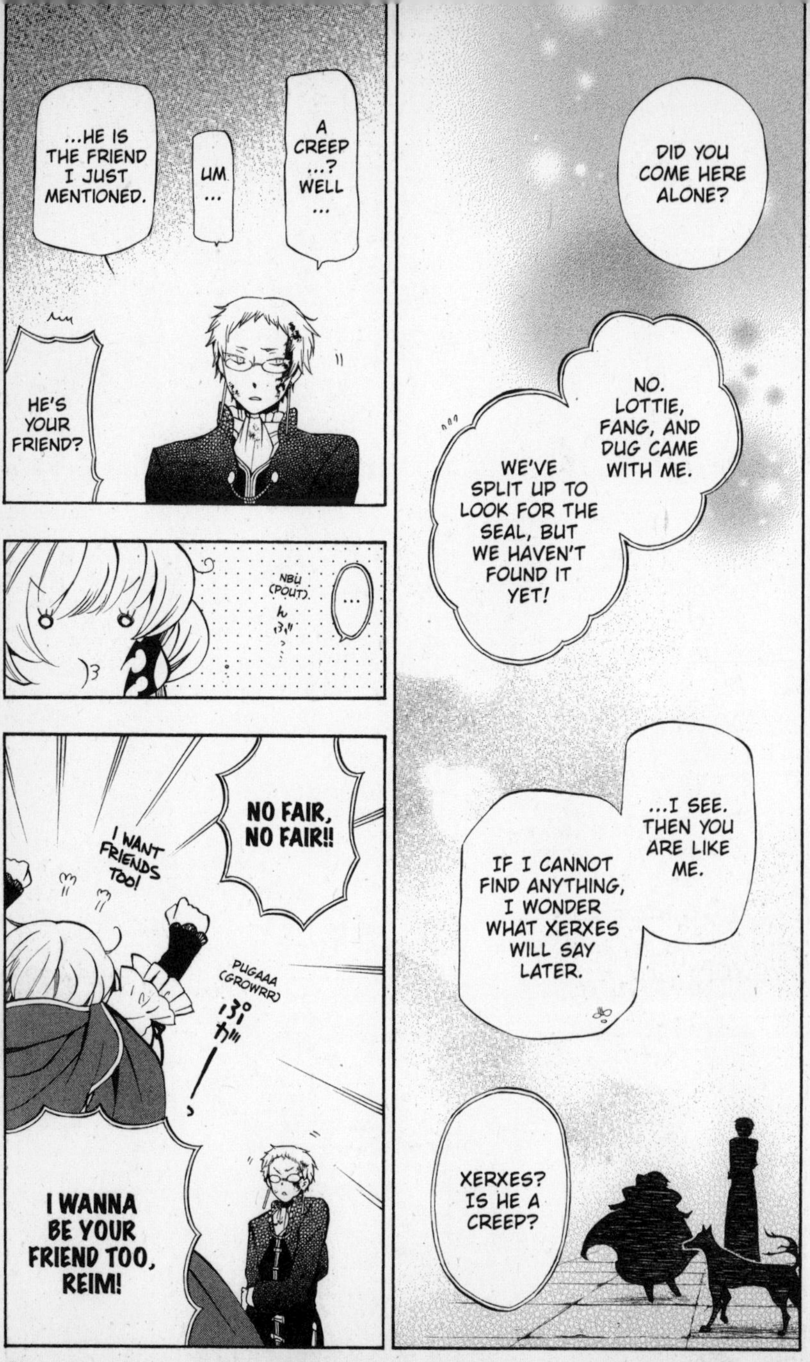
DID YOU COME HERE ALONE?
NO. LOTTIE, FANG, AND DUG CAME WITH ME.
WE'VE SPLIT UP TO LOOK FOR THE SEAL, BUT WE HAVEN'T FOUND IT YET!
...I SEE. THEN YOU ARE LIKE ME.
IF I CANNOT FIND ANYTHING, I WONDER WHAT XERXES WILL SAY LATER.
XERXES? IS HE A CREEP?
A CREEP ...? WELL ...
UM ...
...HE IS THE FRIEND I JUST MENTIONED.
HE'S YOUR FRIEND?
...
NBU (POUT)
NO FAIR, NO FAIR!!
I WANT FRIENDS TOO!
PUGAAA (GROWRR)
I WANNA BE YOUR FRIEND TOO, REIM!

YOU ARE... ERM, AN EMBARRASSING CHILD...

KOHON (KOFF)

......

Y—

...I SEE.

LILY...DO YOU STILL WANT TO SEE MY CHAIN?

I DO! I WON'T LET BANDER-SNATCH BITE, SO SHOW ME, SHOW ME!

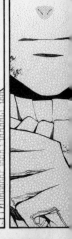

...MY MARCH HARE.

ZAWA (ZWOOSH)

THEN I WILL HAVE YOU SEE...

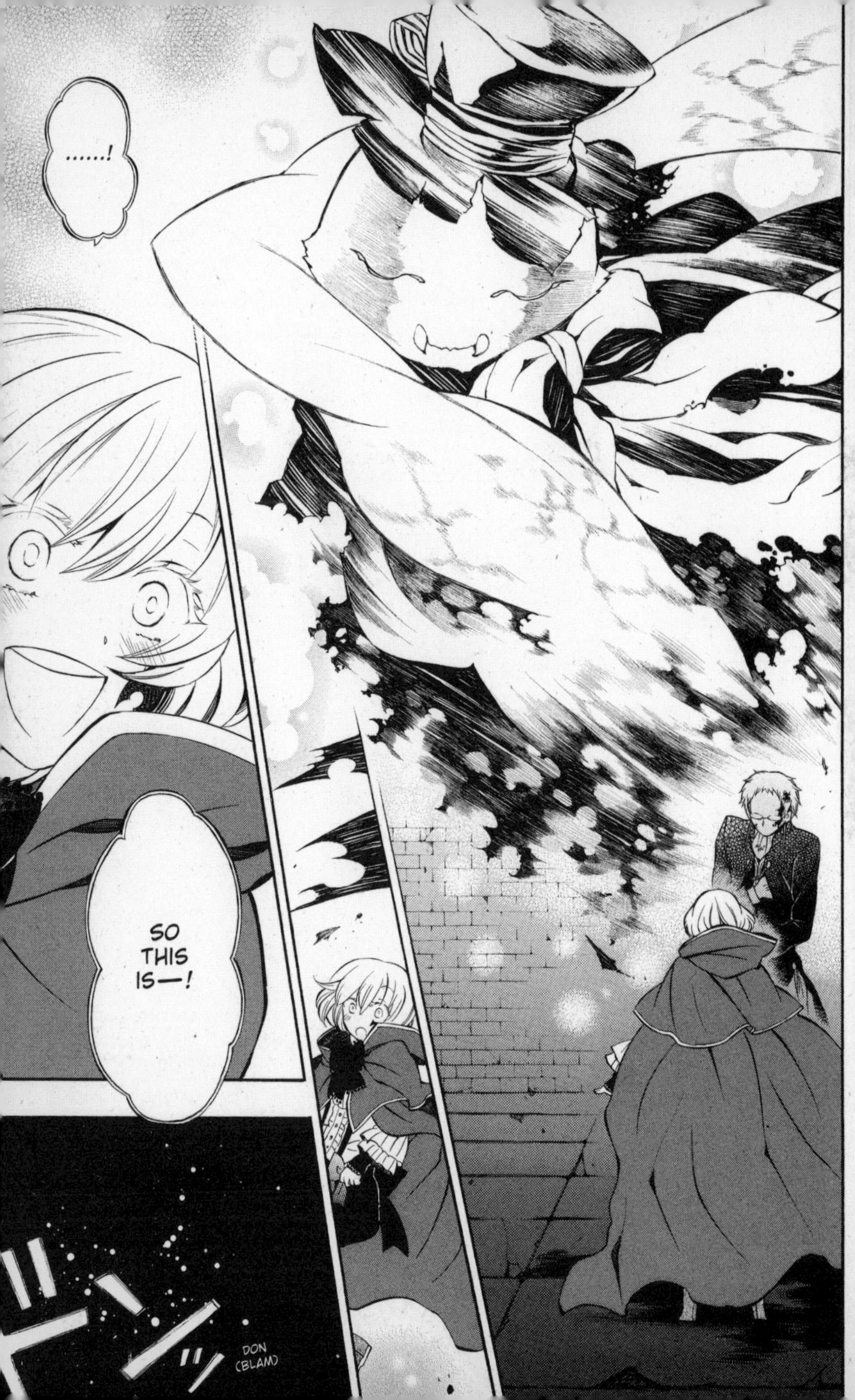
......!
SO THIS IS—!
DON (BLAM)

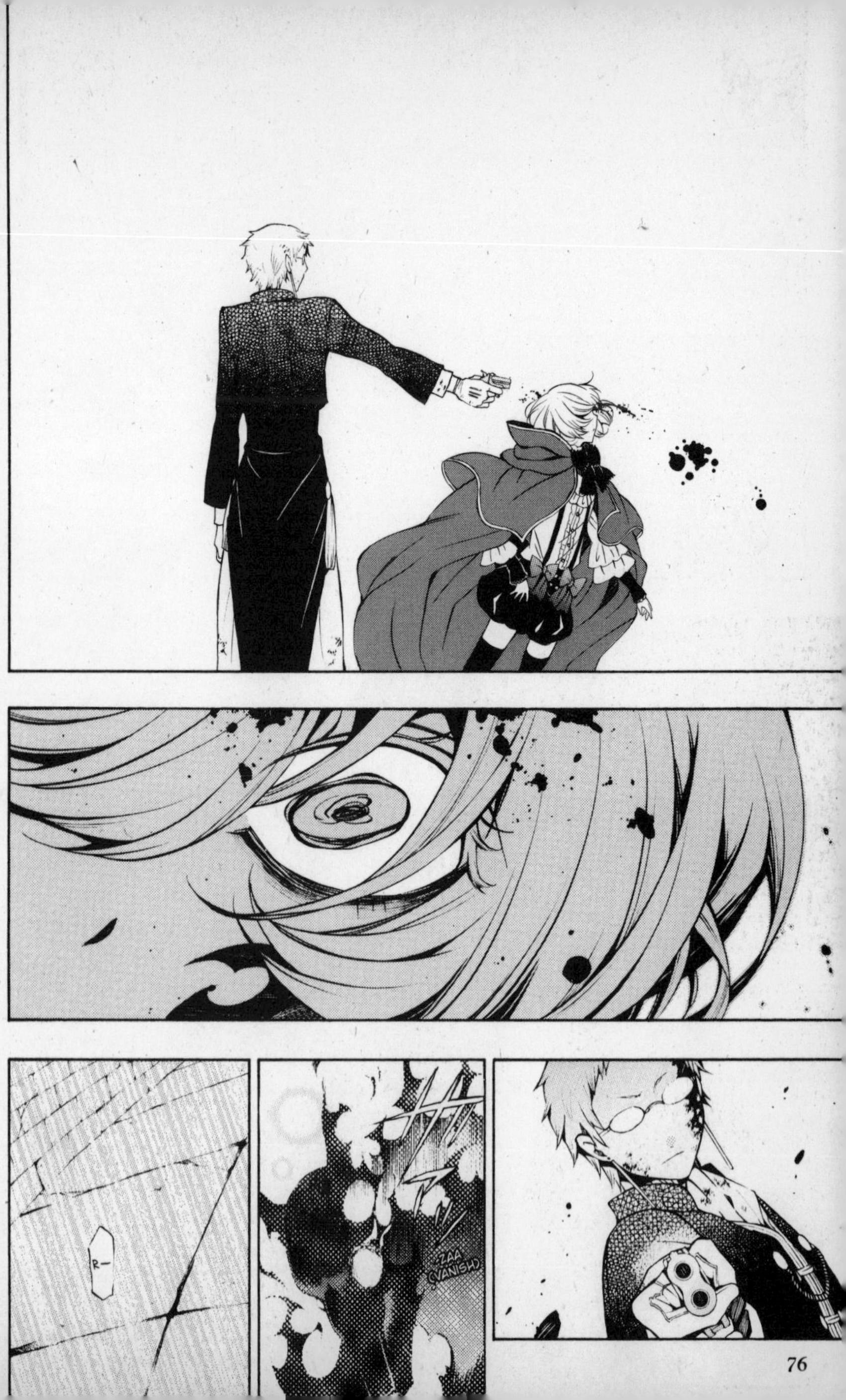
ZAA (VANISH)
R—

DOSA
(THUD)

EVEN IF SHE IS AN INNOCENT CHILD...

...SHE MURDERED MY COLLEAGUES...

...AND IS AN ENEMY WHO WOULD HAVE PLUCKED MANY A LIFE IF I HAD ALLOWED HER TO LIVE.

I MUST HURRY...

I HAVE TO TELL OZ-SAMA THAT THE BASKERVILLES ARE HERE...!

ZA
(STEP)

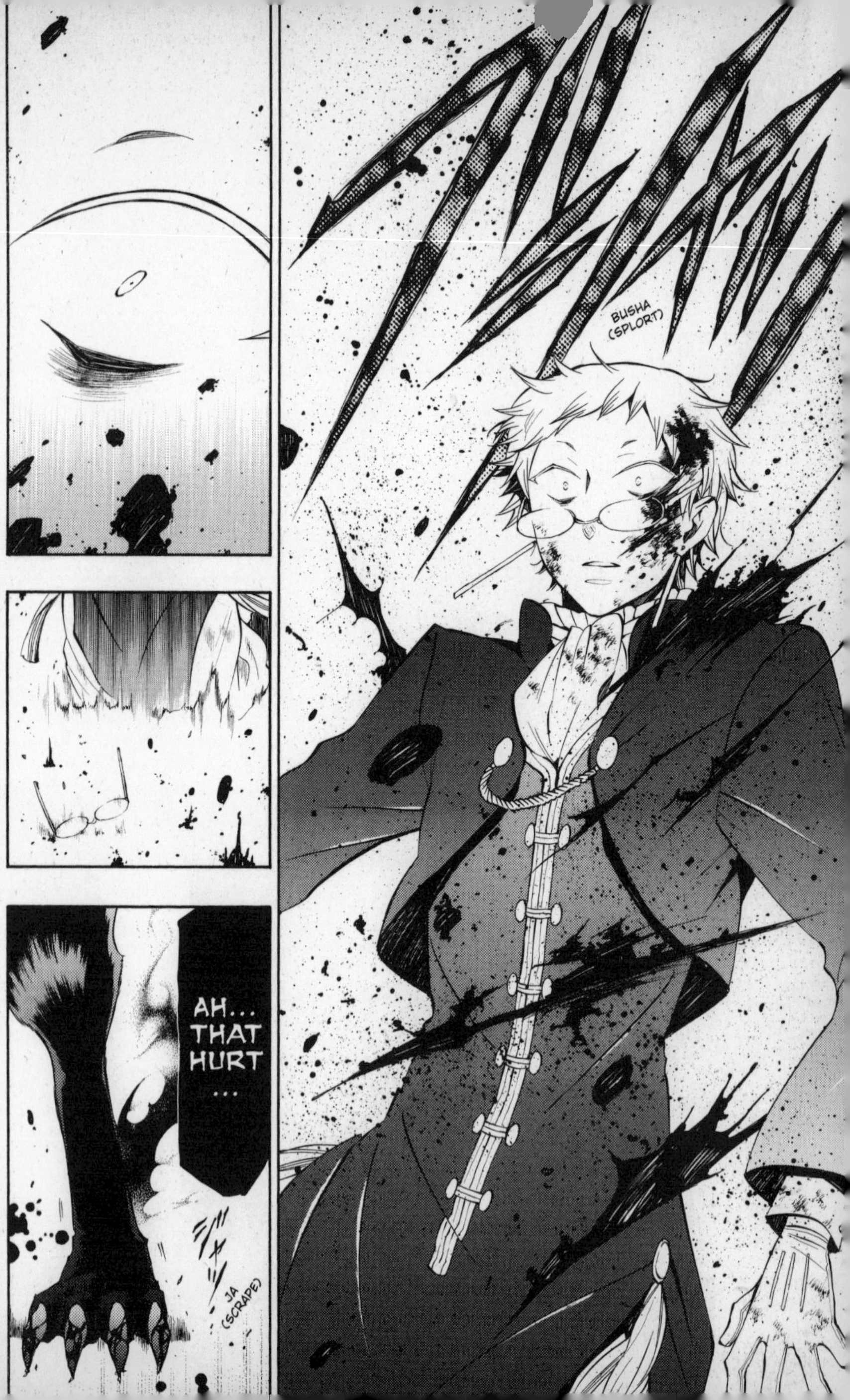
BUSHA
(SPLORT)
AH... THAT HURT ...
JA
(SCRAPE)

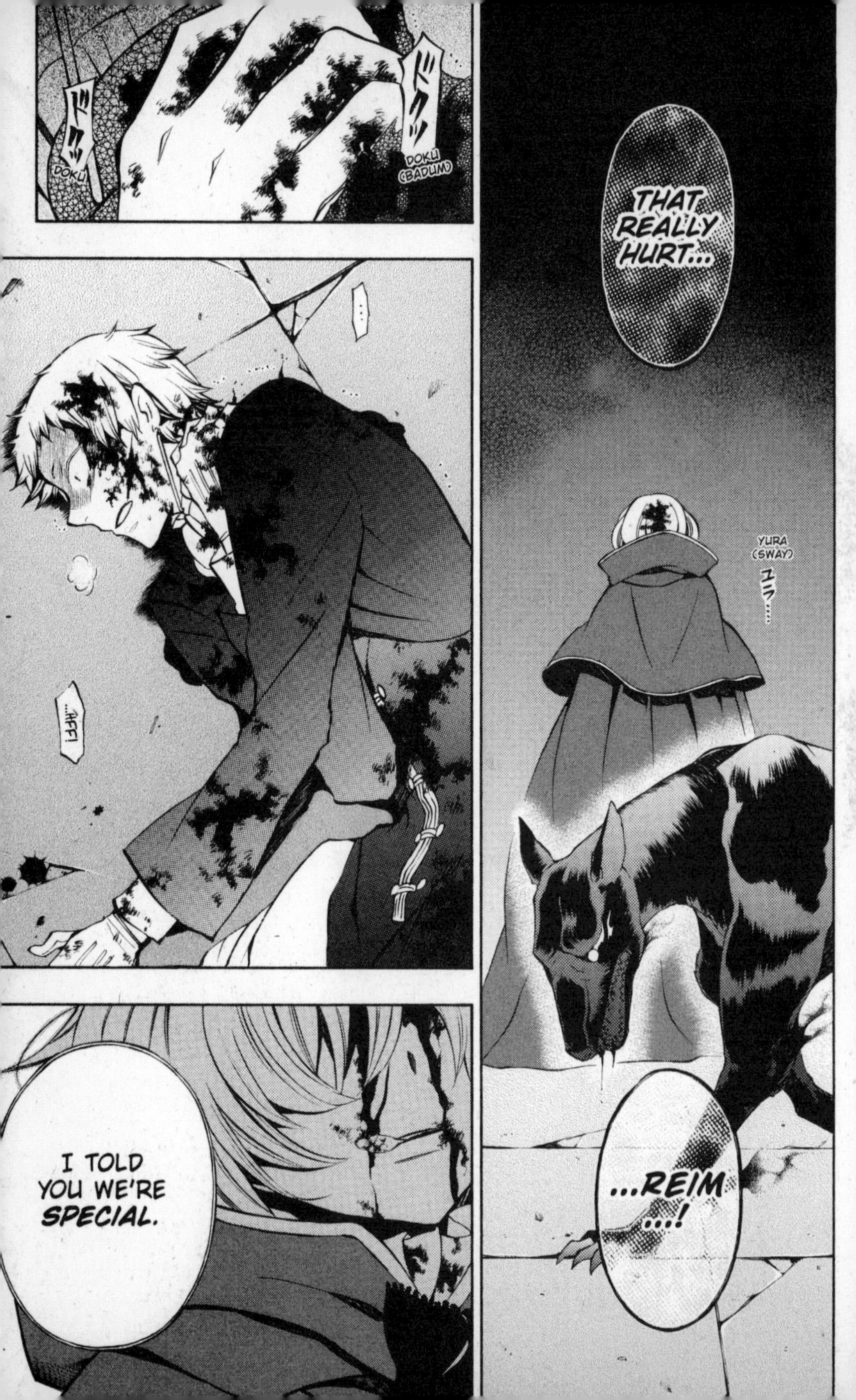
THAT REALLY HURT...
YURA (SWAY)
...REIM ...!
DOKU (BADUM)
DOKU
...
...HFF!
I TOLD YOU WE'RE SPECIAL.

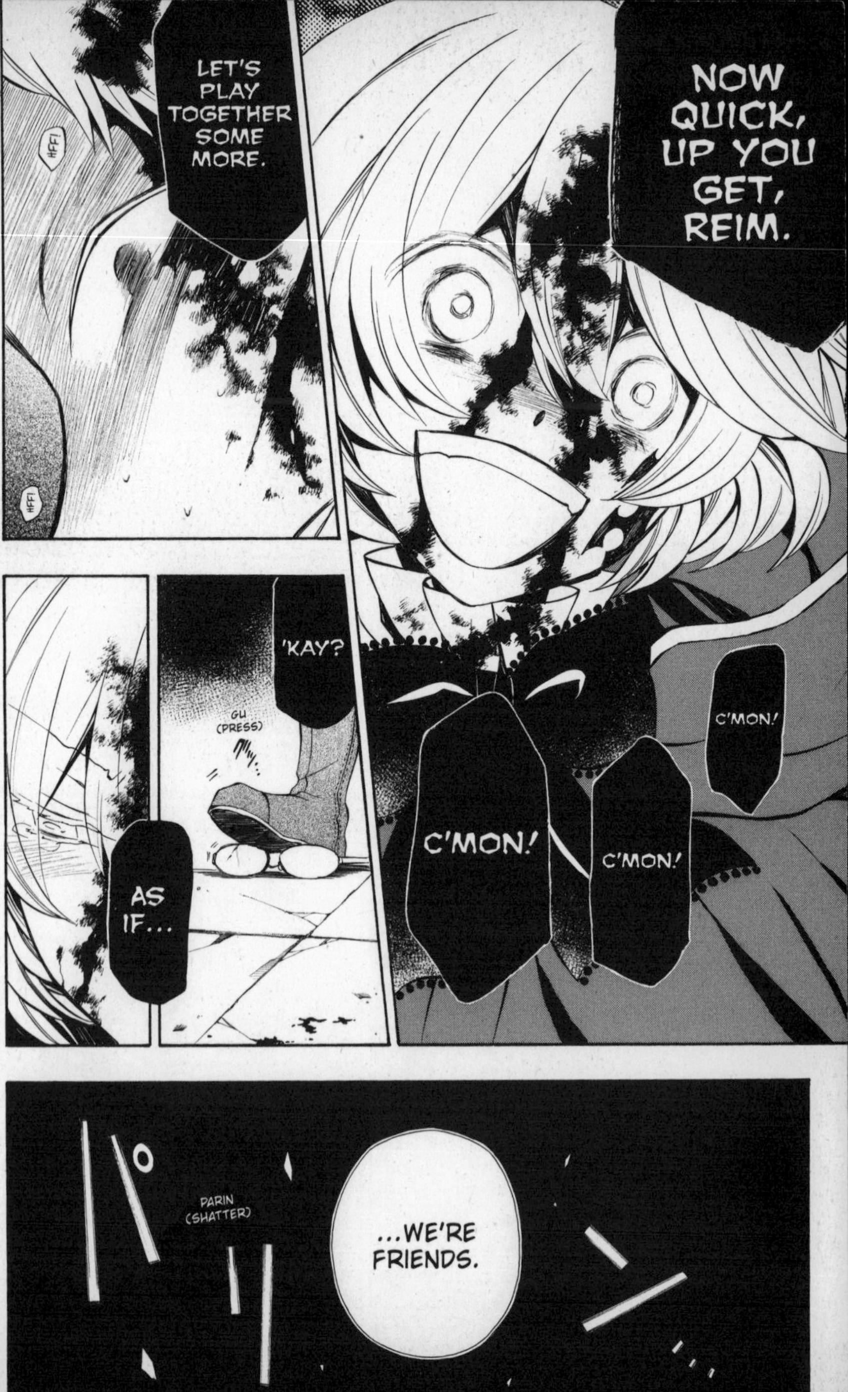
NOW QUICK, UP YOU GET, REIM.
C'MON!
C'MON!
C'MON!
LET'S PLAY TOGETHER SOME MORE.
HFF!
HFF!
'KAY?
GU (PRESS)
AS IF...
PARIN (SHATTER)
...WE'RE FRIENDS.

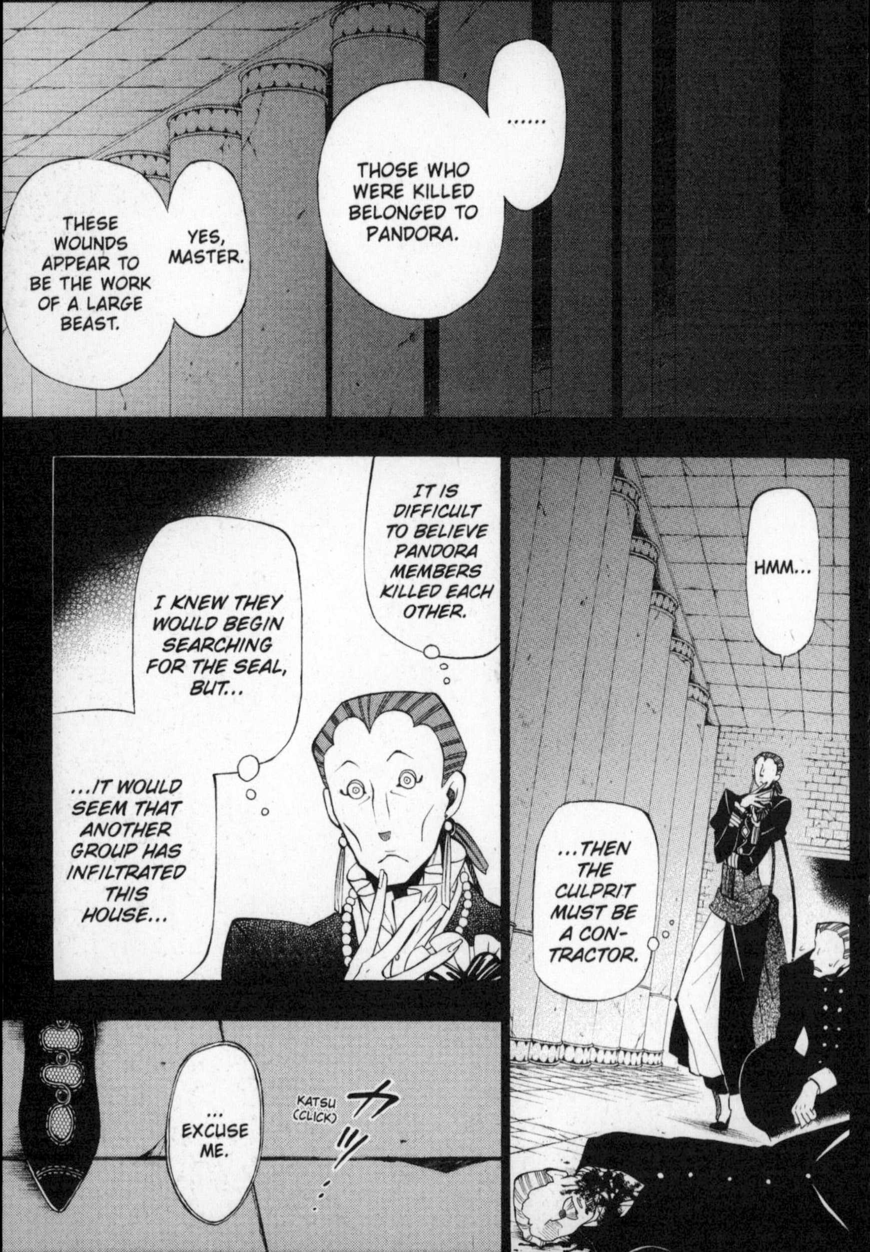
......
THOSE WHO WERE KILLED BELONGED TO PANDORA.
YES, MASTER.
THESE WOUNDS APPEAR TO BE THE WORK OF A LARGE BEAST.
HMM...
...THEN THE CULPRIT MUST BE A CONTRACTOR.
IT IS DIFFICULT TO BELIEVE PANDORA MEMBERS KILLED EACH OTHER.
I KNEW THEY WOULD BEGIN SEARCHING FOR THE SEAL, BUT...
...IT WOULD SEEM THAT ANOTHER GROUP HAS INFILTRATED THIS HOUSE...
KATSU (CLICK)
... EXCUSE ME.

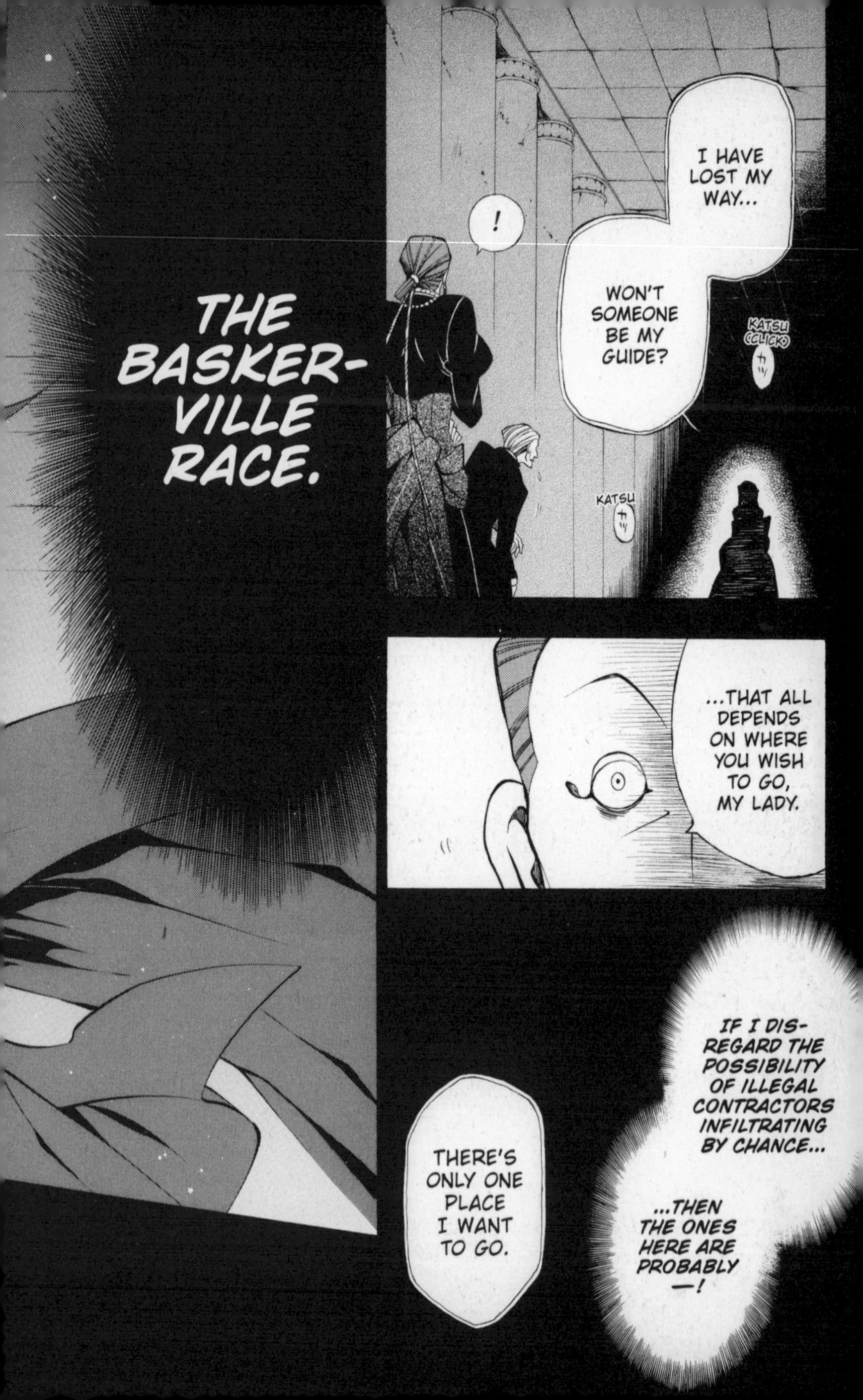
I HAVE LOST MY WAY...
WON'T SOMEONE BE MY GUIDE?
KATSU (CLICK)
!
KATSU
...THAT ALL DEPENDS ON WHERE YOU WISH TO GO, MY LADY.
IF I DISREGARD THE POSSIBILITY OF ILLEGAL CONTRACTORS INFILTRATING BY CHANCE...
...THEN THE ONES HERE ARE PROBABLY—!
THERE'S ONLY ONE PLACE I WANT TO GO.
THE BASKERVILLE RACE.

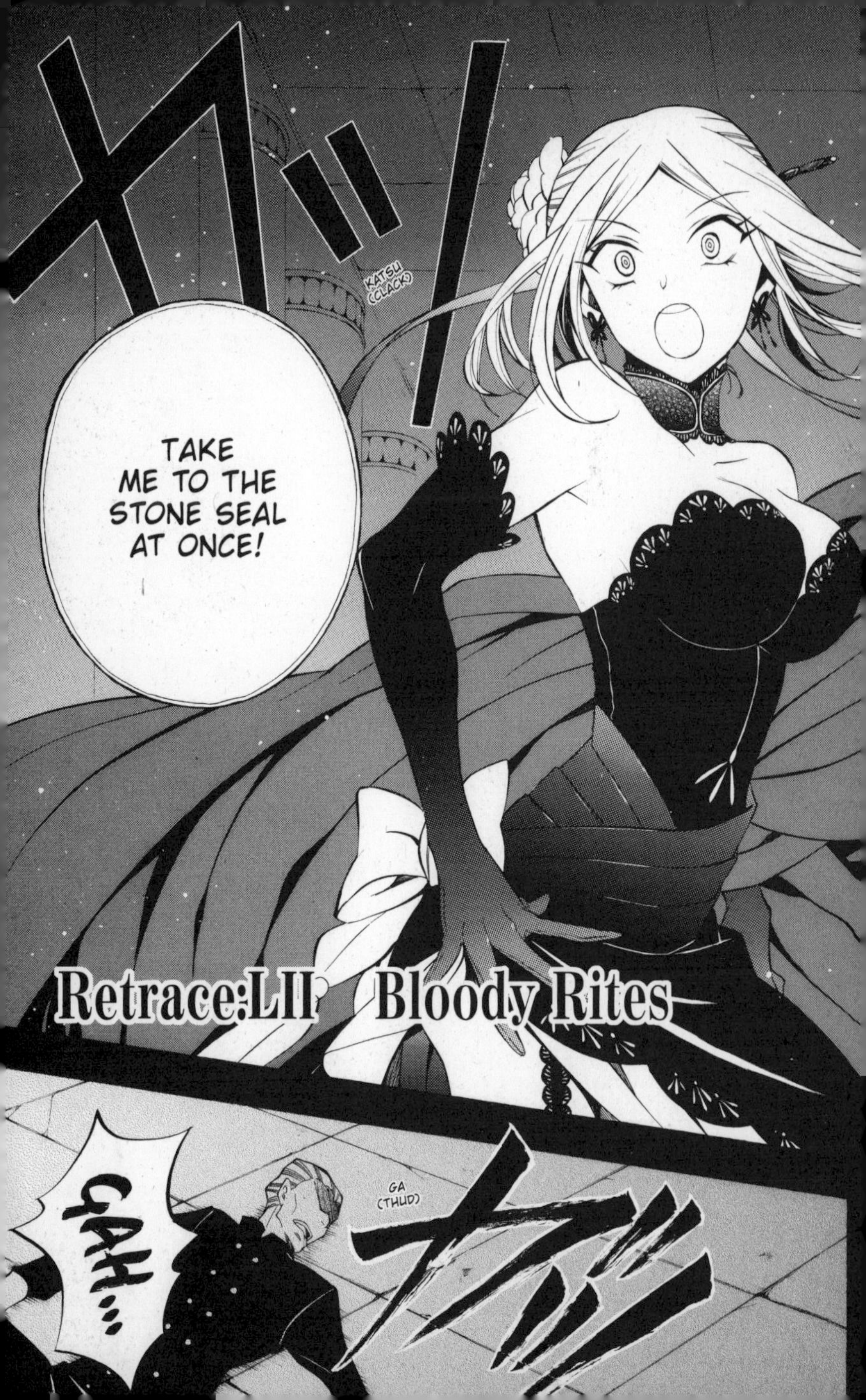
KATSU (CLACK)
TAKE ME TO THE STONE SEAL AT ONCE!
Retrace:LII Bloody Rites
GA (THUD)
GAAH...

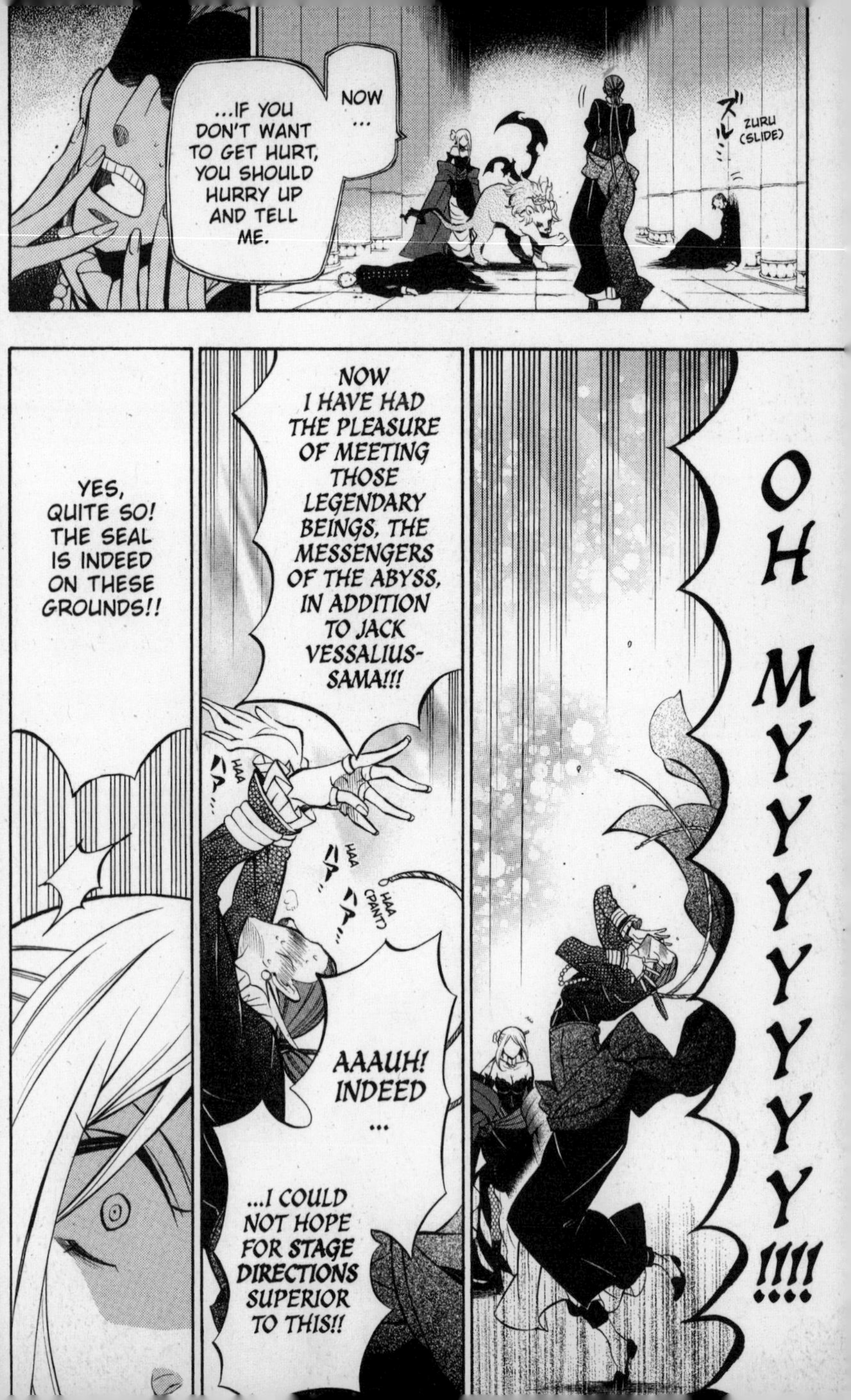

ズル
ZURU (SLIDE)
NOW ...
...IF YOU DON'T WANT TO GET HURT, YOU SHOULD HURRY UP AND TELL ME.
OH MYYYYYY!!!!
NOW I HAVE HAD THE PLEASURE OF MEETING THOSE LEGENDARY BEINGS, THE MESSENGERS OF THE ABYSS, IN ADDITION TO JACK VESSALIUS-SAMA!!!
ハァ HAA
ハァ HAA
ハァ HAA (PANT)
AAAUH! INDEED ...
...I COULD NOT HOPE FOR STAGE DIRECTIONS SUPERIOR TO THIS!!
YES, QUITE SO! THE SEAL IS INDEED ON THESE GROUNDS!!

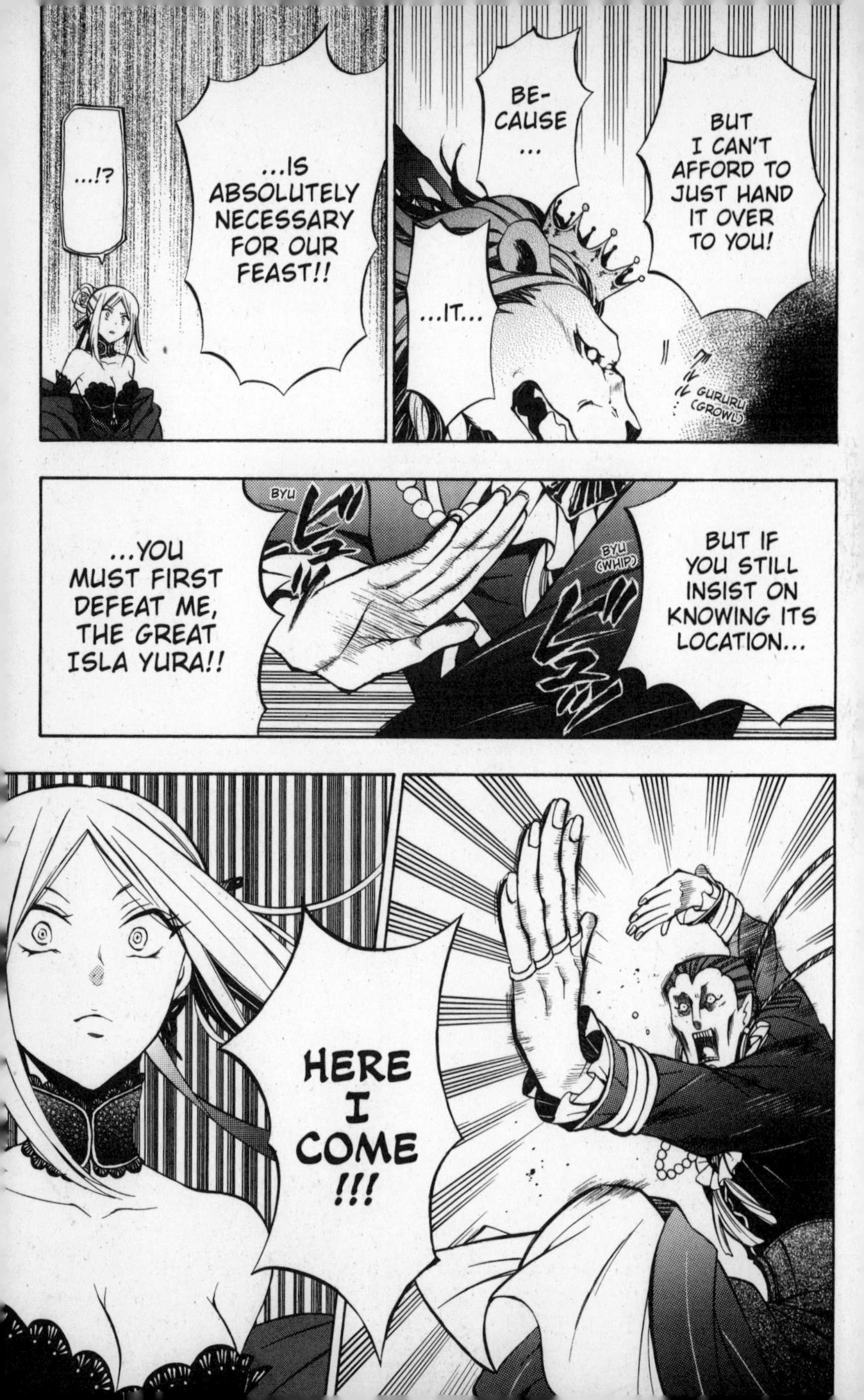
BUT I CAN'T AFFORD TO JUST HAND IT OVER TO YOU!
BE-CAUSE...
...IT...
GURURU (GROWL)
...IS ABSOLUTELY NECESSARY FOR OUR FEAST!!
...!?
BUT IF YOU STILL INSIST ON KNOWING ITS LOCATION...
BYU (WHIP)
BYU
...YOU MUST FIRST DEFEAT ME, THE GREAT ISLA YURA!!
HERE I COME!!!

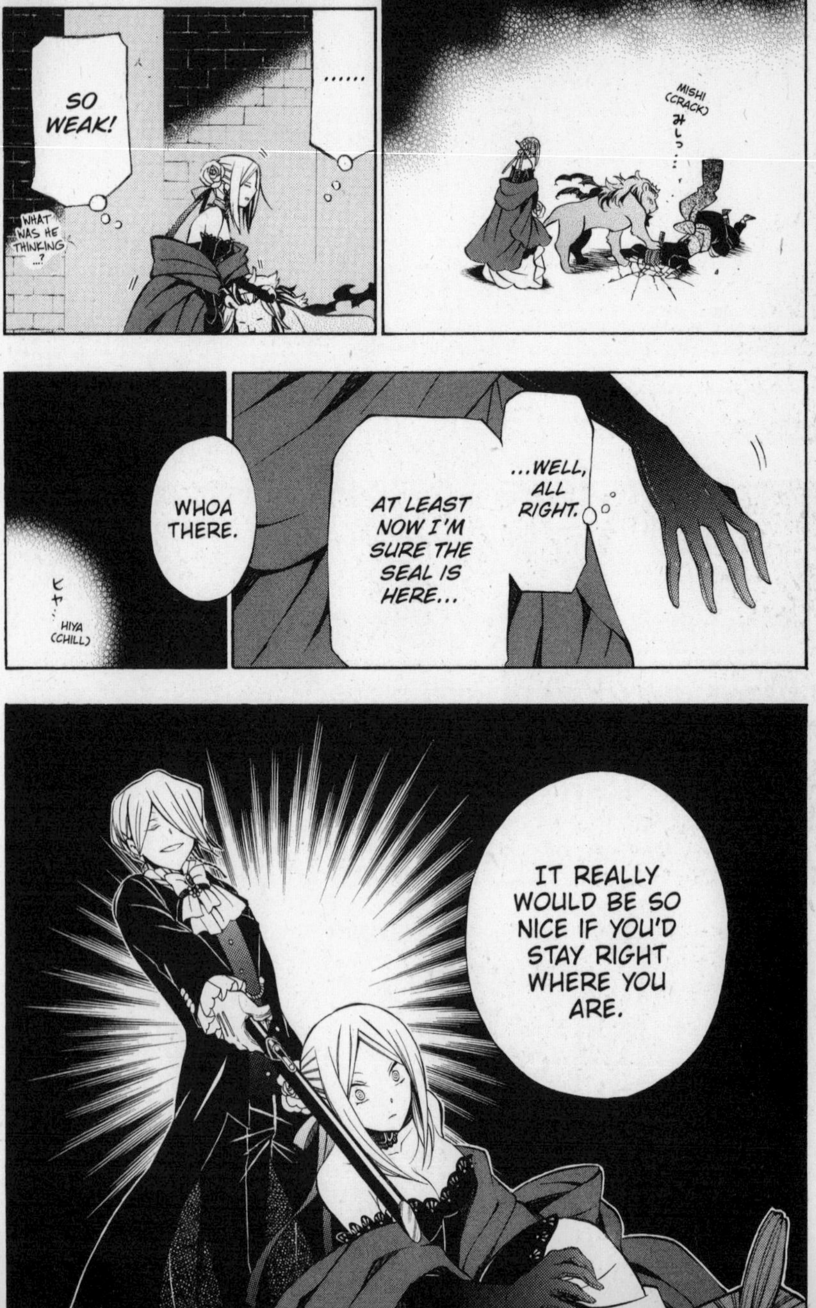
MISHI (CRACK)
みしっ…
......
SO WEAK!
WHAT WAS HE THINKING ...?
...WELL, ALL RIGHT.
AT LEAST NOW I'M SURE THE SEAL IS HERE...
WHOA THERE.
ヒヤ…
HIYA (CHILL)
IT REALLY WOULD BE SO NICE IF YOU'D STAY RIGHT WHERE YOU ARE.

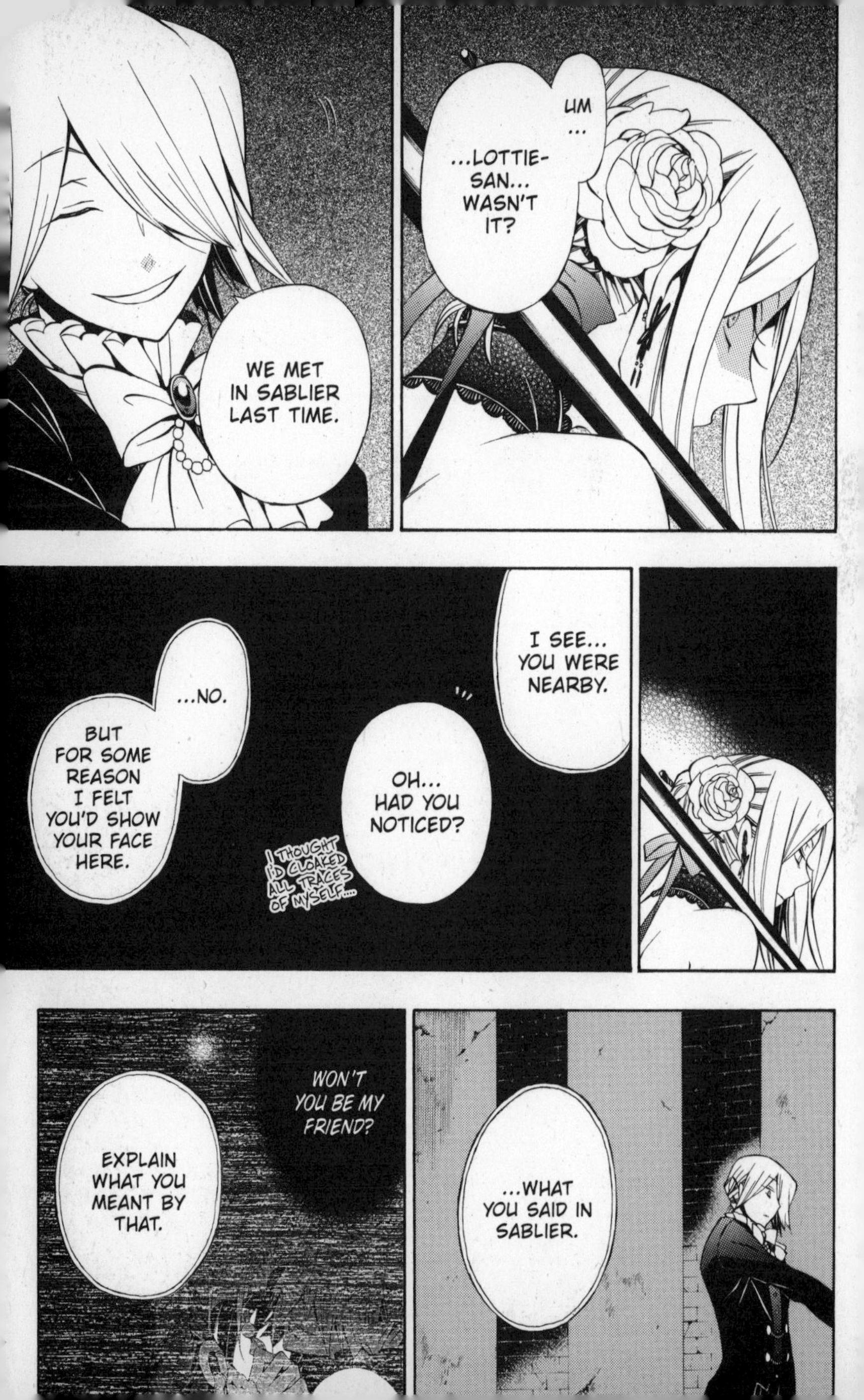
UM...
...LOTTIE-SAN... WASN'T IT?
WE MET IN SABLIER LAST TIME.
I SEE... YOU WERE NEARBY.
OH... HAD YOU NOTICED?
I THOUGHT I'D CLOAKED ALL TRACES OF MYSELF...
...NO.
BUT FOR SOME REASON I FELT YOU'D SHOW YOUR FACE HERE.
...WHAT YOU SAID IN SABLIER.
WON'T YOU BE MY FRIEND?
EXPLAIN WHAT YOU MEANT BY THAT.

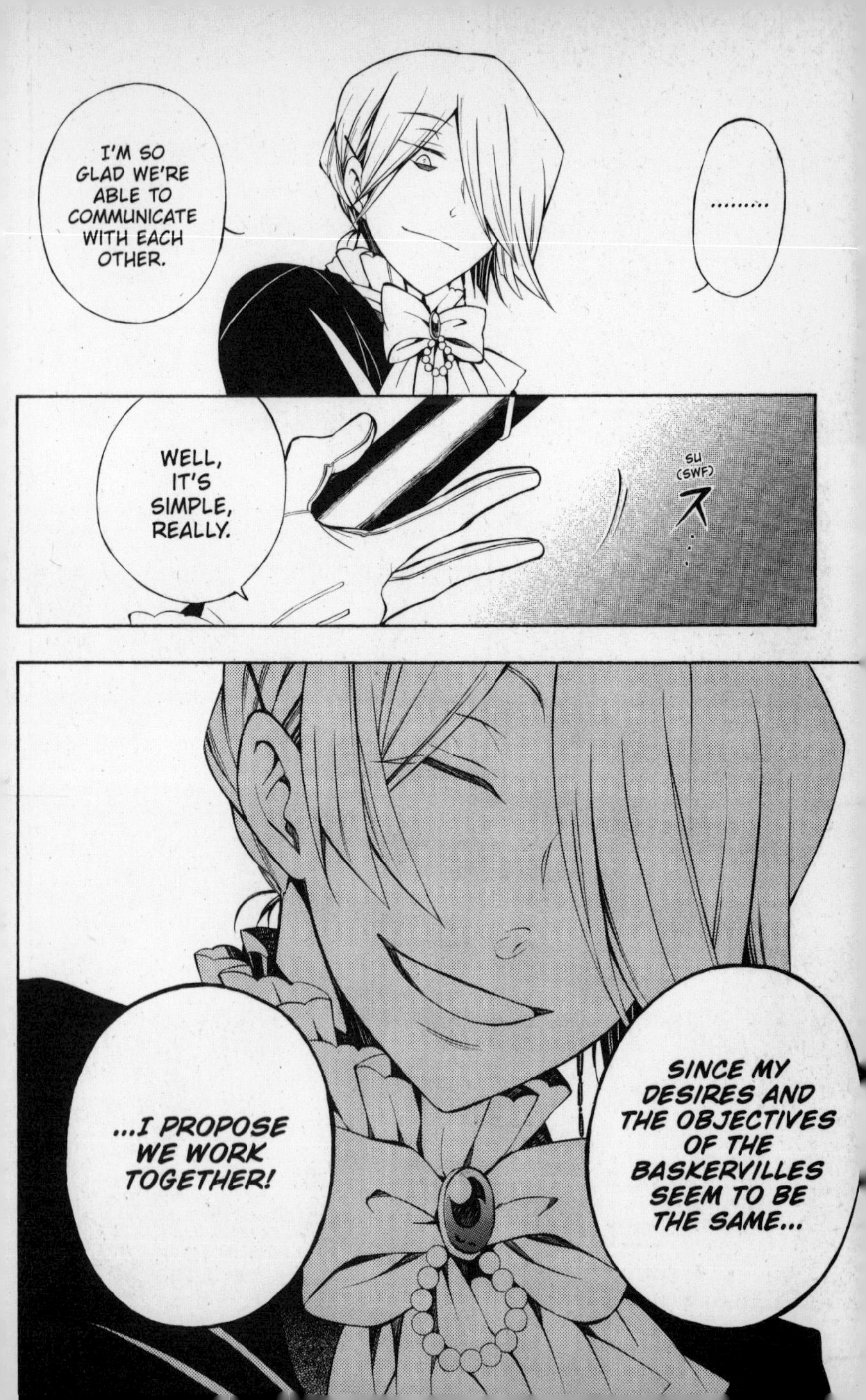
....
I'M SO GLAD WE'RE ABLE TO COMMUNICATE WITH EACH OTHER.
SU (SWF)
WELL, IT'S SIMPLE, REALLY.
SINCE MY DESIRES AND THE OBJECTIVES OF THE BASKERVILLES SEEM TO BE THE SAME...
...I PROPOSE WE WORK TOGETHER!

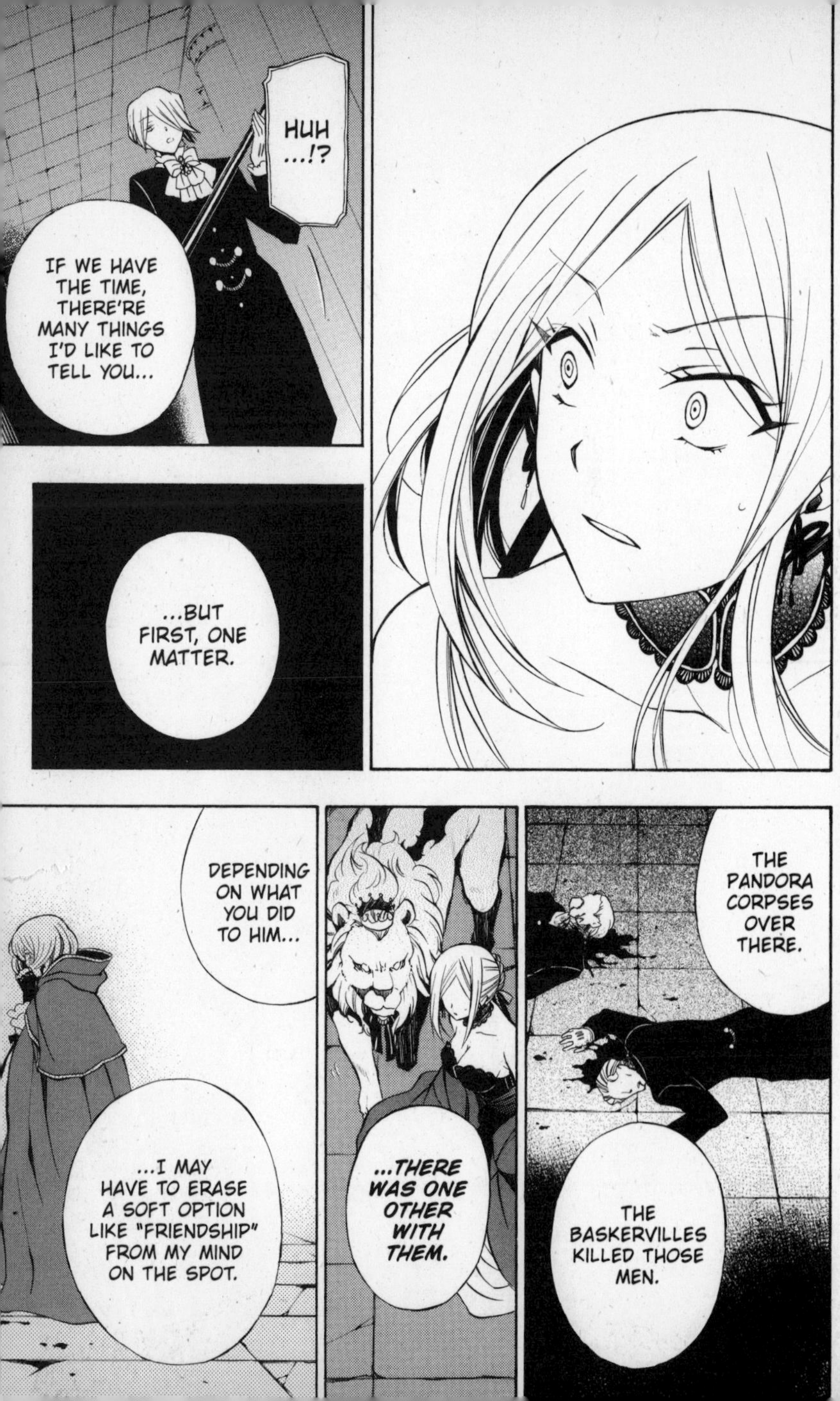
HUH ...!?
IF WE HAVE THE TIME, THERE'RE MANY THINGS I'D LIKE TO TELL YOU...
...BUT FIRST, ONE MATTER.
THE PANDORA CORPSES OVER THERE.
THE BASKERVILLES KILLED THOSE MEN.
...THERE WAS ONE OTHER WITH THEM.
DEPENDING ON WHAT YOU DID TO HIM...
...I MAY HAVE TO ERASE A SOFT OPTION LIKE "FRIENDSHIP" FROM MY MIND ON THE SPOT.

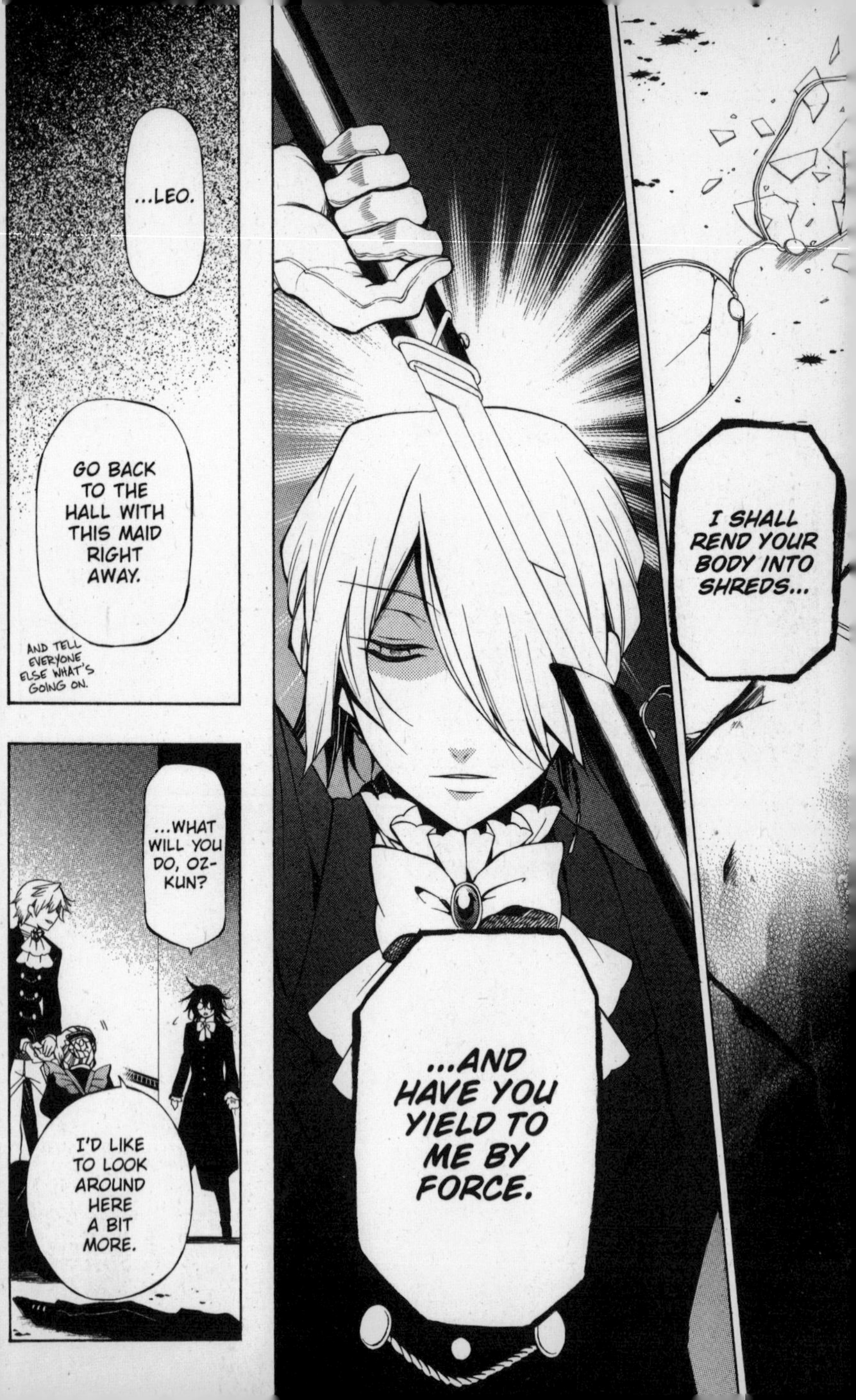
I SHALL REND YOUR BODY INTO SHREDS...
...AND HAVE YOU YIELD TO ME BY FORCE.
...LEO.
GO BACK TO THE HALL WITH THIS MAID RIGHT AWAY.
AND TELL EVERYONE ELSE WHAT'S GOING ON.
...WHAT WILL YOU DO, OZ-KUN?
I'D LIKE TO LOOK AROUND HERE A BIT MORE.

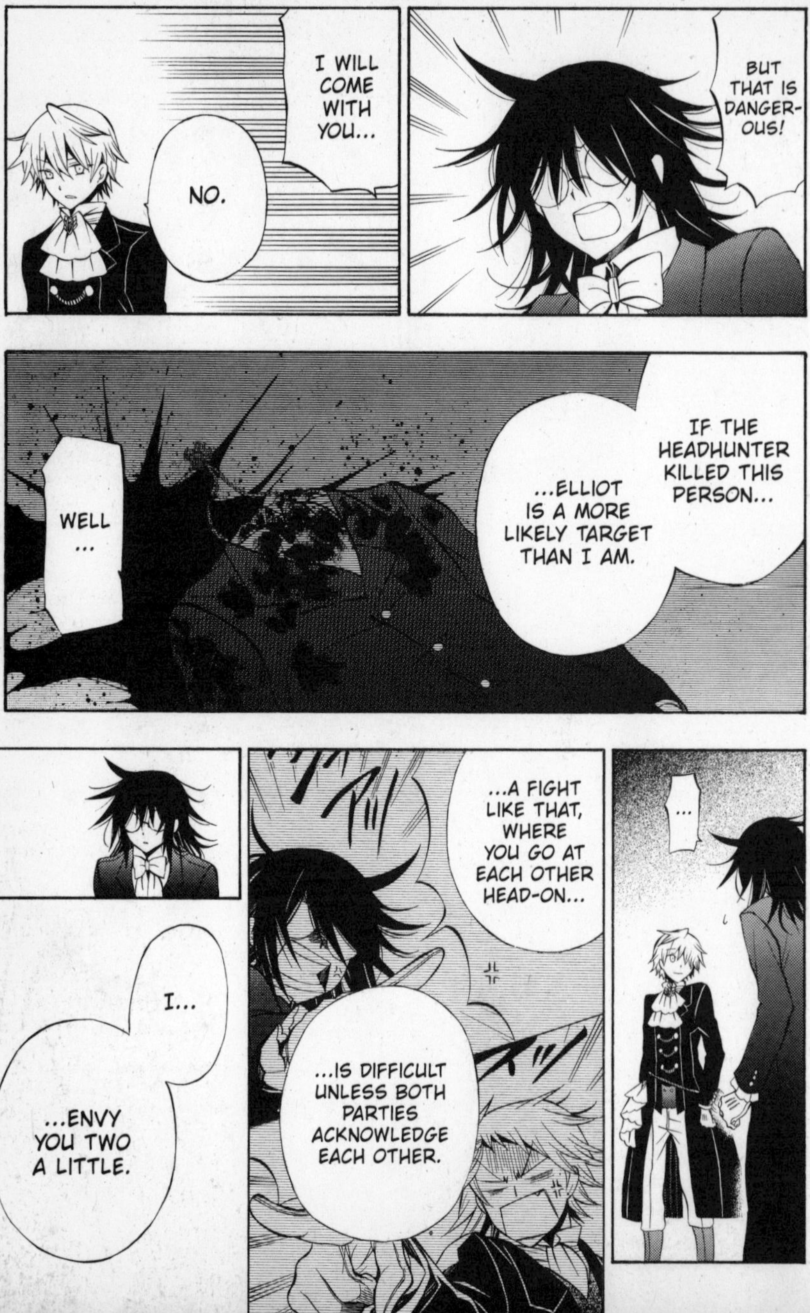
BUT THAT IS DANGER-OUS!
I WILL COME WITH YOU...
NO.
IF THE HEADHUNTER KILLED THIS PERSON...
...ELLIOT IS A MORE LIKELY TARGET THAN I AM.
WELL ...
...
...A FIGHT LIKE THAT, WHERE YOU GO AT EACH OTHER HEAD-ON...
...IS DIFFICULT UNLESS BOTH PARTIES ACKNOWLEDGE EACH OTHER.
I...
...ENVY YOU TWO A LITTLE.

YOU'RE GONNA APOLOGIZE TO ELLIOT, AREN'T YOU?

...GO ON.

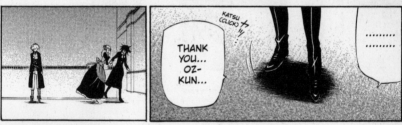

THANK YOU... OZ-KUN...

KATSU (CLICK)

....
....

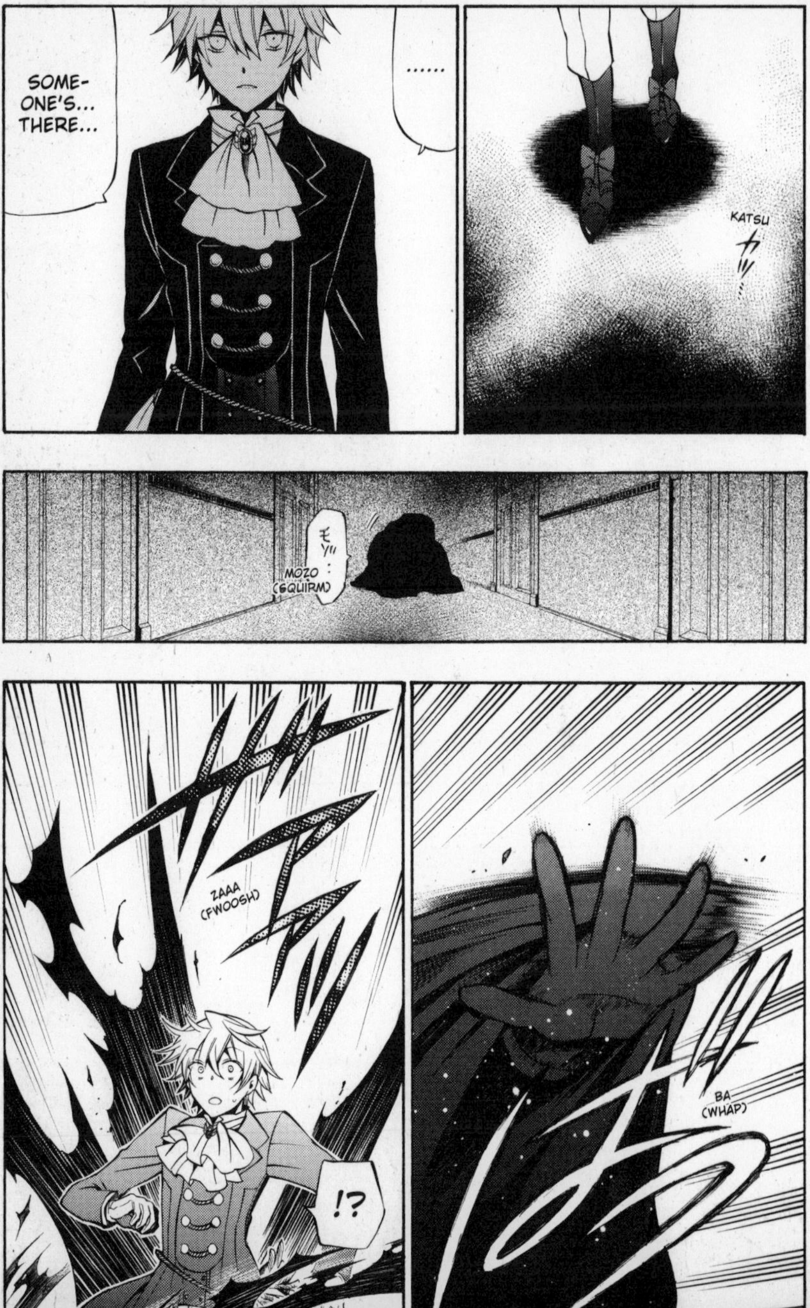
KATSU
カッ…
......
SOME-ONE'S... THERE...
モゾ…
MOZO (SQUIRM)
BA (WHAP)
ZAAA (FWOOSH)
!?

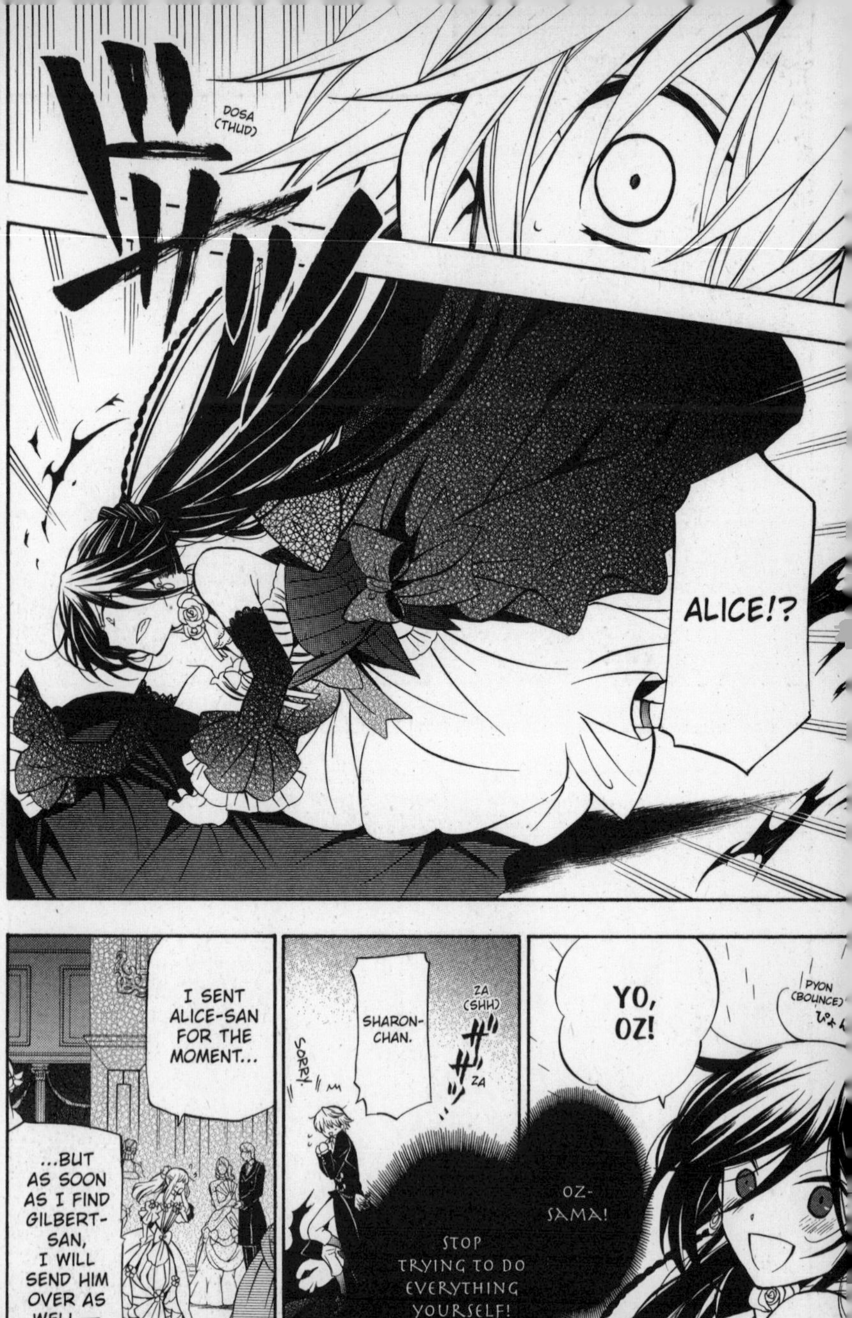
DOSA (THUD)
ALICE!?
PYON (BOUNCE)
YO, OZ!
OZ-SAMA!
SHARON-CHAN.
ZA (SHH)
ZA
SORRY!
STOP TRYING TO DO EVERYTHING YOURSELF!
I SENT ALICE-SAN FOR THE MOMENT...
...BUT AS SOON AS I FIND GILBERT-SAN, I WILL SEND HIM OVER AS WELL—

ザワッ
ZAWA (MURMUR)
......?
?
SHARON-CHAN?
OZ!
HE'S ONE OF YOUR FRIENDS, ISN'T HE?
GUI (YANK)
OW, OW! OW, OW! OW, OW, OW, OW!
PHILIPPE!

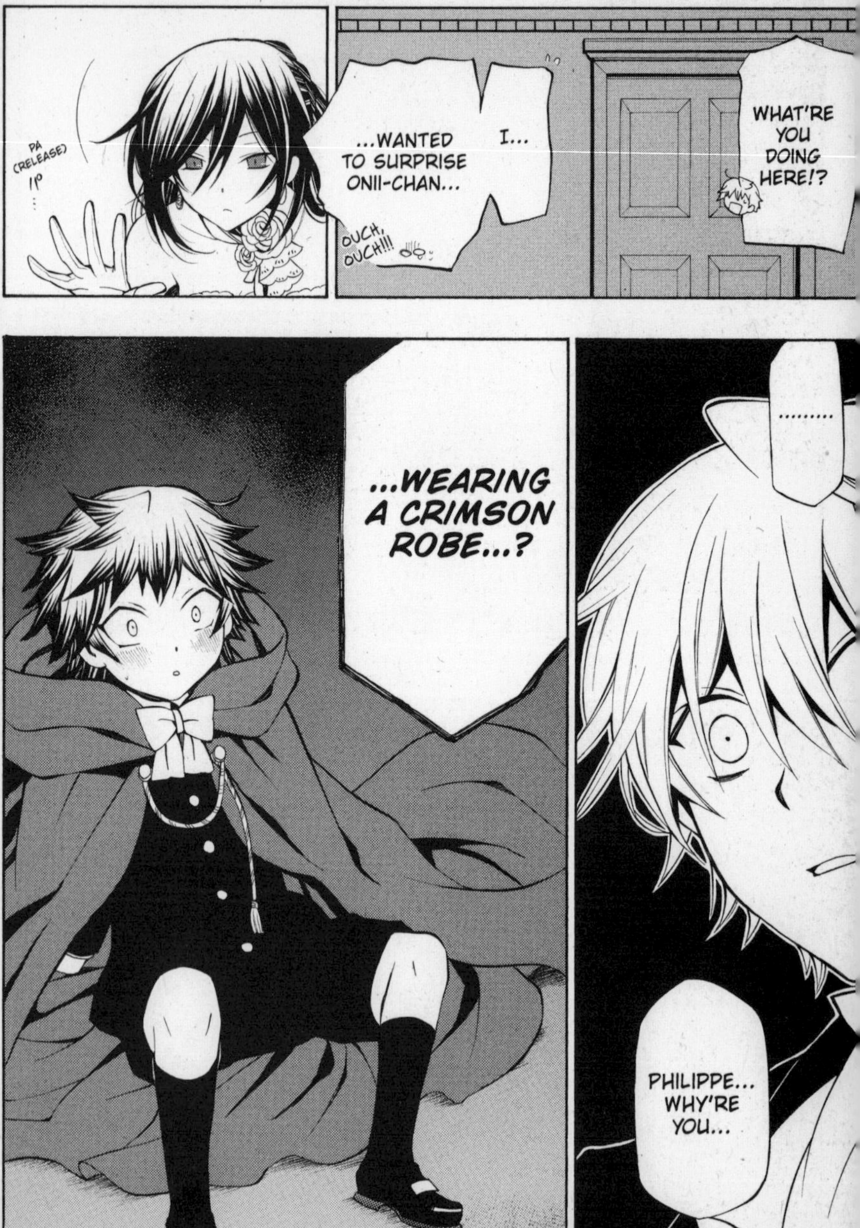
WHAT'RE YOU DOING HERE!?
I...
...WANTED TO SURPRISE ONII-CHAN...
OUCH, OUCH!!!
PA (RELEASE)
....
PHILIPPE... WHY'RE YOU...
...WEARING A CRIMSON ROBE...?

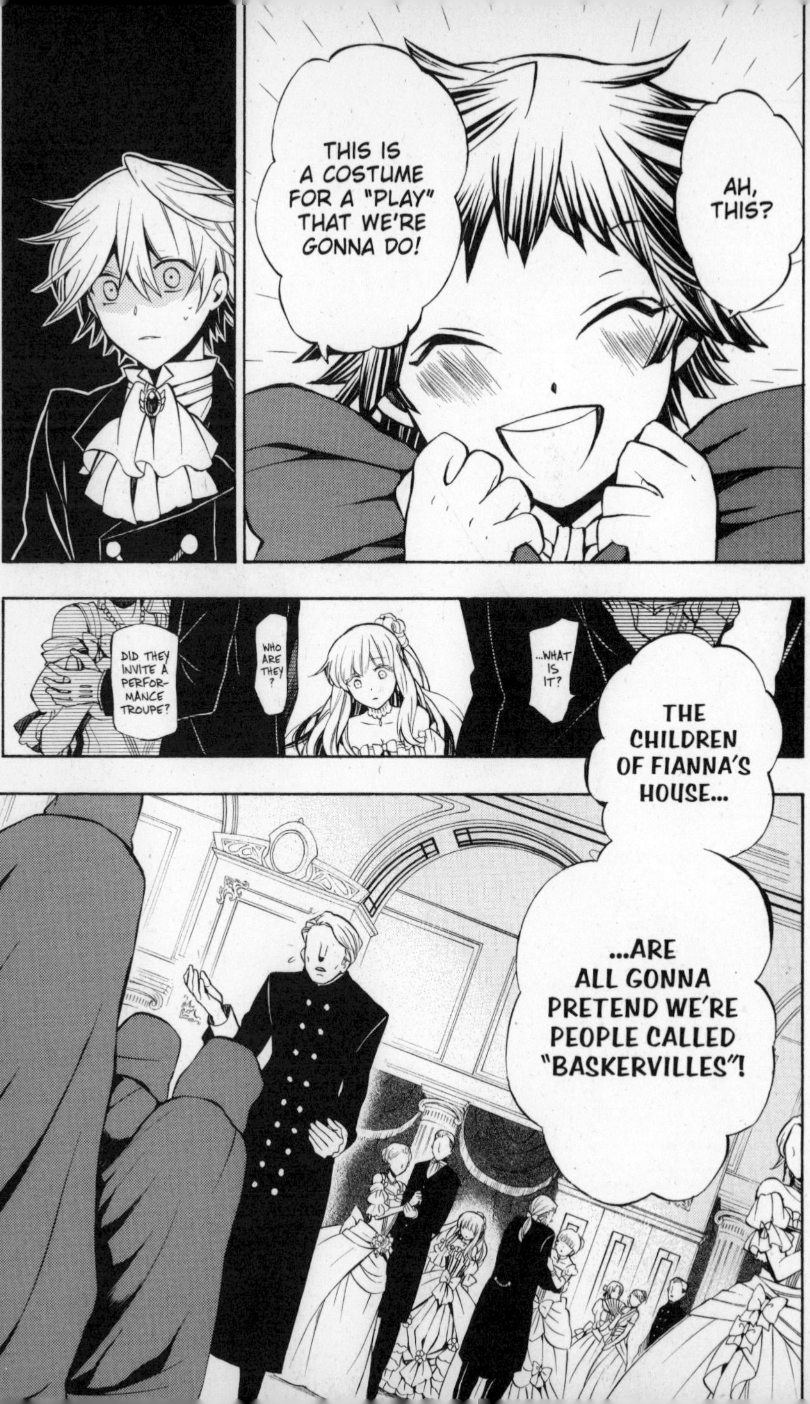
AH, THIS?
THIS IS A COSTUME FOR A "PLAY" THAT WE'RE GONNA DO!
...WHAT IS IT?
WHO ARE THEY?
DID THEY INVITE A PERFORMANCE TROUPE?
THE CHILDREN OF FIANNA'S HOUSE...
...ARE ALL GONNA PRETEND WE'RE PEOPLE CALLED "BASKERVILLES"!

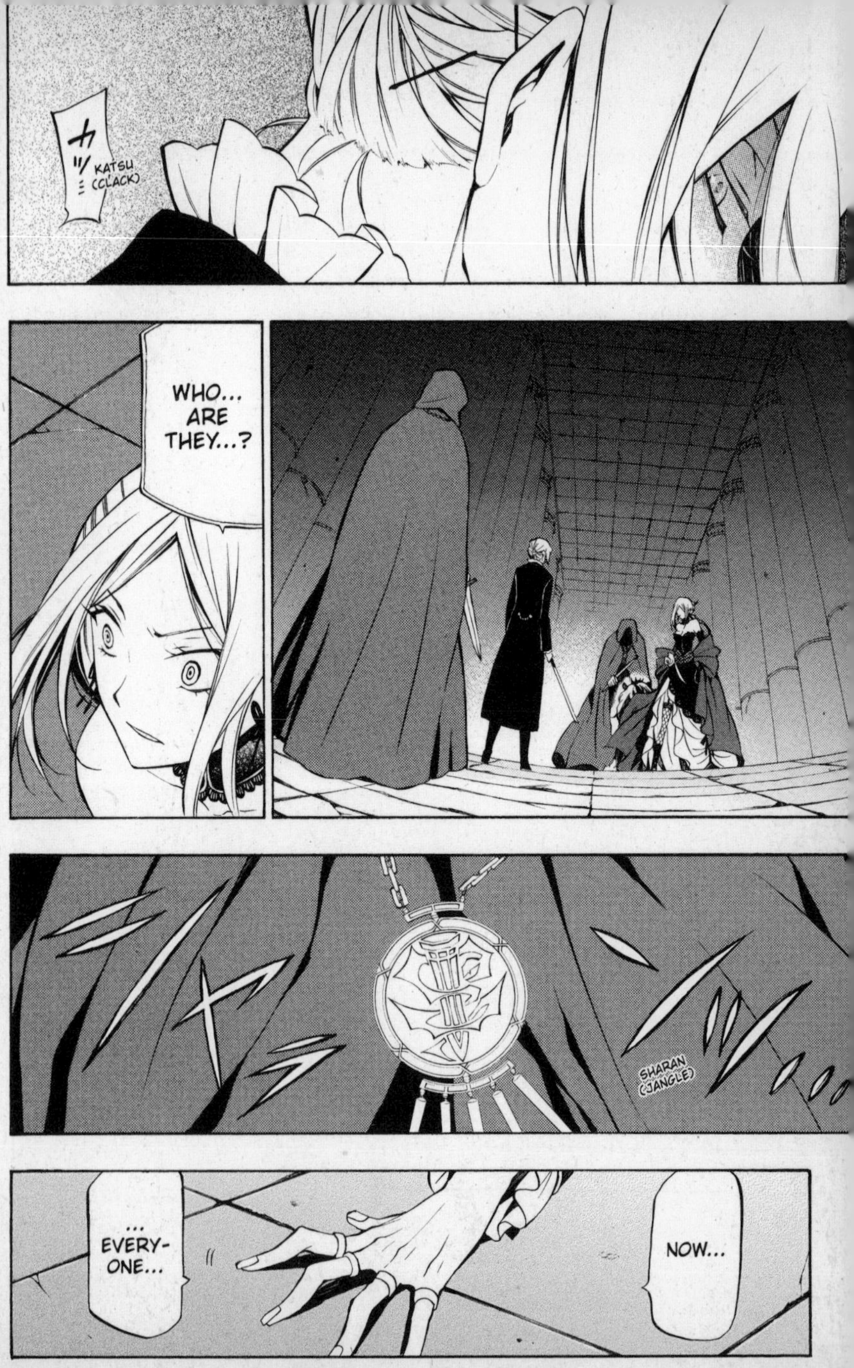
KATSU (CLACK)
WHO... ARE THEY...?
SHARAN (JANGLE)
NOW...
... EVERY-ONE...

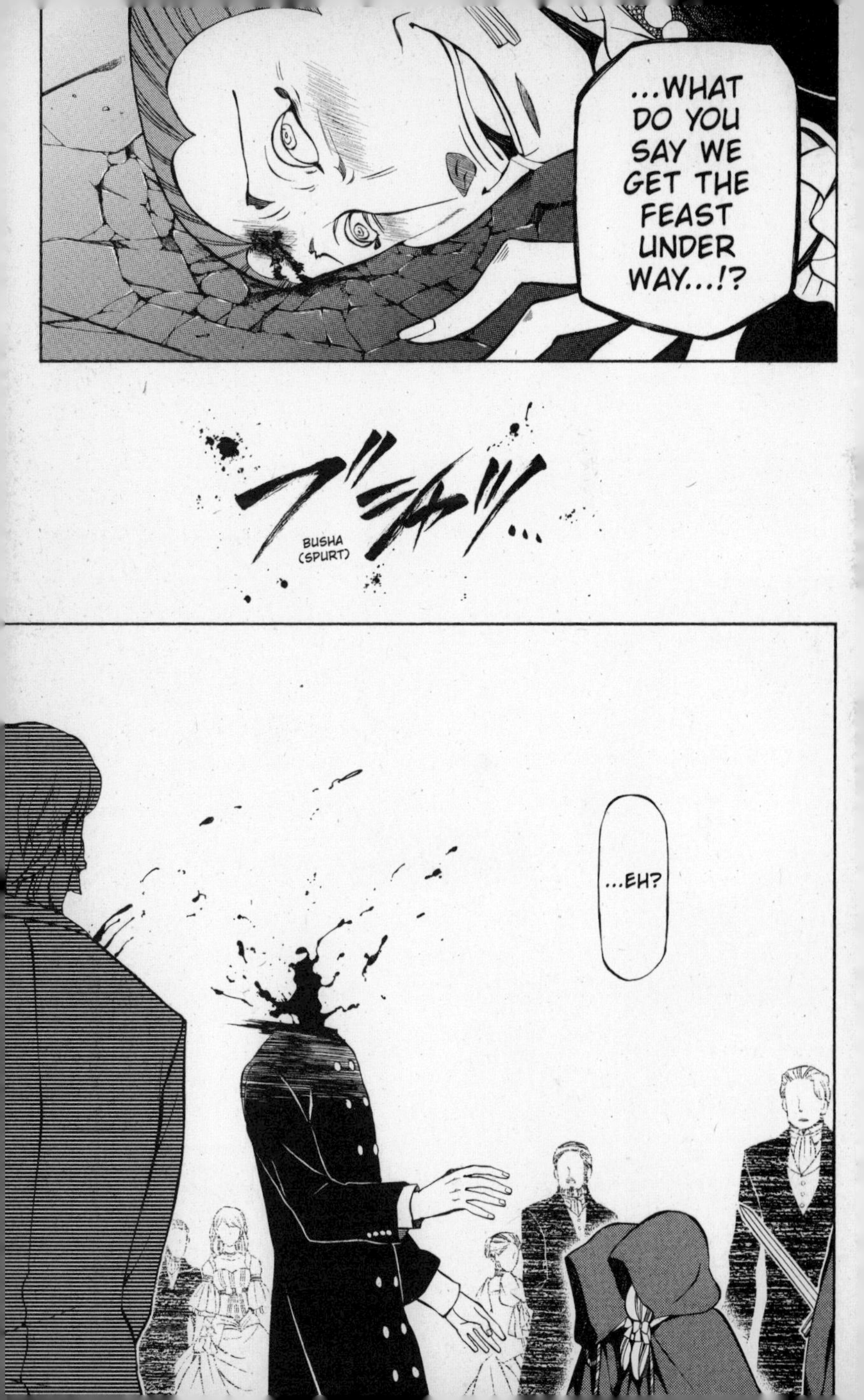
...WHAT DO YOU SAY WE GET THE FEAST UNDER WAY...!?
ブシャッ...
BUSHA (SPURT)
...EH?

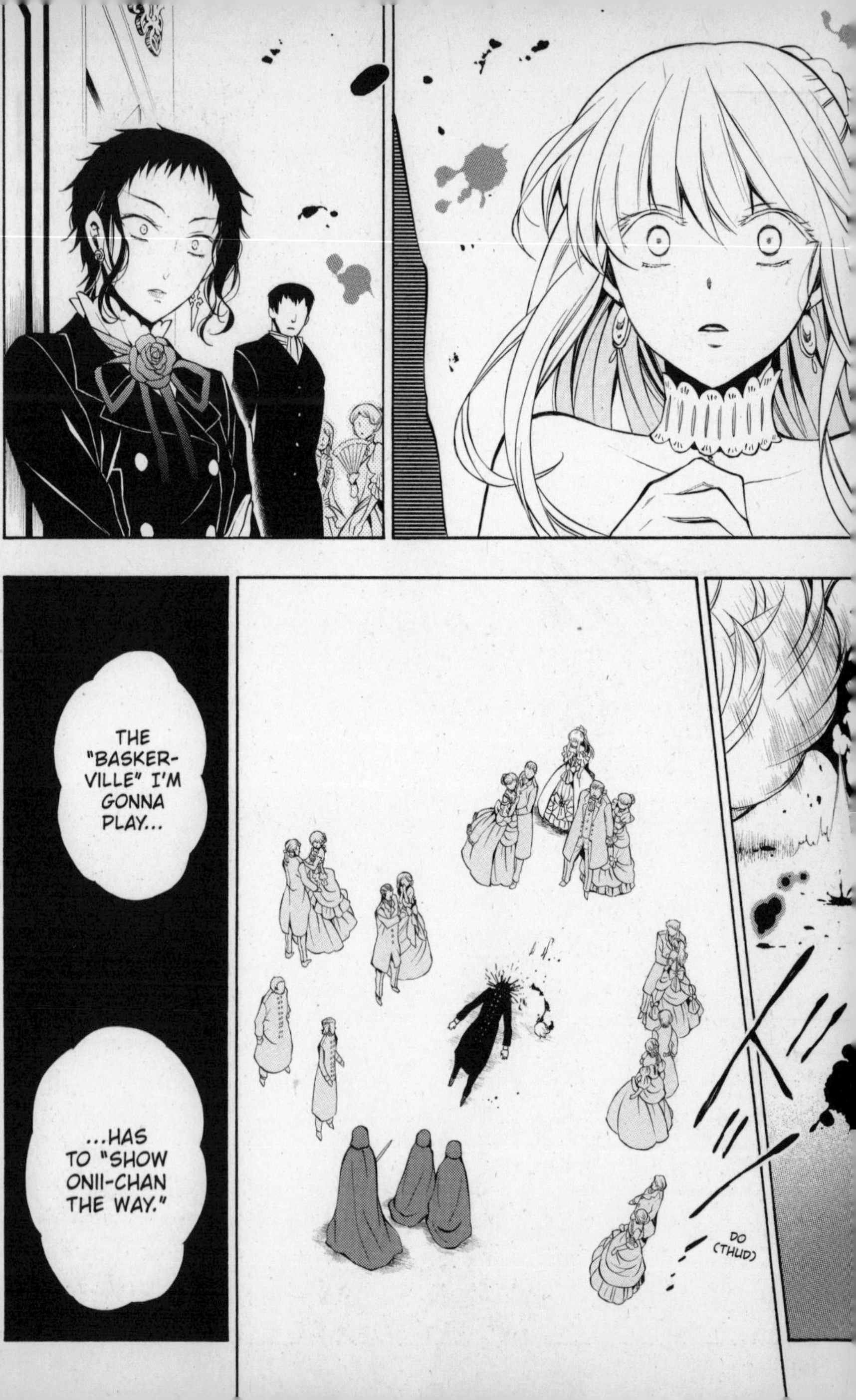
DO
(THUD)
THE "BASKER-VILLE" I'M GONNA PLAY...
...HAS TO "SHOW ONII-CHAN THE WAY."

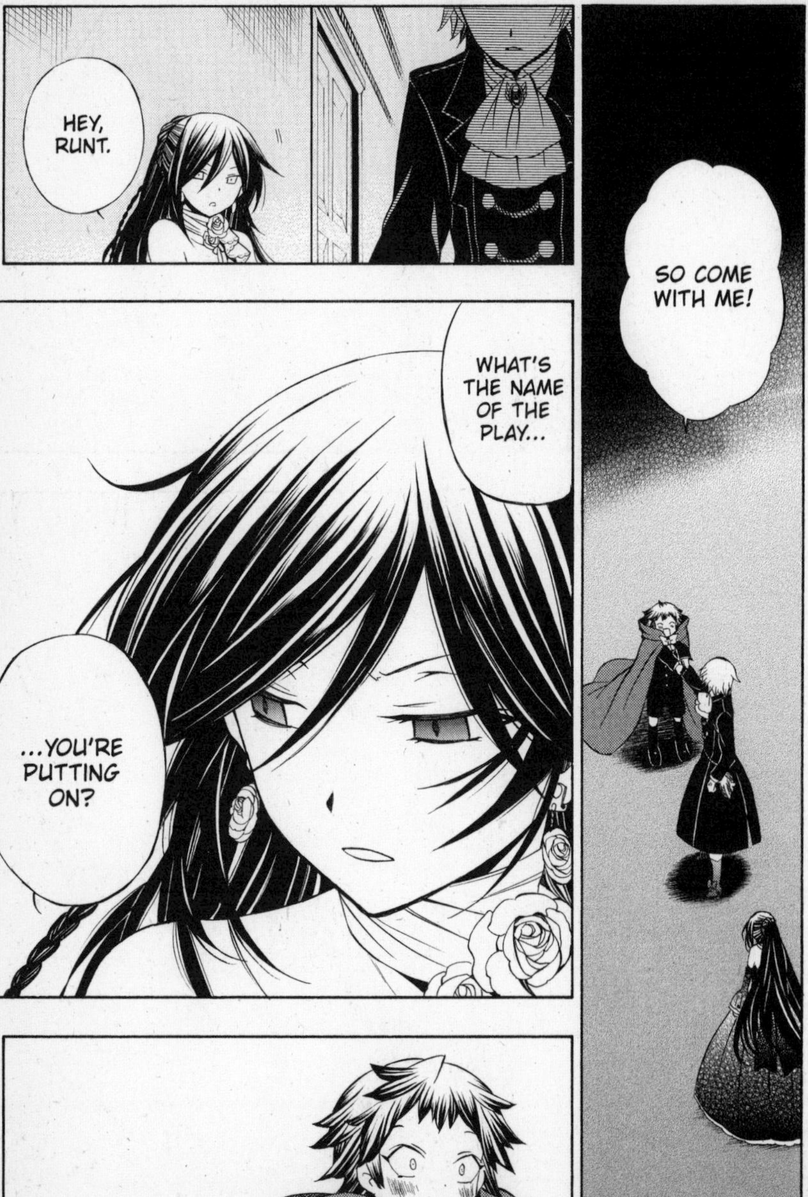
SO COME WITH ME!
HEY, RUNT.
WHAT'S THE NAME OF THE PLAY...
...YOU'RE PUTTING ON?

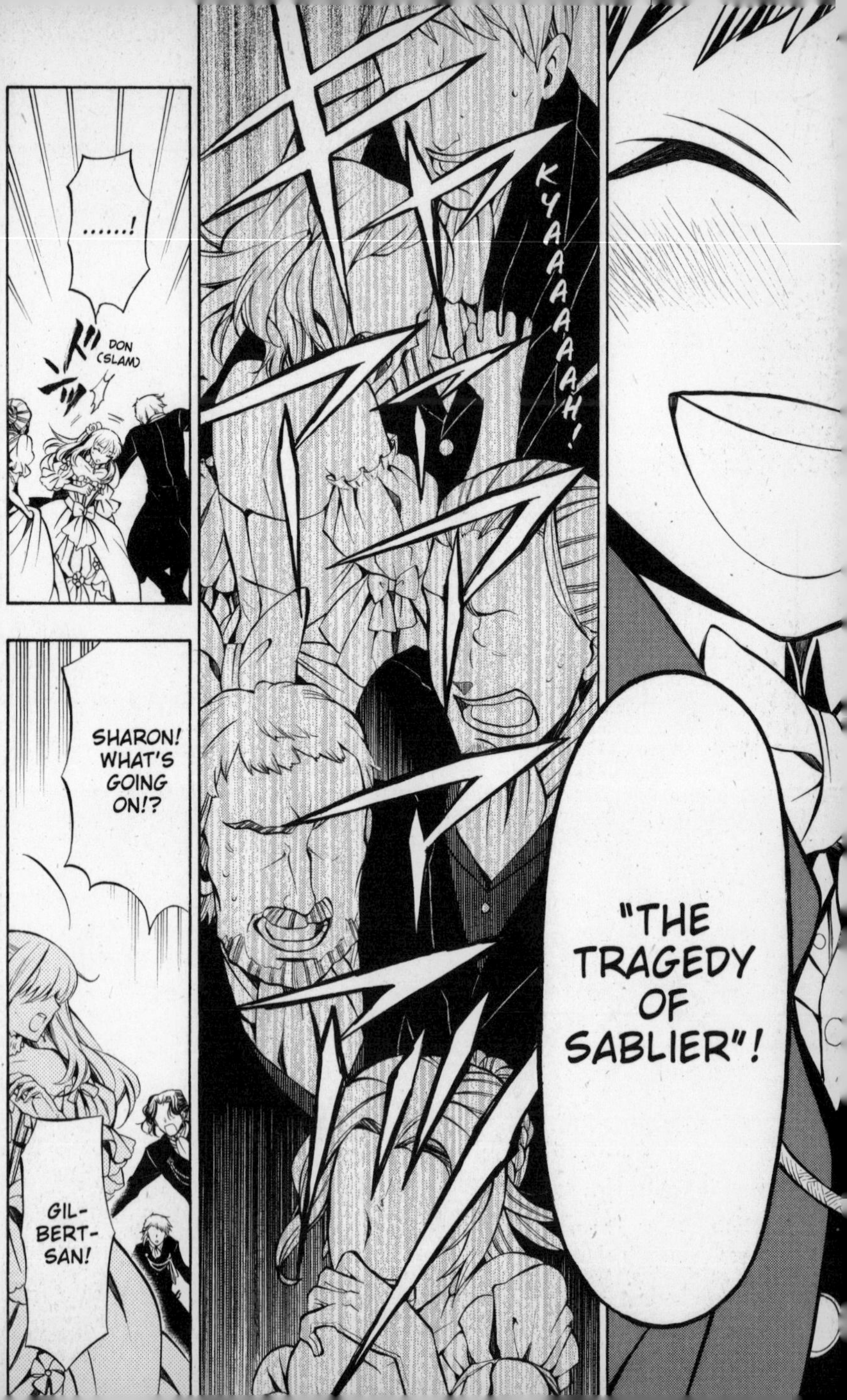
"THE TRAGEDY OF SABLIER"!
KYAAAAAAAH!
......!
DON (SLAM)
SHARON! WHAT'S GOING ON!?
GIL-BERT-SAN!

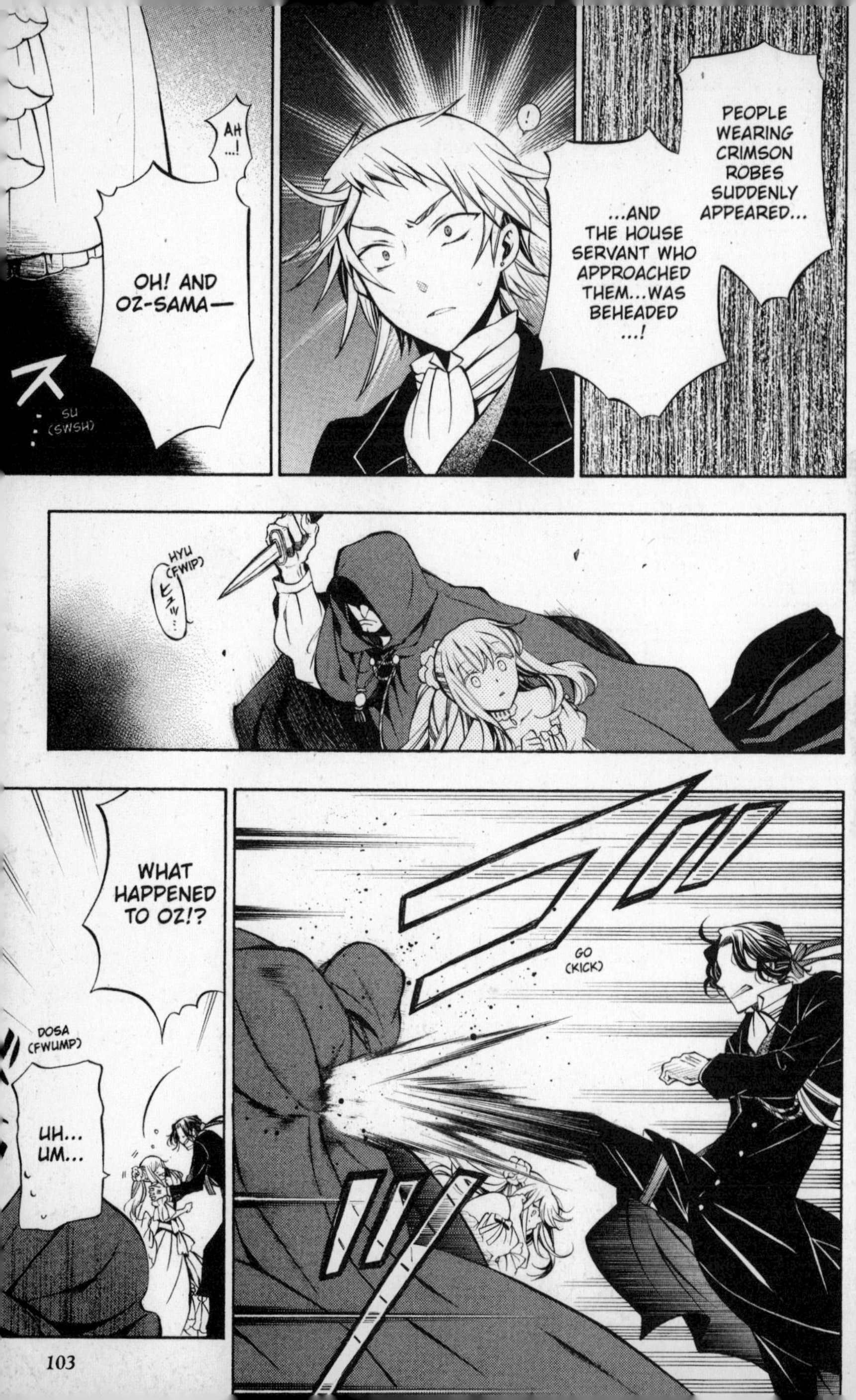
PEOPLE WEARING CRIMSON ROBES SUDDENLY APPEARED...
...AND THE HOUSE SERVANT WHO APPROACHED THEM...WAS BEHEADED ...!
!
AH ...!
OH! AND OZ-SAMA—
ス
SU (SWSH)
HYU (FWIP)
ヒュッ...
GO (KICK)
WHAT HAPPENED TO OZ!?
DOSA (FWUMP)
UH... UM...

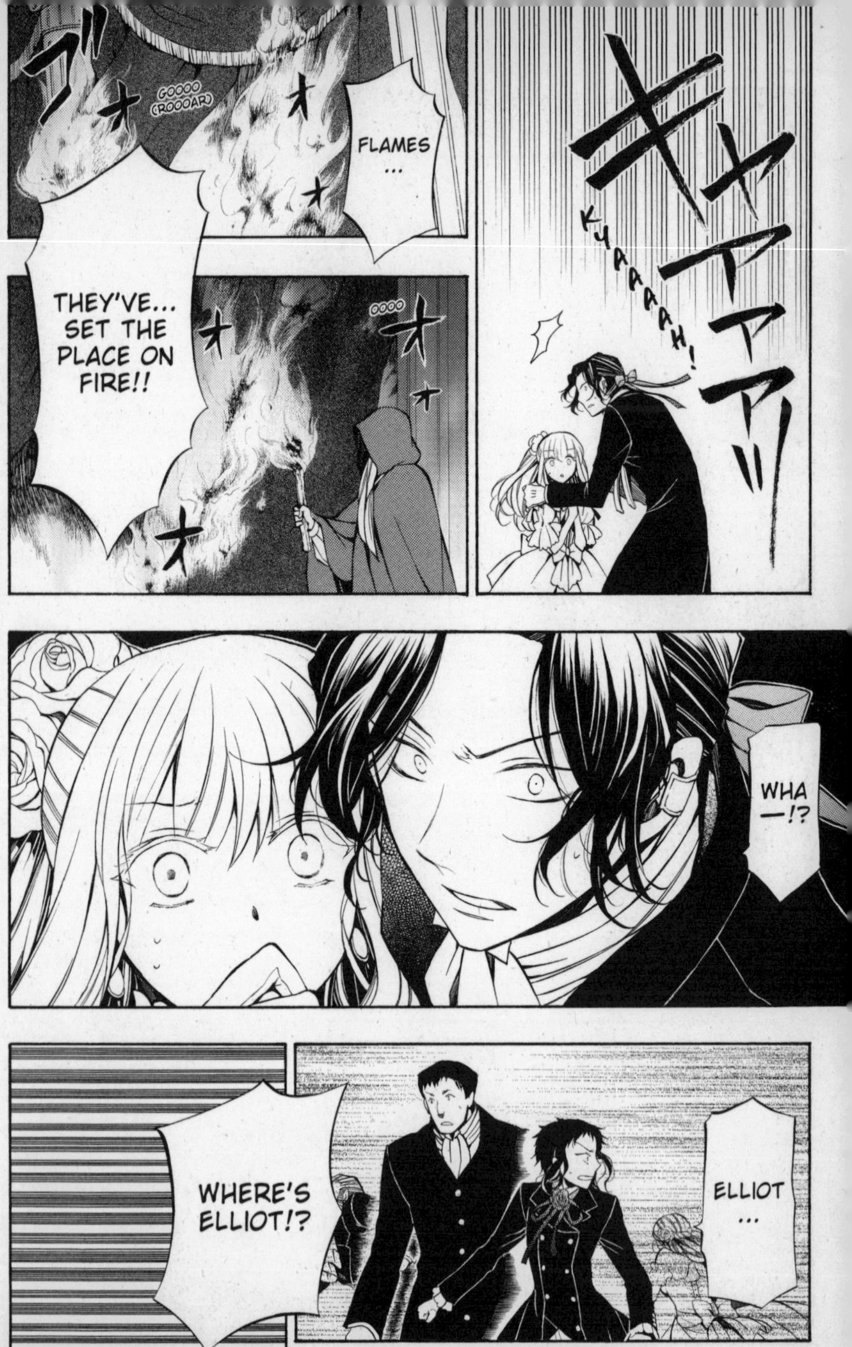
KYAAAAAH!
GOOOO (ROOOAR)
FLAMES ...
THEY'VE... SET THE PLACE ON FIRE!!
OOOO
WHA—!?
ELLIOT ...
WHERE'S ELLIOT!?

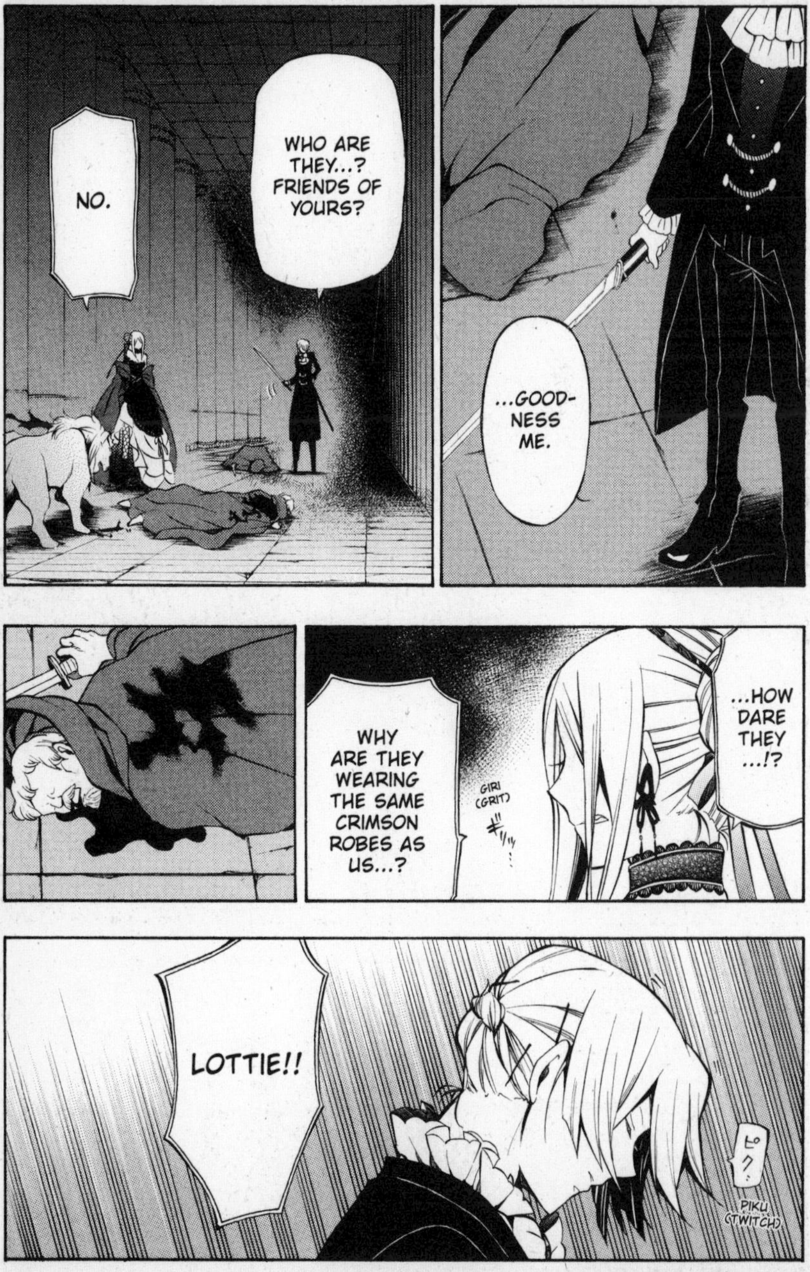
...GOODNESS ME.
WHO ARE THEY...? FRIENDS OF YOURS?
NO.
...HOW DARE THEY ...!?
GIRI (GRIT)
WHY ARE THEY WEARING THE SAME CRIMSON ROBES AS US...?
LOTTIE!!
PIKU (TWITCH)

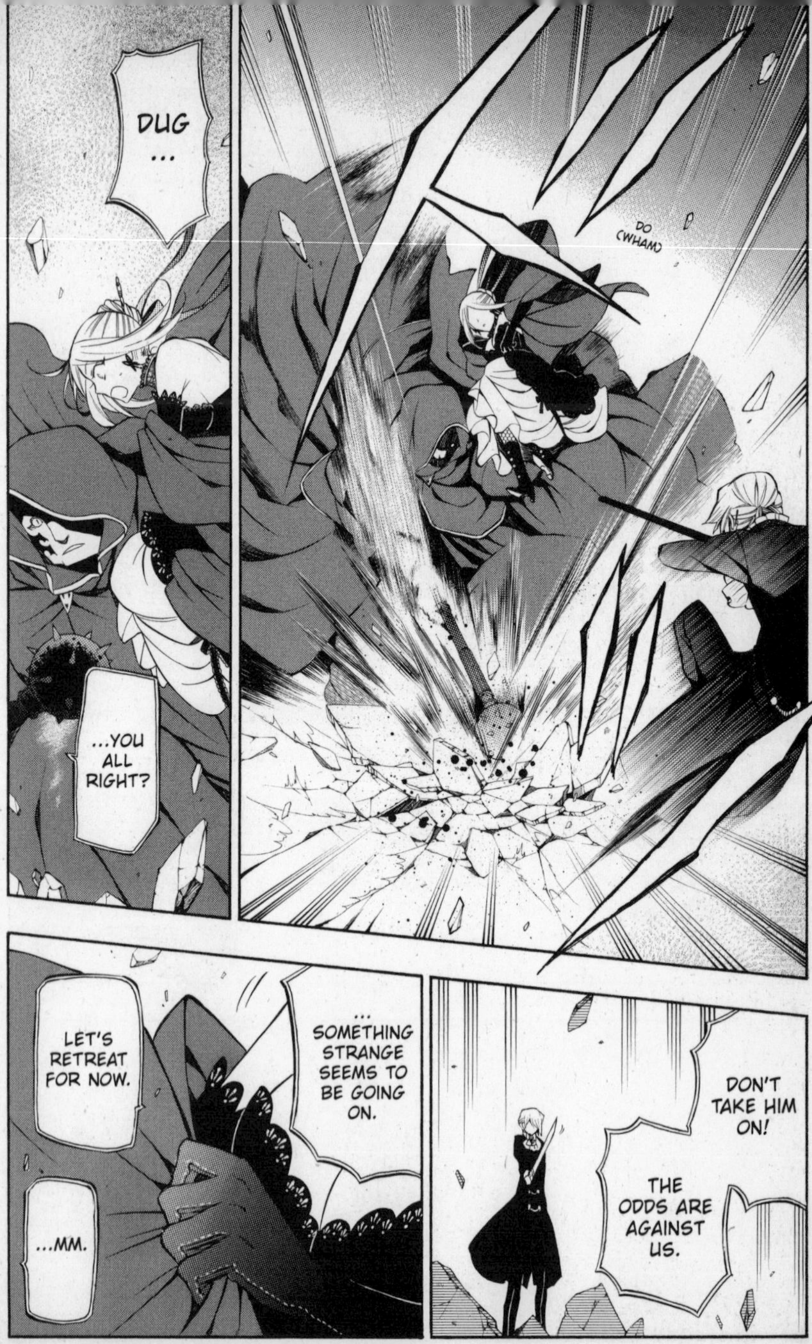
DO (WHAM)
DUG ...
...YOU ALL RIGHT?
DON'T TAKE HIM ON!
THE ODDS ARE AGAINST US.
... SOMETHING STRANGE SEEMS TO BE GOING ON.
LET'S RETREAT FOR NOW.
...MM.

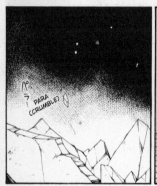

PARA
(CRUMBLE)

TA
(TMP)

TCH...

HE'S GOOD AT RUNNING AWAY, HMM?

ス
SU
(SWF)

WHERE'S YURA...?

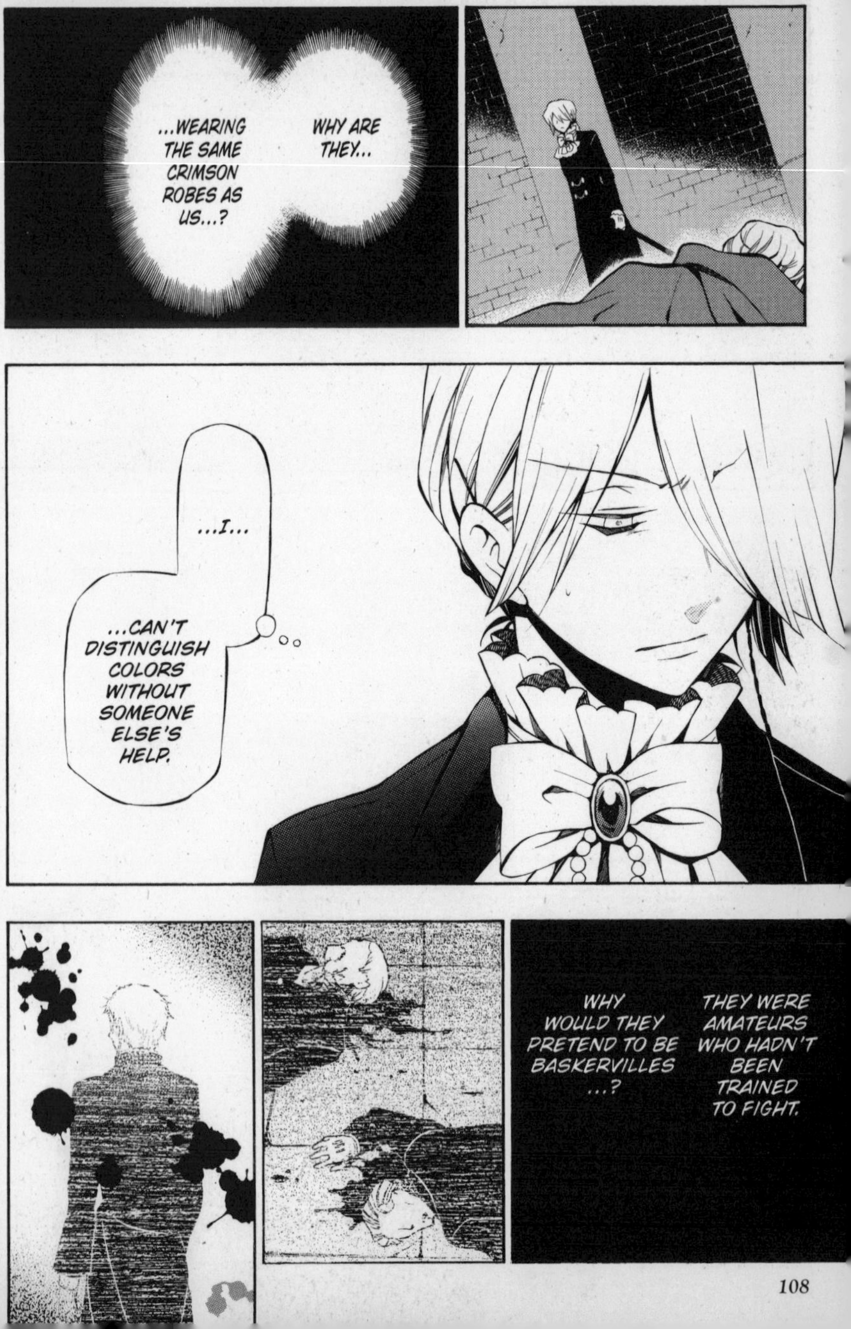
WHY ARE THEY...
...WEARING THE SAME CRIMSON ROBES AS US...?
...I...
...CAN'T DISTINGUISH COLORS WITHOUT SOMEONE ELSE'S HELP.
THEY WERE AMATEURS WHO HADN'T BEEN TRAINED TO FIGHT.
WHY WOULD THEY PRETEND TO BE BASKERVILLES ...?

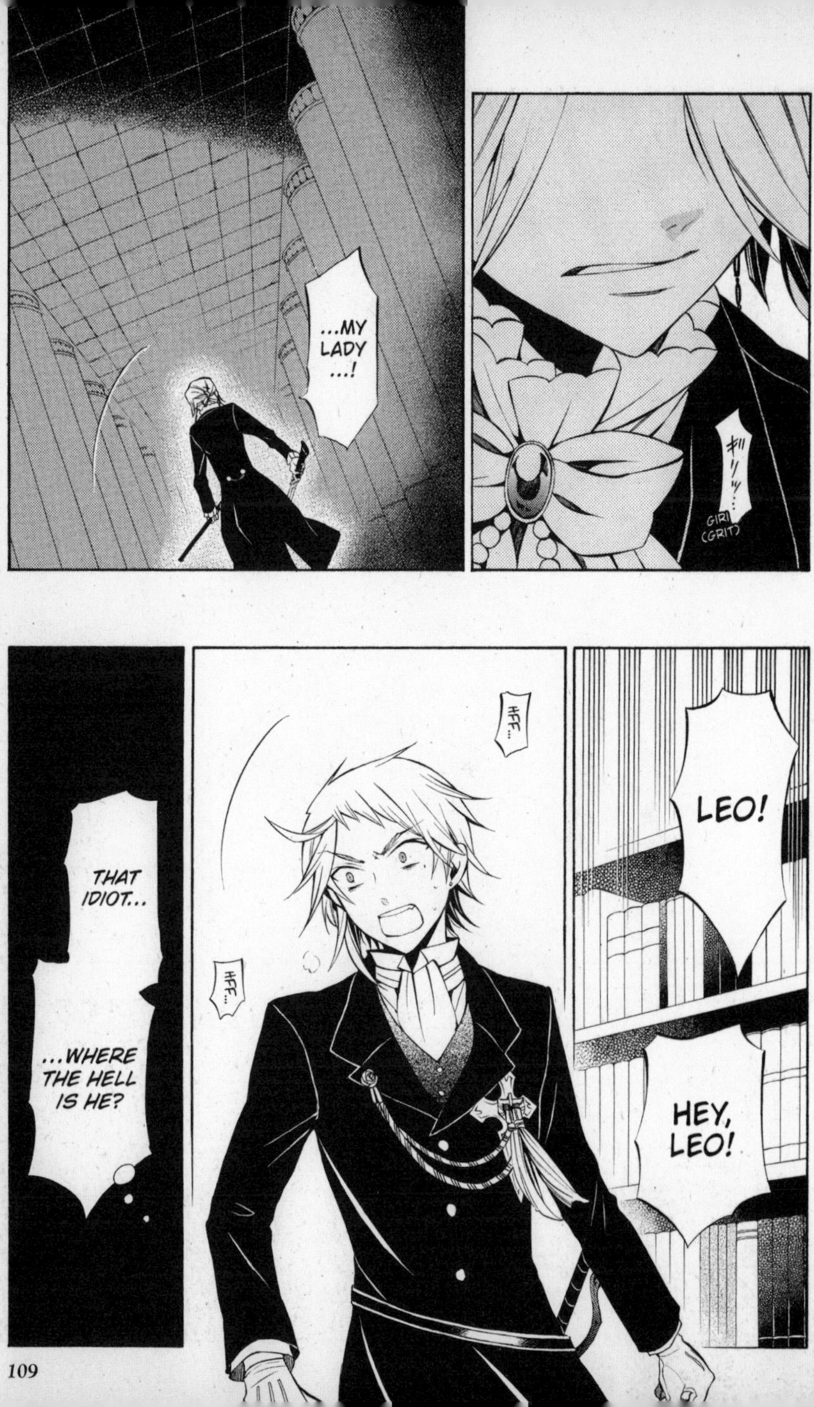
ギリッ…
GIRI (GRIT)
...MY LADY ...!
LEO!
HEY, LEO!
HFF...
HFF...
THAT IDIOT...
...WHERE THE HELL IS HE?

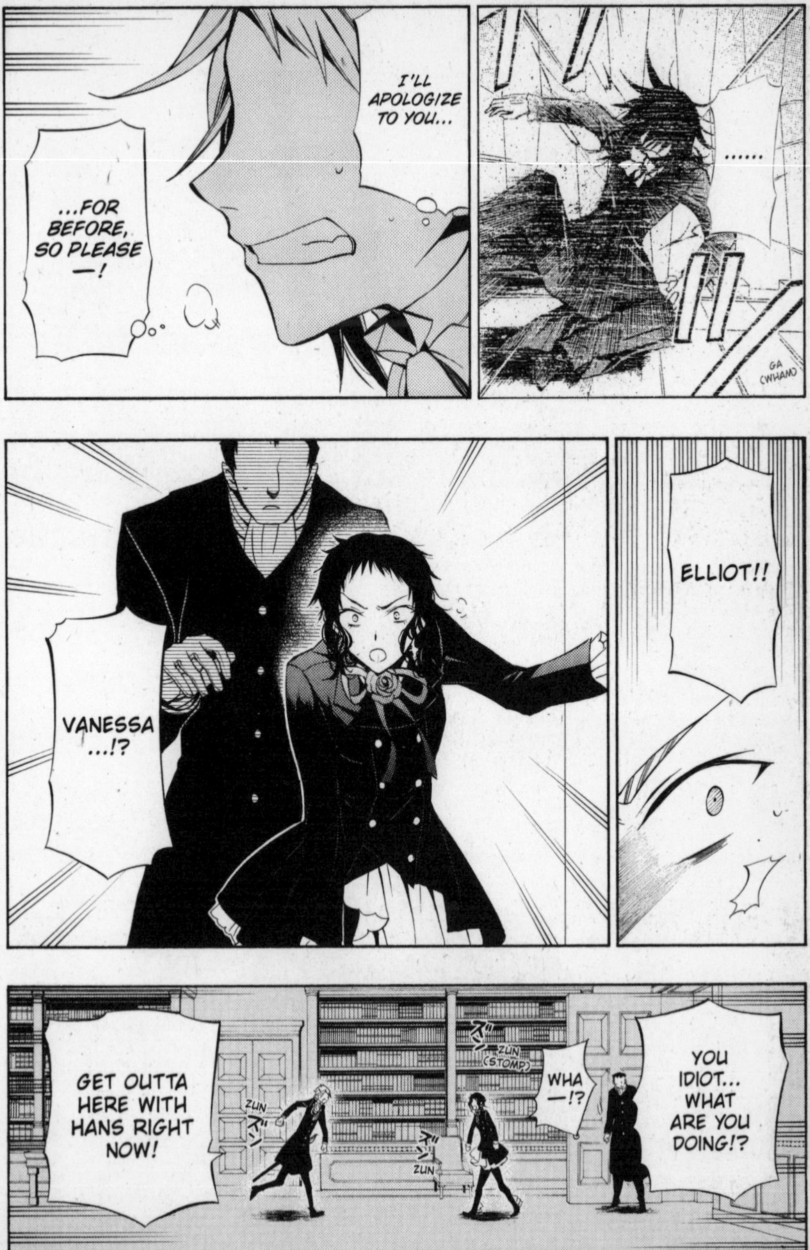
......
GA (WHAM)
I'LL APOLOGIZE TO YOU...
...FOR BEFORE, SO PLEASE—!
ELLIOT!!
VANESSA ...!?
YOU IDIOT... WHAT ARE YOU DOING!?
WHA—!?
ズン ZUN (STOMP)
ズン ZUN
ZUN ズン
GET OUTTA HERE WITH HANS RIGHT NOW!

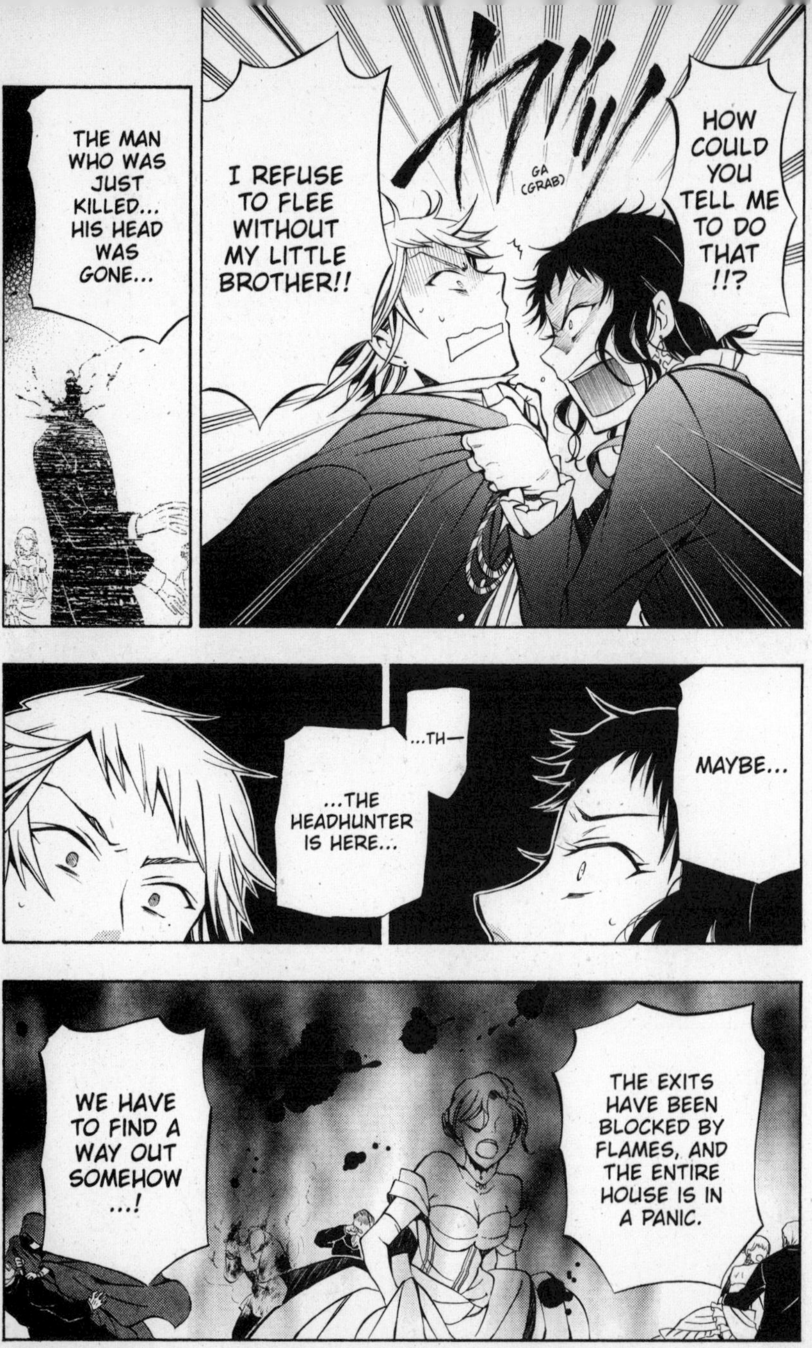
HOW COULD YOU TELL ME TO DO THAT!!?
GA (GRAB)
I REFUSE TO FLEE WITHOUT MY LITTLE BROTHER!!
THE MAN WHO WAS JUST KILLED... HIS HEAD WAS GONE...
MAYBE...
...TH—
...THE HEADHUNTER IS HERE...
THE EXITS HAVE BEEN BLOCKED BY FLAMES, AND THE ENTIRE HOUSE IS IN A PANIC.
WE HAVE TO FIND A WAY OUT SOMEHOW ...!

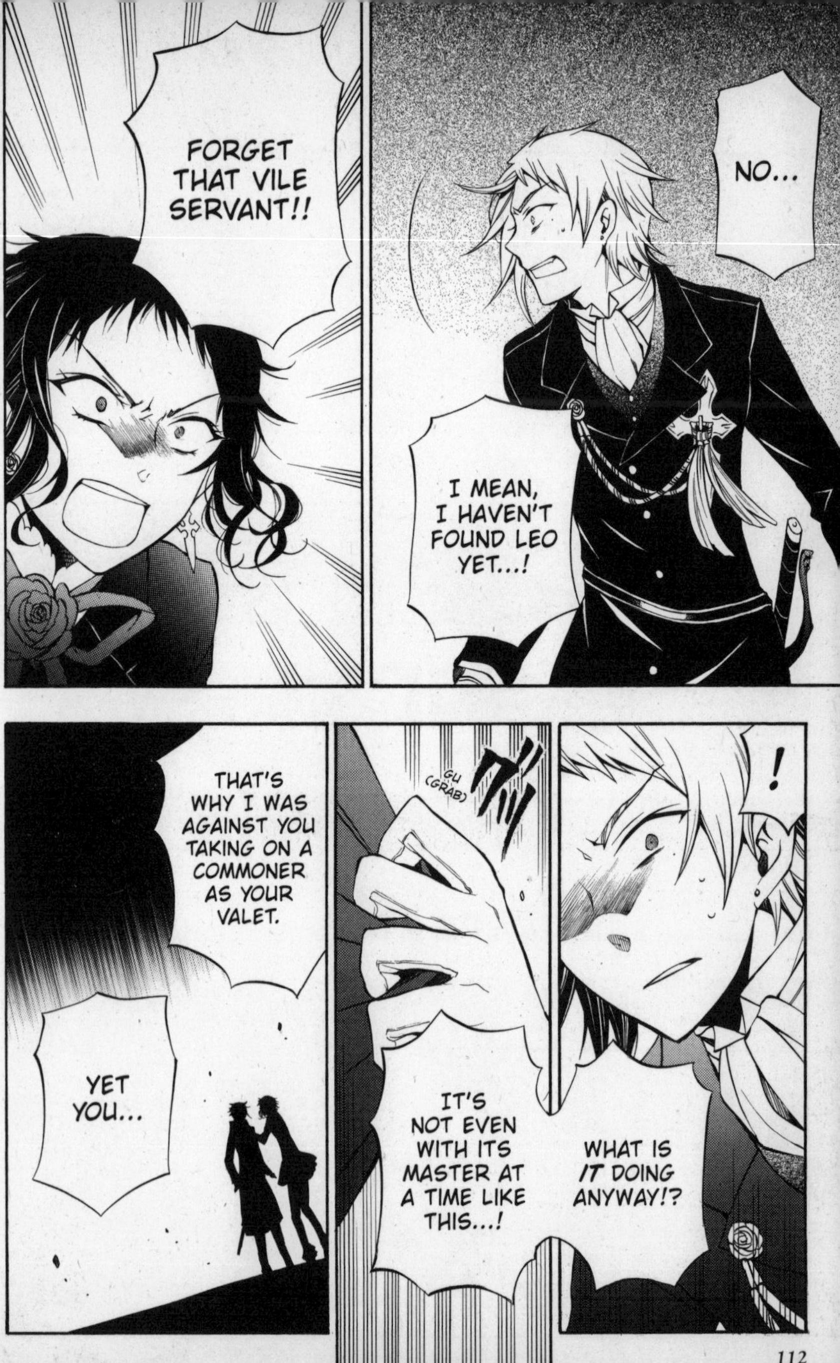
NO...
I MEAN, I HAVEN'T FOUND LEO YET...!
FORGET THAT VILE SERVANT!!
!
WHAT IS *IT* DOING ANYWAY!?
GU (GRAB)
IT'S NOT EVEN WITH ITS MASTER AT A TIME LIKE THIS...!
THAT'S WHY I WAS AGAINST YOU TAKING ON A COMMONER AS YOUR VALET.
YET YOU...

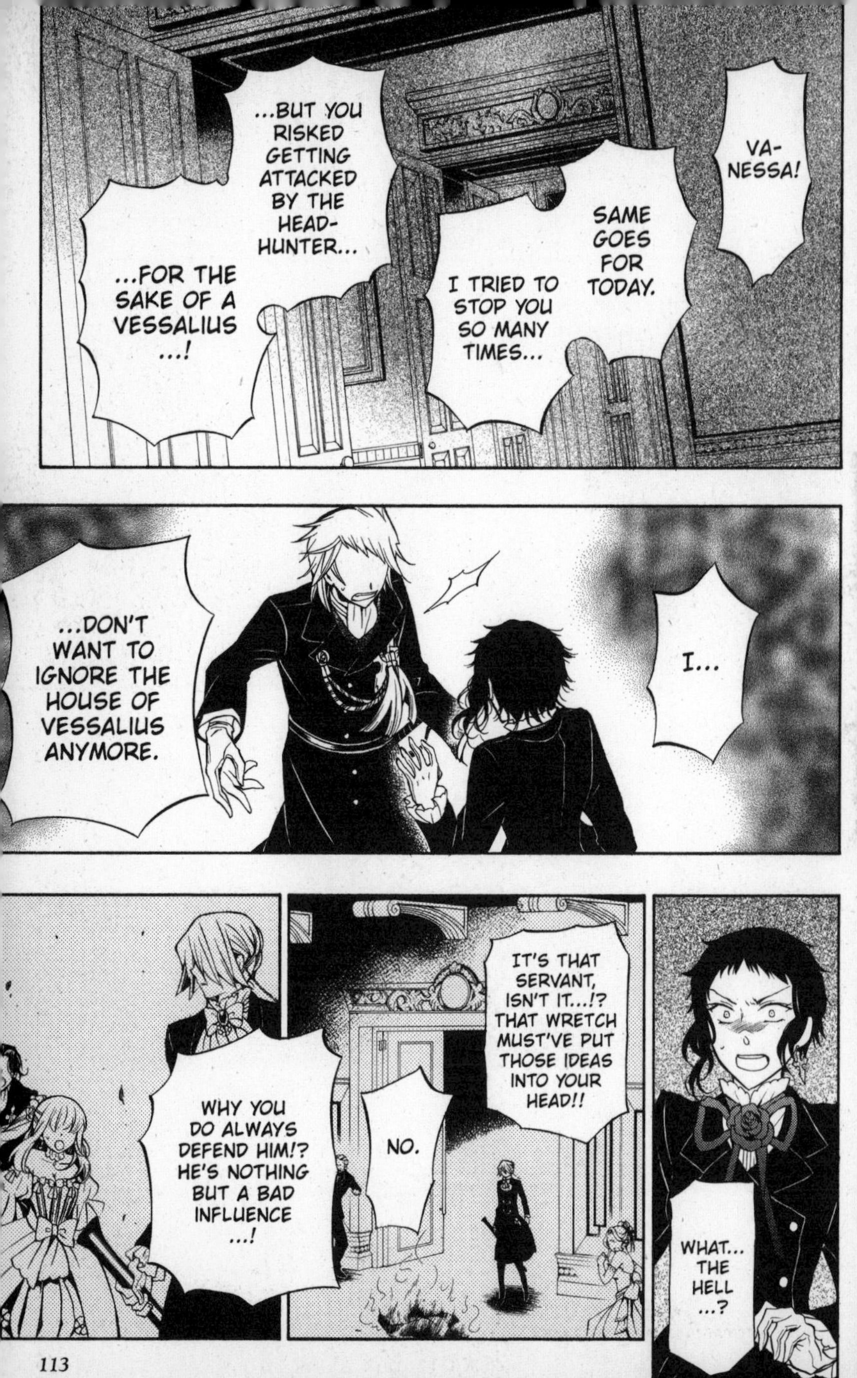
VA-NESSA!
SAME GOES FOR TODAY.
I TRIED TO STOP YOU SO MANY TIMES...
...BUT YOU RISKED GETTING ATTACKED BY THE HEAD-HUNTER...
...FOR THE SAKE OF A VESSALIUS ...!
I...
...DON'T WANT TO IGNORE THE HOUSE OF VESSALIUS ANYMORE.
WHAT... THE HELL ...?
IT'S THAT SERVANT, ISN'T IT...!? THAT WRETCH MUST'VE PUT THOSE IDEAS INTO YOUR HEAD!!
NO.
WHY YOU DO ALWAYS DEFEND HIM!? HE'S NOTHING BUT A BAD INFLUENCE ...!

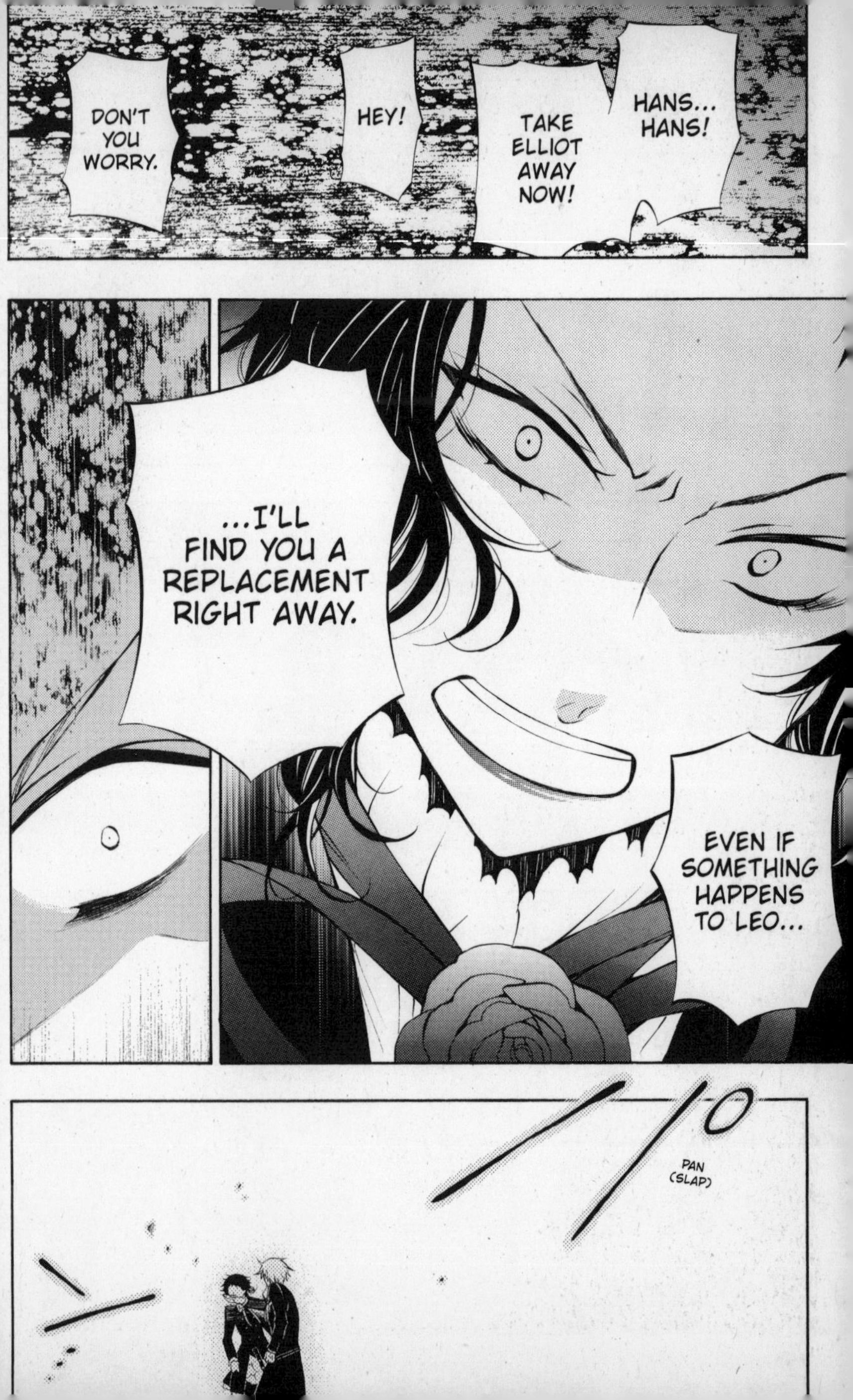
HANS... HANS!
TAKE ELLIOT AWAY NOW!
HEY!
DON'T YOU WORRY.
EVEN IF SOMETHING HAPPENS TO LEO...
...I'LL FIND YOU A REPLACEMENT RIGHT AWAY.
PAN (SLAP)

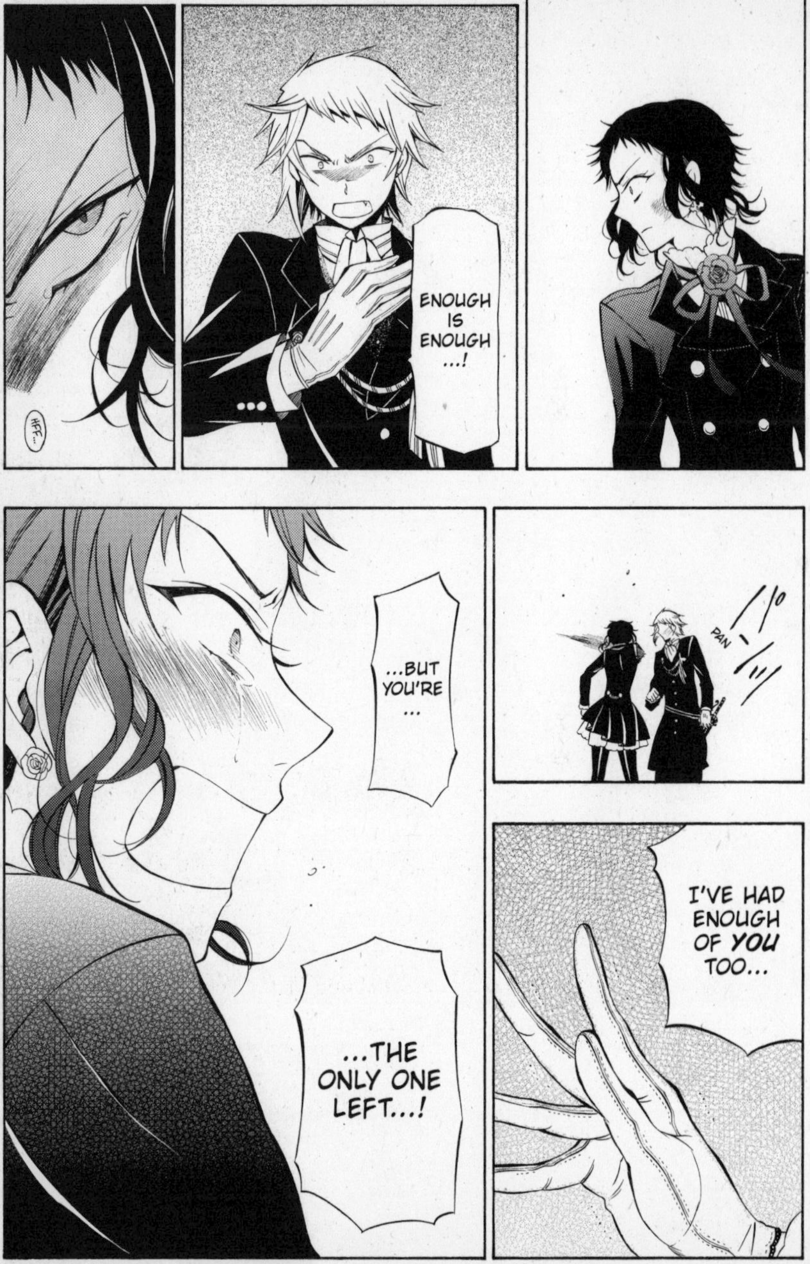
ENOUGH IS ENOUGH ...!
HFF...
PAN
I'VE HAD ENOUGH OF *YOU* TOO...
...BUT YOU'RE ...
...THE ONLY ONE LEFT...!

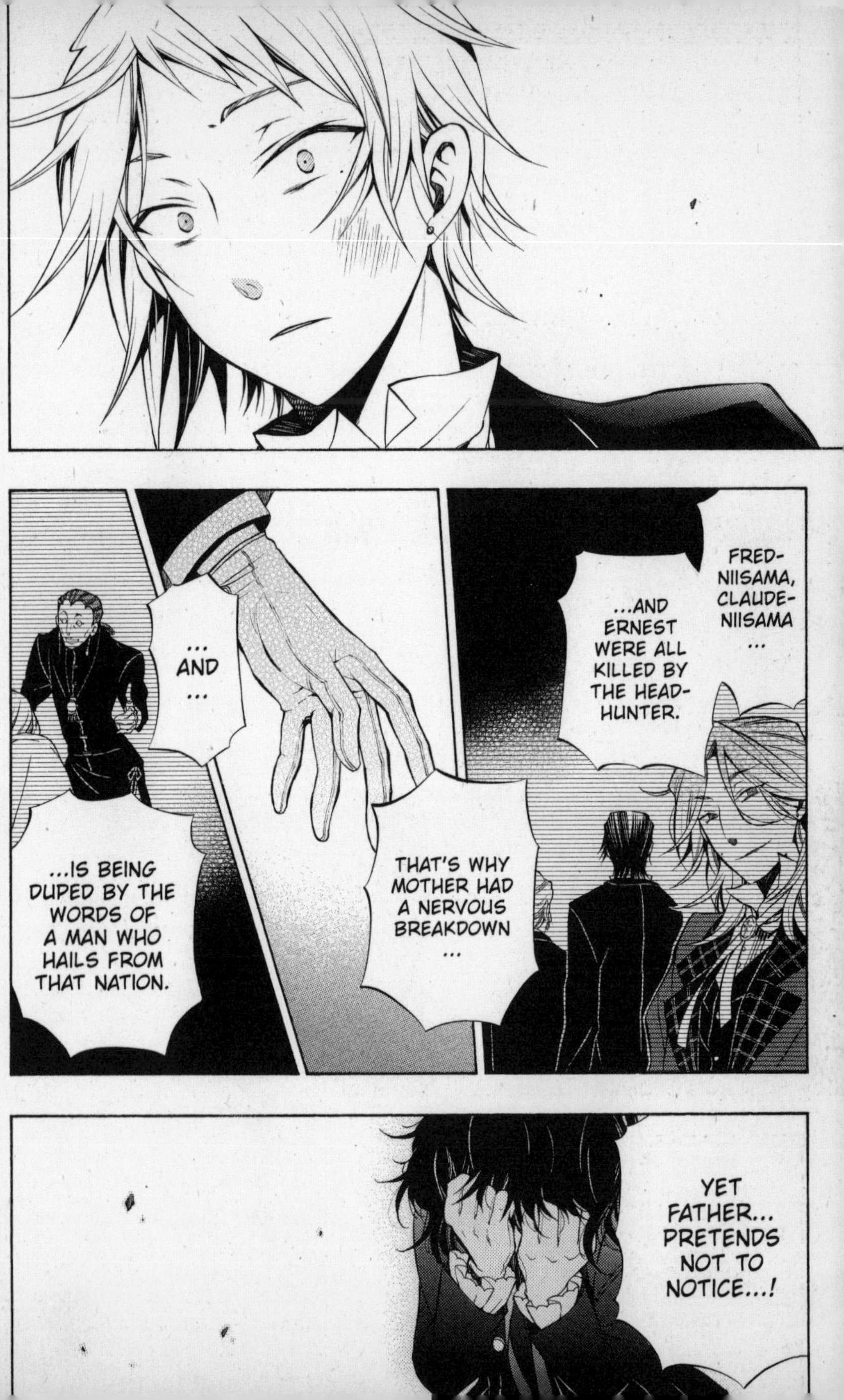
FRED-NIISAMA, CLAUDE-NIISAMA...
...AND ERNEST WERE ALL KILLED BY THE HEAD-HUNTER.
THAT'S WHY MOTHER HAD A NERVOUS BREAKDOWN...
...AND...
...IS BEING DUPED BY THE WORDS OF A MAN WHO HAILS FROM THAT NATION.
YET FATHER... PRETENDS NOT TO NOTICE...!

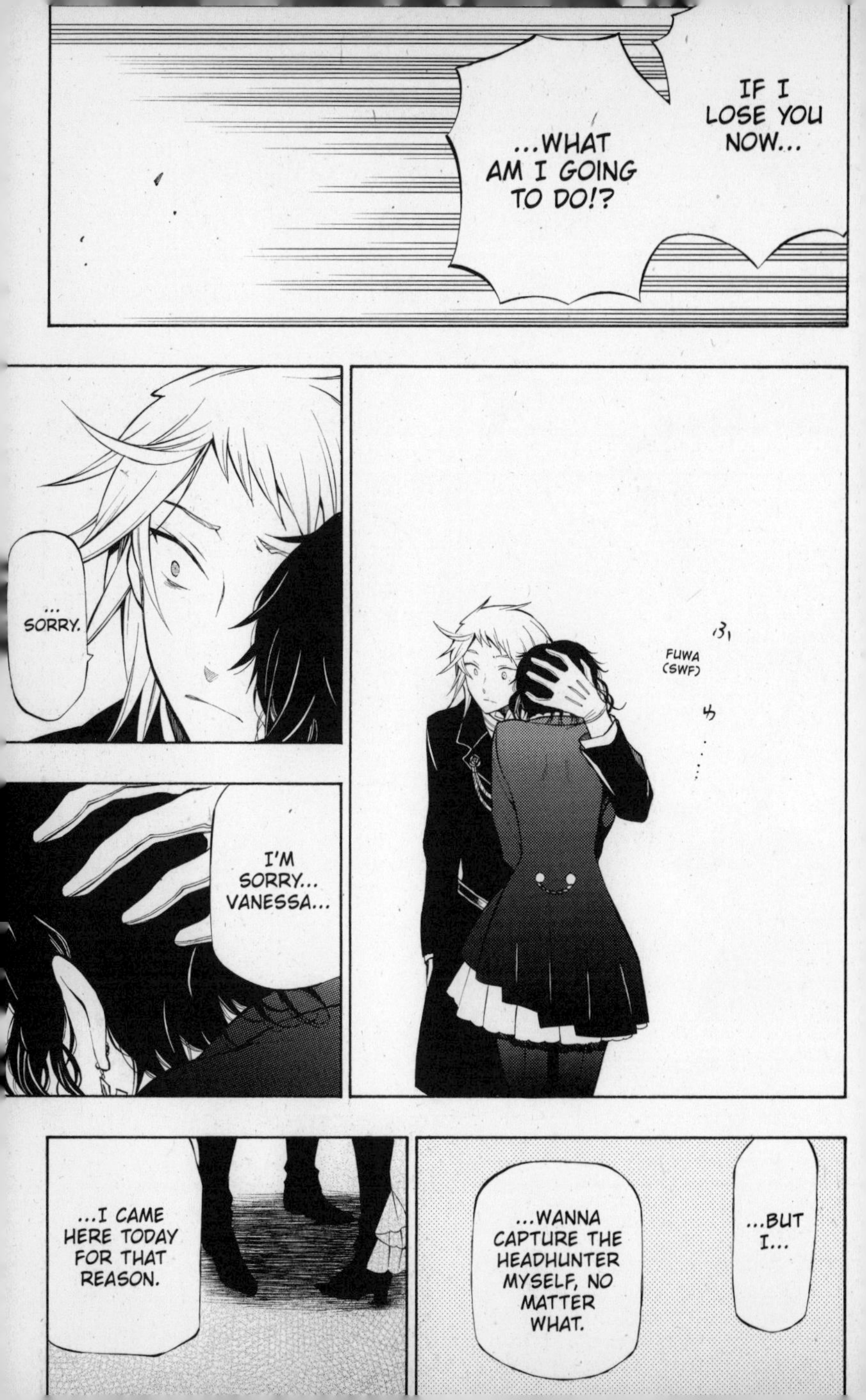
IF I LOSE YOU NOW...
...WHAT AM I GOING TO DO!?
FUWA (SWF)
... SORRY.
I'M SORRY... VANESSA...
...BUT I...
...WANNA CAPTURE THE HEADHUNTER MYSELF, NO MATTER WHAT.
...I CAME HERE TODAY FOR THAT REASON.

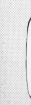

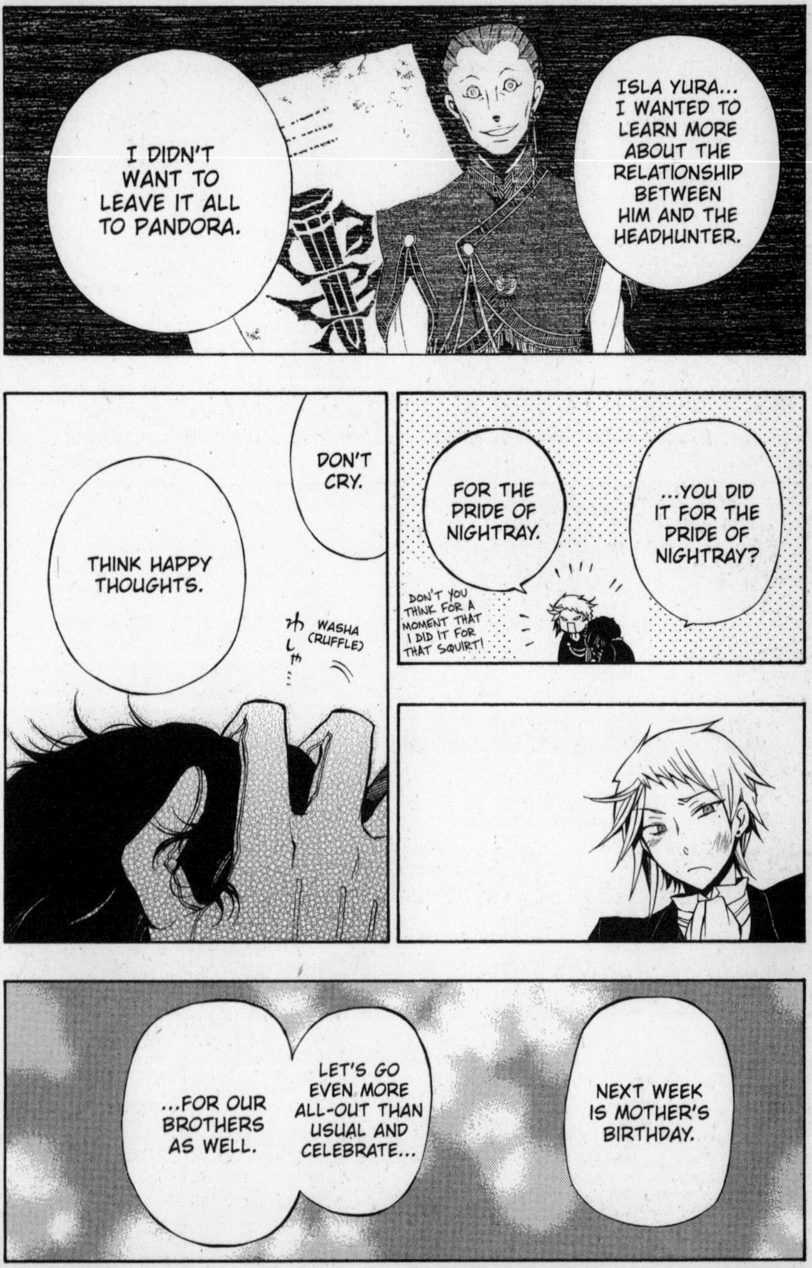
ISLA YURA... I WANTED TO LEARN MORE ABOUT THE RELATIONSHIP BETWEEN HIM AND THE HEADHUNTER.
I DIDN'T WANT TO LEAVE IT ALL TO PANDORA.
...YOU DID IT FOR THE PRIDE OF NIGHTRAY?
FOR THE PRIDE OF NIGHTRAY.
DON'T YOU THINK FOR A MOMENT THAT I DID IT FOR THAT SQUIRT!
DON'T CRY.
THINK HAPPY THOUGHTS.
WASHA (RUFFLE)
NEXT WEEK IS MOTHER'S BIRTHDAY.
LET'S GO EVEN MORE ALL-OUT THAN USUAL AND CELEBRATE...
...FOR OUR BROTHERS AS WELL.

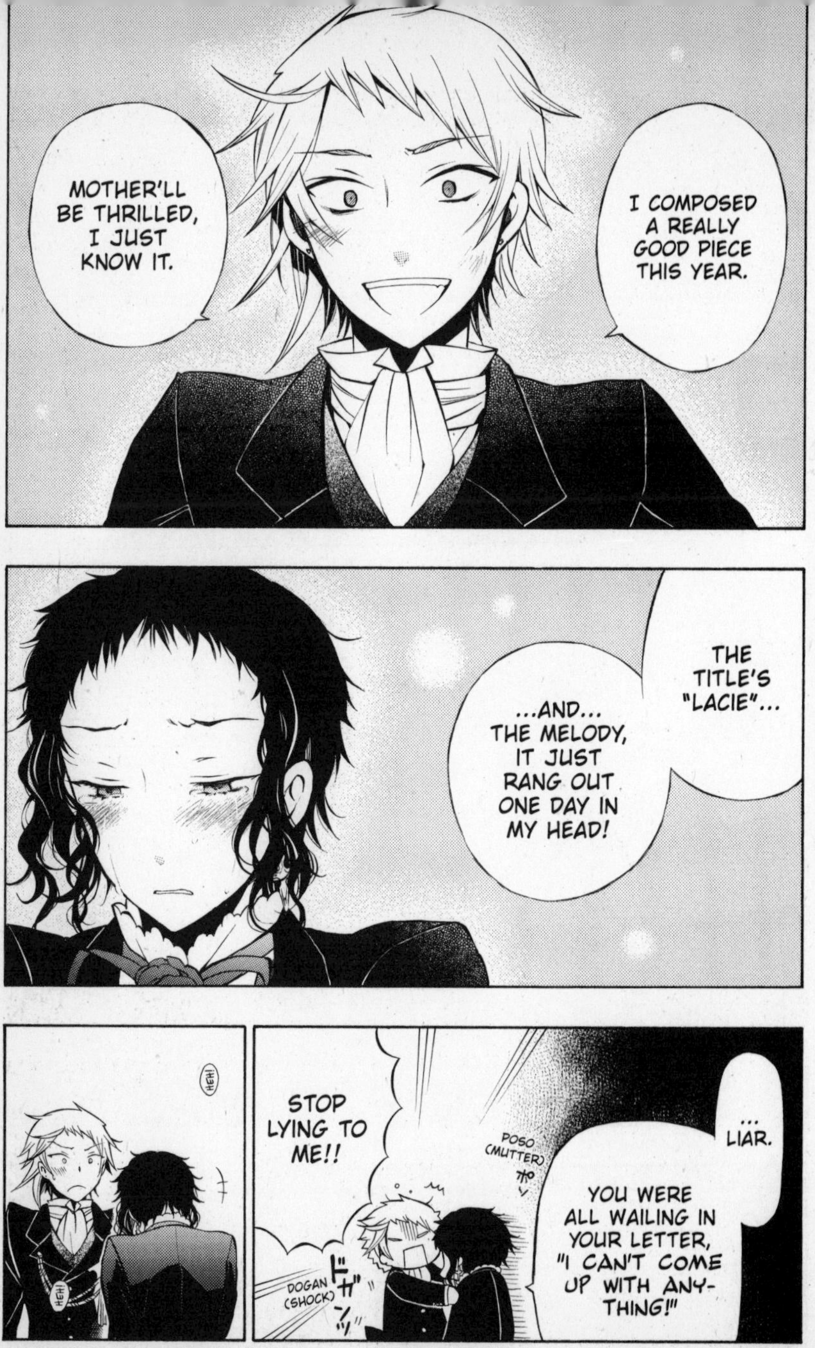
I COMPOSED A REALLY GOOD PIECE THIS YEAR.
MOTHER'LL BE THRILLED, I JUST KNOW IT.
THE TITLE'S "LACIE"...
...AND... THE MELODY, IT JUST RANG OUT ONE DAY IN MY HEAD!
... LIAR.
YOU WERE ALL WAILING IN YOUR LETTER, "I CAN'T COME UP WITH ANY-THING!"
POSO (MUTTER)
STOP LYING TO ME!!
DOGAN (SHOCK)
HEH!
HEH!

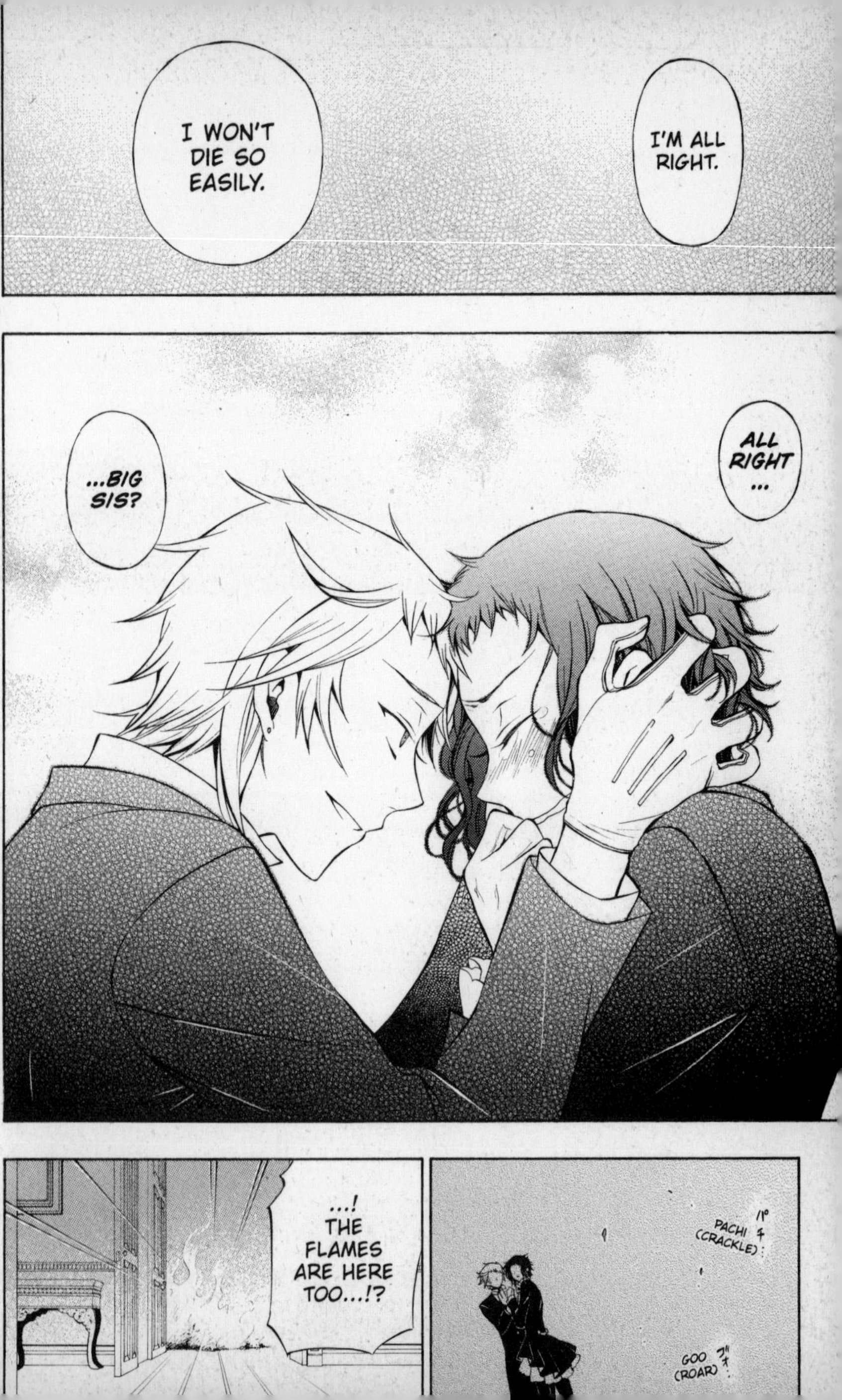
I'M ALL RIGHT.
I WON'T DIE SO EASILY.
ALL RIGHT ...
...BIG SIS?
PACHI (CRACKLE)
GOO (ROAR)
...! THE FLAMES ARE HERE TOO...!?

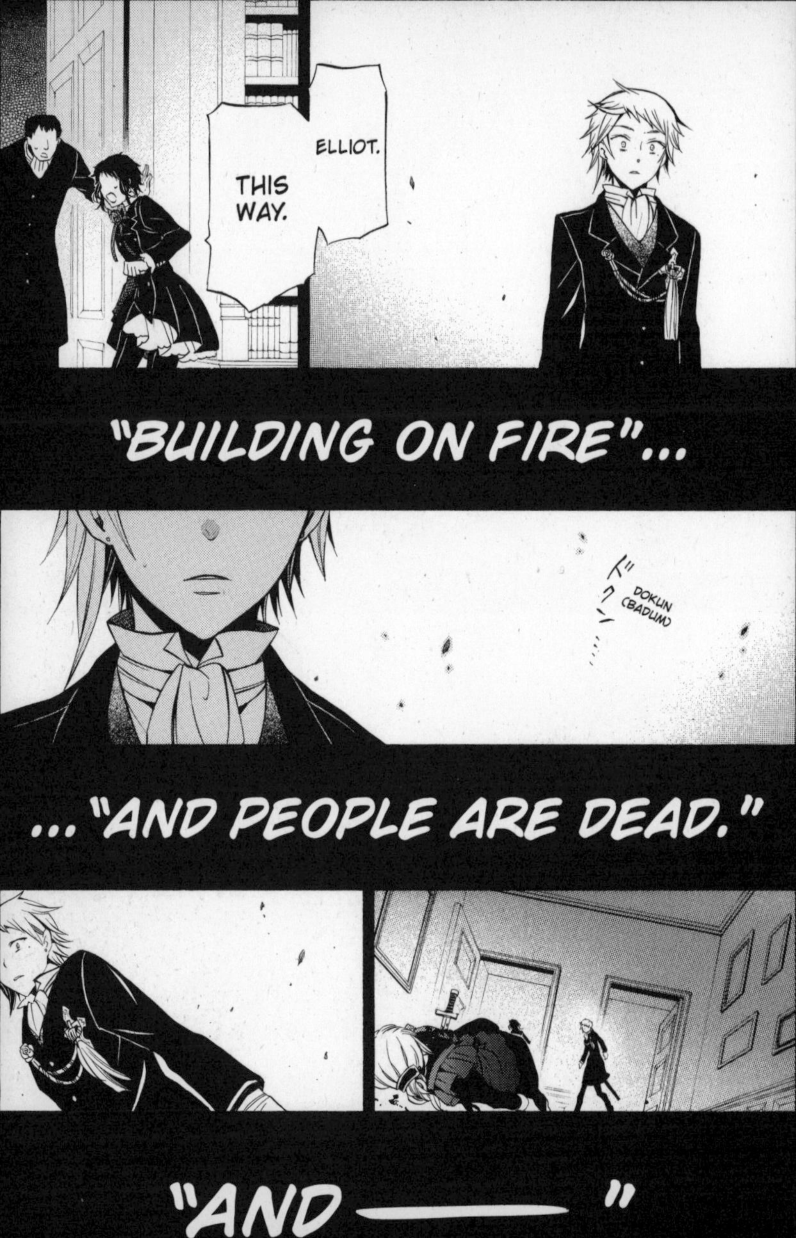
ELLIOT.
THIS WAY.
"BUILDING ON FIRE"...
DOKUN (BADUM)
..."AND PEOPLE ARE DEAD."
"AND——"

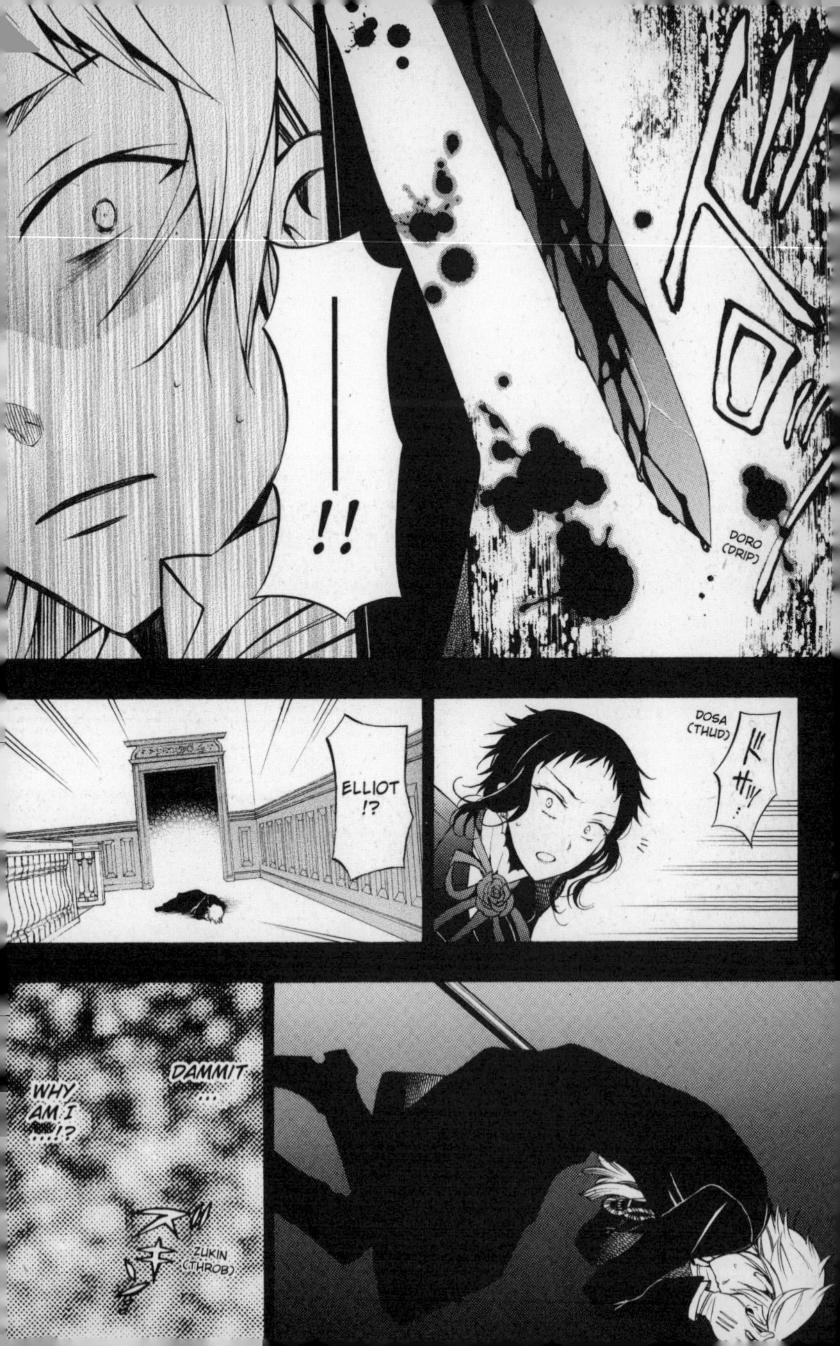
DORO (DRIP)
—!!
DOSA (THUD)
ELLIOT !?
DAMMIT ...
WHY AM I ....!?
ZUKIN (THROB)

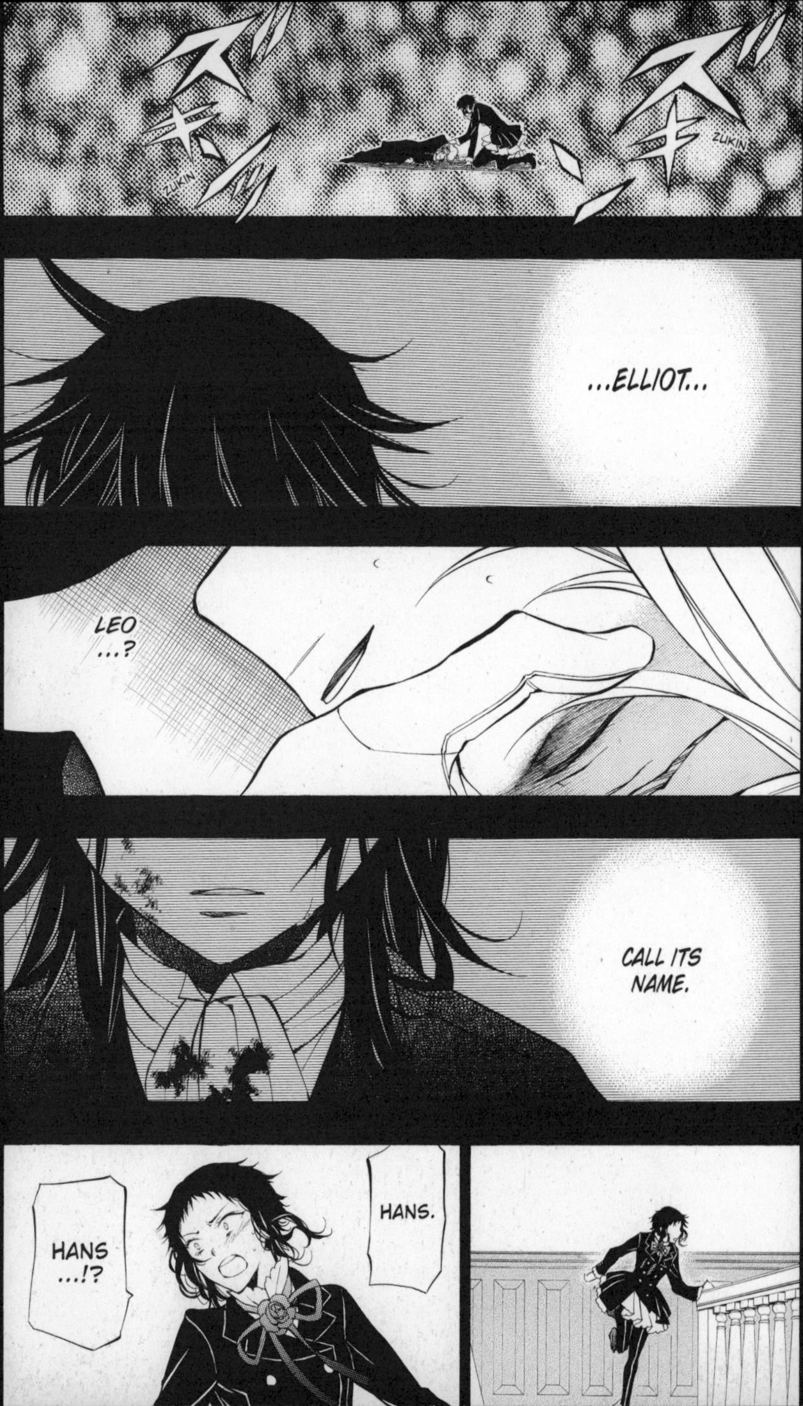
ZUKIN
ZUKIN
...ELLIOT...
LEO
...?
CALL ITS
NAME.
HANS.
HANS
...!?

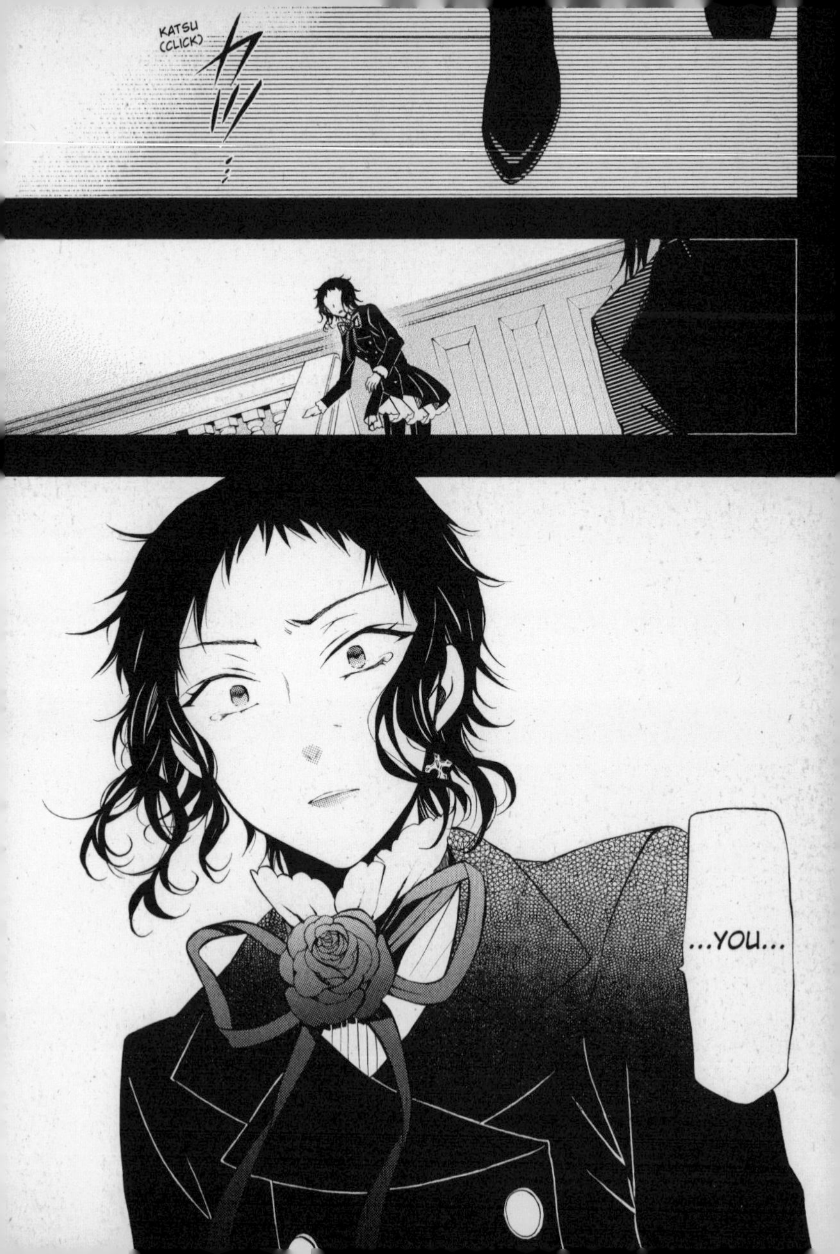
KATSU (CLICK)
カツ…
...YOU...

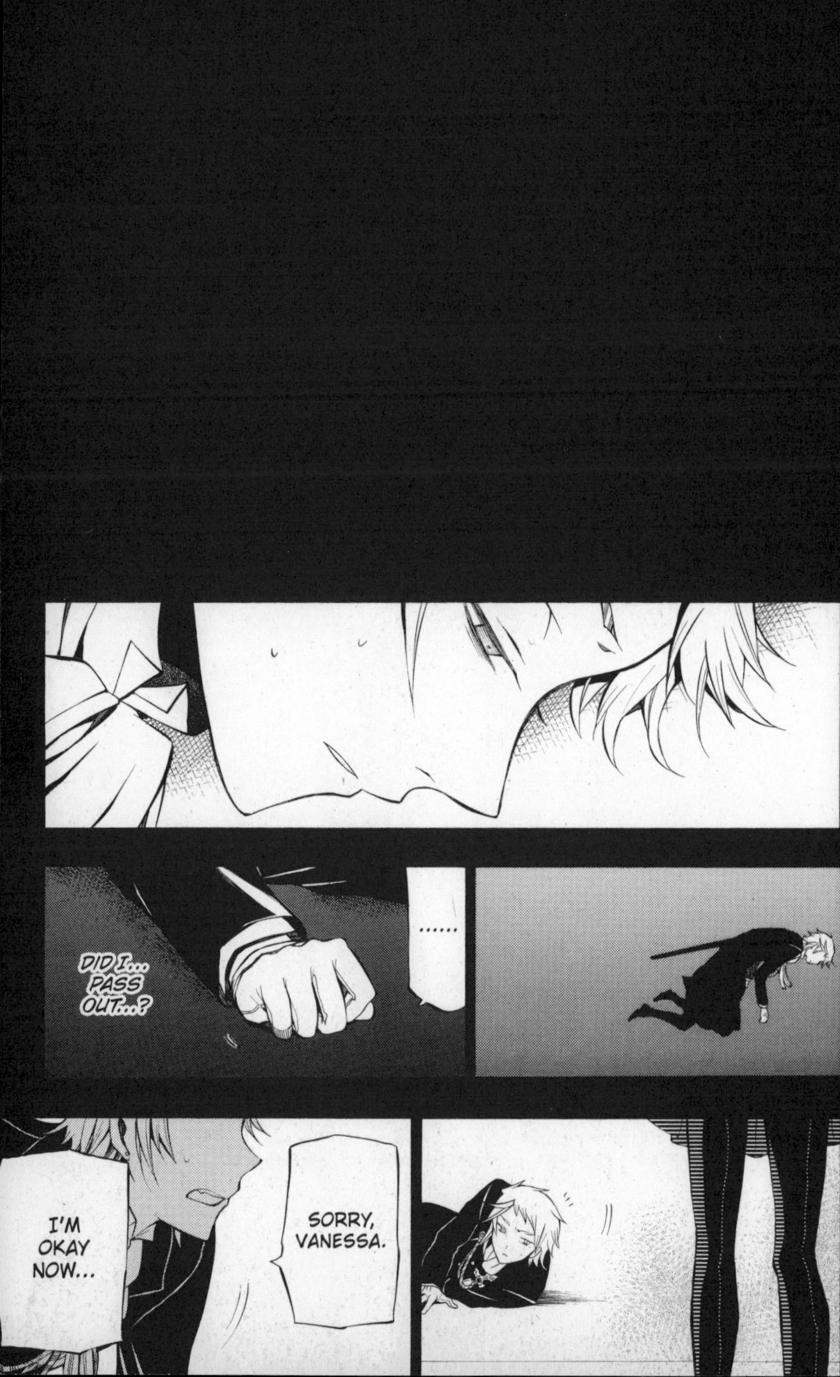
......
DID I... PASS OUT...?
SORRY, VANESSA.
I'M OKAY NOW...

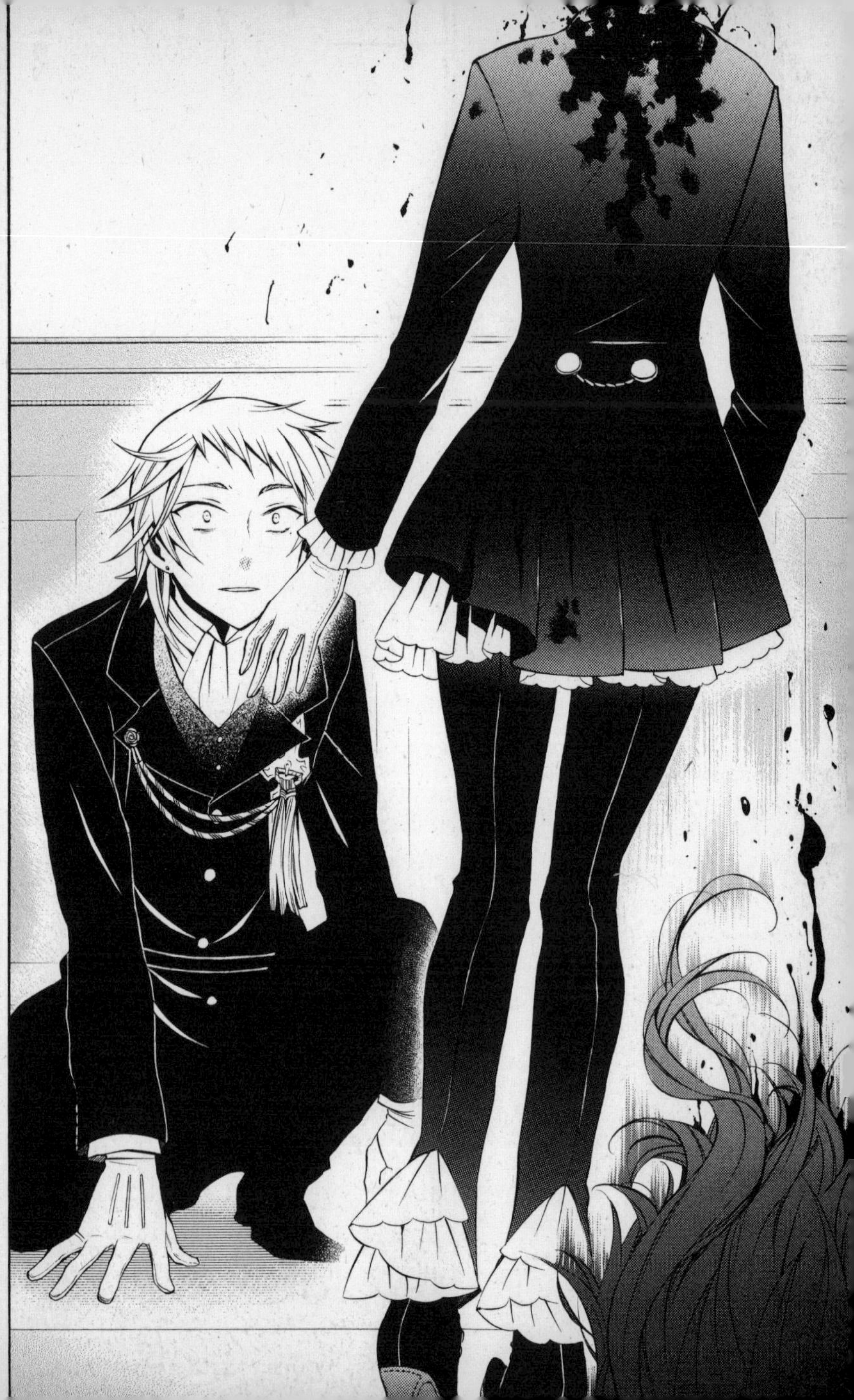

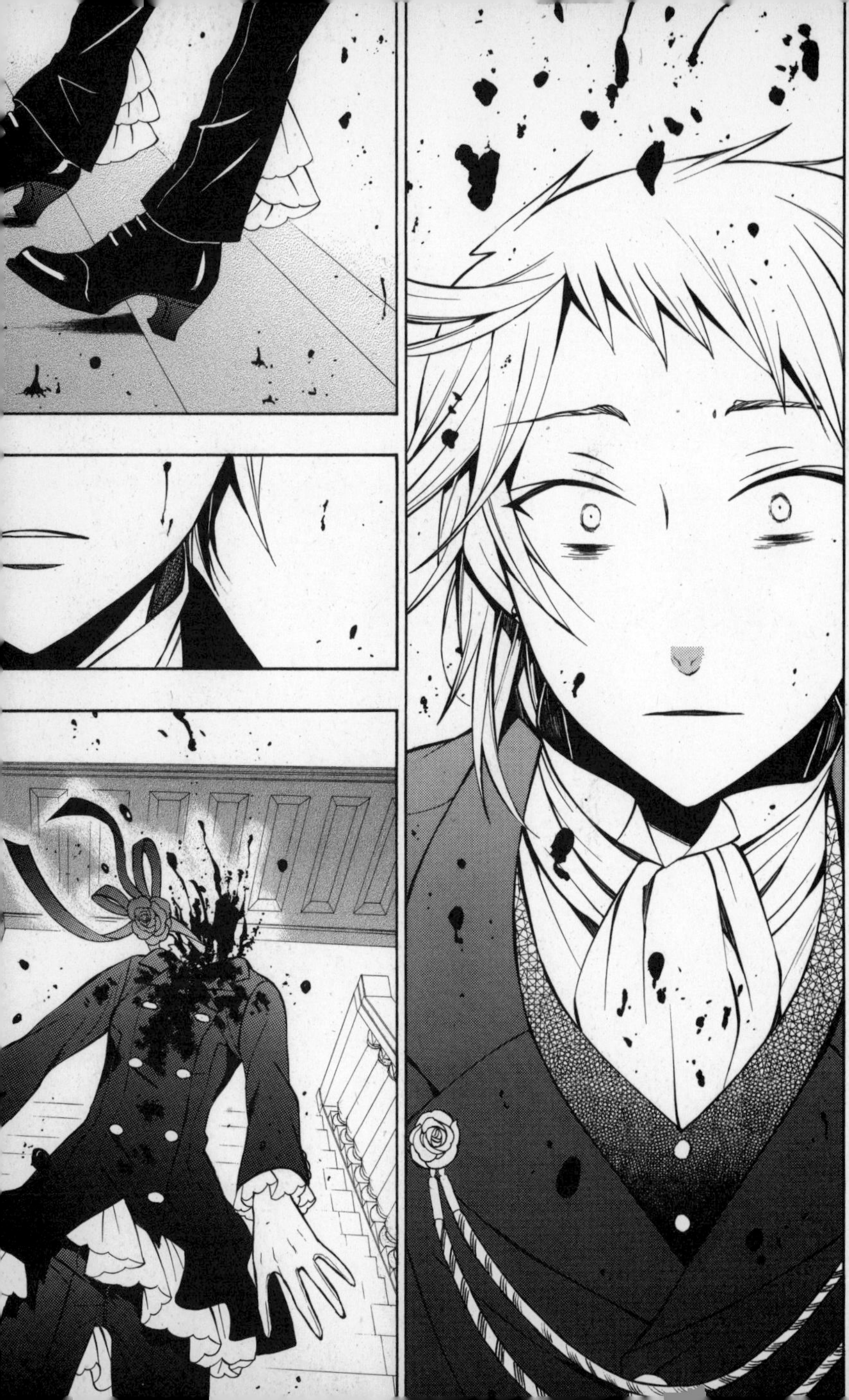

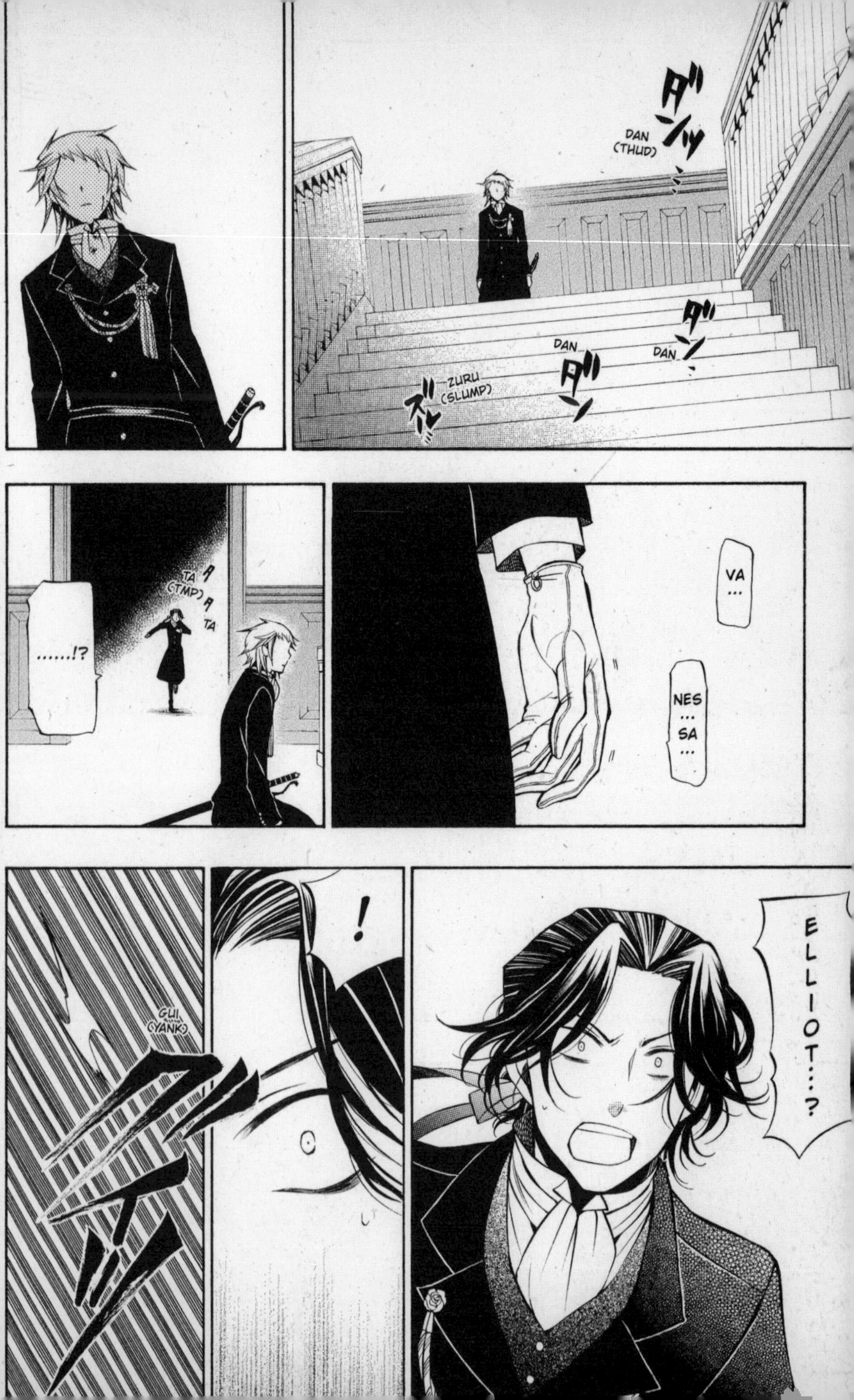
DAN (THUD)
DAN
DAN
ZURU (SLUMP)
VA...
NES... SA...
TA (TMP) TA TA
......!?
ELLIOT...?
!
GUI (YANK)

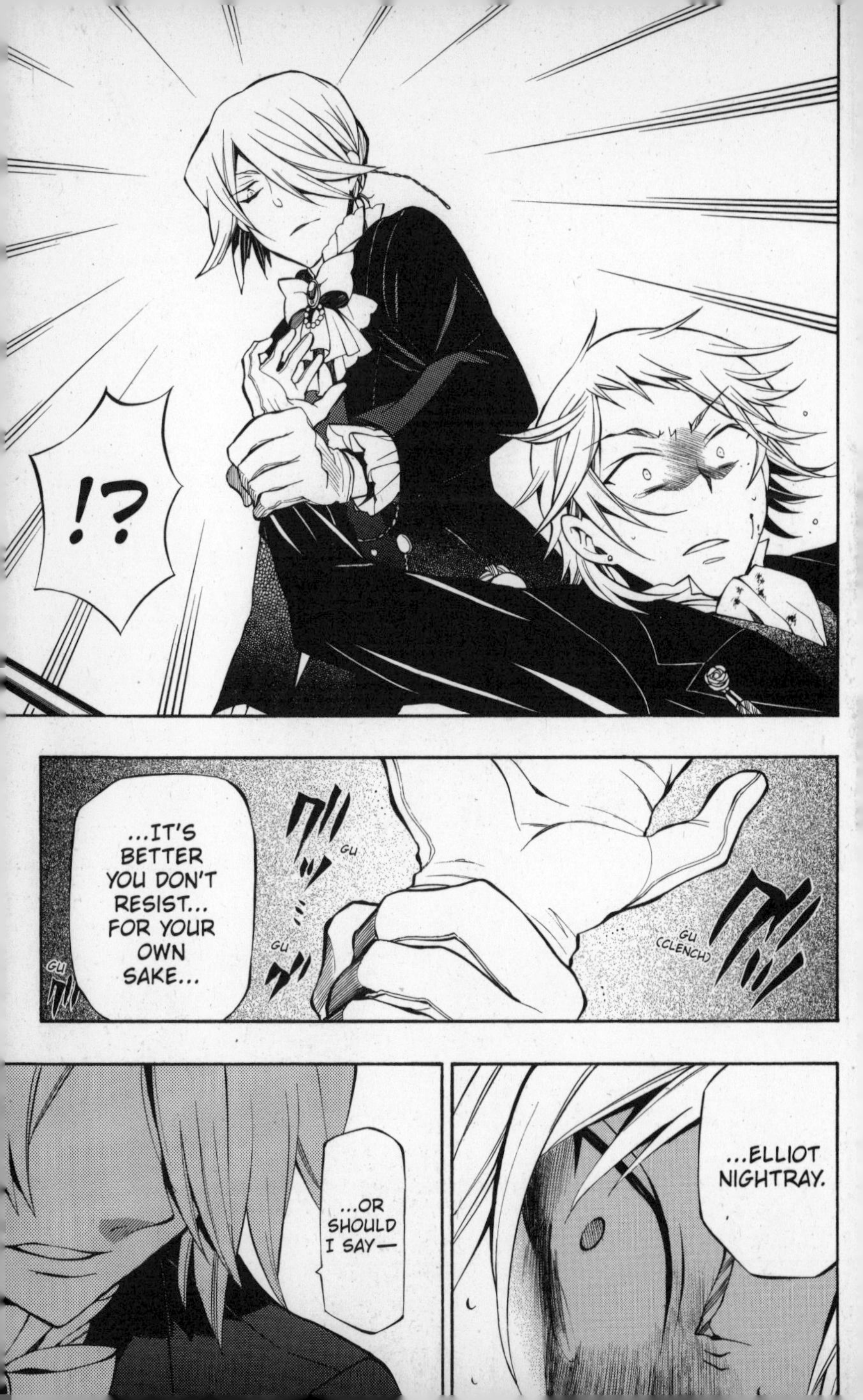
!?
GU (CLENCH)
GU
GU
...IT'S BETTER YOU DON'T RESIST... FOR YOUR OWN SAKE...
GU
...OR SHOULD I SAY—
...ELLIOT NIGHTRAY.

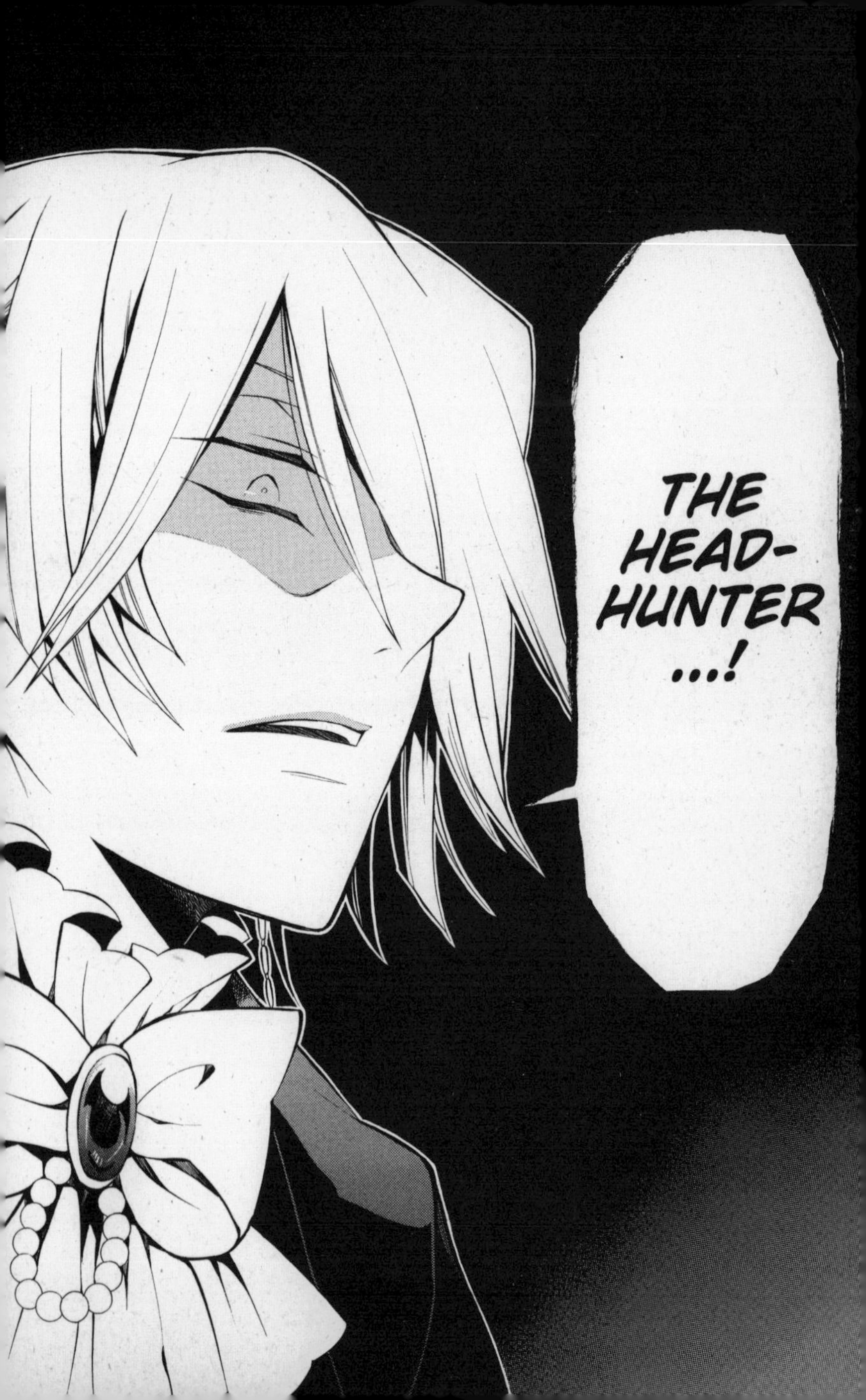
THE HEAD-HUNTER ...!

"I YIELD TO THEE ONE IMPORTANT SNIPPET OF INFORMATION, MAD HATTER."

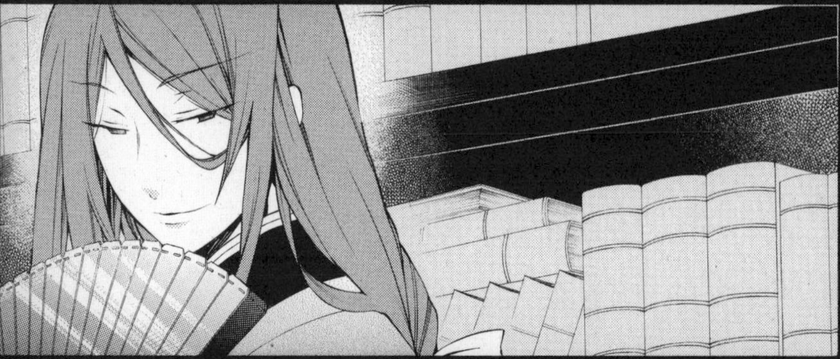

Retrace:LIII

Humpty Dumpty Sat On A Wall

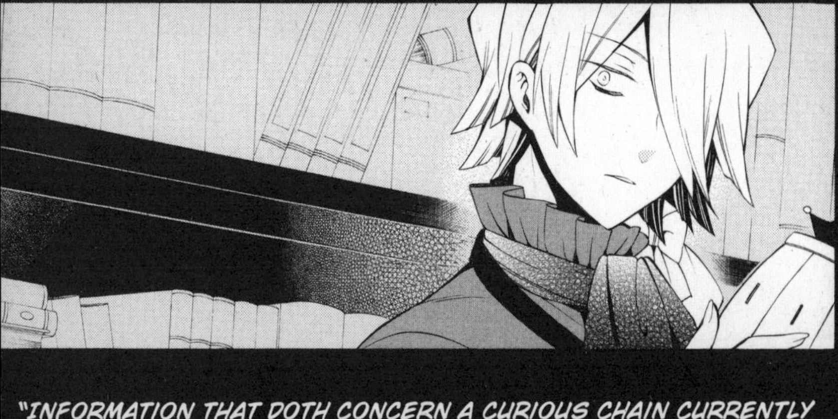

"INFORMATION THAT DOTH CONCERN A CURIOUS CHAIN CURRENTLY UNDER INVESTIGATION BY THE HOUSE OF NIGHTRAY."

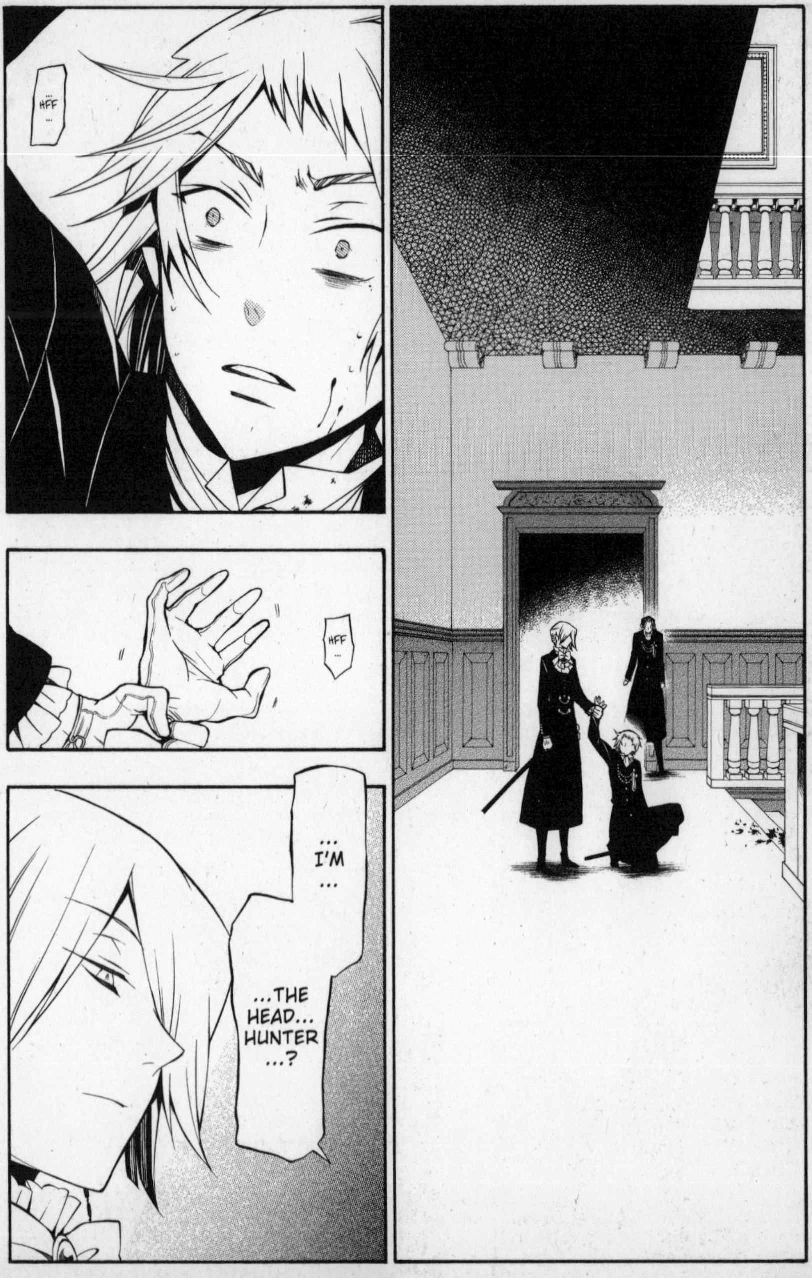
...HFF...
HFF...
...I'M...
...THE HEAD... HUNTER...?

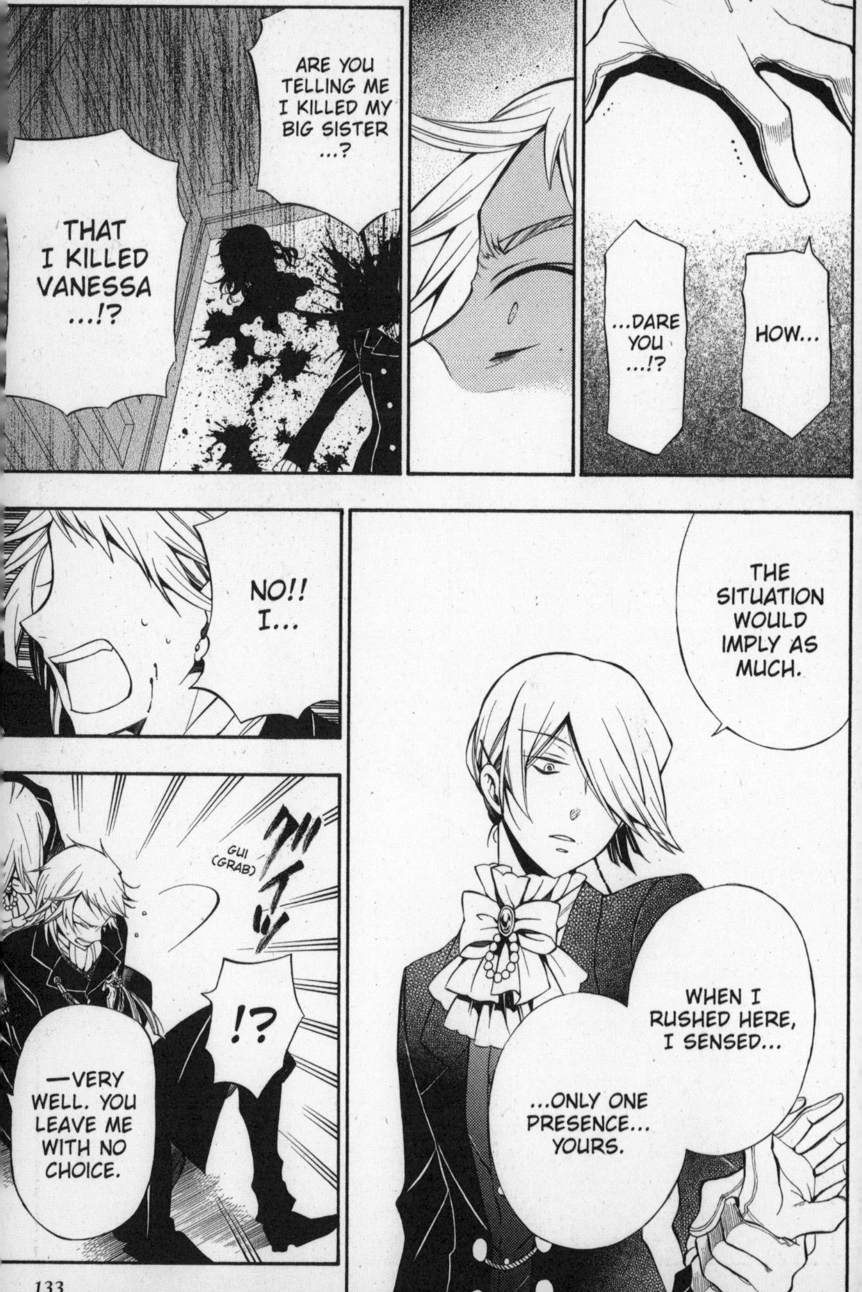
HOW...
...DARE YOU ...!?
ARE YOU TELLING ME I KILLED MY BIG SISTER ...?
THAT I KILLED VANESSA ...!?
THE SITUATION WOULD IMPLY AS MUCH.
WHEN I RUSHED HERE, I SENSED...
...ONLY ONE PRESENCE... YOURS.
NO!! I...
GUI (GRAB)
!?
—VERY WELL. YOU LEAVE ME WITH NO CHOICE.

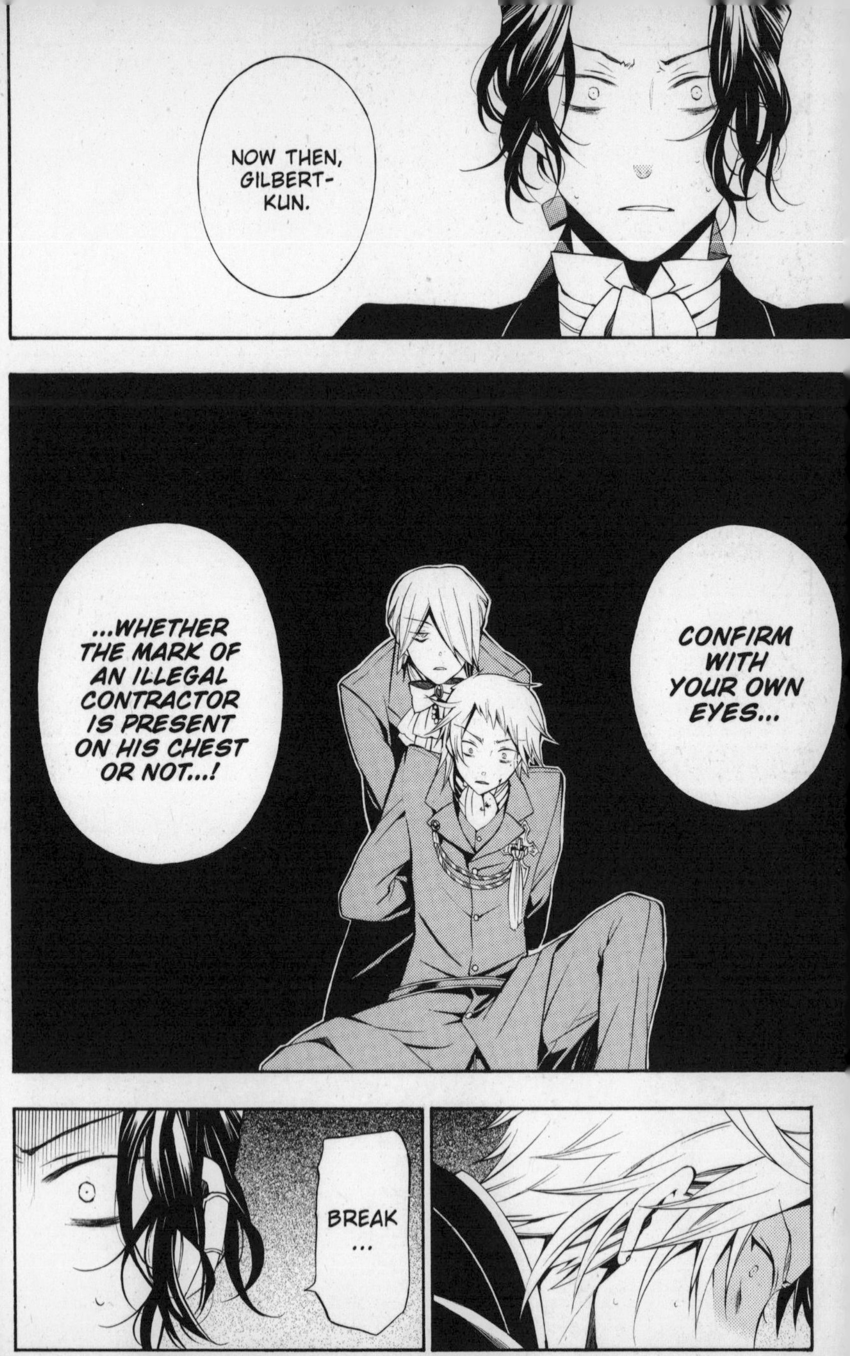
NOW THEN, GILBERT-KUN.
CONFIRM WITH YOUR OWN EYES...
...WHETHER THE MARK OF AN ILLEGAL CONTRACTOR IS PRESENT ON HIS CHEST OR NOT...!
BREAK ...

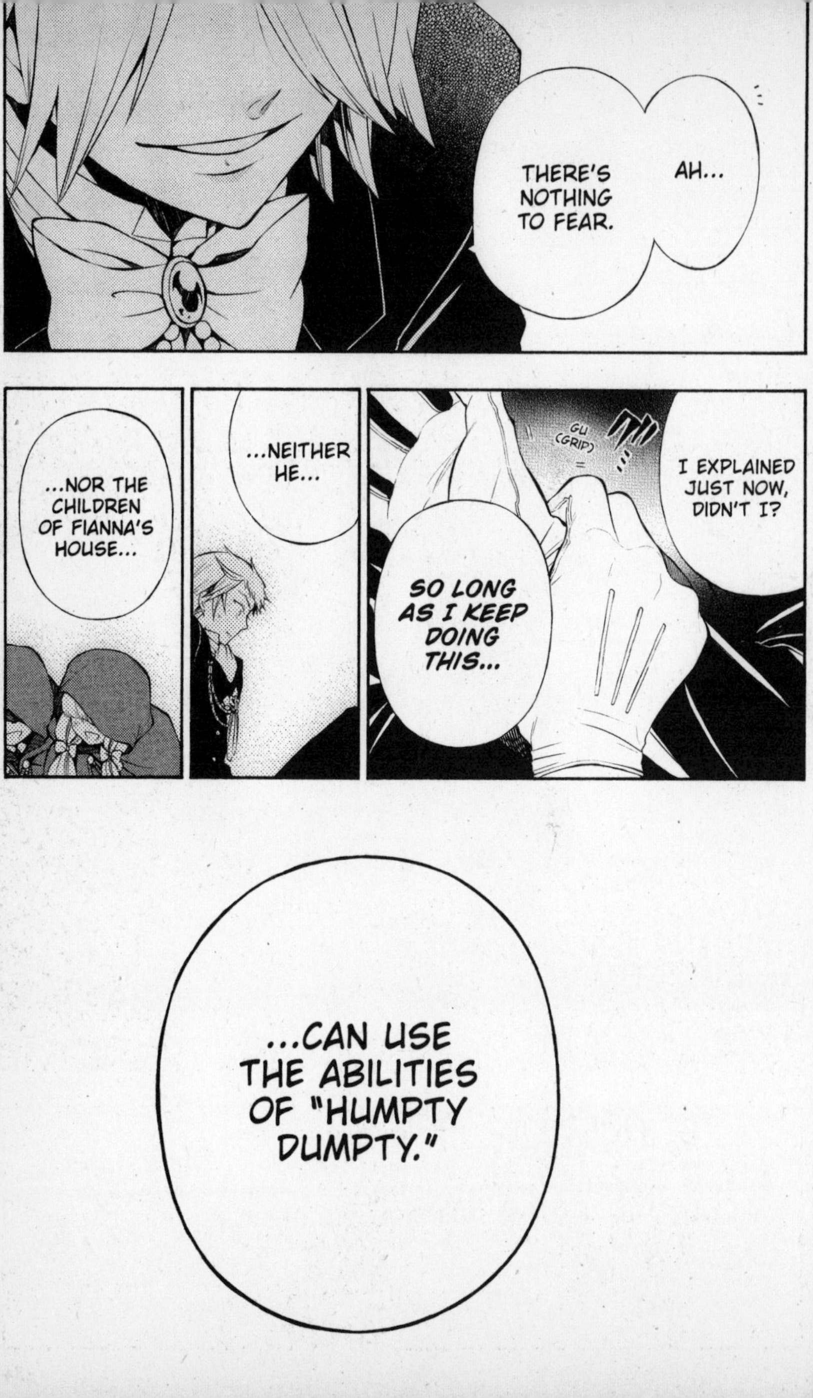
AH...
THERE'S NOTHING TO FEAR.
I EXPLAINED JUST NOW, DIDN'T I?
GU (GRIP)
SO LONG AS I KEEP DOING THIS...
...NEITHER HE...
...NOR THE CHILDREN OF FIANNA'S HOUSE...
...CAN USE THE ABILITIES OF "HUMPTY DUMPTY."

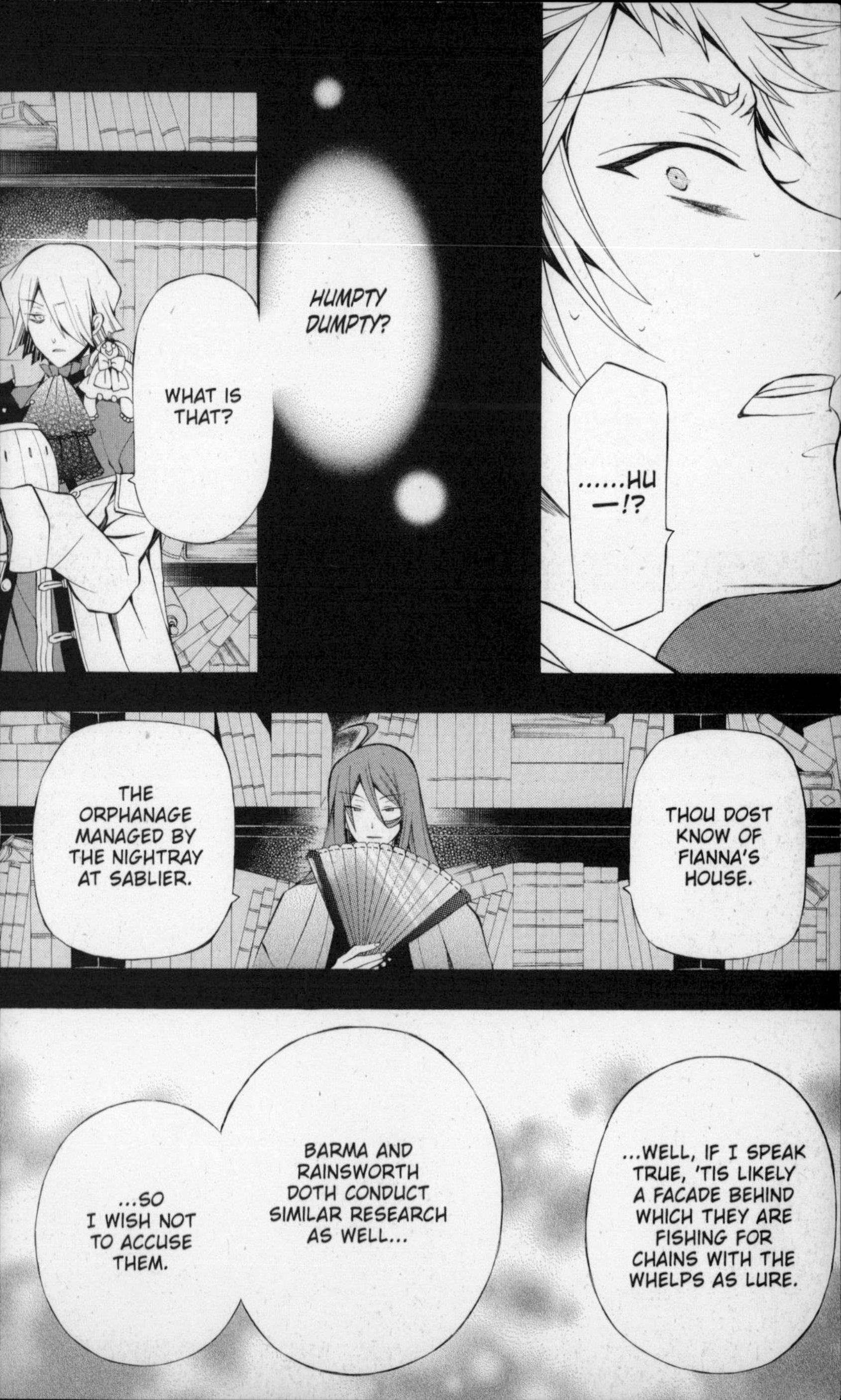
......HU—!?
HUMPTY DUMPTY?
WHAT IS THAT?
THOU DOST KNOW OF FIANNA'S HOUSE.
THE ORPHANAGE MANAGED BY THE NIGHTRAY AT SABLIER.
...WELL, IF I SPEAK TRUE, 'TIS LIKELY A FACADE BEHIND WHICH THEY ARE FISHING FOR CHAINS WITH THE WHELPS AS LURE.
BARMA AND RAINSWORTH DOTH CONDUCT SIMILAR RESEARCH AS WELL...
...SO I WISH NOT TO ACCUSE THEM.

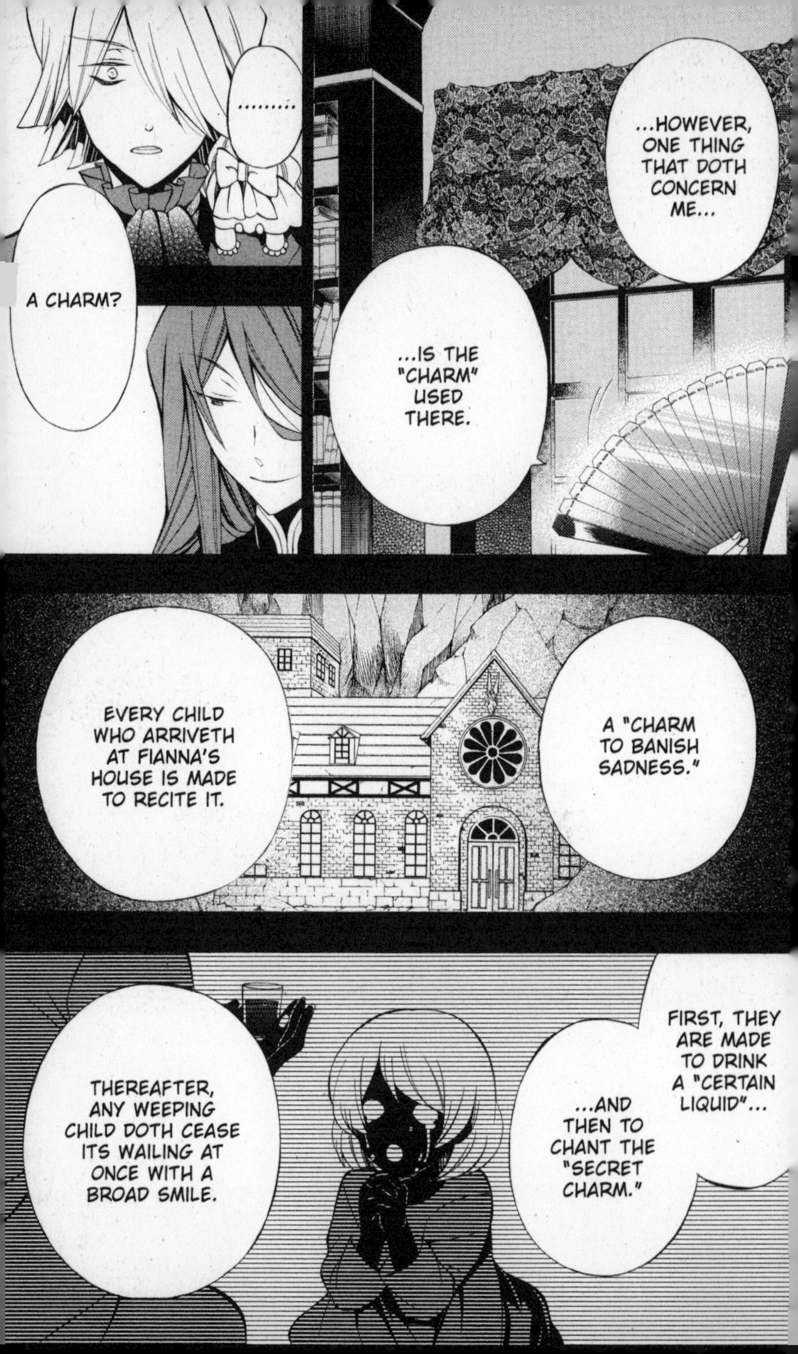
...HOWEVER, ONE THING THAT DOTH CONCERN ME...
...IS THE "CHARM" USED THERE.
....
A CHARM?
A "CHARM TO BANISH SADNESS."
EVERY CHILD WHO ARRIVETH AT FIANNA'S HOUSE IS MADE TO RECITE IT.
FIRST, THEY ARE MADE TO DRINK A "CERTAIN LIQUID"...
...AND THEN TO CHANT THE "SECRET CHARM."
THEREAFTER, ANY WEEPING CHILD DOTH CEASE ITS WAILING AT ONCE WITH A BROAD SMILE.

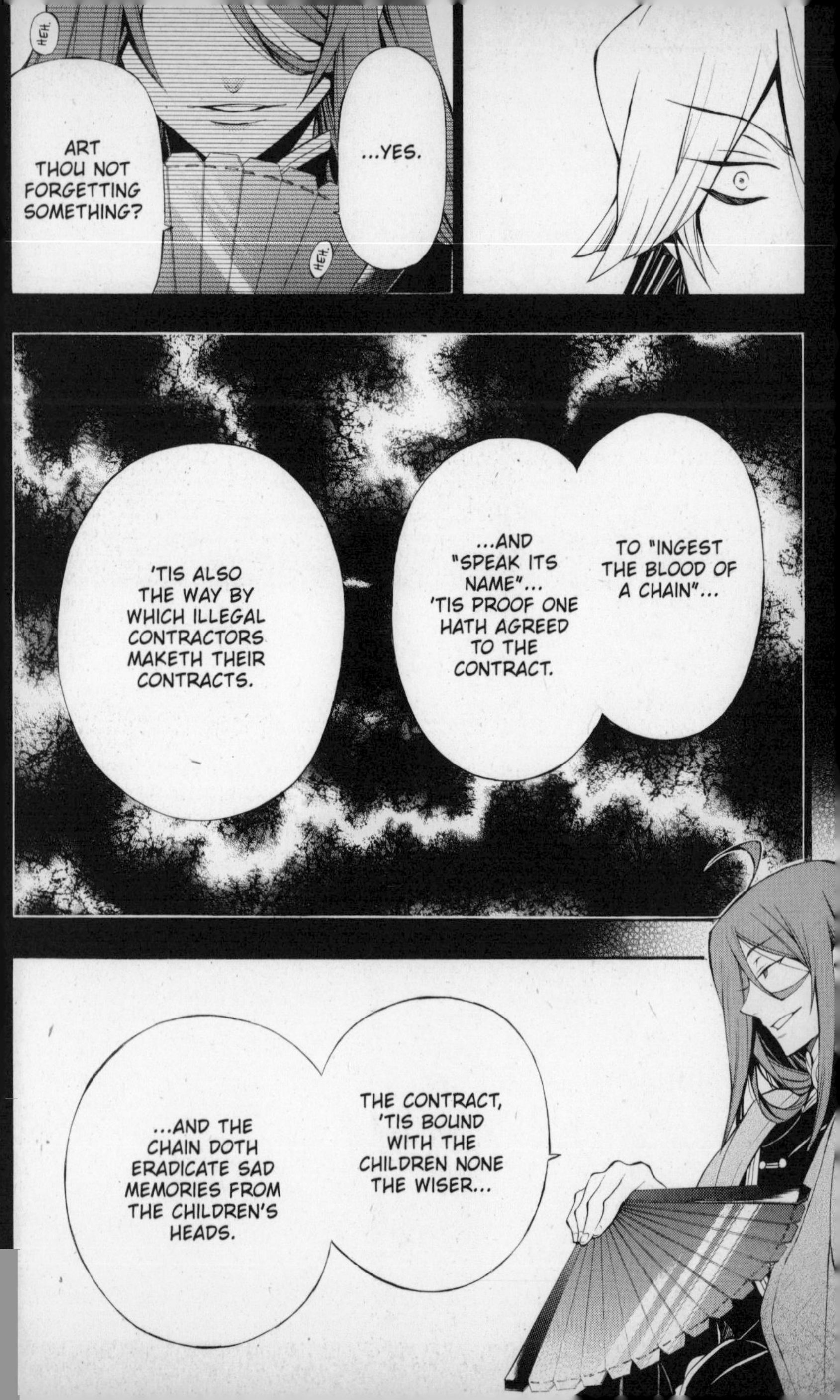
...YES.
HEH.
ART THOU NOT FORGETTING SOMETHING?
HEH.
TO "INGEST THE BLOOD OF A CHAIN"...
...AND "SPEAK ITS NAME"... 'TIS PROOF ONE HATH AGREED TO THE CONTRACT.
'TIS ALSO THE WAY BY WHICH ILLEGAL CONTRACTORS MAKETH THEIR CONTRACTS.
THE CONTRACT, 'TIS BOUND WITH THE CHILDREN NONE THE WISER...
...AND THE CHAIN DOTH ERADICATE SAD MEMORIES FROM THE CHILDREN'S HEADS.

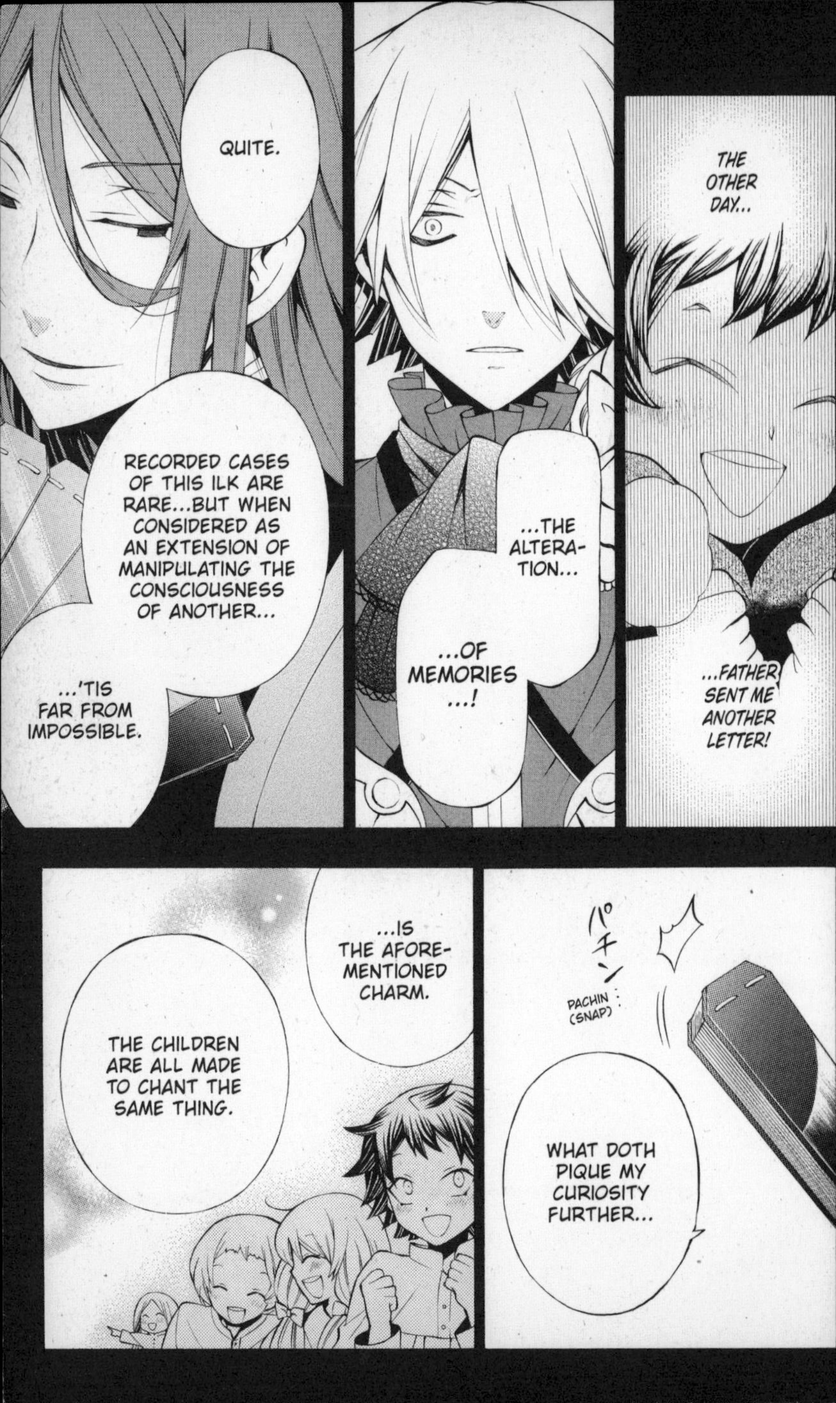
THE OTHER DAY...
...FATHER SENT ME ANOTHER LETTER!
...THE ALTERATION...
...OF MEMORIES...!
QUITE.
RECORDED CASES OF THIS ILK ARE RARE...BUT WHEN CONSIDERED AS AN EXTENSION OF MANIPULATING THE CONSCIOUSNESS OF ANOTHER...
...'TIS FAR FROM IMPOSSIBLE.
パチン
PACHIN (SNAP)
WHAT DOTH PIQUE MY CURIOSITY FURTHER...
...IS THE AFOREMENTIONED CHARM.
THE CHILDREN ARE ALL MADE TO CHANT THE SAME THING.

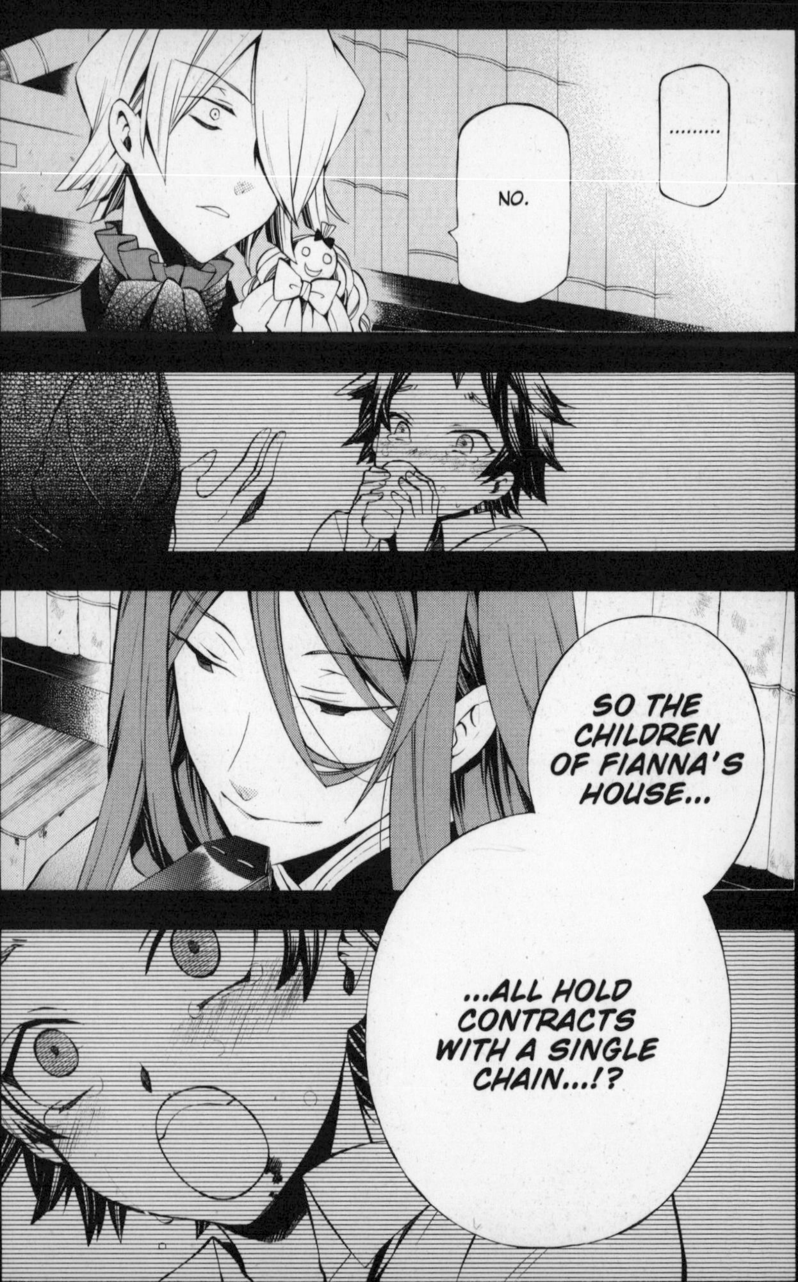
....
NO.
SO THE CHILDREN OF FIANNA'S HOUSE...
...ALL HOLD CONTRACTS WITH A SINGLE CHAIN...!?

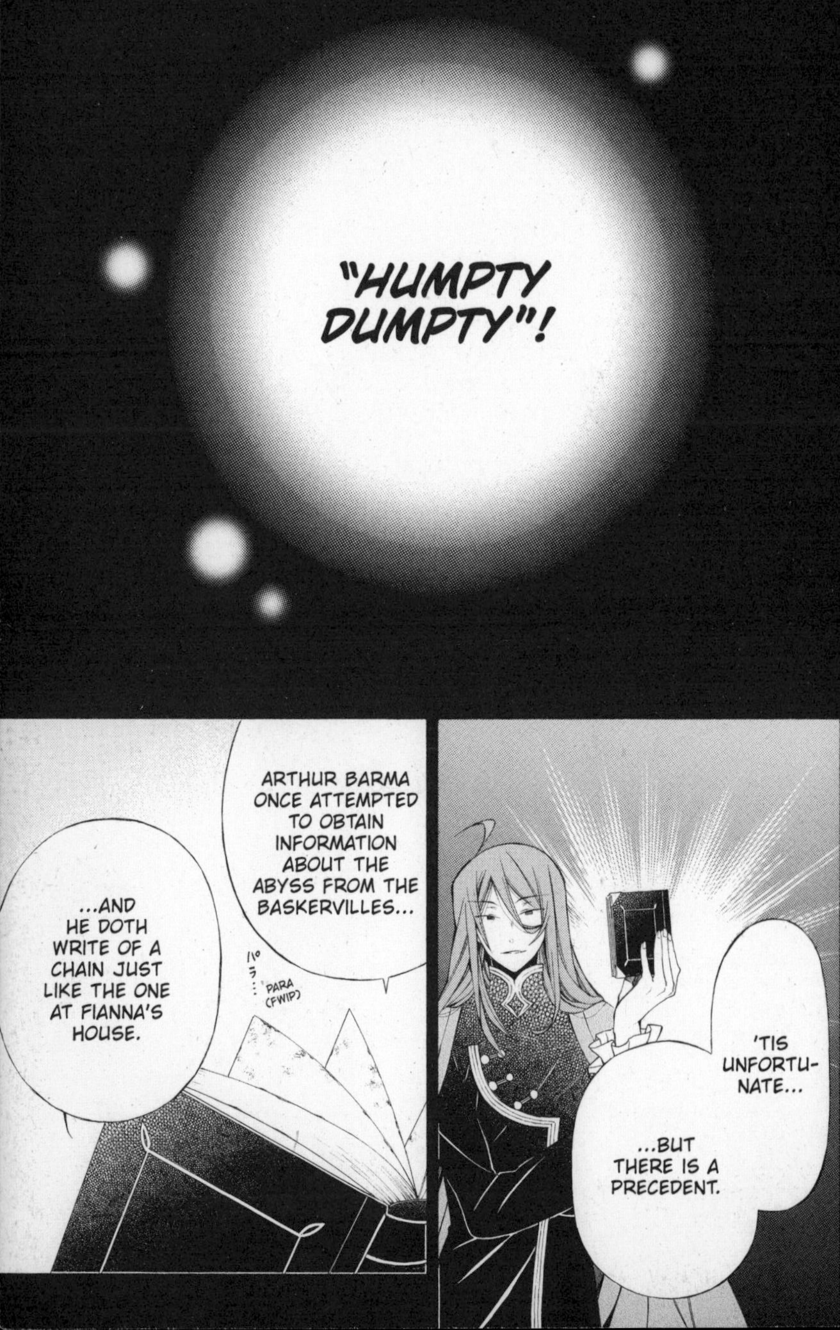
"HUMPTY DUMPTY"!
'TIS UNFORTUNATE...
...BUT THERE IS A PRECEDENT.
ARTHUR BARMA ONCE ATTEMPTED TO OBTAIN INFORMATION ABOUT THE ABYSS FROM THE BASKERVILLES...
...AND HE DOTH WRITE OF A CHAIN JUST LIKE THE ONE AT FIANNA'S HOUSE.
パラ…
PARA (FWIP)

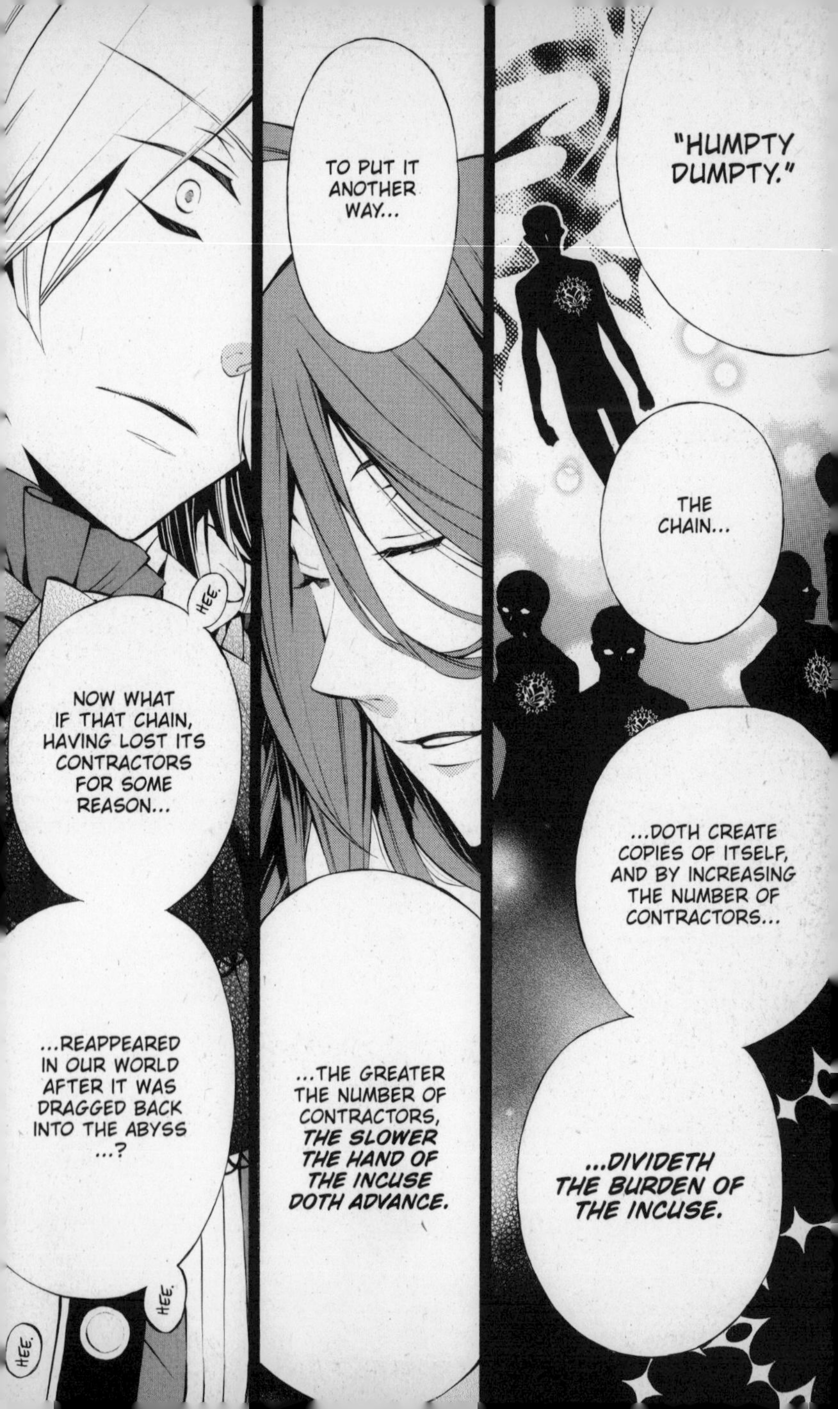
"HUMPTY DUMPTY."
THE CHAIN...
...DOTH CREATE COPIES OF ITSELF, AND BY INCREASING THE NUMBER OF CONTRACTORS...
...DIVIDETH THE BURDEN OF THE INCUSE.
TO PUT IT ANOTHER WAY...
...THE GREATER THE NUMBER OF CONTRACTORS, *THE SLOWER THE HAND OF THE INCUSE DOTH ADVANCE.*
HEE.
NOW WHAT IF THAT CHAIN, HAVING LOST ITS CONTRACTORS FOR SOME REASON...
...REAPPEARED IN OUR WORLD AFTER IT WAS DRAGGED BACK INTO THE ABYSS ...?
HEE.
HEE.

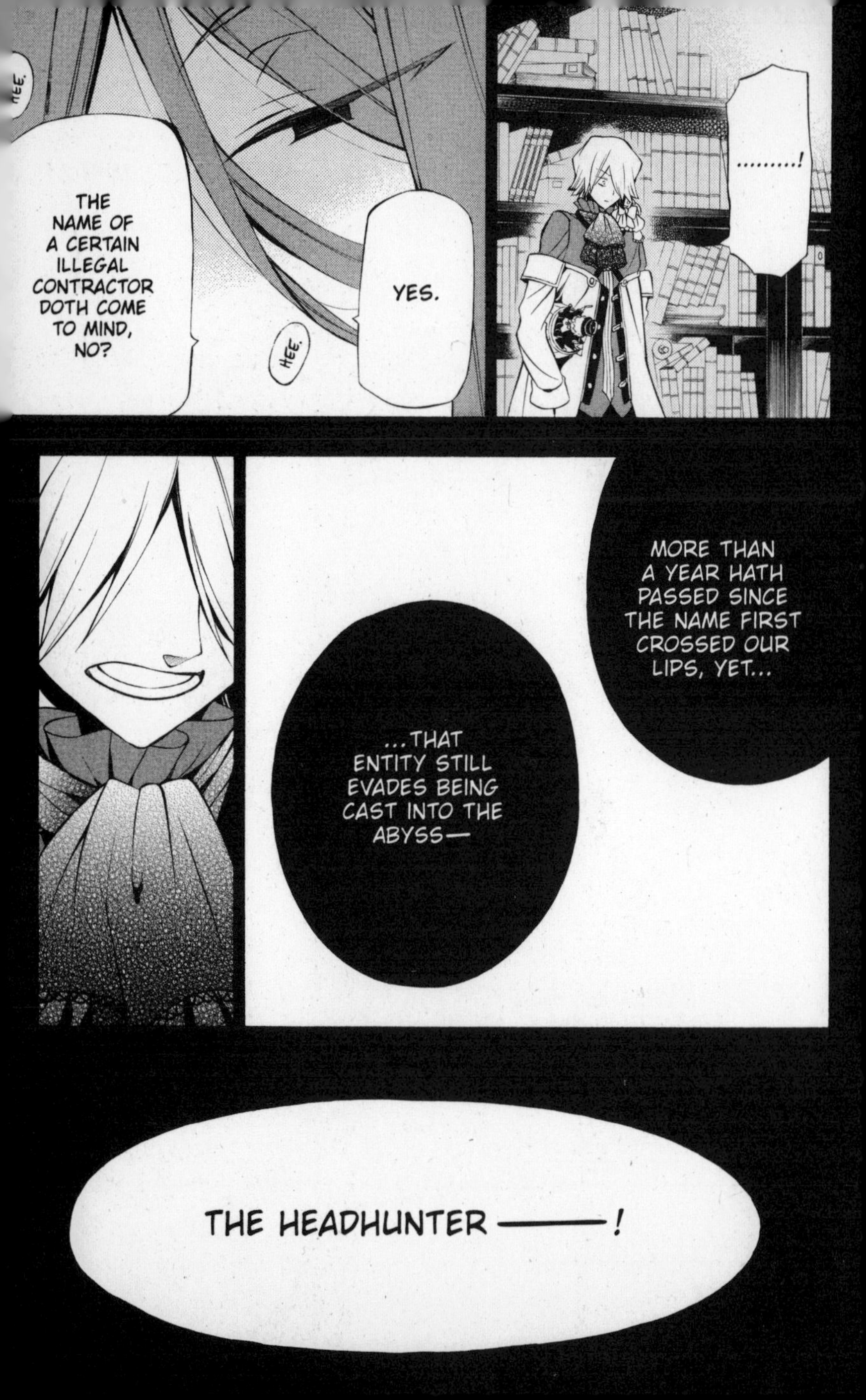
..........!
HEE.
THE NAME OF A CERTAIN ILLEGAL CONTRACTOR DOTH COME TO MIND, NO?
YES.
HEE.
MORE THAN A YEAR HATH PASSED SINCE THE NAME FIRST CROSSED OUR LIPS, YET...
...THAT ENTITY STILL EVADES BEING CAST INTO THE ABYSS—
THE HEADHUNTER——!

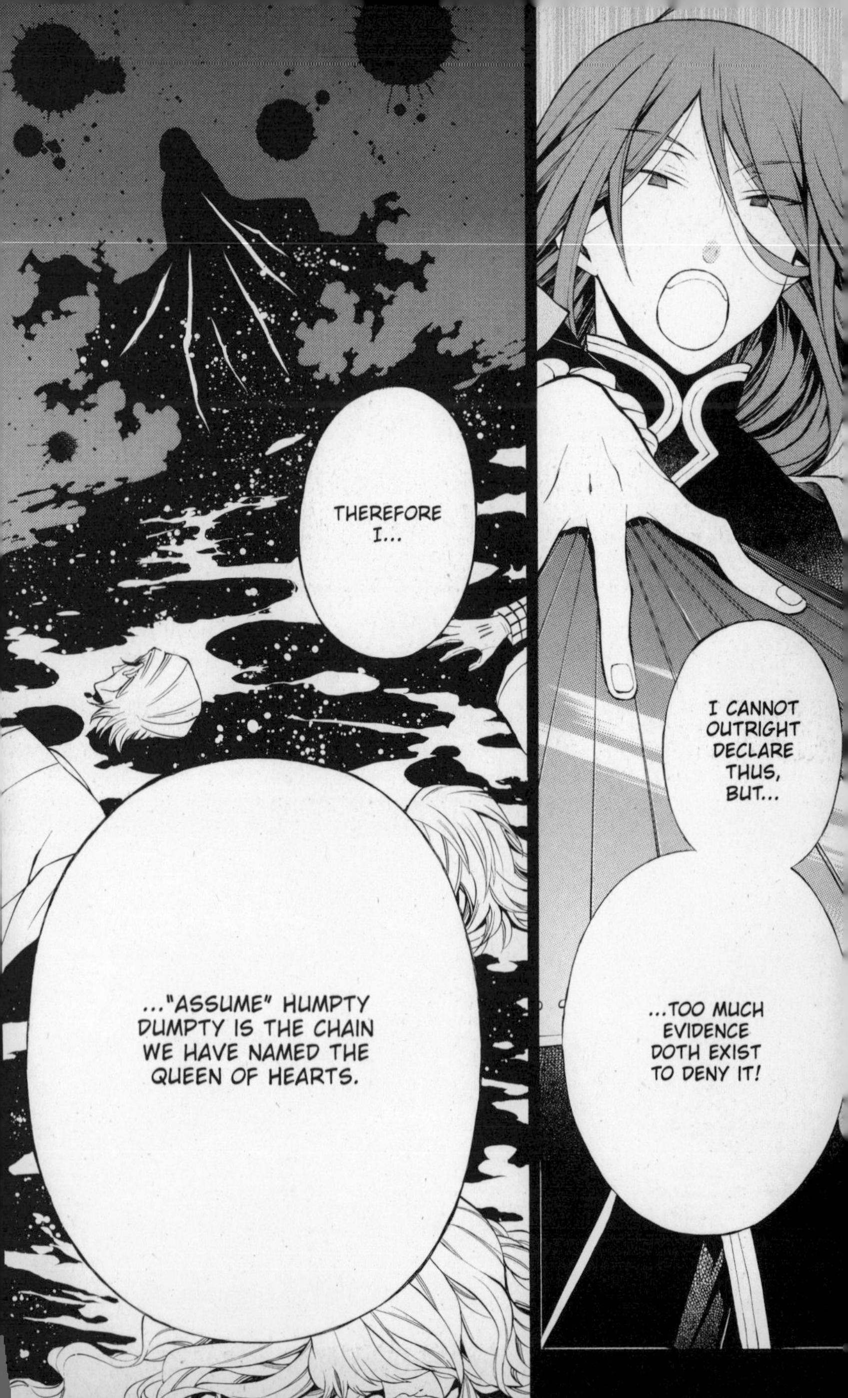
I CANNOT OUTRIGHT DECLARE THUS, BUT...
...TOO MUCH EVIDENCE DOTH EXIST TO DENY IT!
THEREFORE I...
..."ASSUME" HUMPTY DUMPTY IS THE CHAIN WE HAVE NAMED THE QUEEN OF HEARTS.

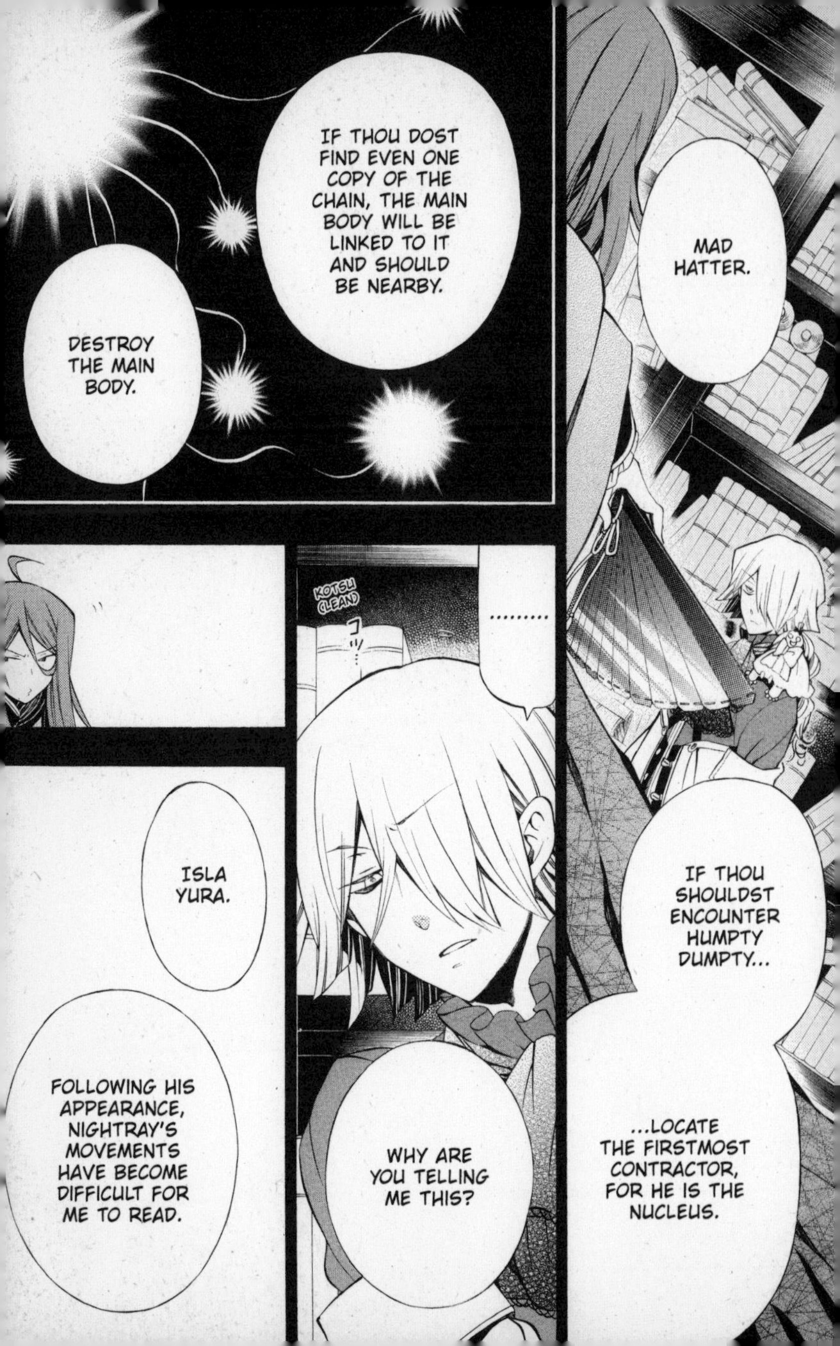
MAD HATTER.
IF THOU SHOULDST ENCOUNTER HUMPTY DUMPTY...
...LOCATE THE FIRSTMOST CONTRACTOR, FOR HE IS THE NUCLEUS.
IF THOU DOST FIND EVEN ONE COPY OF THE CHAIN, THE MAIN BODY WILL BE LINKED TO IT AND SHOULD BE NEARBY.
DESTROY THE MAIN BODY.
KOTSU (CLEAN)
....
WHY ARE YOU TELLING ME THIS?
ISLA YURA.
FOLLOWING HIS APPEARANCE, NIGHTRAY'S MOVEMENTS HAVE BECOME DIFFICULT FOR ME TO READ.

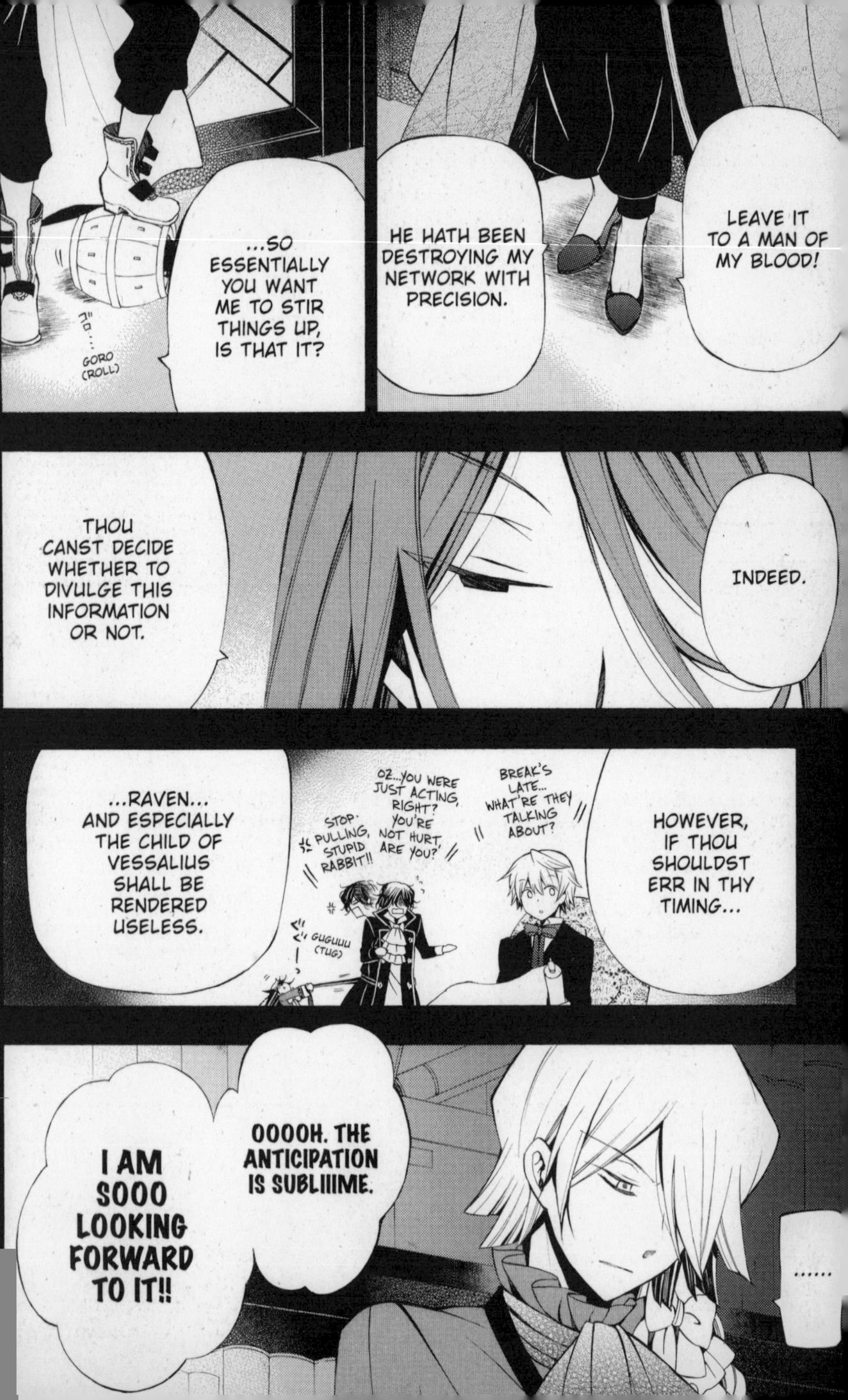
LEAVE IT TO A MAN OF MY BLOOD!
HE HATH BEEN DESTROYING MY NETWORK WITH PRECISION.
...SO ESSENTIALLY YOU WANT ME TO STIR THINGS UP, IS THAT IT?
ゴロ…
GORO (ROLL)
INDEED.
THOU CANST DECIDE WHETHER TO DIVULGE THIS INFORMATION OR NOT.
HOWEVER, IF THOU SHOULDST ERR IN THY TIMING...
BREAK'S LATE... WHAT'RE THEY TALKING ABOUT?
OZ...YOU WERE JUST ACTING, RIGHT? YOU'RE NOT HURT, ARE YOU?
STOP PULLING, STUPID RABBIT!!
GUGUUU (TUG)
...RAVEN... AND ESPECIALLY THE CHILD OF VESSALIUS SHALL BE RENDERED USELESS.
......
OOOOH. THE ANTICIPATION IS SUBLIIIME.
I AM SOOO LOOKING FORWARD TO IT!!

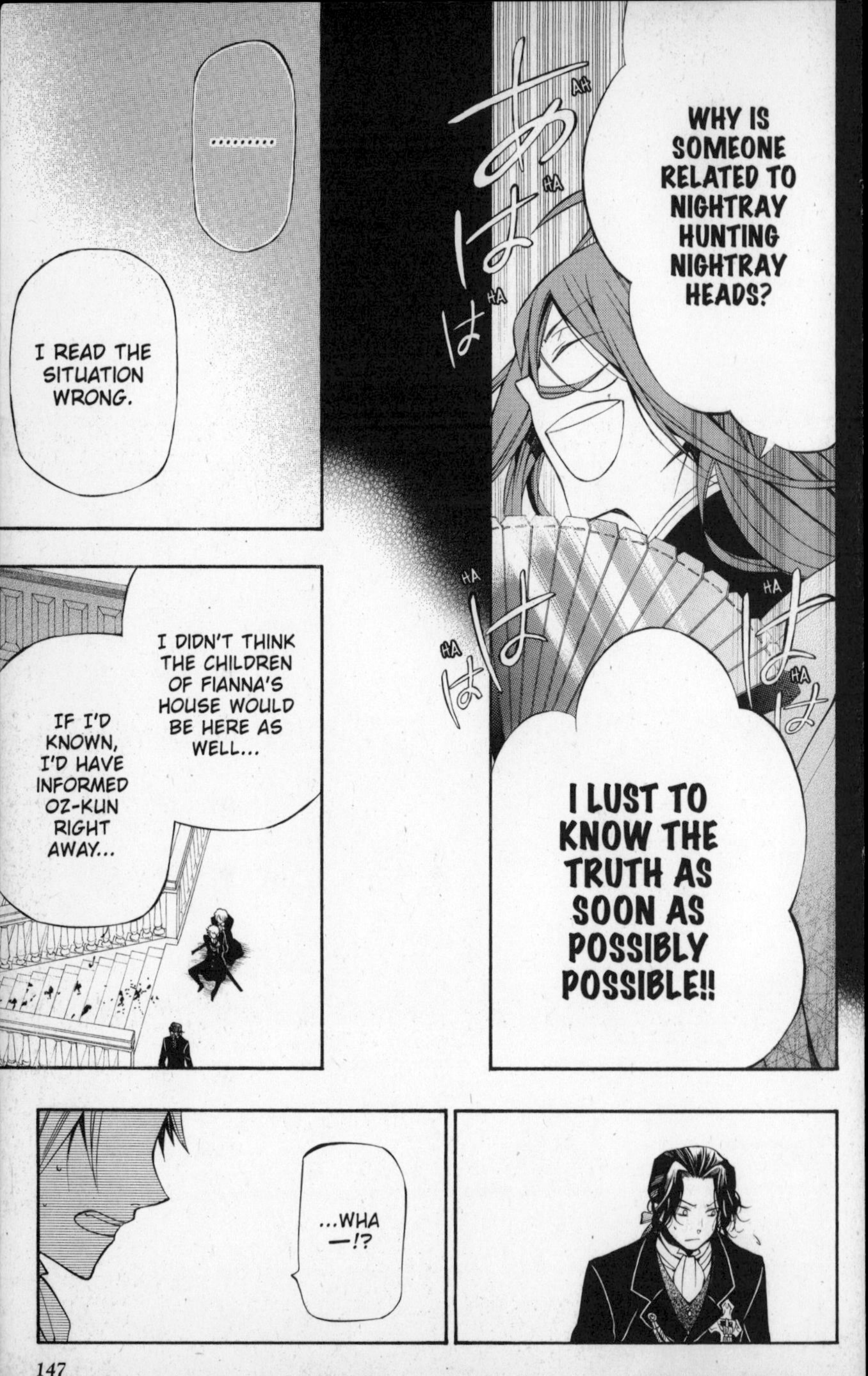

あ AH
は HA
は HA
WHY IS SOMEONE RELATED TO NIGHTRAY HUNTING NIGHTRAY HEADS?
は HA
は HA
は HA
は HA
I LUST TO KNOW THE TRUTH AS SOON AS POSSIBLY POSSIBLE!!
....
I READ THE SITUATION WRONG.
I DIDN'T THINK THE CHILDREN OF FIANNA'S HOUSE WOULD BE HERE AS WELL...
IF I'D KNOWN, I'D HAVE INFORMED OZ-KUN RIGHT AWAY...
...WHA—!?

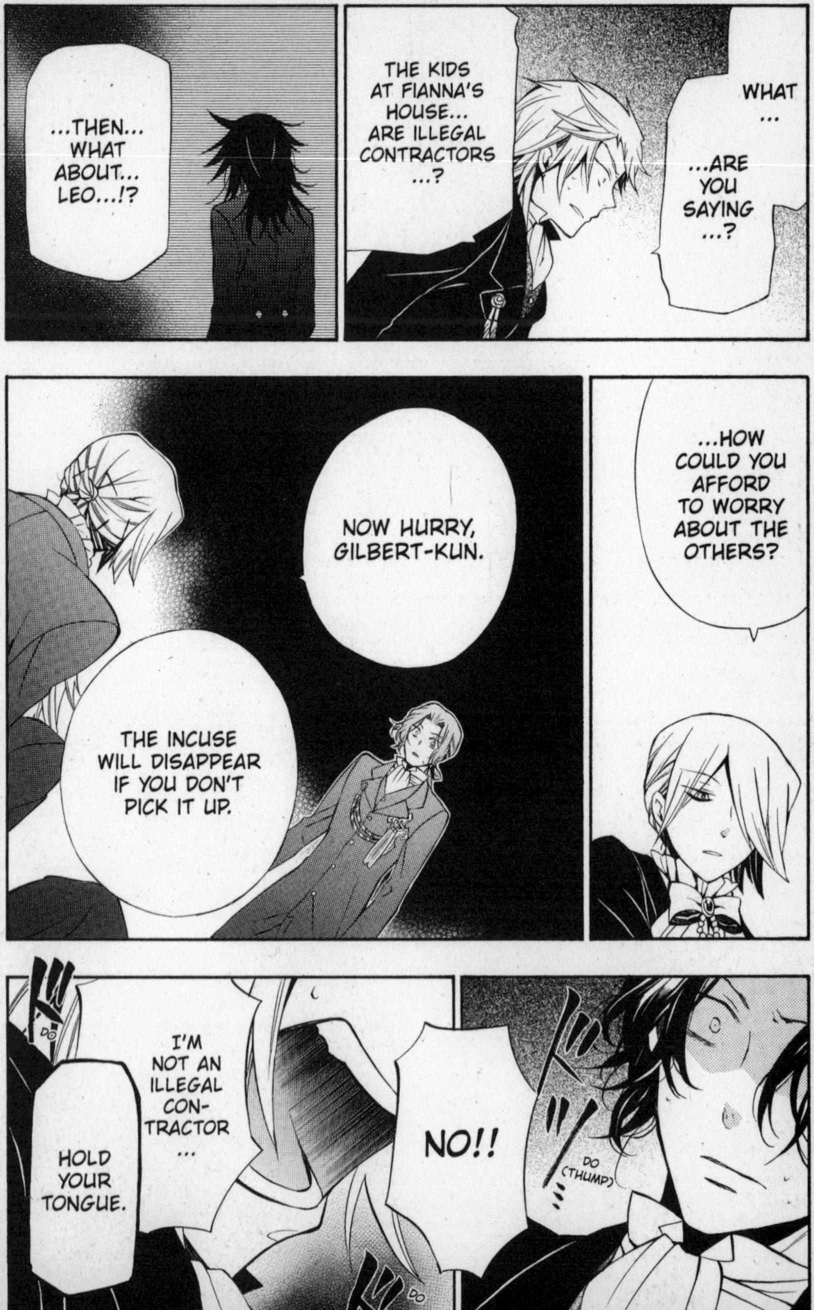
WHAT ... ...ARE YOU SAYING ...?
THE KIDS AT FIANNA'S HOUSE... ARE ILLEGAL CONTRACTORS ...?
...THEN... WHAT ABOUT... LEO...!?
...HOW COULD YOU AFFORD TO WORRY ABOUT THE OTHERS?
NOW HURRY, GILBERT-KUN.
THE INCUSE WILL DISAPPEAR IF YOU DON'T PICK IT UP.
DO (THUMP)
NO!!
I'M NOT AN ILLEGAL CONTRACTOR ...
HOLD YOUR TONGUE.
DO
DO

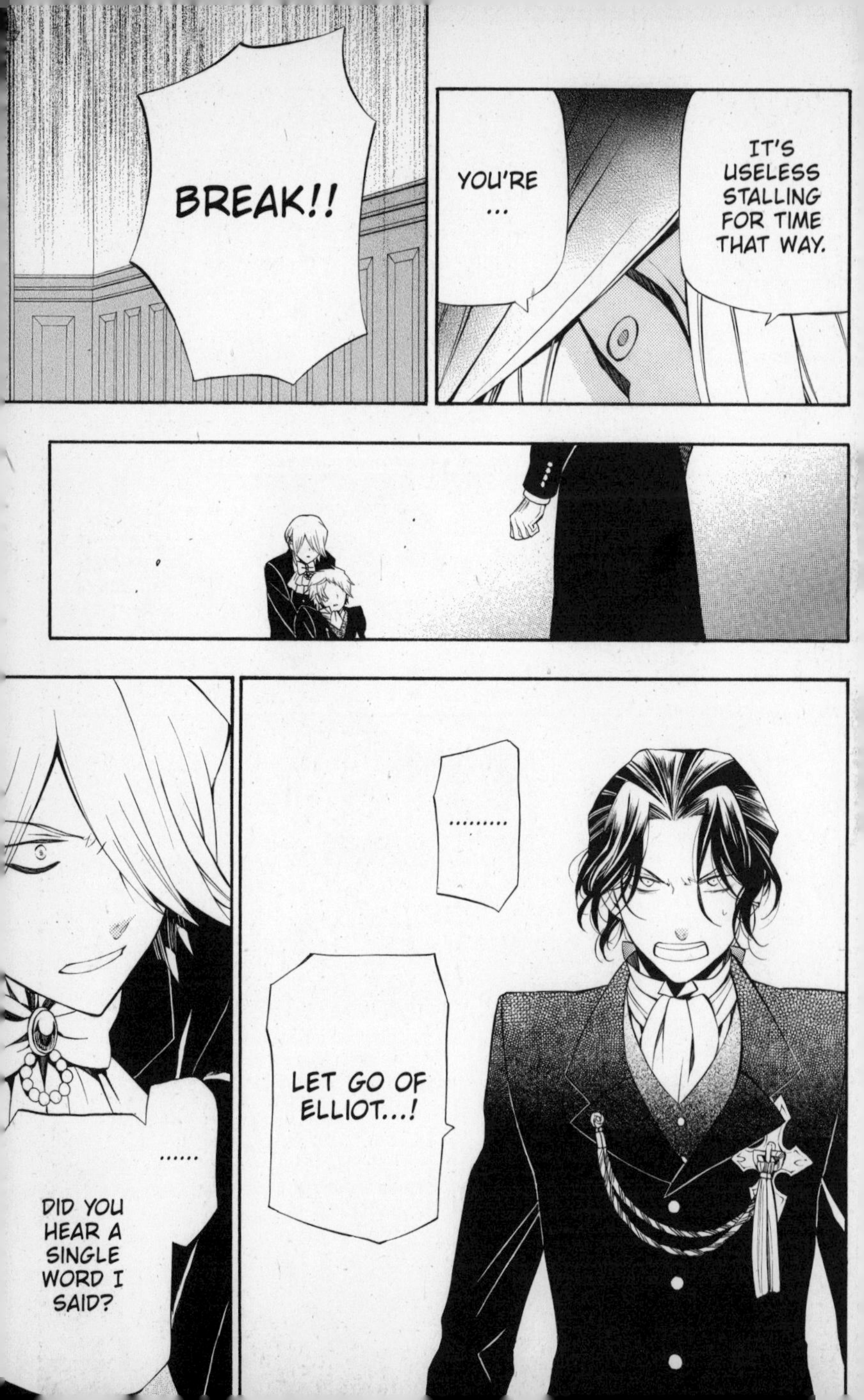
IT'S USELESS STALLING FOR TIME THAT WAY.
YOU'RE ...
BREAK!!
....
LET GO OF ELLIOT...!
......
DID YOU HEAR A SINGLE WORD I SAID?

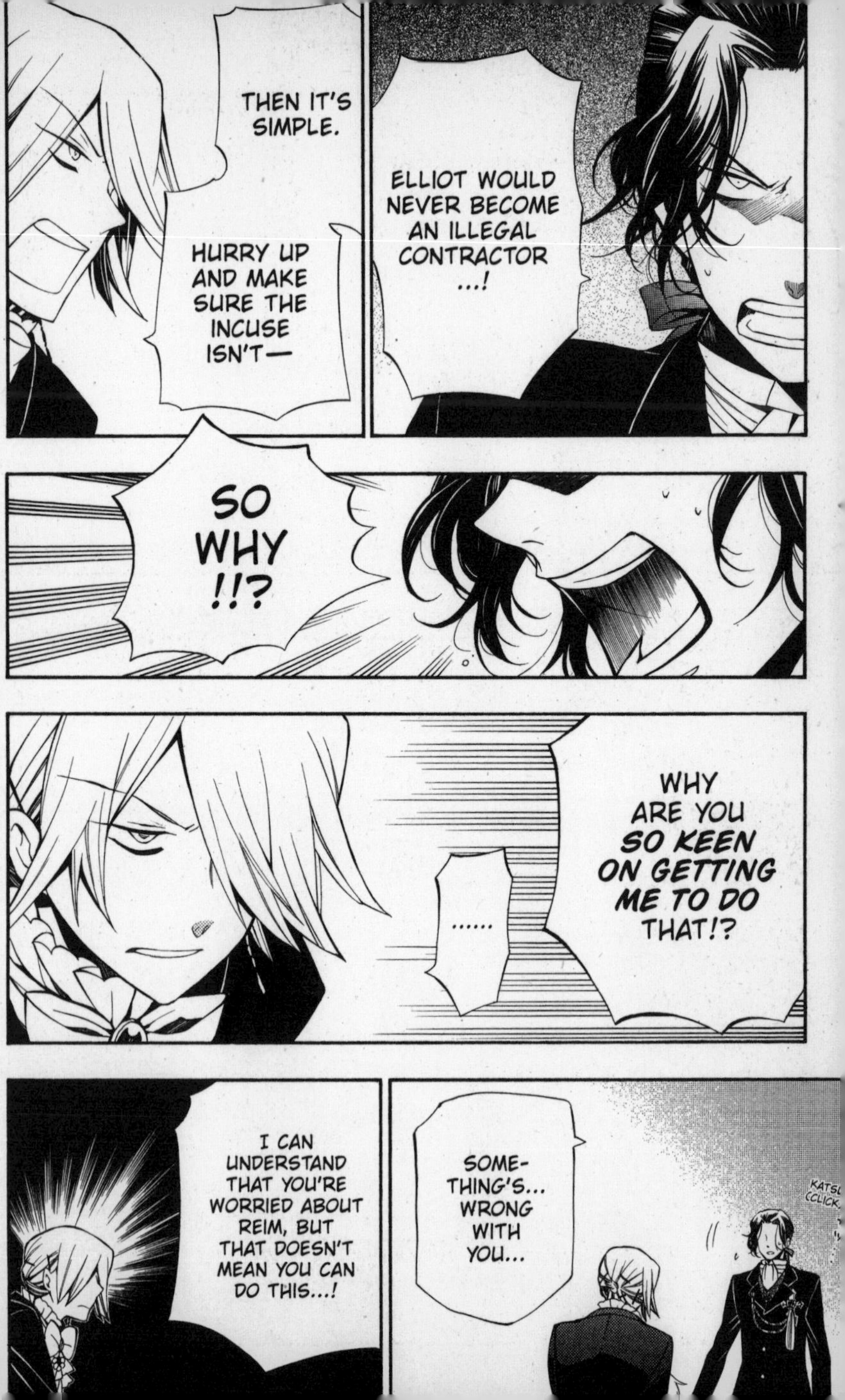
ELLIOT WOULD NEVER BECOME AN ILLEGAL CONTRACTOR ...!
THEN IT'S SIMPLE.
HURRY UP AND MAKE SURE THE INCUSE ISN'T—
SO WHY !!?
WHY ARE YOU SO KEEN ON GETTING ME TO DO THAT!?
......
SOME-THING'S... WRONG WITH YOU...
I CAN UNDERSTAND THAT YOU'RE WORRIED ABOUT REIM, BUT THAT DOESN'T MEAN YOU CAN DO THIS...!

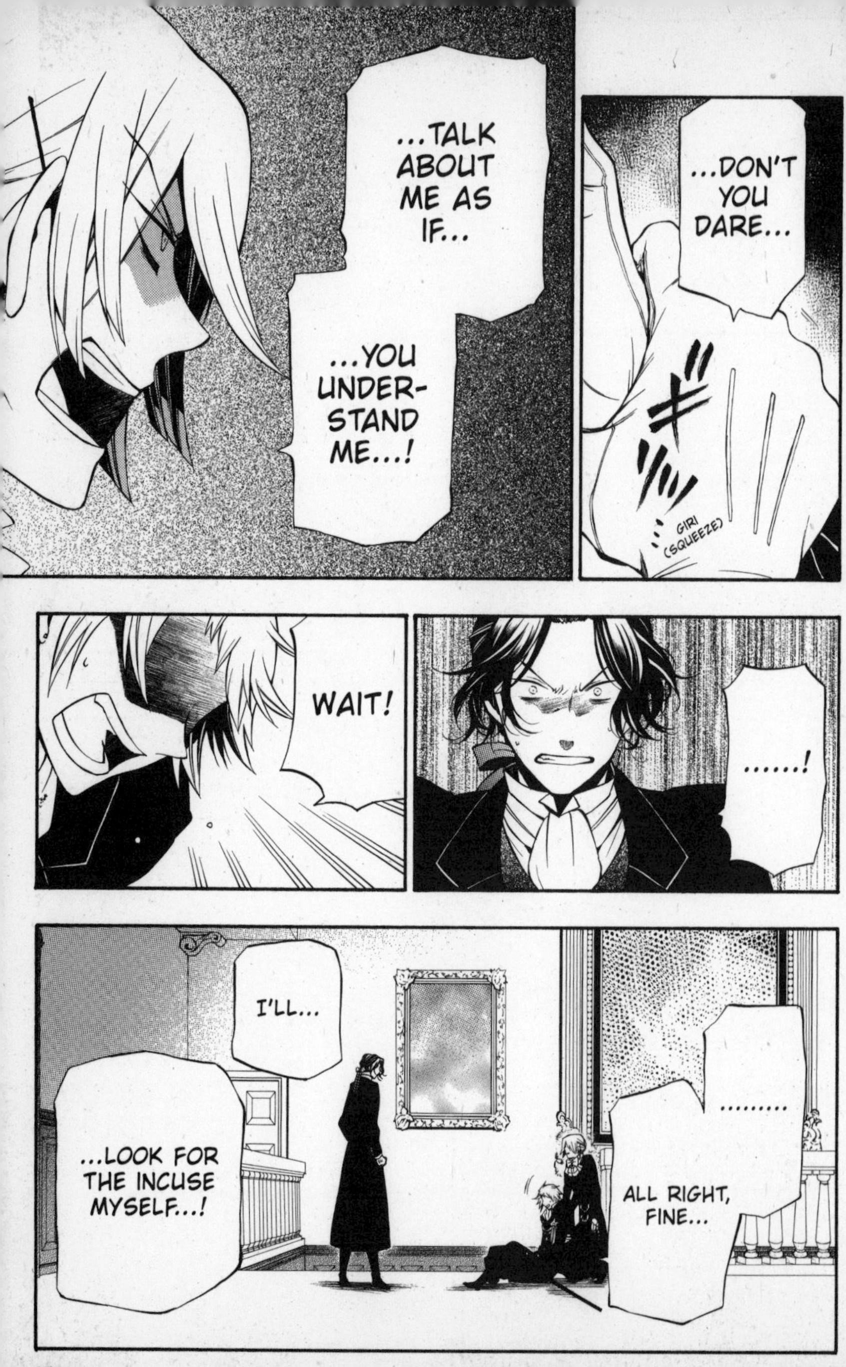
...DON'T YOU DARE...
GIRI (SQUEEZE)
...TALK ABOUT ME AS IF...
...YOU UNDERSTAND ME...!
......!
WAIT!
....
ALL RIGHT, FINE...
I'LL...
...LOOK FOR THE INCUSE MYSELF...!

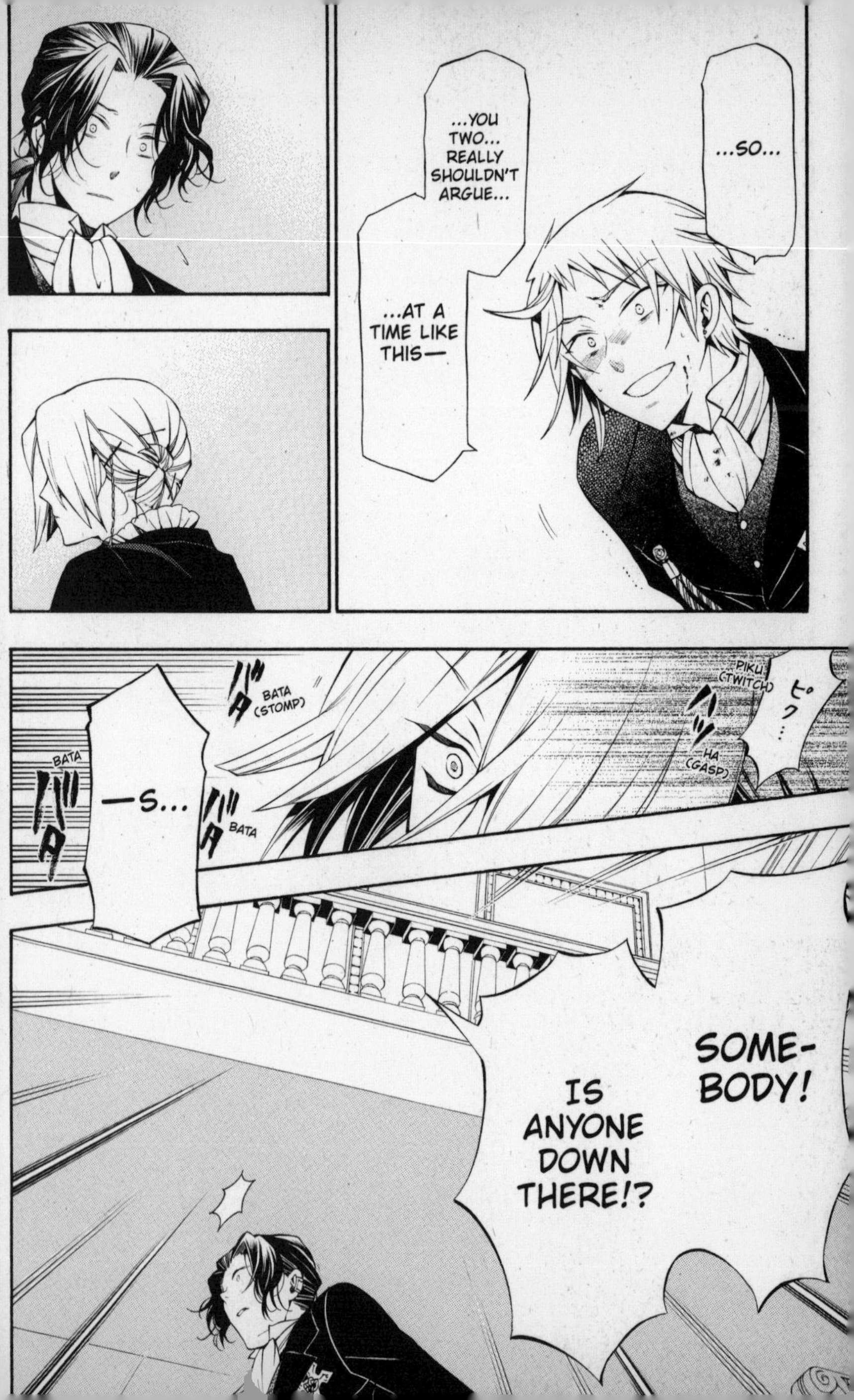
...SO...
...YOU TWO... REALLY SHOULDN'T ARGUE...
...AT A TIME LIKE THIS—
ピク...
PIKU (TWITCH)
HA (GASP)
BATA (STOMP)
—S...
BATA
BATA
SOME-BODY!
IS ANYONE DOWN THERE!?

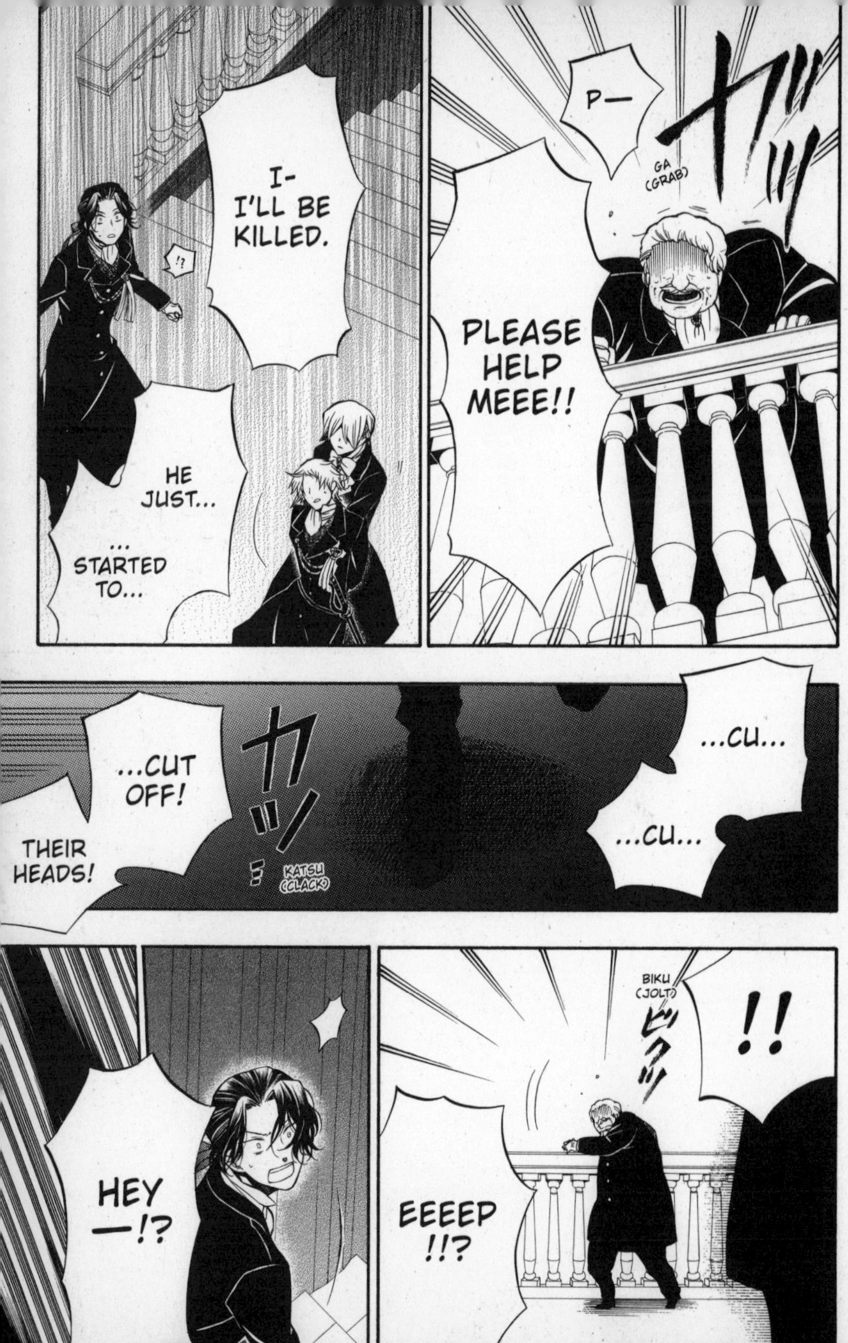
P—
GA (GRAB)
PLEASE HELP MEEE!!
I- I'LL BE KILLED.
!?
HE JUST...
... STARTED TO...
...CU...
...CU...
KATSU (CLACK)
...CUT OFF!
THEIR HEADS!
BIKU (JOLT)
!!
EEEEP !!?
HEY—!?

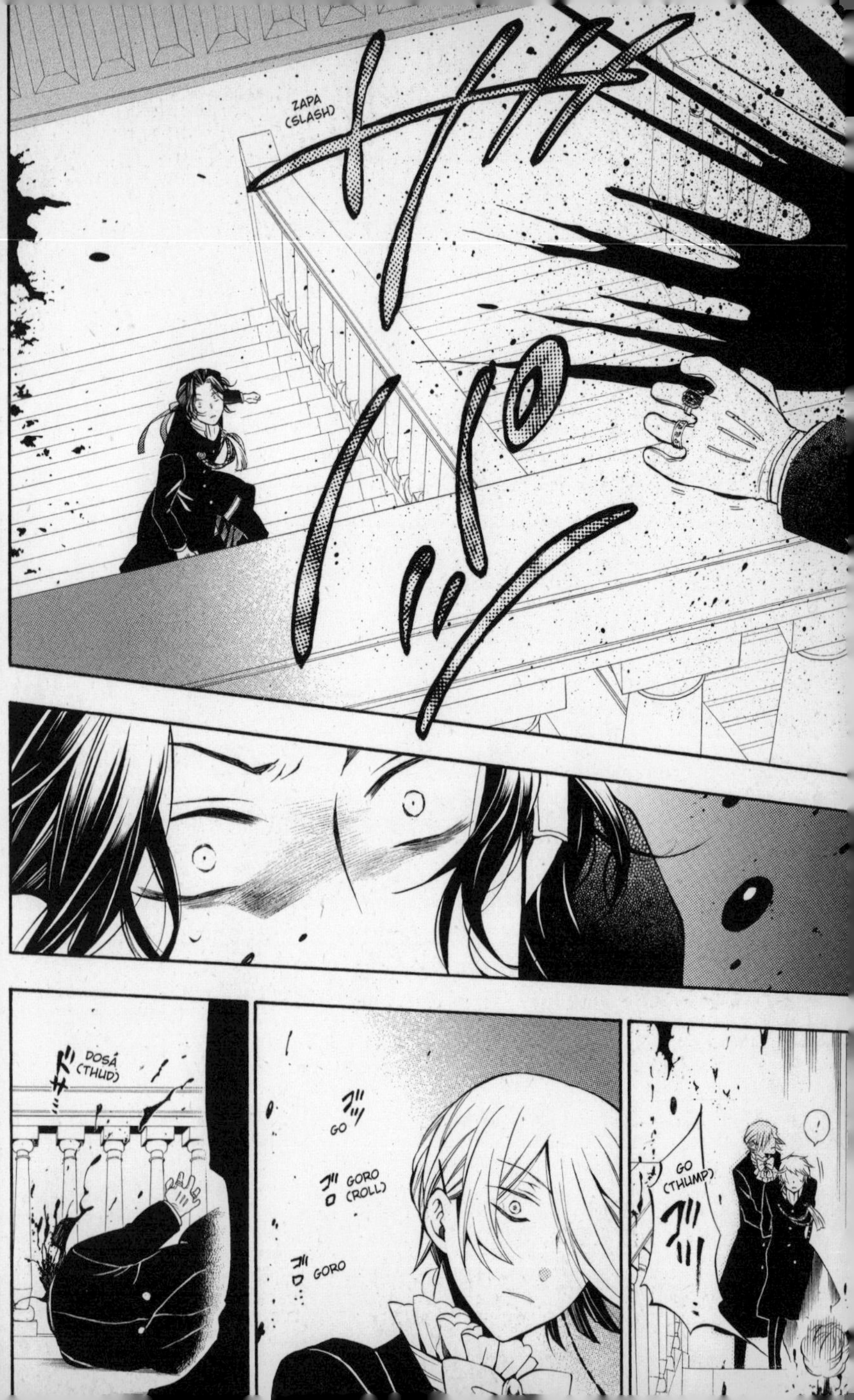
ZAPA (SLASH)
!
GO (THUMP)
GO
GORO (ROLL)
GORO
DOSA (THUD)

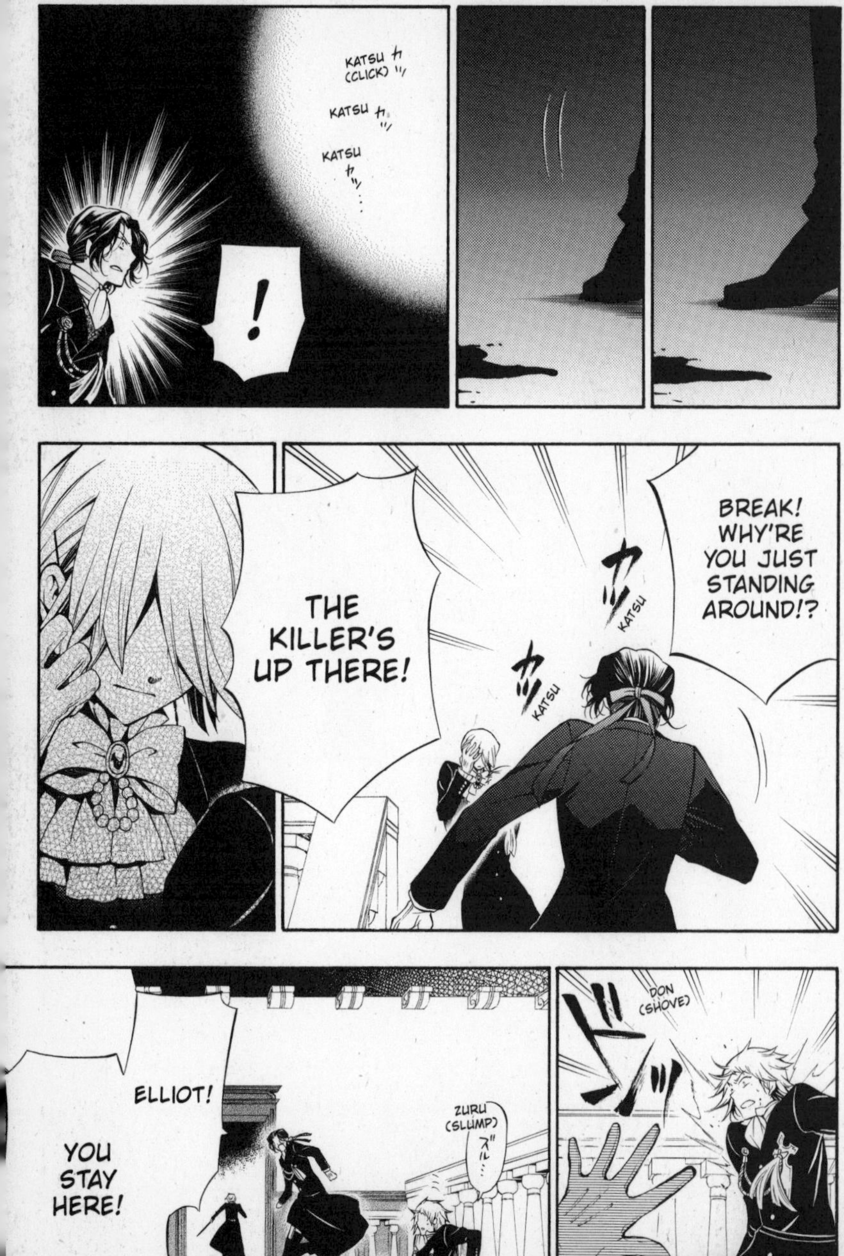
KATSU カッ (CLICK)
KATSU カッ
KATSU カッ...
!
BREAK! WHY'RE YOU JUST STANDING AROUND!?
カッ KATSU
カッ KATSU
THE KILLER'S UP THERE!
DON (SHOVE)
ドンッ
ZURU (SLUMP) ズル...
ELLIOT!
YOU STAY HERE!

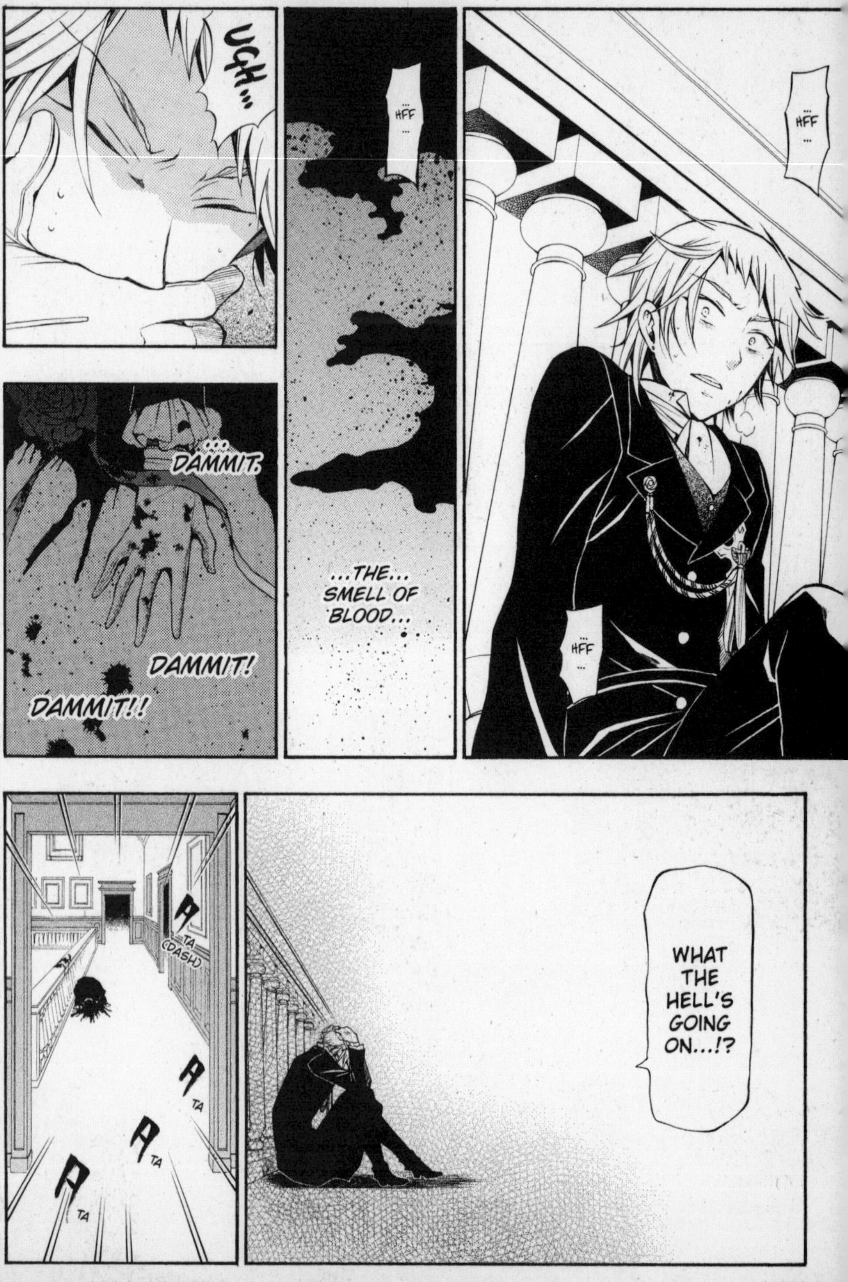
...HFF...
...HFF...
...HFF...
...THE... SMELL OF BLOOD...
UGH...
...DAMMIT.
DAMMIT!
DAMMIT!!
WHAT THE HELL'S GOING ON...!?
TA (DASH)
TA
TA
TA

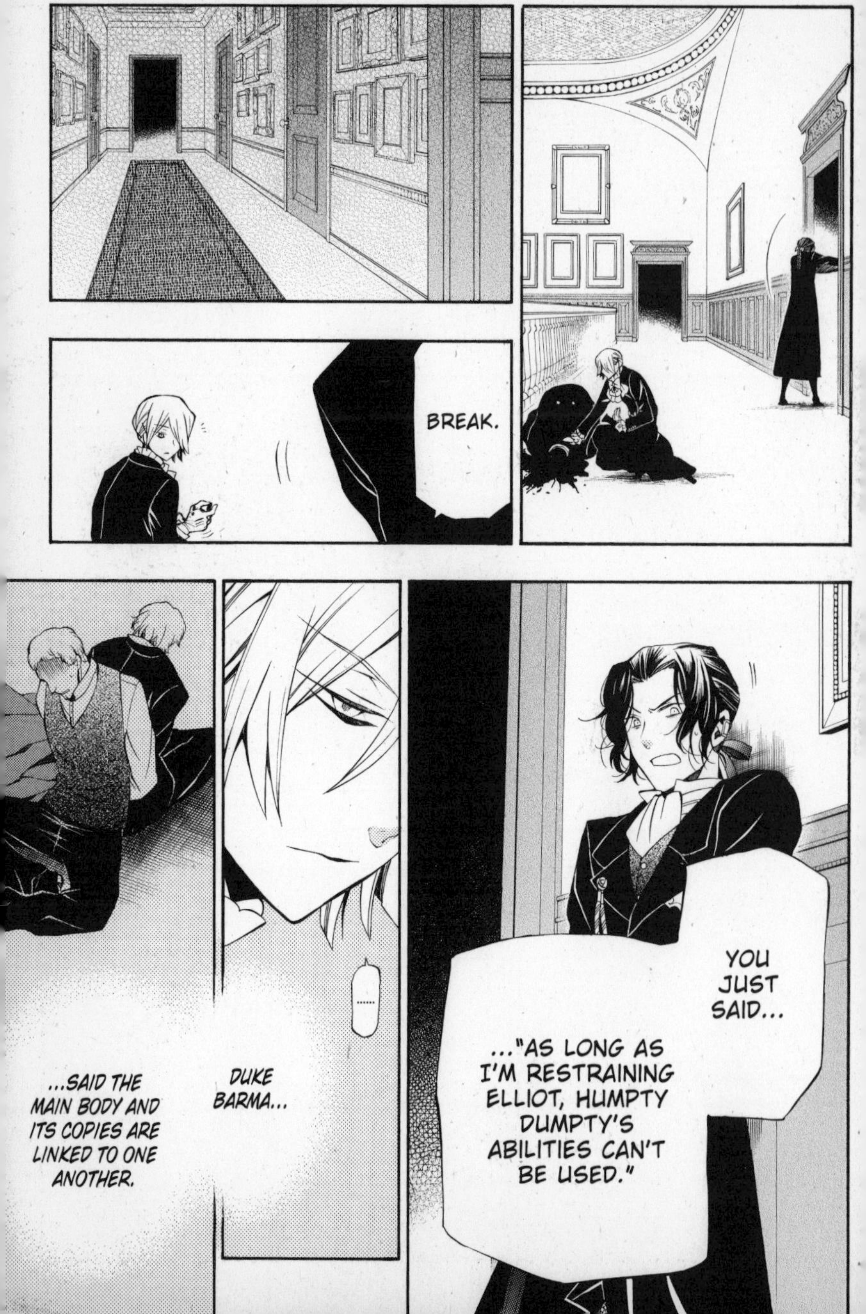
BREAK.
YOU JUST SAID...
..."AS LONG AS I'M RESTRAINING ELLIOT, HUMPTY DUMPTY'S ABILITIES CAN'T BE USED."
......
DUKE BARMA...
...SAID THE MAIN BODY AND ITS COPIES ARE LINKED TO ONE ANOTHER.

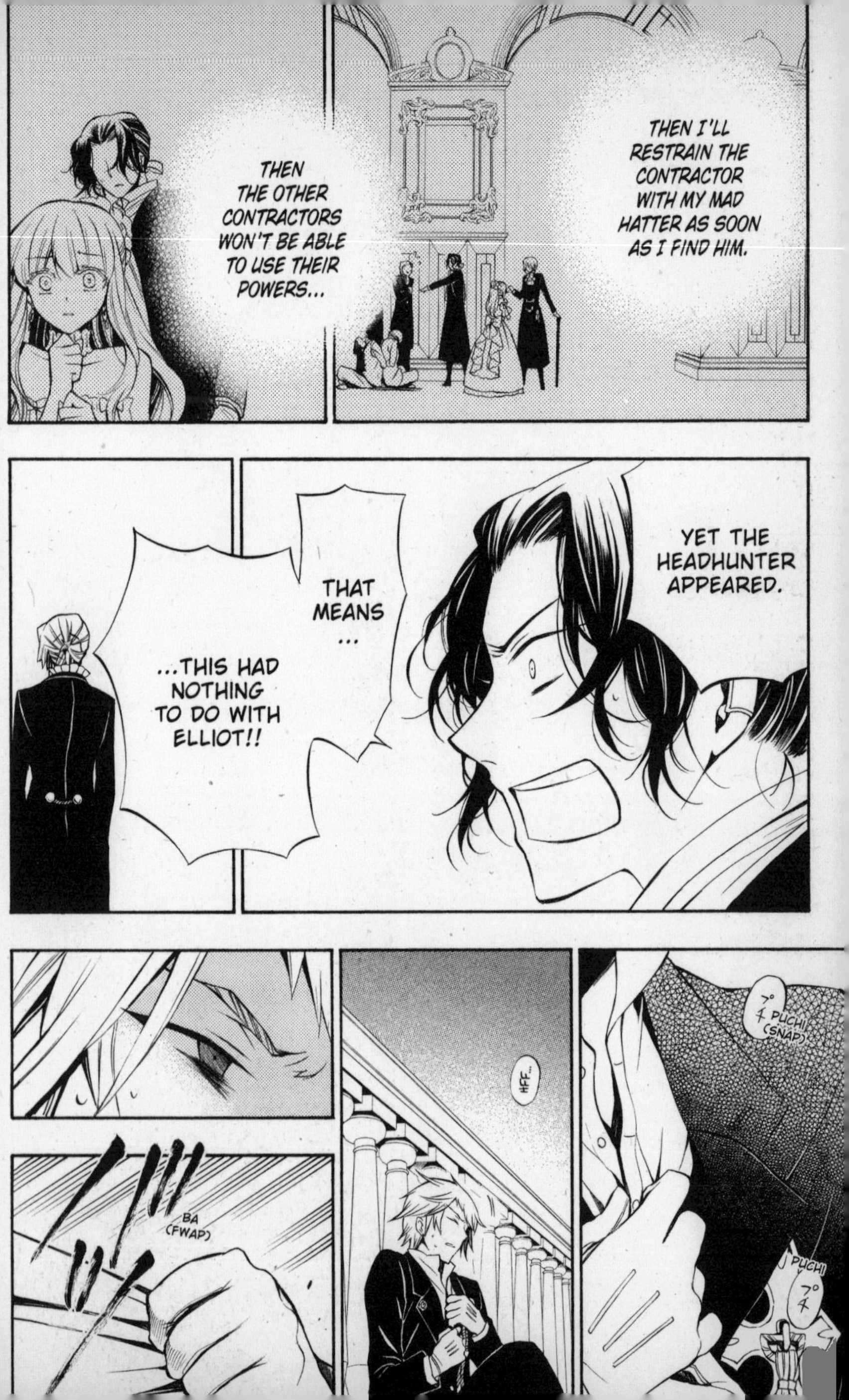
THEN I'LL RESTRAIN THE CONTRACTOR WITH MY MAD HATTER AS SOON AS I FIND HIM.
THEN THE OTHER CONTRACTORS WON'T BE ABLE TO USE THEIR POWERS...
YET THE HEADHUNTER APPEARED.
THAT MEANS ...
...THIS HAD NOTHING TO DO WITH ELLIOT!!
プチ PUCHI (SNAP)
PUCHI プチ
HFF...
BA (FWAP)

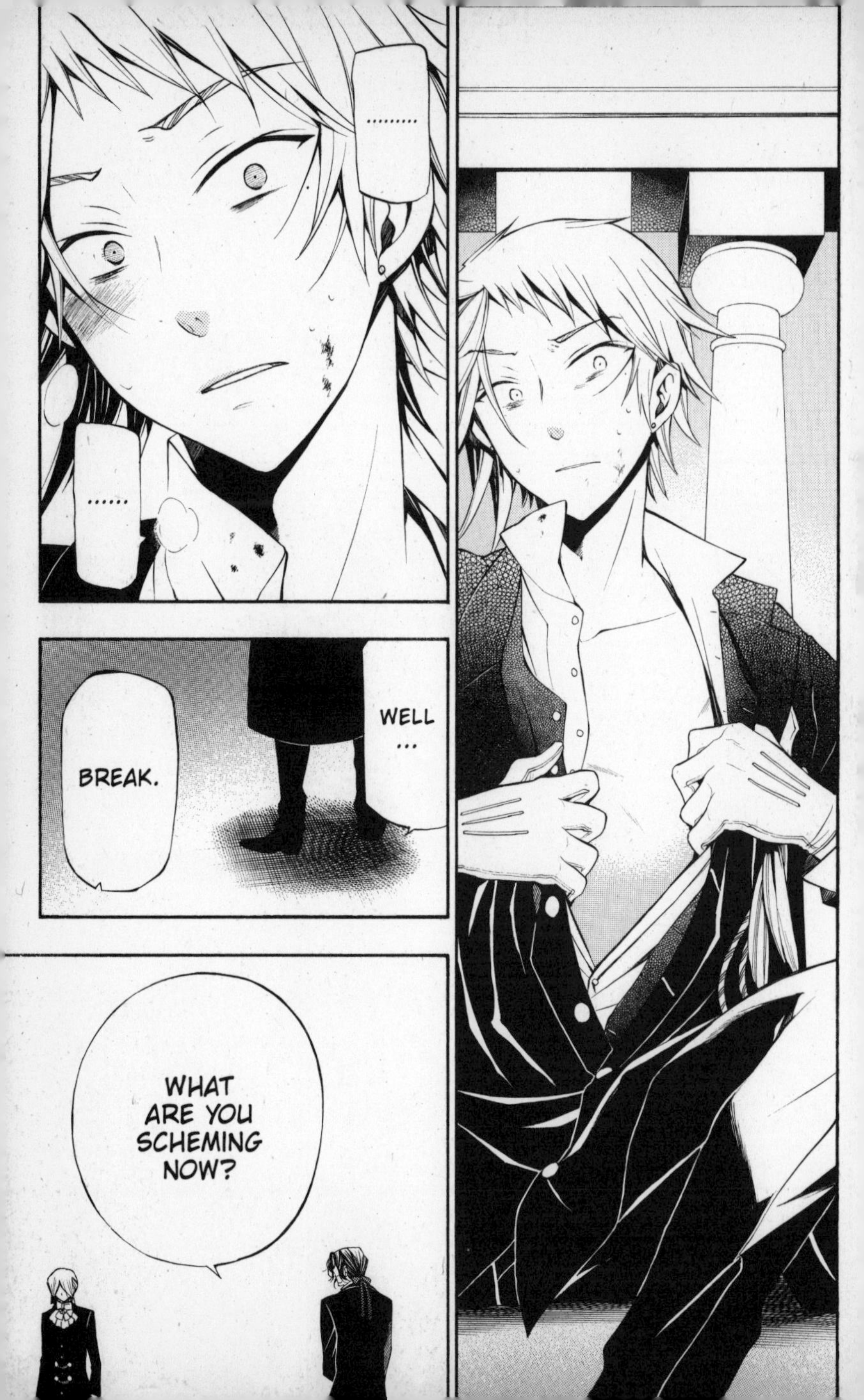
....
......
WELL ...
BREAK.
WHAT ARE YOU SCHEMING NOW?

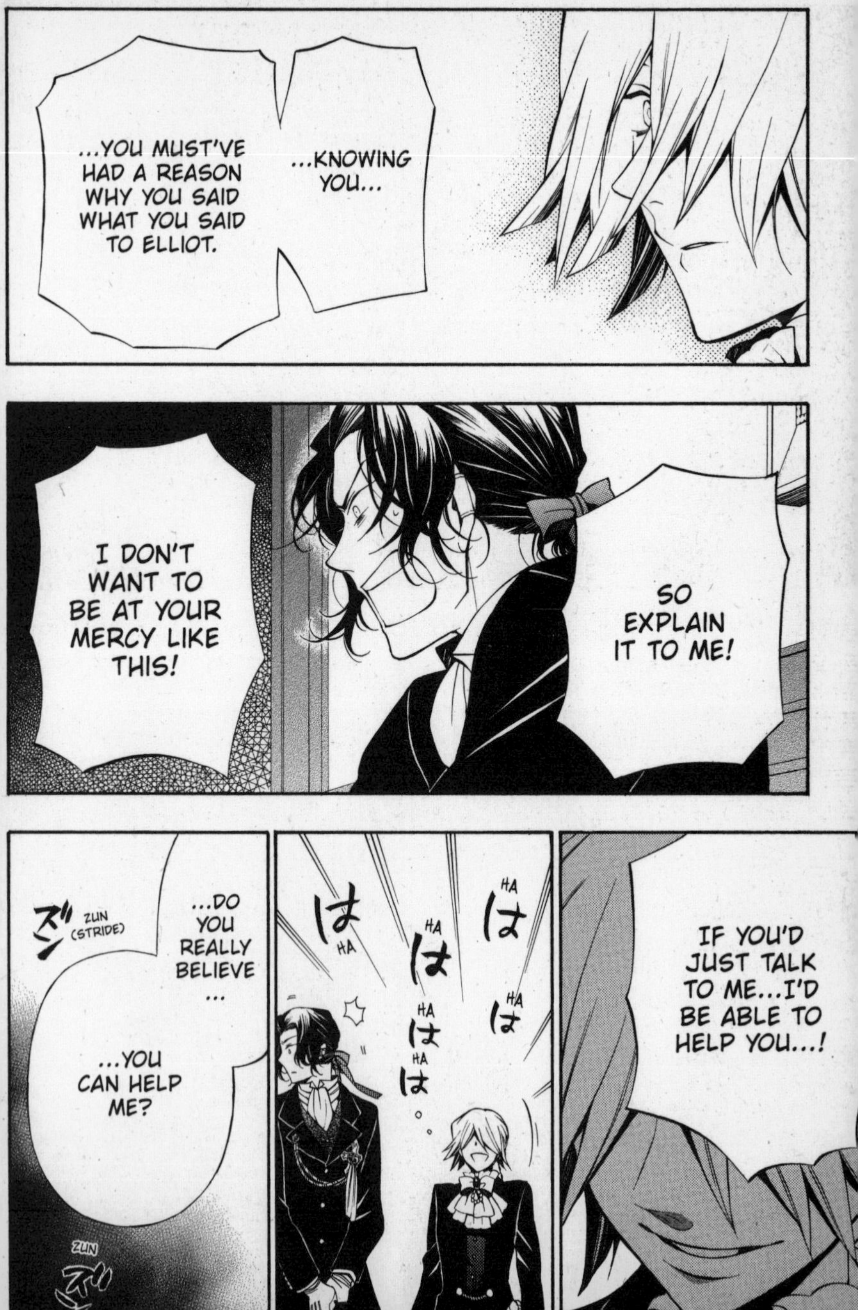
...KNOWING YOU...
...YOU MUST'VE HAD A REASON WHY YOU SAID WHAT YOU SAID TO ELLIOT.
SO EXPLAIN IT TO ME!
I DON'T WANT TO BE AT YOUR MERCY LIKE THIS!
IF YOU'D JUST TALK TO ME...I'D BE ABLE TO HELP YOU...!
は HA
は HA
は HA
は HA
は HA
は HA
...DO YOU REALLY BELIEVE ...
ズン ZUN (STRIDE)
...YOU CAN HELP ME?
ZUN ズン

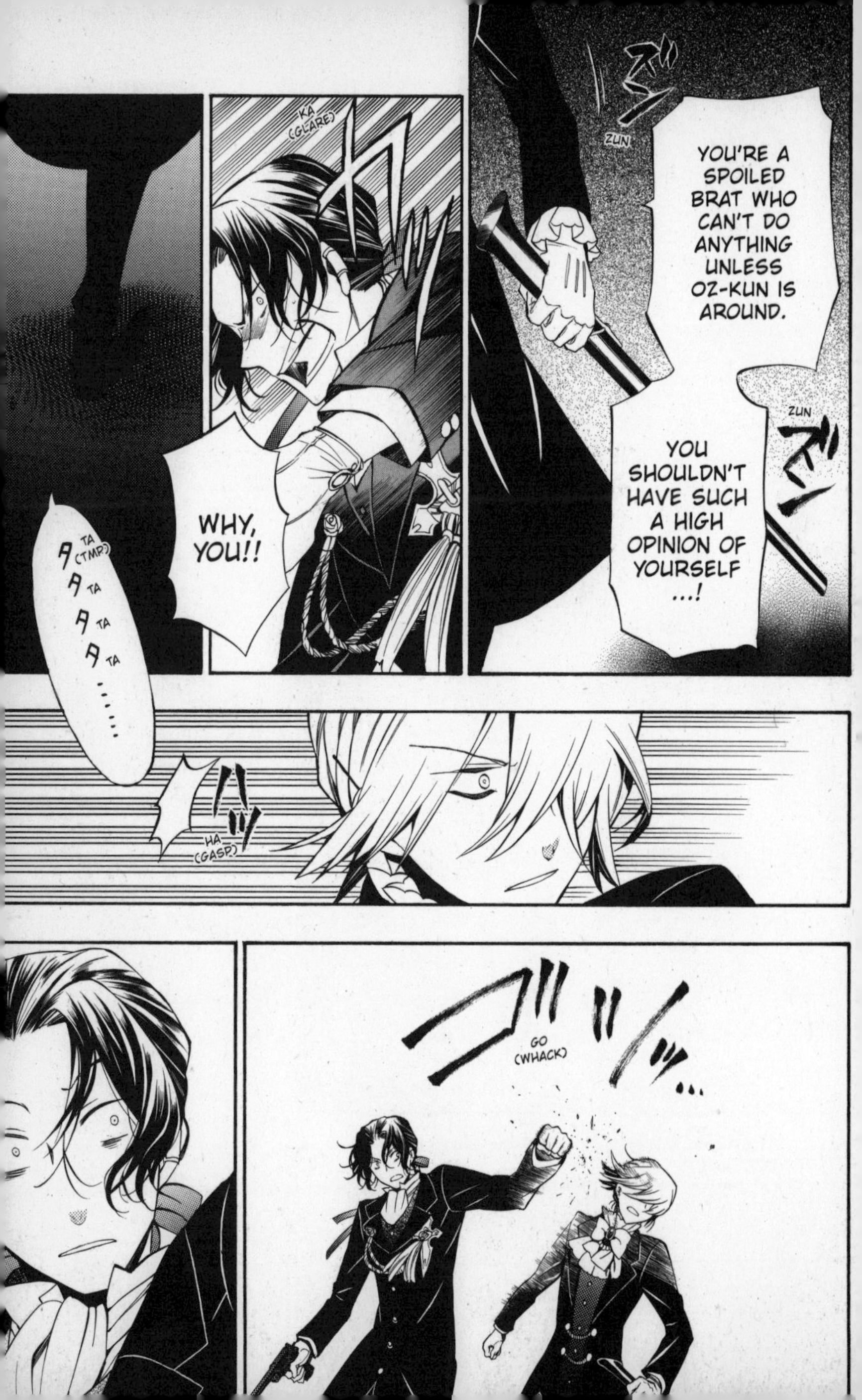
ZUN
YOU'RE A SPOILED BRAT WHO CAN'T DO ANYTHING UNLESS OZ-KUN IS AROUND.
ZUN
YOU SHOULDN'T HAVE SUCH A HIGH OPINION OF YOURSELF ...!
KA (GLARE)
WHY, YOU!!
TA (TMP) TA TA TA ......
HA (GASP)
GO (WHACK)

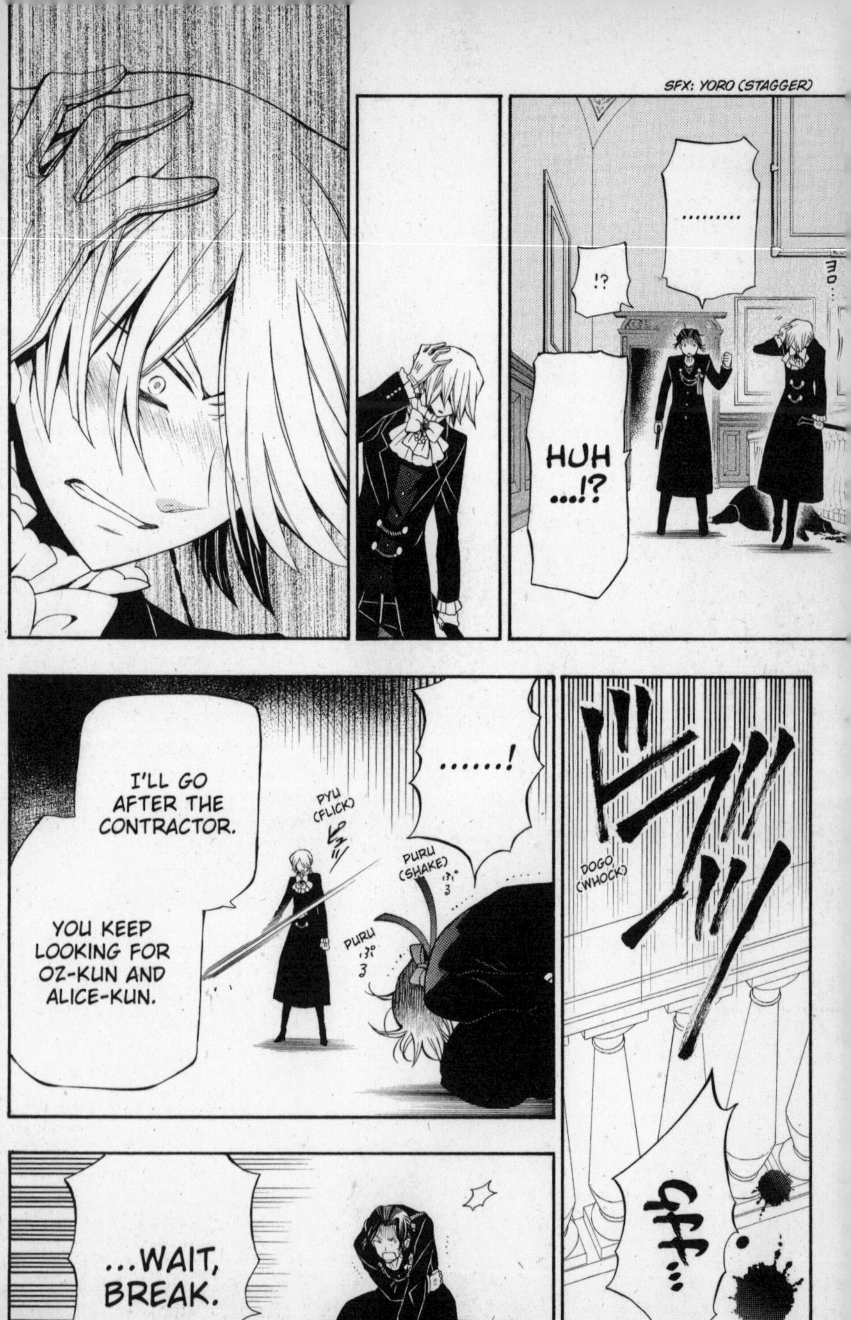
SFX: YORO (STAGGER)
....
!?
HUH ...!?
DOGO (WHOCK)
GFF...
......!
PURU (SHAKE)
PURU
PYU (FLICK)
I'LL GO AFTER THE CONTRACTOR.
YOU KEEP LOOKING FOR OZ-KUN AND ALICE-KUN.
...WAIT, BREAK.

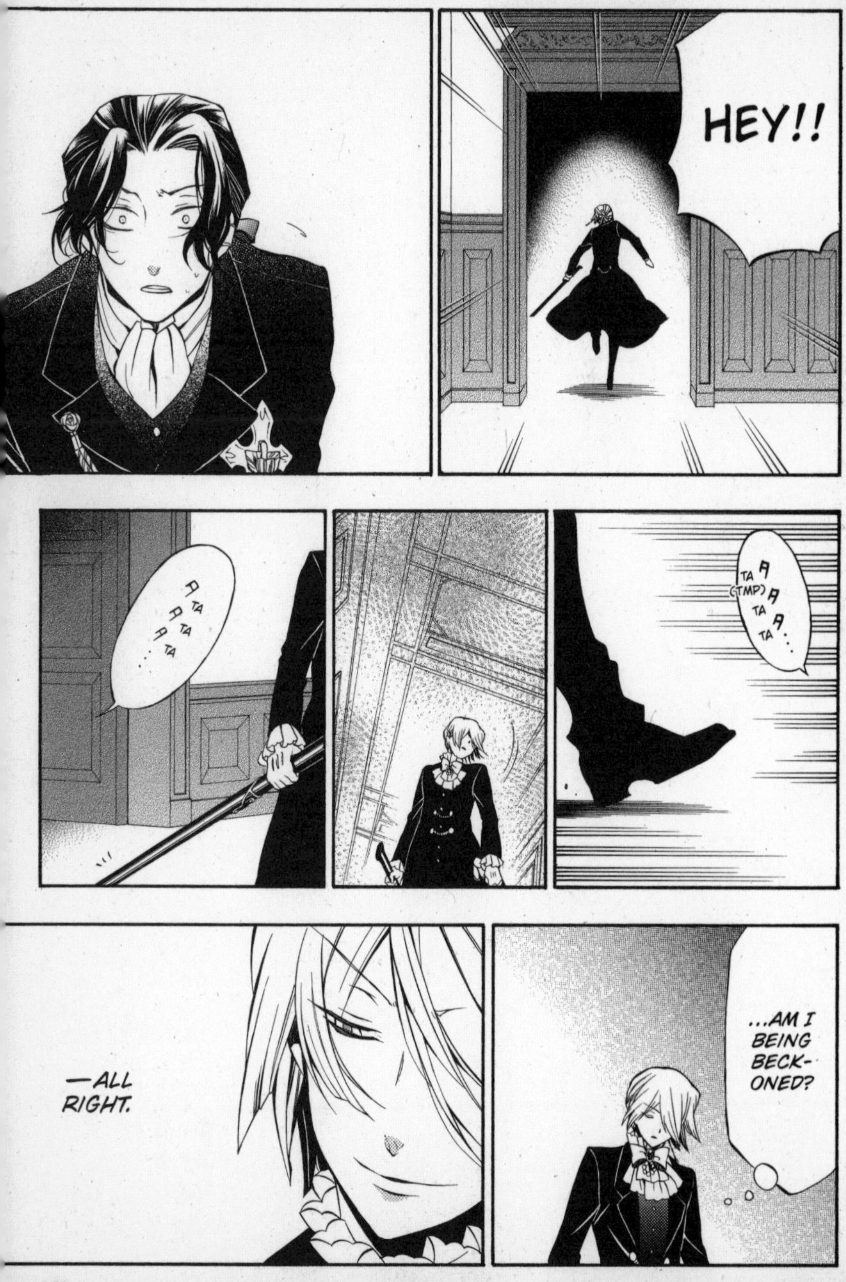
HEY!!
TA (TMP) TA TA TA...
TA TA TA...
...AM I BEING BECK-ONED?
—ALL RIGHT.

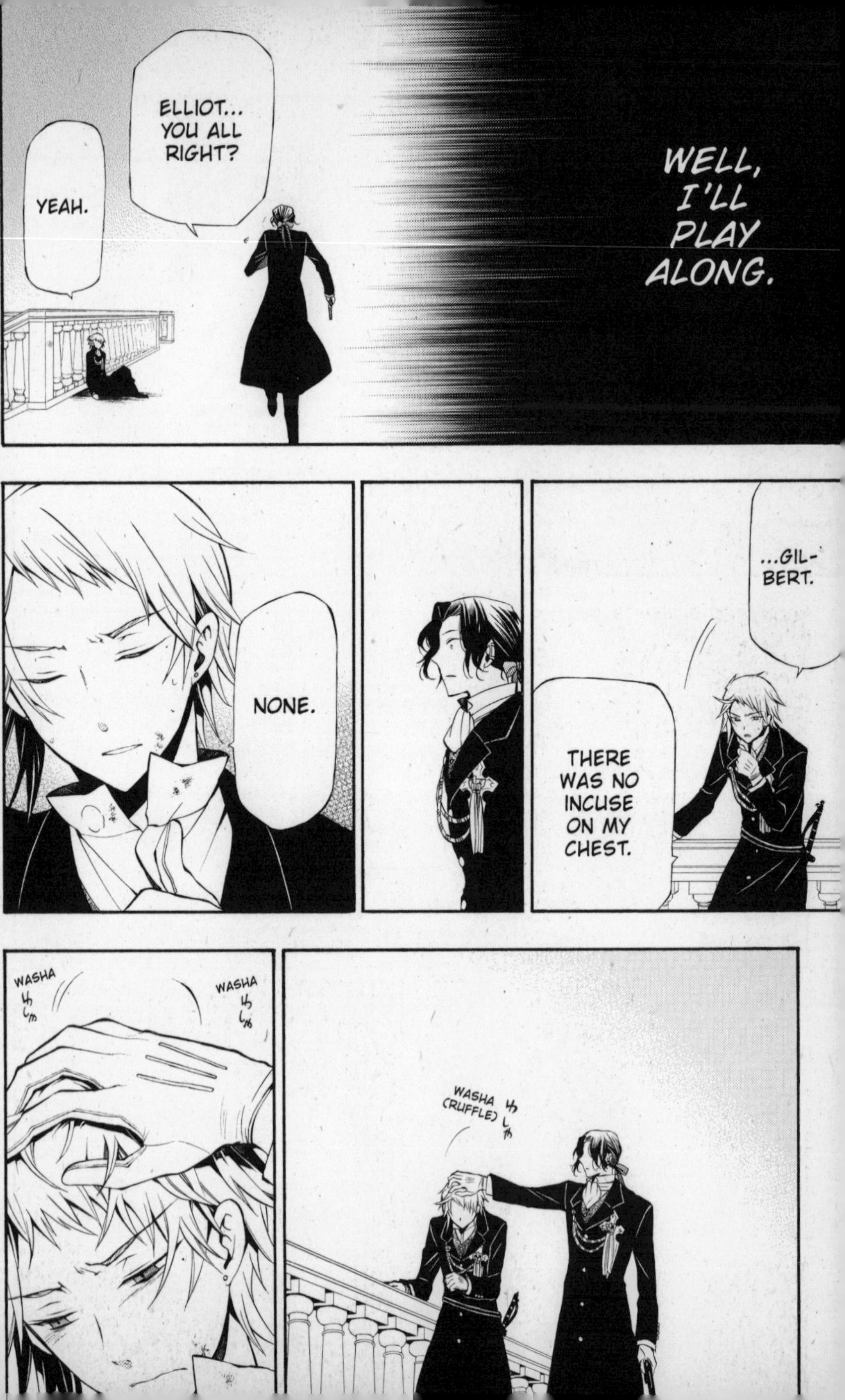
WELL, I'LL PLAY ALONG.
ELLIOT... YOU ALL RIGHT?
YEAH.
...GIL-BERT.
THERE WAS NO INCUSE ON MY CHEST.
NONE.
WASHA (RUFFLE)
WASHA
WASHA

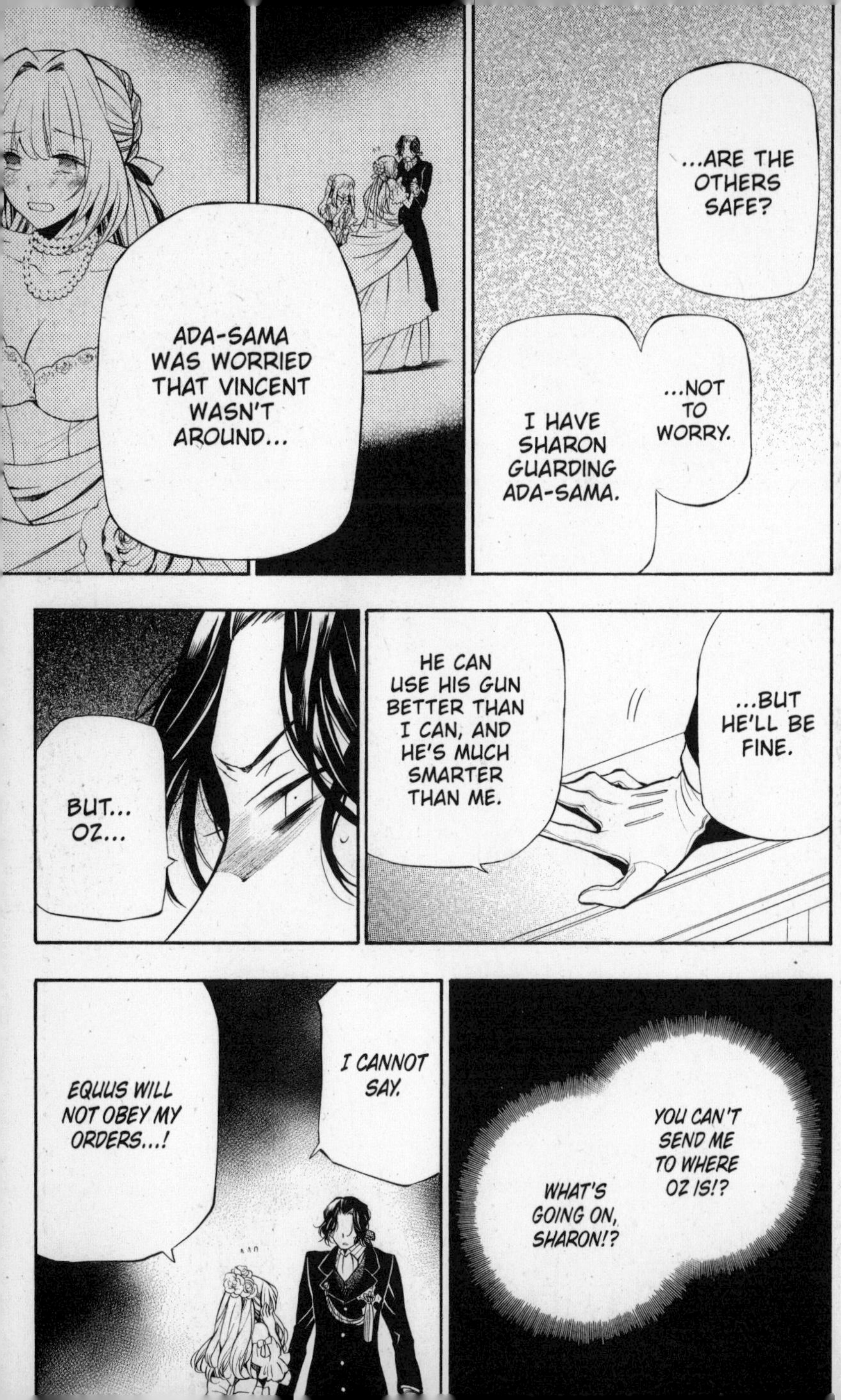
...ARE THE OTHERS SAFE?
...NOT TO WORRY.
I HAVE SHARON GUARDING ADA-SAMA.
ADA-SAMA WAS WORRIED THAT VINCENT WASN'T AROUND...
...BUT HE'LL BE FINE.
HE CAN USE HIS GUN BETTER THAN I CAN, AND HE'S MUCH SMARTER THAN ME.
BUT... OZ...
YOU CAN'T SEND ME TO WHERE OZ IS!?
WHAT'S GOING ON, SHARON!?
I CANNOT SAY.
EQUUS WILL NOT OBEY MY ORDERS...!

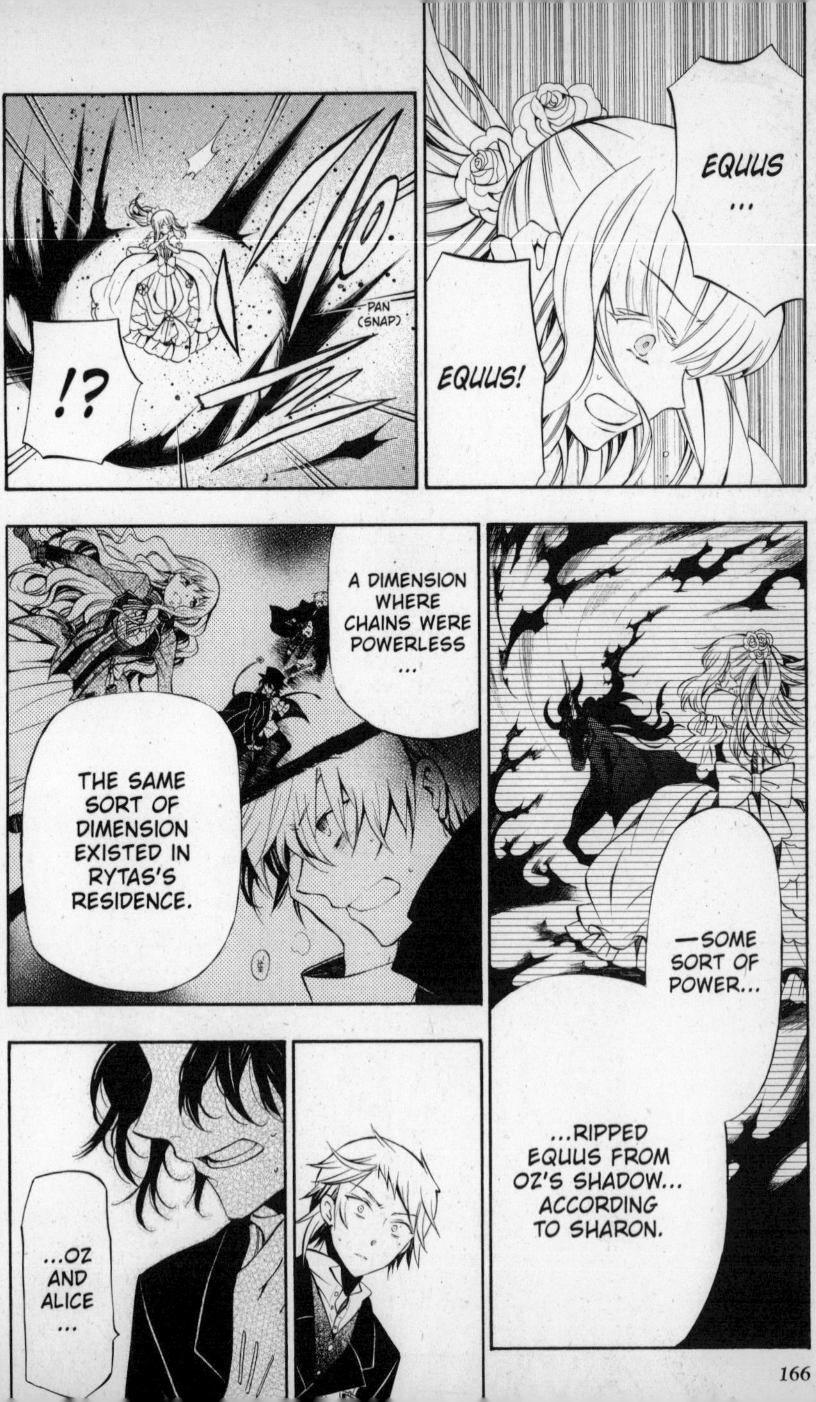
EQUUS ...
EQUUS!
PAN (SNAP)
!?
—SOME SORT OF POWER...
...RIPPED EQUUS FROM OZ'S SHADOW... ACCORDING TO SHARON.
A DIMENSION WHERE CHAINS WERE POWERLESS ...
THE SAME SORT OF DIMENSION EXISTED IN RYTAS'S RESIDENCE.
...OZ AND ALICE ...

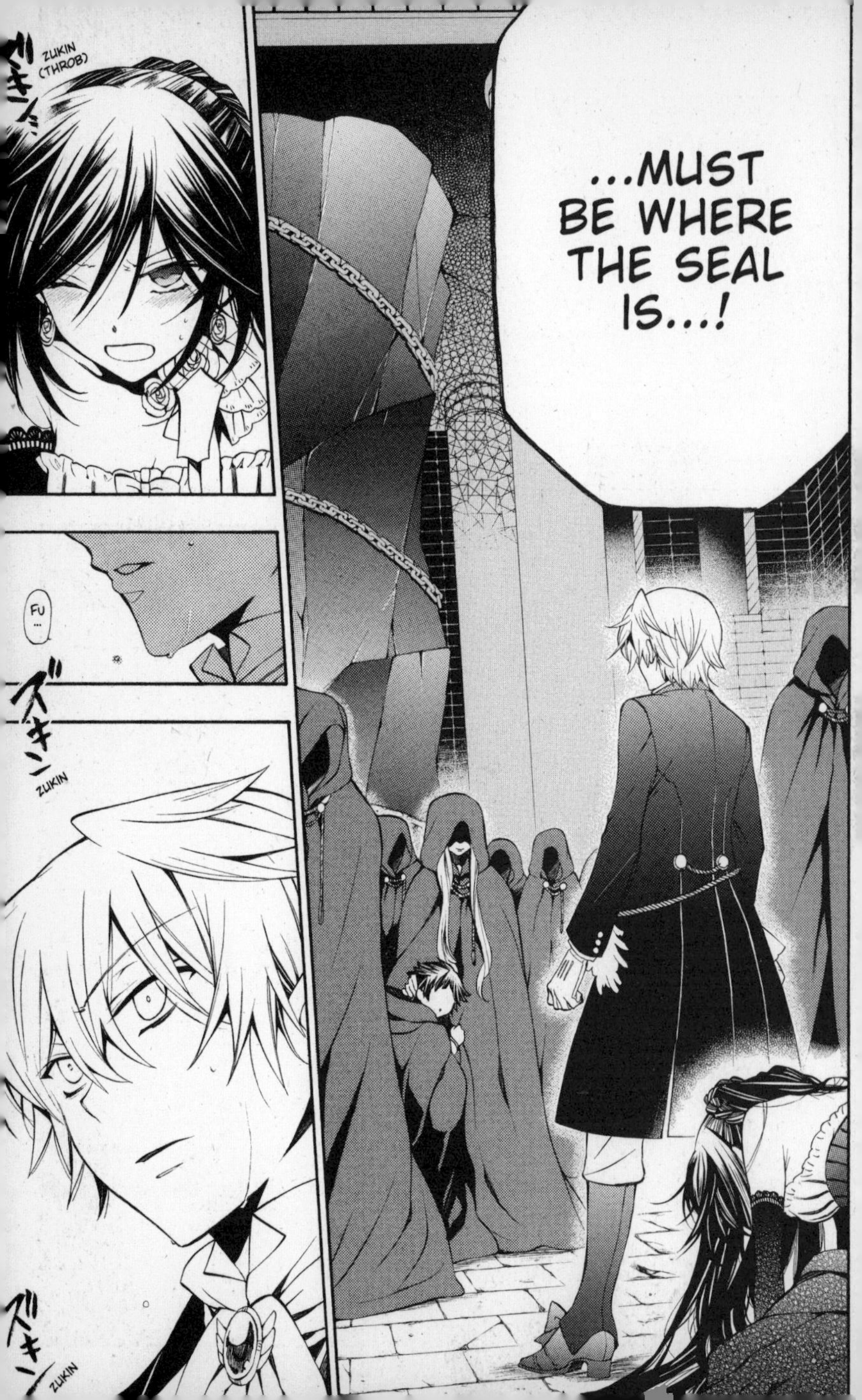

...MUST BE WHERE THE SEAL IS...!
ZUKIN (THROB)
FU ...
ズキン
ZUKIN
ズキン
ZUKIN

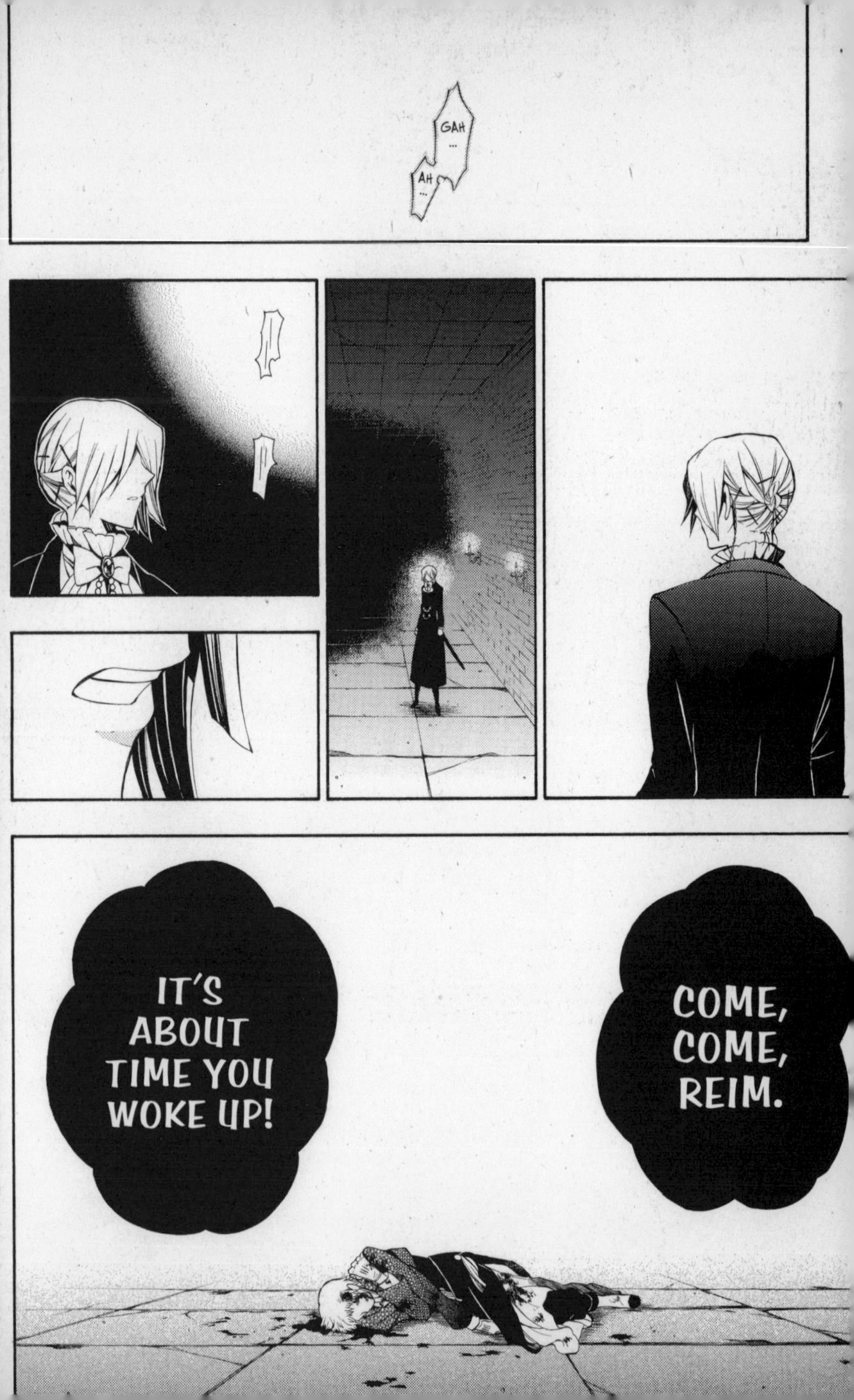
GAH...
AH...
COME, COME, REIM.
IT'S ABOUT TIME YOU WOKE UP!

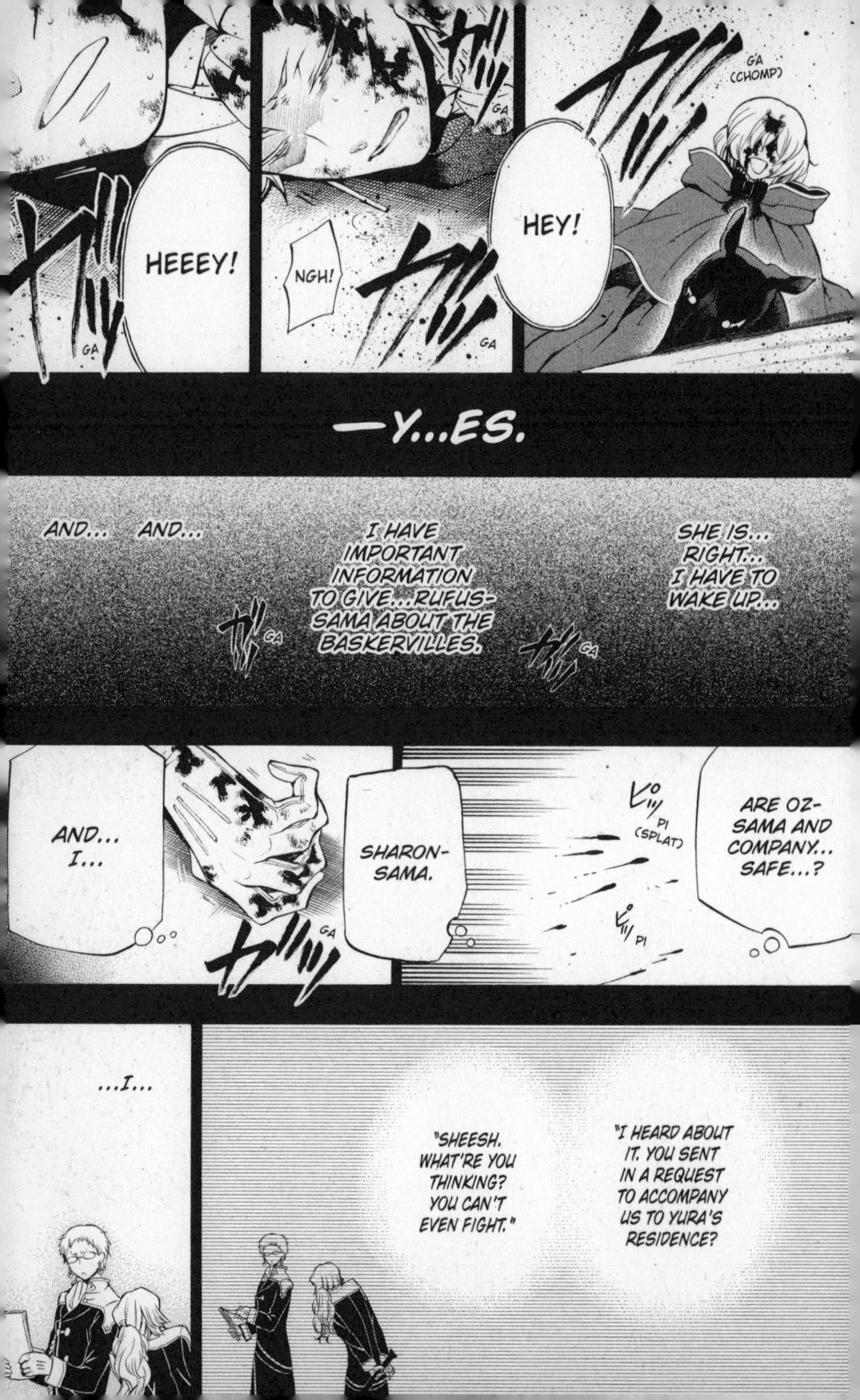
GA (CHOMP)
HEY!
GA
NGH!
GA
HEEEY!
GA
—Y...ES.
SHE IS... RIGHT... I HAVE TO WAKE UP...
GA
I HAVE IMPORTANT INFORMATION TO GIVE...RUFUS-SAMA ABOUT THE BASKERVILLES.
GA
AND...
AND...
ARE OZ-SAMA AND COMPANY... SAFE...?
PI (SPLAT)
PI
SHARON-SAMA.
GA
AND... I...
"I HEARD ABOUT IT. YOU SENT IN A REQUEST TO ACCOMPANY US TO YURA'S RESIDENCE?
"SHEESH. WHAT'RE YOU THINKING? YOU CAN'T EVEN FIGHT."
...I...

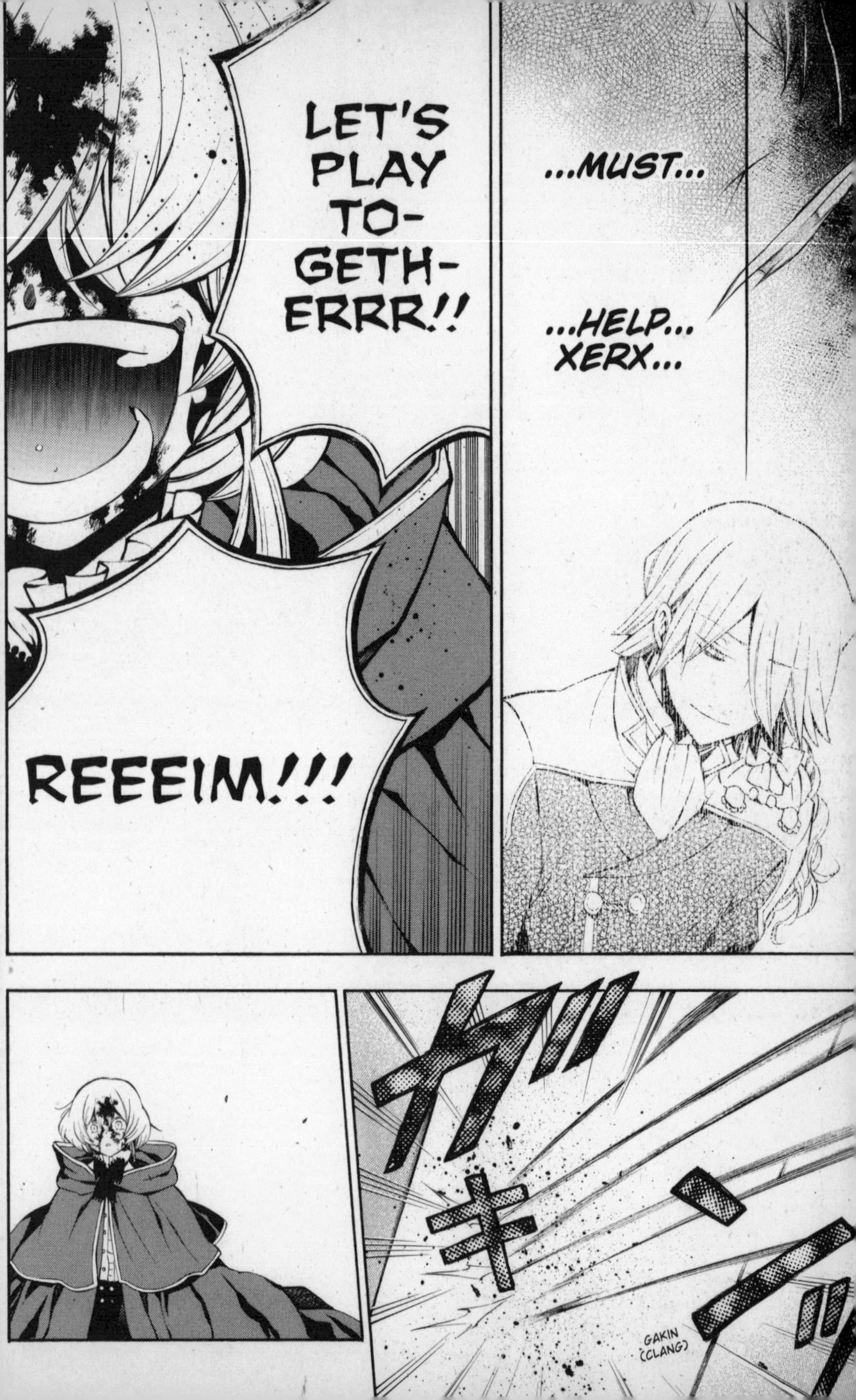
...MUST...
...HELP... XERX...
LET'S PLAY TO-GETH-ERRR!!
REEEIM!!!
GAKIN (CLANG)

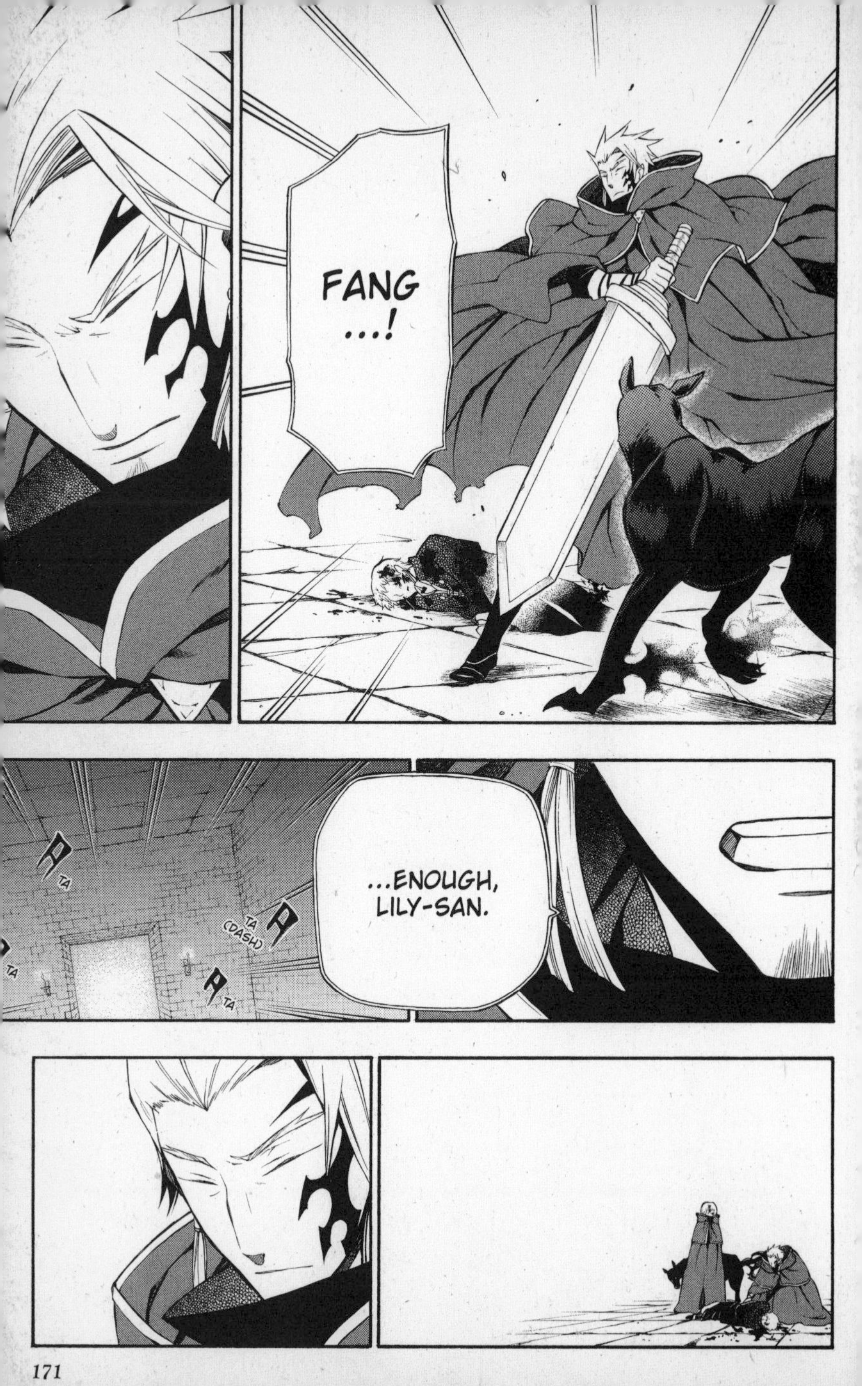
FANG ...!
...ENOUGH, LILY-SAN.
TA (DASH)
TA
TA
TA

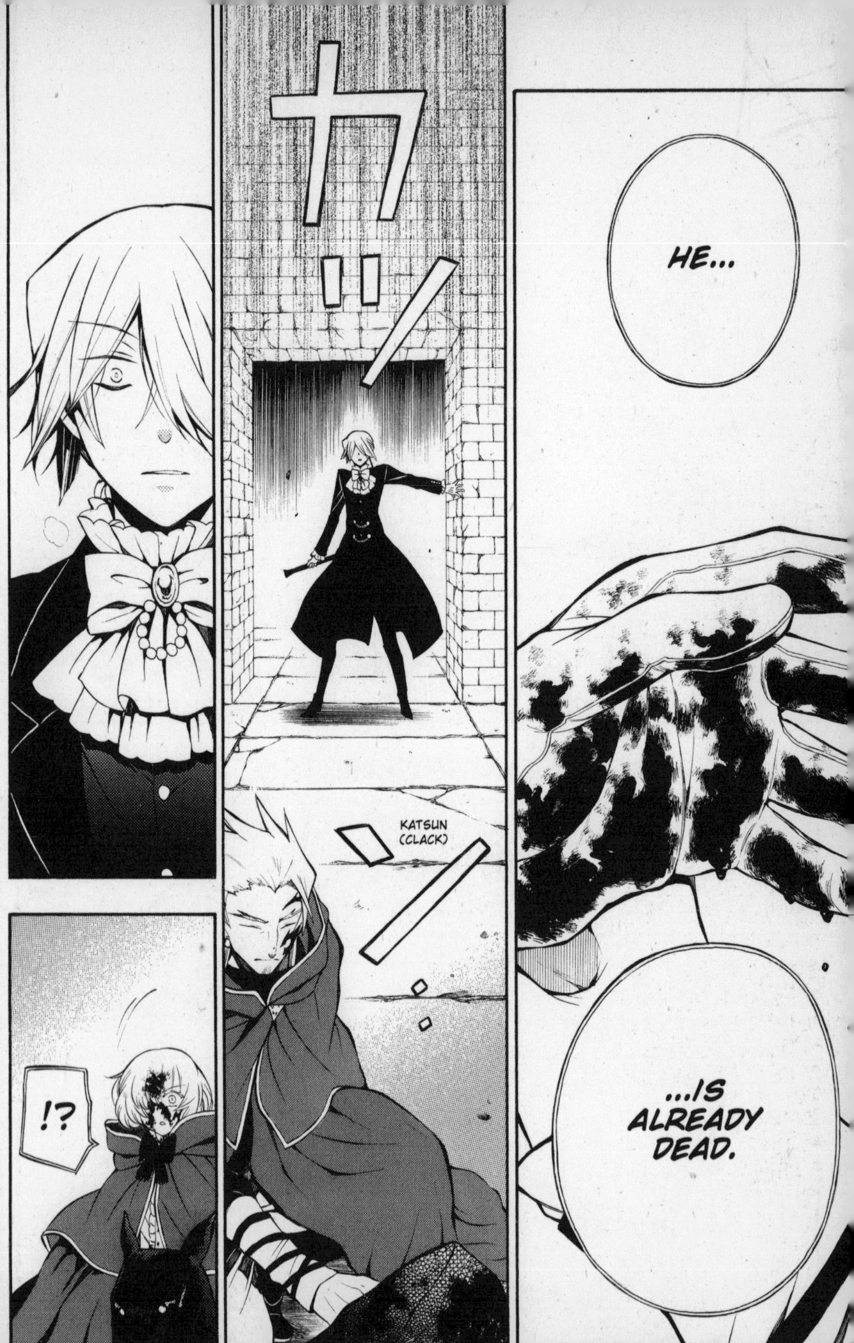
HE...
...IS ALREADY DEAD.
カッ
KATSUN (CLACK)
!?

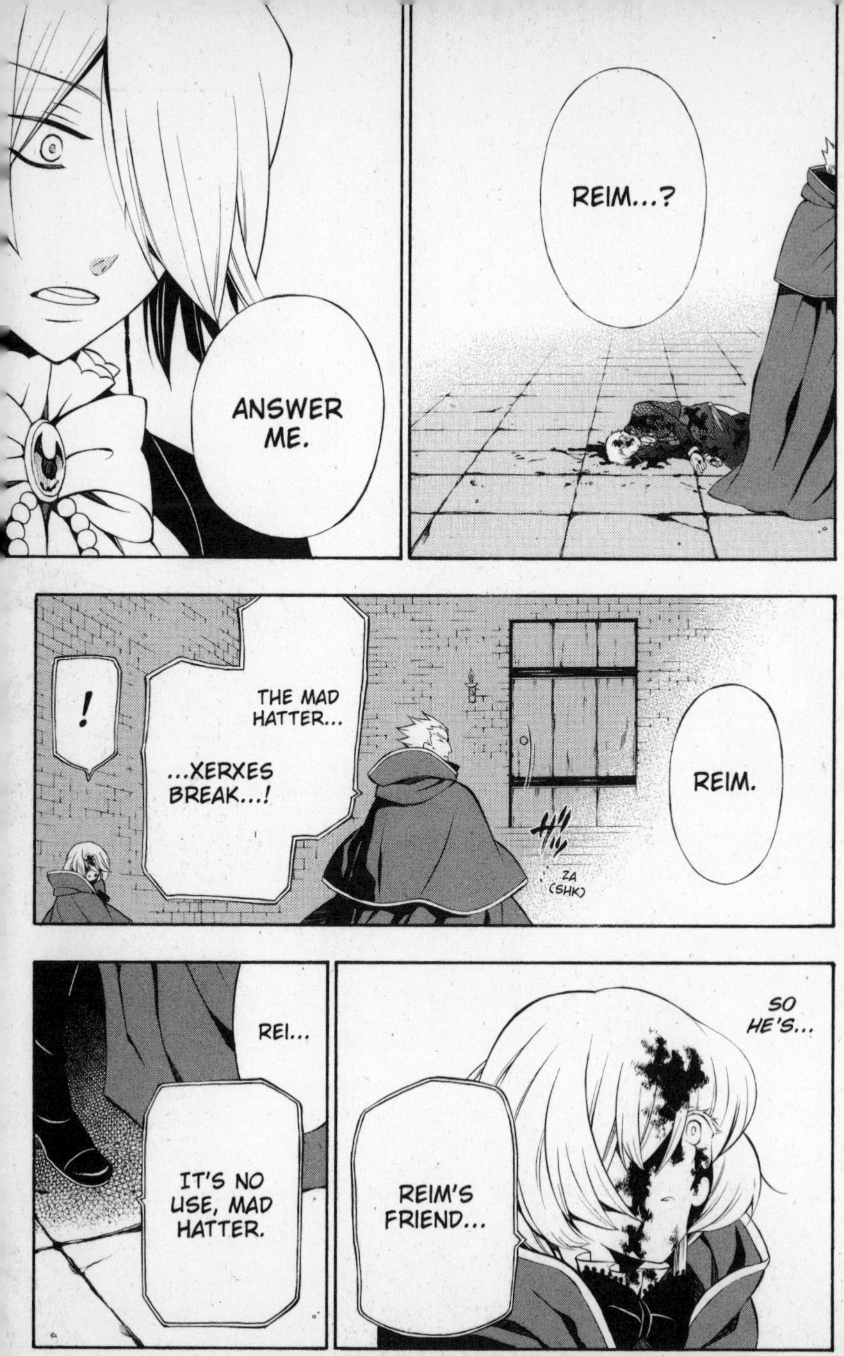
REIM...?
ANSWER ME.
REIM.
ZA (SHK)
THE MAD HATTER...
...XERXES BREAK...!
!
SO HE'S...
REIM'S FRIEND...
REI...
IT'S NO USE, MAD HATTER.

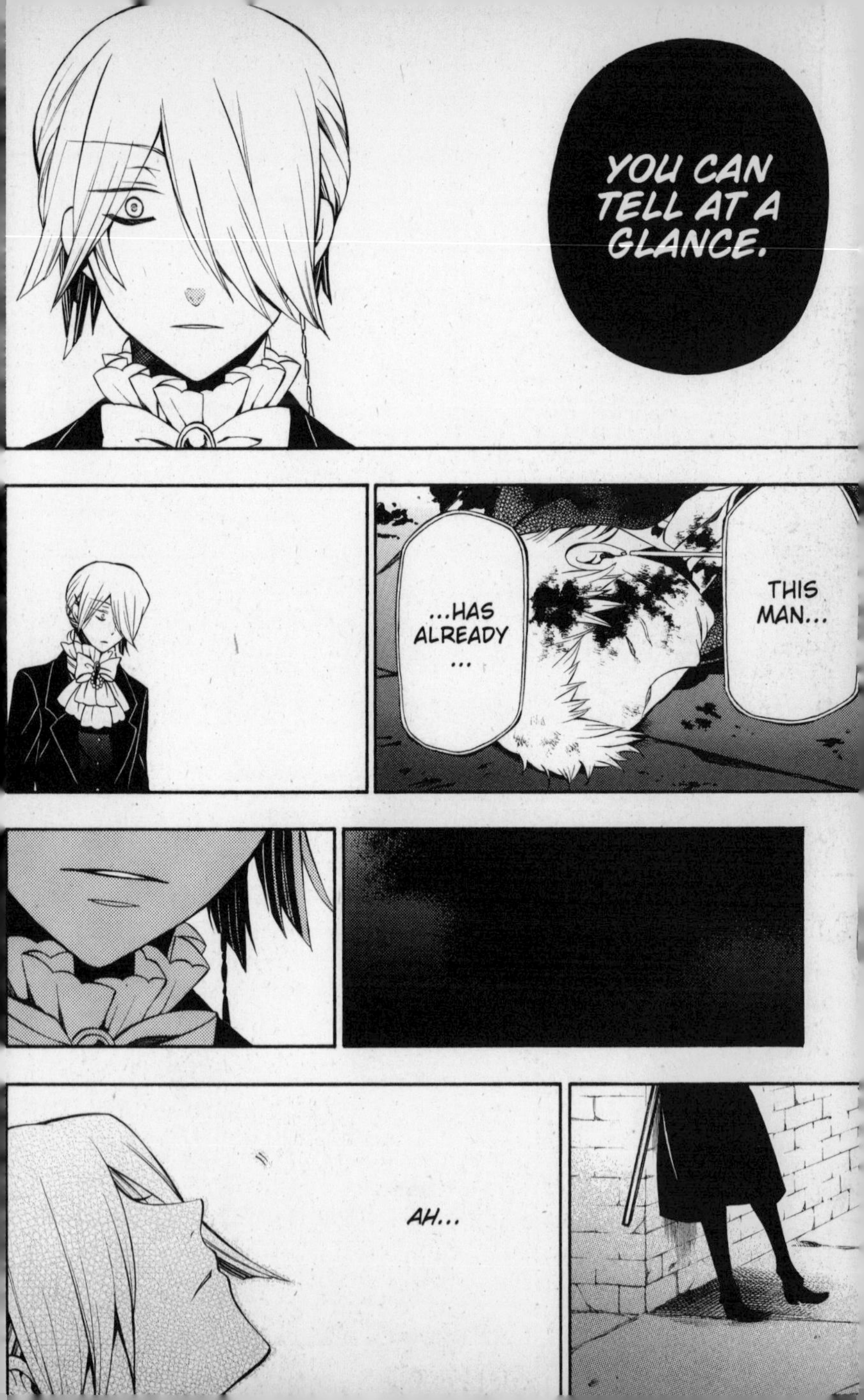
YOU CAN TELL AT A GLANCE.
THIS MAN...
...HAS ALREADY ...
AH...

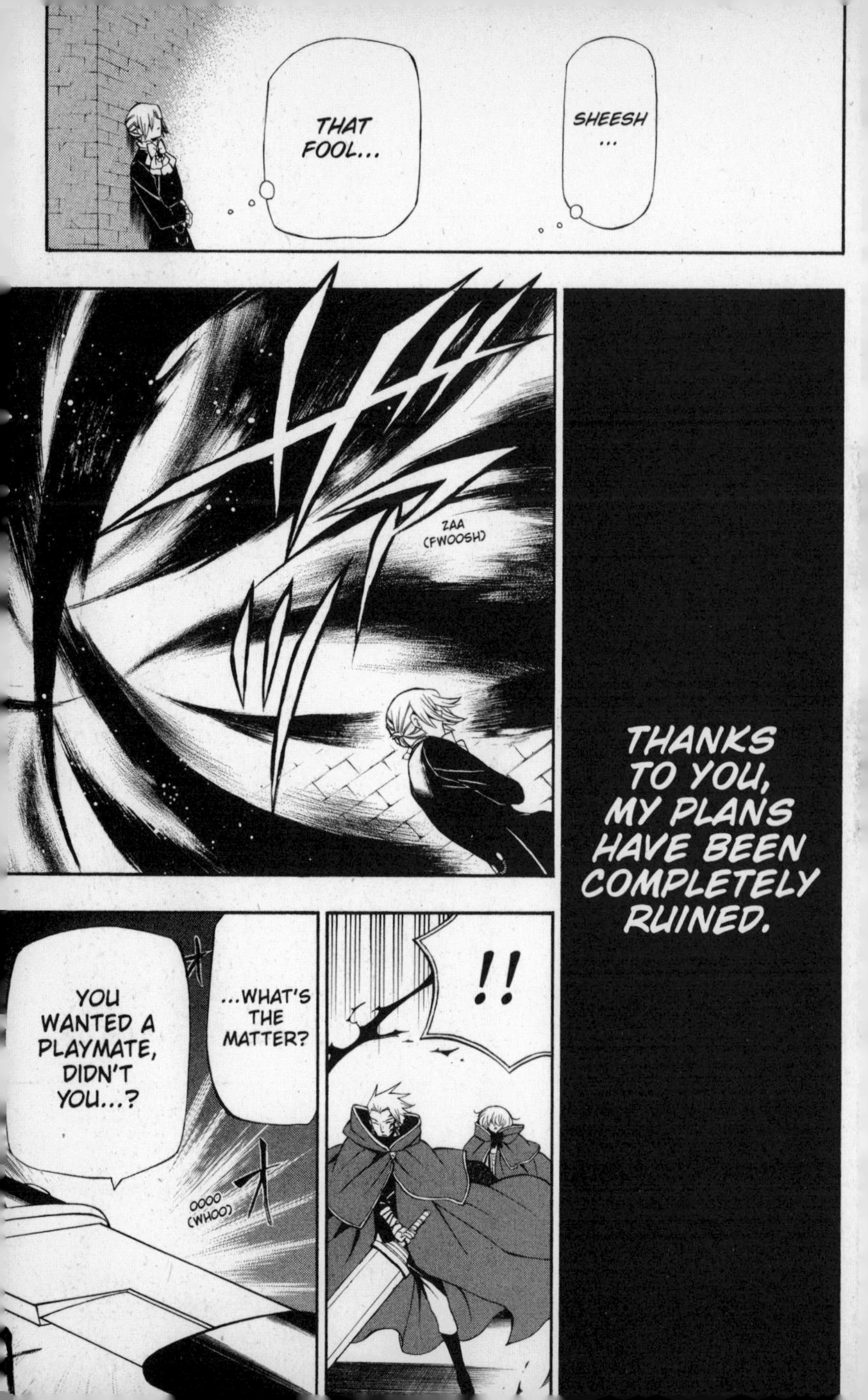
SHEESH ...
THAT FOOL...
THANKS TO YOU, MY PLANS HAVE BEEN COMPLETELY RUINED.
ZAA (FWOOSH)
!!
...WHAT'S THE MATTER?
YOU WANTED A PLAYMATE, DIDN'T YOU...?
OOOO (WHOO)

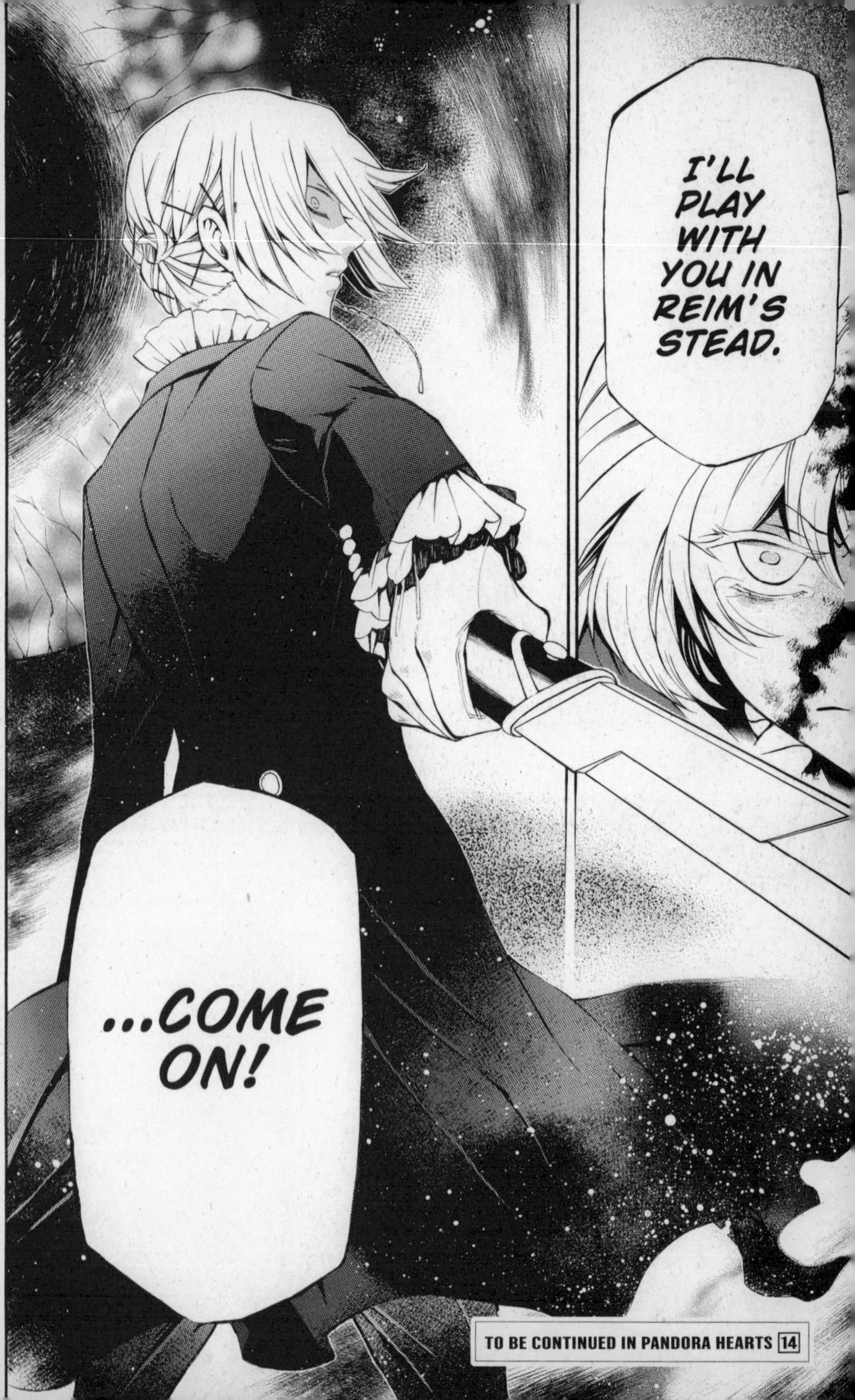
I'LL PLAY WITH YOU IN REIM'S STEAD.
...COME ON!
TO BE CONTINUED IN PANDORA HEARTS 14

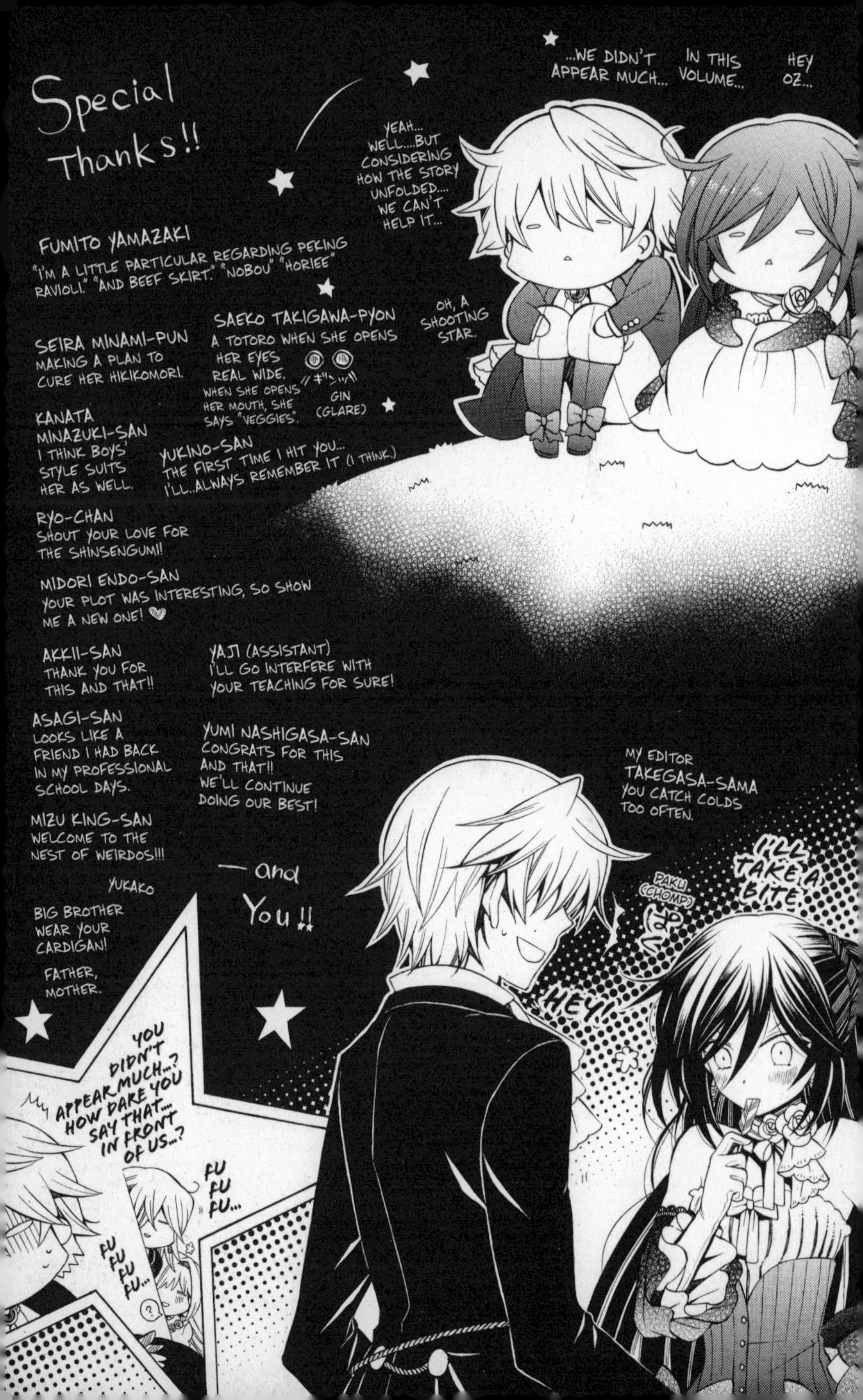
HEY OZ...
IN THIS VOLUME...
...WE DIDN'T APPEAR MUCH...
YEAH... WELL....BUT CONSIDERING HOW THE STORY UNFOLDED.... WE CAN'T HELP IT...
OH, A SHOOTING STAR.
Special Thanks!!
FUMITO YAMAZAKI
"I'M A LITTLE PARTICULAR REGARDING PEKING RAVIOLI." "AND BEEF SKIRT." "NOBOU" "HORIEE"
SAEKO TAKIGAWA-PYON
A TOTORO WHEN SHE OPENS HER EYES REAL WIDE.
WHEN SHE OPENS HER MOUTH, SHE SAYS "VEGGIES".
GIN (GLARE)
SEIRA MINAMI-PUN
MAKING A PLAN TO CURE HER HIKIKOMORI.
KANATA MINAZUKI-SAN
I THINK BOYS' STYLE SUITS HER AS WELL.
YUKINO-SAN
THE FIRST TIME I HIT YOU... I'LL..ALWAYS REMEMBER IT (I THINK.)
RYO-CHAN
SHOUT YOUR LOVE FOR THE SHINSENGUMI!
MIDORI ENDO-SAN
YOUR PLOT WAS INTERESTING, SO SHOW ME A NEW ONE!
AKKII-SAN
THANK YOU FOR THIS AND THAT!!
YAJI (ASSISTANT)
I'LL GO INTERFERE WITH YOUR TEACHING FOR SURE!
ASAGI-SAN
LOOKS LIKE A FRIEND I HAD BACK IN MY PROFESSIONAL SCHOOL DAYS.
YUMI NASHIGASA-SAN
CONGRATS FOR THIS AND THAT!! WE'LL CONTINUE DOING OUR BEST!
MIZU KING-SAN
WELCOME TO THE NEST OF WEIRDOS!!!
YUKAKO
BIG BROTHER WEAR YOUR CARDIGAN!
FATHER, MOTHER.
MY EDITOR TAKEGASA-SAMA
YOU CATCH COLDS TOO OFTEN.
—and You!!
I'LL TAKE A BITE
PAKU (CHOMP)
HEY!
YOU DIDN'T APPEAR MUCH...? HOW DARE YOU SAY THAT... IN FRONT OF US...?
FU FU FU...
FU FU FU FU...

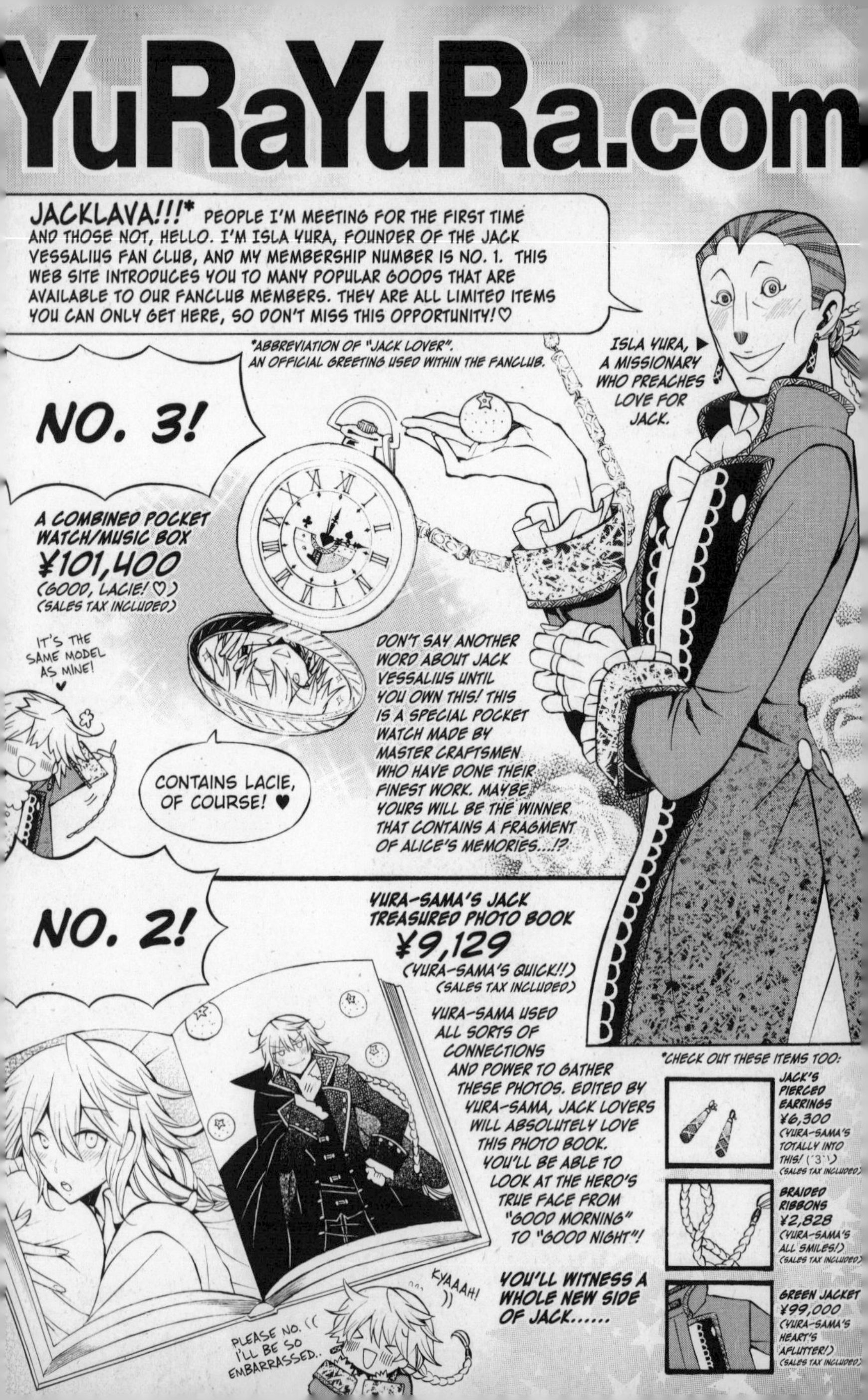
YuRaYuRa.com
JACKLAVA!!!* PEOPLE I'M MEETING FOR THE FIRST TIME AND THOSE NOT, HELLO. I'M ISLA YURA, FOUNDER OF THE JACK VESSALIUS FAN CLUB, AND MY MEMBERSHIP NUMBER IS NO. 1. THIS WEB SITE INTRODUCES YOU TO MANY POPULAR GOODS THAT ARE AVAILABLE TO OUR FANCLUB MEMBERS. THEY ARE ALL LIMITED ITEMS YOU CAN ONLY GET HERE, SO DON'T MISS THIS OPPORTUNITY! ♡
*ABBREVIATION OF "JACK LOVER". AN OFFICIAL GREETING USED WITHIN THE FANCLUB.
ISLA YURA, ▶ A MISSIONARY WHO PREACHES LOVE FOR JACK.
NO. 3!
A COMBINED POCKET WATCH/MUSIC BOX
¥101,400
(GOOD, LACIE! ♡)
(SALES TAX INCLUDED)
DON'T SAY ANOTHER WORD ABOUT JACK VESSALIUS UNTIL YOU OWN THIS! THIS IS A SPECIAL POCKET WATCH MADE BY MASTER CRAFTSMEN WHO HAVE DONE THEIR FINEST WORK. MAYBE YOURS WILL BE THE WINNER THAT CONTAINS A FRAGMENT OF ALICE'S MEMORIES...!?
IT'S THE SAME MODEL AS MINE! ♥
CONTAINS LACIE, OF COURSE! ♥
NO. 2!
YURA-SAMA'S JACK TREASURED PHOTO BOOK
¥9,129
(YURA-SAMA'S QUICK!!)
(SALES TAX INCLUDED)
YURA-SAMA USED ALL SORTS OF CONNECTIONS AND POWER TO GATHER THESE PHOTOS. EDITED BY YURA-SAMA, JACK LOVERS WILL ABSOLUTELY LOVE THIS PHOTO BOOK. YOU'LL BE ABLE TO LOOK AT THE HERO'S TRUE FACE FROM "GOOD MORNING" TO "GOOD NIGHT"!
YOU'LL WITNESS A WHOLE NEW SIDE OF JACK......
KYAAAH!
PLEASE NO. I'LL BE SO EMBARRASSED..
*CHECK OUT THESE ITEMS TOO:
JACK'S PIERCED EARRINGS
¥6,300
(YURA-SAMA'S TOTALLY INTO THIS! ('3'))
(SALES TAX INCLUDED)
BRAIDED RIBBONS
¥2,828
(YURA-SAMA'S ALL SMILES!)
(SALES TAX INCLUDED)
GREEN JACKET
¥99,000
(YURA-SAMA'S HEART'S AFLUTTER!)
(SALES TAX INCLUDED)

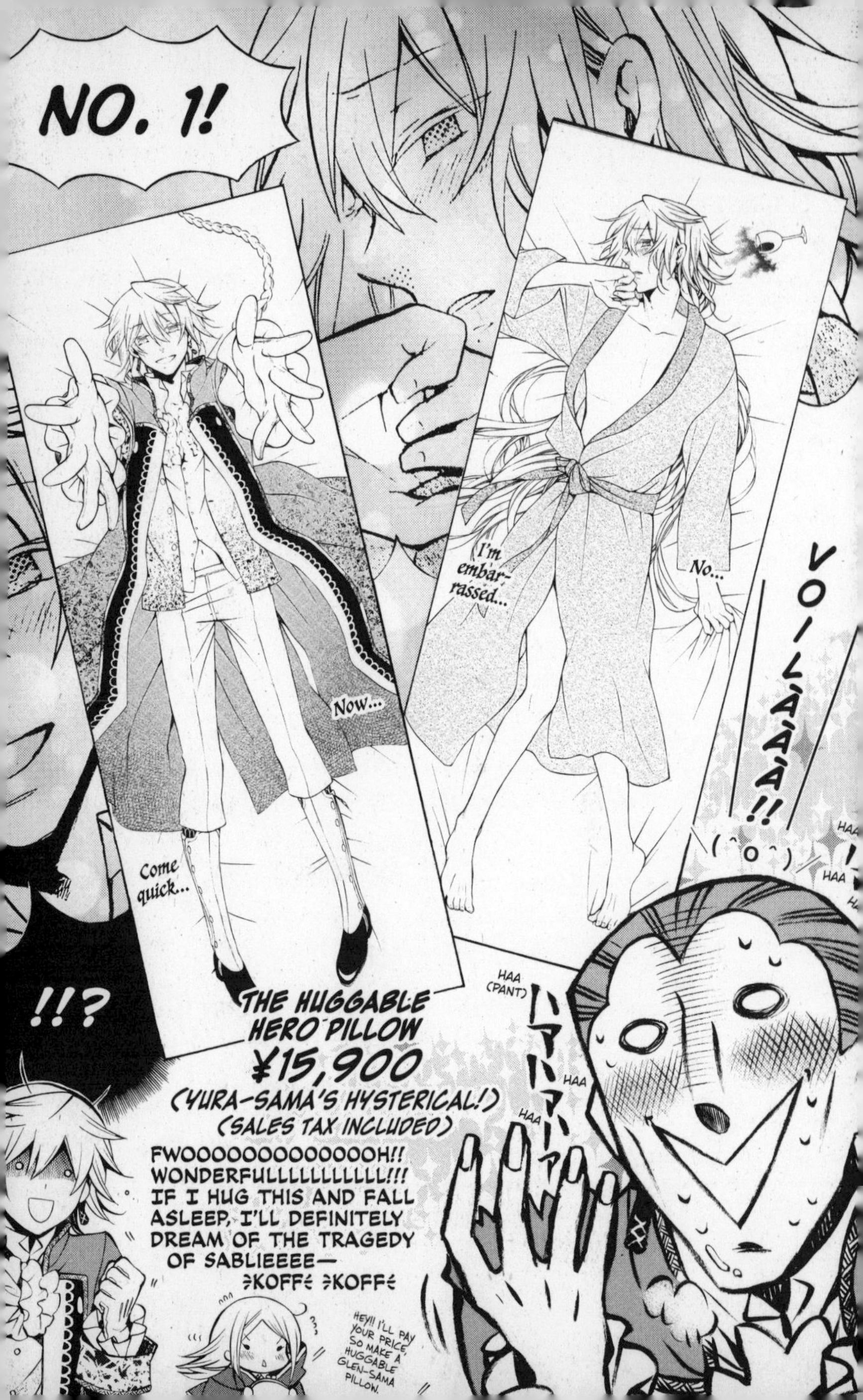
NO. 1!
No...
I'm embarrassed...
Now...
Come quick...
VOILÀÀÀÀ!!
(^o^)
HAA HAA
HAA (PANT)
ハアハアーア
HAA
HAA
!!?
THE HUGGABLE HERO PILLOW
¥15,900
(YURA-SAMA'S HYSTERICAL!)
(SALES TAX INCLUDED)
FWOOOOOOOOOOOOOH!! WONDERFULLLLLLLLLLL!!! IF I HUG THIS AND FALL ASLEEP, I'LL DEFINITELY DREAM OF THE TRAGEDY OF SABLIEEEE— *KOFF* *KOFF*
HEY!! I'LL PAY YOUR PRICE, SO MAKE A HUGGABLE GLEN-SAMA PILLOW.

COMMON HONORIFICS

no honorific: Indicates familiarity or closeness; if used without permission or reason, addressing someone in this manner would constitute an insult.

-san: The Japanese equivalent of Mr./Mrs./Miss. If a situation calls for politeness, this is the fail-safe honorific.

-sama: Conveys great respect; may also indicate that the social status of the speaker is lower than that of the addressee.

-kun: Used most often when referring to boys (though it can be applied to girls as well), this indicates affection or familiarity. Occasionally used by older men among their peers, but it may also be used by anyone referring to a person of lower standing.

-chan: An affectionate honorific indicating familiarity used mostly in reference to girls; also used in reference to cute persons or animals of either gender.

Good, Lacie!   page 178

The price of the pocket watch can be read as *Ii ne, Lacie*, or "Good, Lacie."

Yura-sama's Quick!!   page 178

The price of the photo book can be read as *Kyuikkyu*, or "Quick."

Yura-sama's Totally Into This!!   page 178

The first two numbers in the price of the earrings can be read as *Muchuu*, or "obsessed."

Yura-sama's All Smiles!!   page 178

The price of the ribbons can be read *Niya-Niya*, or "Grin-Grin."

Yura-sama's Heart's Aflutter!!   page 178

The price on the jacket can be read as *Kyun-Kyun*. *Kyun* is the feeling of something or someone tugging at one's heartstrings.

Yura-sama's Hysterical!!   page 179

The 5 and 9 in the price of the pillow can be read as *Goukyuu*, a word that can mean "crying aloud, hysterical."

PandoraHearts

MOCHIZUKI'S MUSINGS

VOLUME 13

I finally stepped on foreign soil. I managed to defy that weak-hearted comment in Volume 11. Things were so comfortable abroad that I still say "I want to go back to Paris" and "I want to live in Chatsworth." But now I can tell because I've gone abroad...miso soup truly is the soul food of all Japanese people!

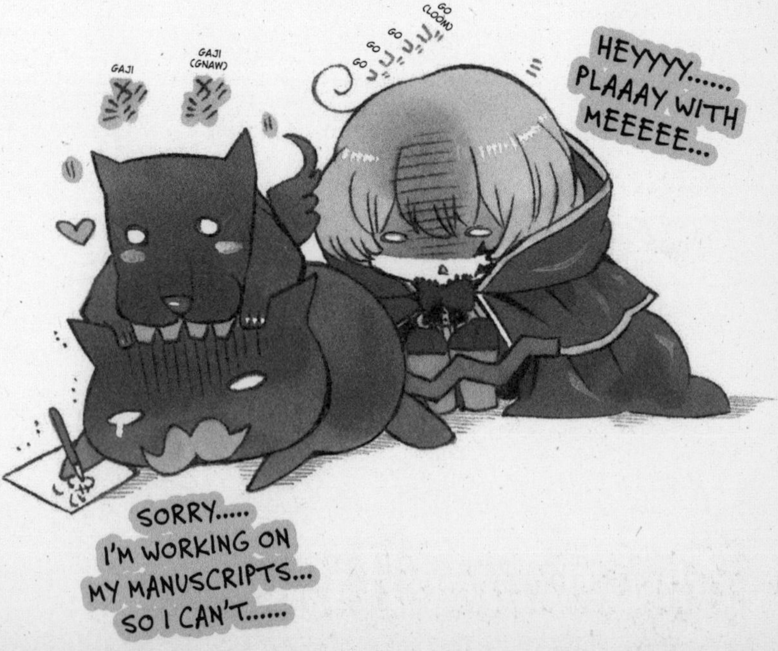
HEYYYY...... PLAAAY WITH MEEEEE...
GO GO GO GO (LOOM)
GAJI (GNAW)
GAJI
SORRY..... I'M WORKING ON MY MANUSCRIPTS... SO I CAN'T......

PandoraHearts

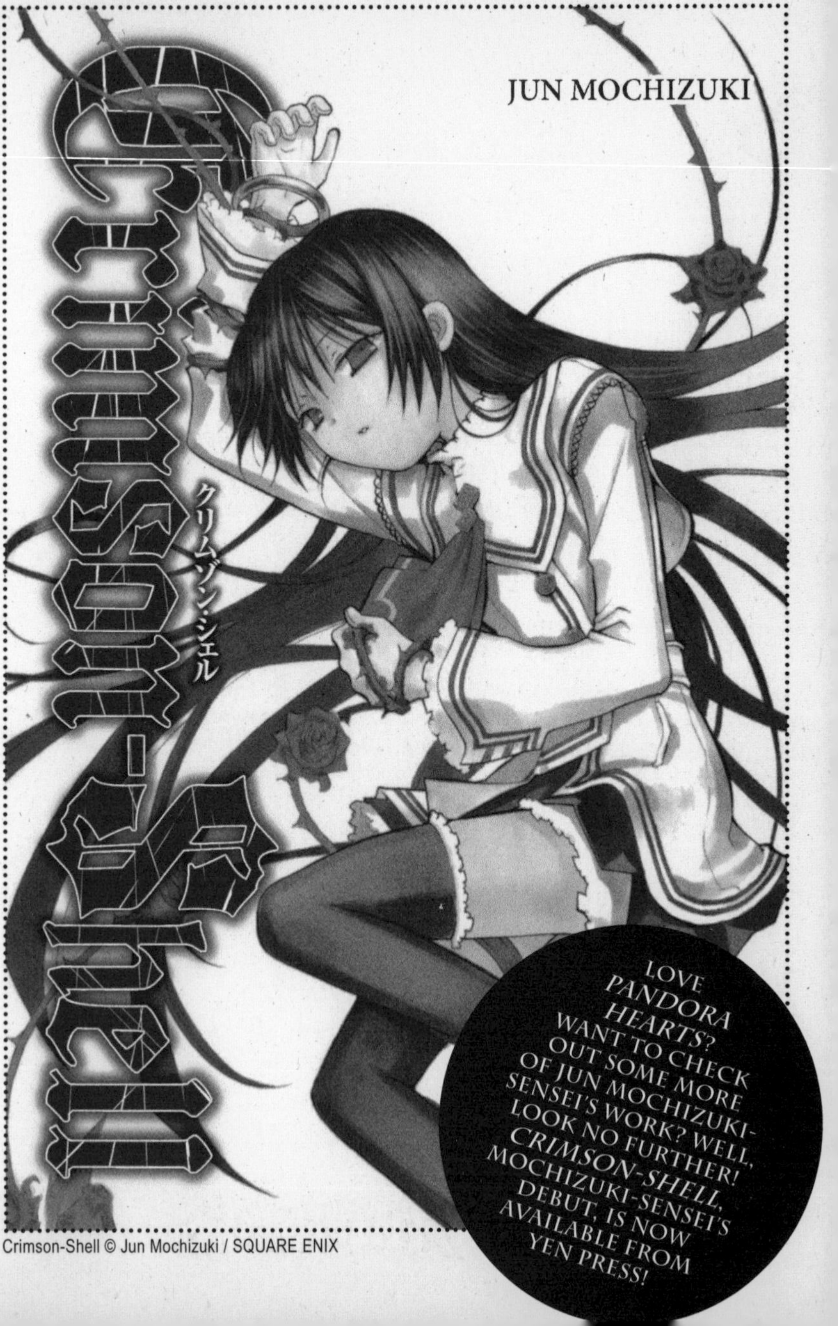
Crimson-Shell
クリムゾン・シェル
JUN MOCHIZUKI

PandoraHearts

Can't wait for the next volume? You don't have to!

Keep up with the latest chapters of some of your favorite manga every month online in the pages of YEN PLUS!

READ IT THE SAME DAY AS JAPAN!

SOUL EATER NOT?

MAXIMUM RIDE

SOULLESS

WITCH & WIZARD

THE INFERNAL DEVICES
CLOCKWORK ANGEL

Visit us at
www.yenplus.com
for details!

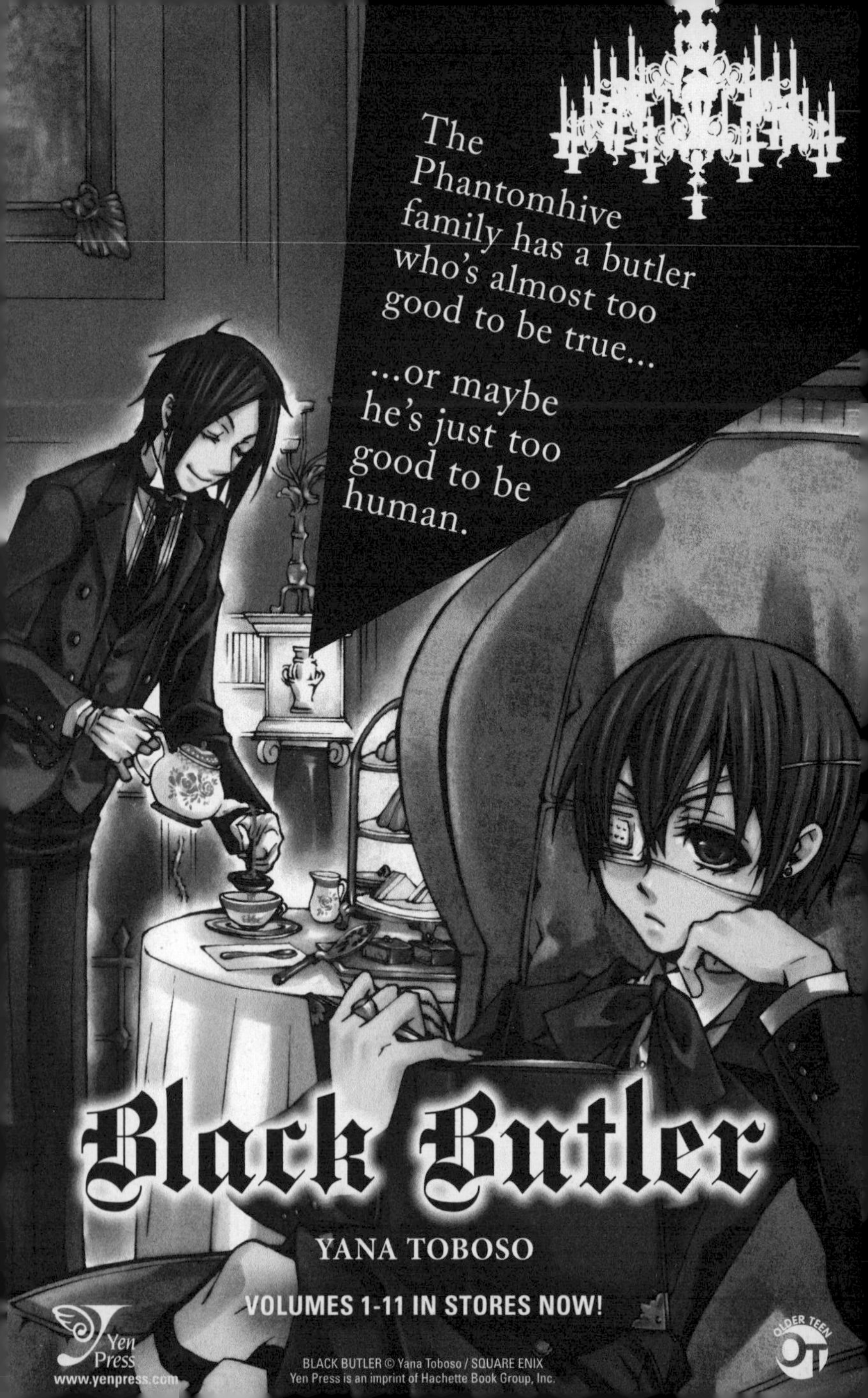
The Phantomhive family has a butler who's almost too good to be true...
...or maybe he's just too good to be human.
Black Butler
YANA TOBOSO
VOLUMES 1-11 IN STORES NOW!
Yen Press
www.yenpress.com
OLDER TEEN OT
BLACK BUTLER © Yana Toboso / SQUARE ENIX
Yen Press is an imprint of Hachette Book Group, Inc.

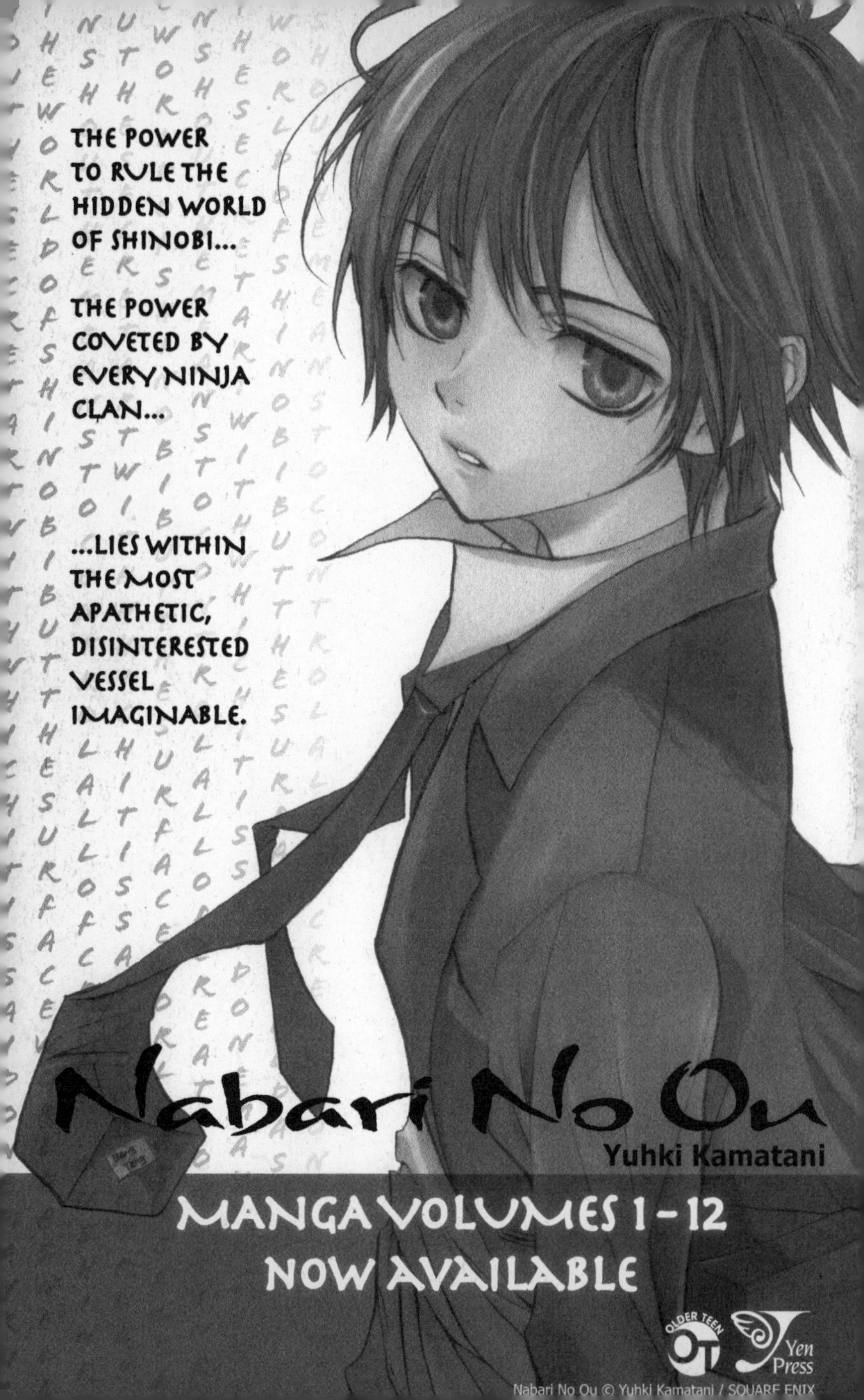
THE POWER TO RULE THE HIDDEN WORLD OF SHINOBI...
THE POWER COVETED BY EVERY NINJA CLAN...
...LIES WITHIN THE MOST APATHETIC, DISINTERESTED VESSEL IMAGINABLE.
Nabari No Ou
Yuhki Kamatani
MANGA VOLUMES 1-12 NOW AVAILABLE
OLDER TEEN OT
Yen Press
Nabari No Ou © Yuhki Kamatani / SQUARE ENIX

DEALING WITH THE DEAD IS EVEN WORSE THAN DEALING WITH THE DEVIL!

ZOMBIE-LOAN

BY PEACH-PIT

AVAILABLE NOW.

www.yenpress.com

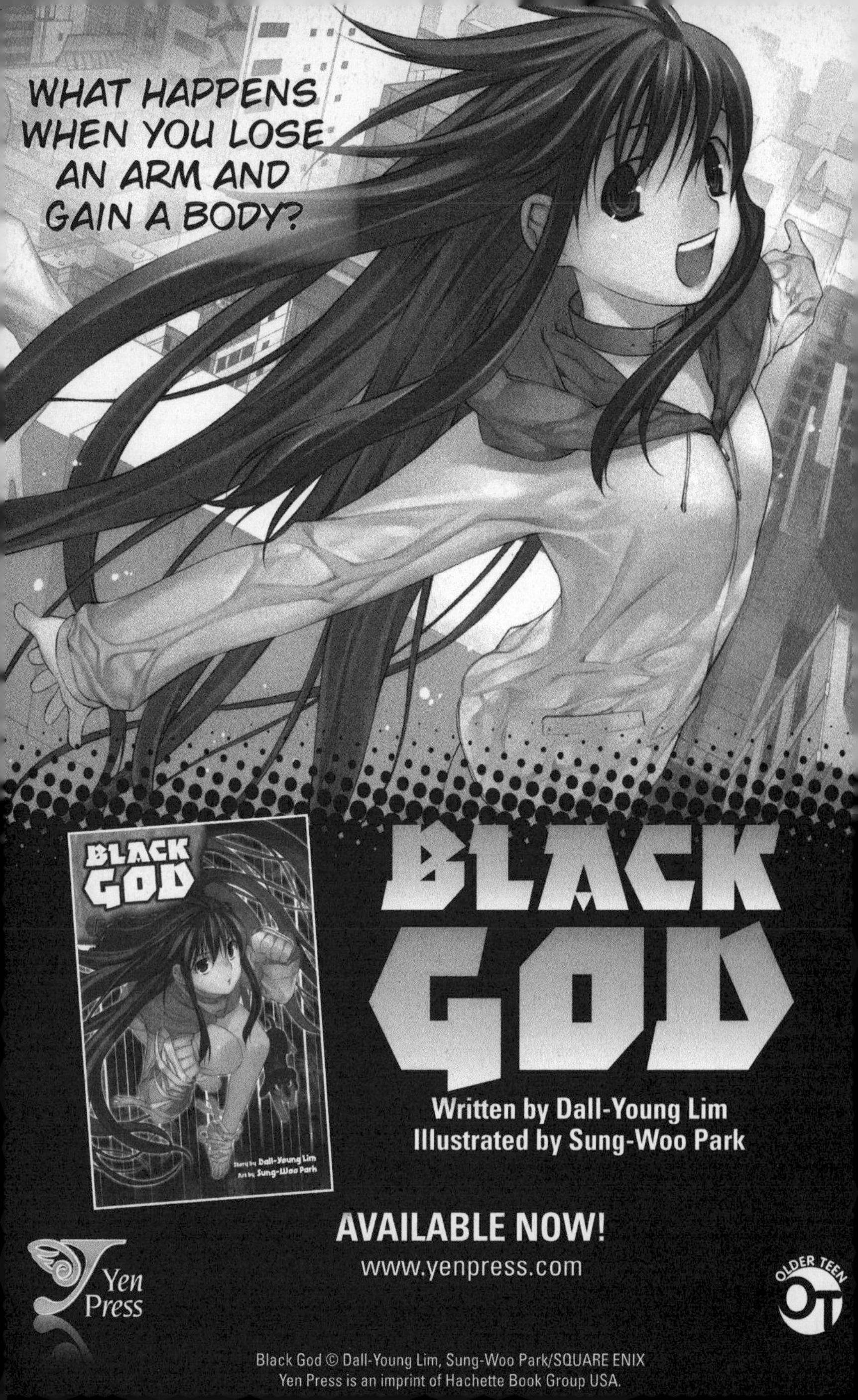
WHAT HAPPENS WHEN YOU LOSE AN ARM AND GAIN A BODY?
BLACK GOD
Story by Dall-Young Lim
Art by Sung-Woo Park
BLACK GOD
Written by Dall-Young Lim
Illustrated by Sung-Woo Park
AVAILABLE NOW!
www.yenpress.com
Yen Press
OLDER TEEN
OT
Black God © Dall-Young Lim, Sung-Woo Park/SQUARE ENIX
Yen Press is an imprint of Hachette Book Group USA.

PANDORA HEARTS ⓭

JUN MOCHIZUKI

Translation: Tomo Kimura • Lettering: Alexis Eckerman

PANDORA HEARTS Vol. 13 © 2010 Jun Mochizuki / SQUARE ENIX CO., LTD. All rights reserved. First published in Japan in 2010 by SQUARE ENIX CO., LTD. English translation rights arranged with SQUARE ENIX CO., LTD. and Hachette Book Group through Tuttle-Mori Agency, Inc.

Translation © 2012 by SQUARE ENIX CO., LTD.

Yen Press
Hachette Book Group
237 Park Avenue, New York, NY 10017

www.HachetteBookGroup.com
www.YenPress.com

Yen Press is an imprint of Hachette Book Group, Inc. The Yen Press name and logo are trademarks of Hachette Book Group, Inc.

First Yen Press Edition: December 2012

ISBN: 978-0-316-19733-5

10 9 8 7 6 5 4 3 2 1

BVG

Printed in the United States of America